A History of Philosophy
in the Twentieth Century

A History
of Philosophy
in the Twentieth
Century

Christian Delacampagne

Translated by
M. B. DeBevoise

The Johns Hopkins University Press
Baltimore and London

The translation was prepared with the generous
assistance of the French Ministry of Culture.

Originally published as *Histoire de la philosophie au
XXᵉ siècle*. © September 1995 Éditions du Seuil

The Johns Hopkins University Press
2715 North Charles Street
Baltimore, Maryland 21218-4363
www.press.jhu.edu

Library of Congress Cataloging-in-Publication
Data will be found at the end of this book.
A catalog record for this book is available from
the British Library.

ISBN 0-8018-6016-4

In memory of my father,

and of our conversation

interrupted on 24 October 1991

C.D.

Contents

Preface to the English-Language Edition

When may a text be said to fully belong, or not belong, to philosophy? The question has never been a simple one to answer, and it is still less so today than it was one hundred years ago.

Until the beginning of the last century, Western philosophy was by definition European. But since Emerson and his famous "declaration of intellectual independence" in *The American Scholar* (1837), there has been an American philosophy as well. And even if American philosophy was not fated to develop in a different direction than that of European philosophy, the fact remains that from the end of the nineteenth century (with the pragmatism of Peirce and James) and, still more so, from the end of the 1940s (with the logical empiricism of Quine and Goodman) the idea of philosophy that grew up among the academic elite in the United States has become increasingly difficult to square with the dominant conception of it in Europe—or, at least, on the Continent.

By an amusing paradox, the so-called American conception of philosophy is actually an Anglo-American conception. It derives in large part from the work of an aristocratic British philosopher, Bertrand Russell. Russell's work, of course, did not itself appear ex nihilo. It drew its inspiration not only from the English empiricist tradition (which runs from Locke through Hume and so on up to Moore) but also from Leibniz and Kant as well as Bolzano and Meinong and the subsequent work by Frege and Peano on the foundations of mathematics. Nonetheless, since Moore and Russell, which is to say since the beginning of the twentieth century, and above all since Austin, Great Britain has felt the need to defend and illustrate a much more rigorous conception of philosophy than that which prevailed on the other side of the

Channel—on the Continent, to which, as everyone knows, the English in particular have always had some trouble attaching themselves.

It was from the United Kingdom, then, that the expression "Continental philosophy" came—the expression American philosophers still use today to refer to a style of philosophy that is not their own and that, for the most part, they hold to be mistaken. We therefore find ourselves at the end of the present century in a somewhat awkward situation, with the Western world (to say nothing of the other regions of the planet) divided between two definitions of philosophy that coexist only with difficulty.

The Anglo-American definition, due to Russell, conceives of philosophy as a technical or scientific activity whose exercise is reserved to a relatively small number of specialists, most of them found in universities. The European definition considers philosophy to be a reflective practice of a more general sort, having variable rules and multiple forms, that shows far greater generosity in attributing the title "philosopher"—witness the fact that many authors regarded as philosophers in the present work, written by a European, would no doubt in the United States be classified under other rubrics (literary theory, cultural studies, social science, and so on).

These two conceptions, both of them matters of convention and therefore debatable, are nonetheless not unrelated. This is not only because, as I have just indicated, the Anglo-American conception is partly derived from Kant and Frege and because one could show, furthermore, that it owes a debt to other Continental philosophers, chiefly German (as in the case of Carnap) and Austrian (Wittgenstein, although he passed his adult life in England, was essentially a product of Vienna). It is also because the philosophical dialogue between Europe and America was never actually broken off (even if at certain times—as, for example, in the 1950s and 1960s—it did go through critical periods) and because it has in fact experienced a spectacular revival over the last two decades (to the benefit mainly of authors such as Rawls, Cavell, and Rorty, on the one side, and, on the other, Habermas, Foucault, and Derrida).

It is because I have wished to take these things into account that the present work is limited neither to Continental philosophy nor to Anglo-American philosophy. It tries instead to follow the course of both, from their common source and along their simultaneous and parallel paths of evolution up through their most recent stages of development. I have sometimes insisted, more than is usually done in works of this kind, on the many bridges that in every area of philosophy have been built from one side of the

Atlantic Ocean to the other—by thinkers who felt (and rightly so, it seems to me) that they would best understand themselves by understanding their colleagues across the sea.

PHILOSOPHY IS ESSENTIALLY a political activity: this was one of the fundamental convictions of the ancient Greek philosophers. It is still in our own day the conviction of the majority of Continental philosophers. Anglo-American philosophers are far from agreeing with them, however. For some, such as Rawls, political philosophy is only one among several branches of philosophy. For others, such as Quine, properly political questions—which, on their view, ought to be submitted to rigorous and experimental analysis as part of a science of politics that remains to be fully elaborated—cannot be regarded as falling under the head of philosophy, whose specific subject is the study of the most general features of reality.

It has not been possible for me in this book to adopt all of these contradictory points of view. I have therefore chosen one of them: the view of ancient Greek and modern European philosophy, that all philosophical thought, even when it does not explicitly speak of politics, involves questions of a political nature or else conceals assumptions—or entails consequences—of this nature. I was led to choose this perspective by a simple observation with which I think everyone can agree, namely, that our understanding of the history of philosophy is greatly enlarged by placing this history within the context of the history of the world as a whole—its political, social, and cultural history. This claim holds true, I believe, for all periods and most especially for the twentieth century, given that philosophy in our time continues to maintain complex but close relations with the history—above all, with the *political* history—of our time.

This history has, of course, been dominated by a dual adventure, or rather misadventure: Nazism and Communism. In this connection, I would ask the American reader, along with all other non-European readers, not to forget that Nazism and Communism were born in Europe and that they have weighed very heavily upon the life of this continent—more than that of any other—for several decades. I would also ask these readers to keep in mind that Nazism and Communism—two very different realities, for which the single category "totalitarian regime" is really not adequate—are not phenomena of the same kind. Whereas Communism aimed at improving the lot of humanity (even if it failed in this enterprise), Nazism aimed above all

at exterminating a part of humanity (an enterprise in which it largely succeeded) and at reducing another part to slavery. This, it will be admitted, is
something more than a simple matter of "nuance."

I wish also to emphasize that at the present juncture our attitude toward
these two phenomena must take into account recent developments. Since
1989, Communism is dead—and all the evidence suggests that it will not be
reborn in the forms that historically, until now, it has assumed. By contrast,
Nazism, or, more precisely, forms of nationalism and racism that closely re-
semble the one actually assumed by Nazism, have reared their heads almost
everywhere. These forms have surfaced in the ideologies of various parties
of the extreme Right that have gained support over the last decade in a number of European countries. Additionally, they have directly inspired the Ser-
bian campaign for "ethnic purification," which has reawakened painful
memories in Europe, to say the least. Other regions of the world, such as the
lake region of East Africa, are now, alas, suffering from tendencies analogous to those that have recently ravaged the former Yugoslavia.

All of this shows that philosophy cannot help but feel directly concerned—today more than ever—by history and politics. The question of its
moral and political responsibilities is one that in any case cannot be dismissed out of hand.

IT REMAINS FOR ME, finally, to explain briefly why the English-language
edition differs in many places from the first French edition of this work.

It is always a duty, and a pleasure, for an author to thank his translator.
Translation is, in itself, a very difficult task that verges on the impossible.
Malcolm DeBevoise has done a remarkable job in this respect. But he has at
the same time done much more—so much more, in fact, that I cannot bring
myself to consider him only as the translator of this book.

He has, on the one hand, been of great help to me in correcting—and, I
trust, improving—almost every page of the French edition, whose gaps I
have done my best to fill and whose errors I have tried as far as possible to
rectify. On the other hand, his careful reading and candid queries have made
me realize that in several places my way of posing or of explaining philosophical problems was not always as clear or as rigorous as it should have
been. If I have succeeded, as I hope, in better formulating these problems for
the English-language edition, it is therefore to his properly philosophical—
and not only linguistic—contribution that I am indebted. But is it not exactly

this circumstance—that the linguistic and the philosophical are so closely linked they cannot be separated from each other—that constitutes one of the great philosophical discoveries of our century?

Apart from Malcolm DeBevoise's valuable criticisms, this edition has also benefited from the sound advice of other American friends, among whom I am pleased to thank, in particular, Arthur Goldhammer, Lawrence Kritzman, and Jeffrey Mehlman.

My gratitude extends as well to Marc Shell and Willis G. Regier, without whose intervention I should no doubt never have had the pleasure of seeing my book find a new life in English.

Preface to the Original Edition

Must philosophers take an interest in the history of their own discipline? Most Anglo-American philosophers reply in the negative, either because they think that philosophy has no history, that it is the eternal development of a single question to which no definitive answer can be given and that each philosopher therefore needs to start over again from scratch, or because they believe that philosophy is a science in its own right, promised a slow but certain progress, on account of which the study of its past errors is less useful than the search for new truths.

Other philosophers—practitioners for the most part of what in Great Britain and the United States is called Continental, or European, philosophy—feel, to the contrary, that philosophy does not exist apart from its own history, that it is inextricably bound up with the corpus of texts through which it has expressed itself over the centuries, and that philosophizing consists primarily in carrying on an argument with these texts. On this view, philosophy is a matter of confronting the problems raised by past works and evaluating the claims these works assert, either adopting them as one's own or subjecting them to criticism. Since no philosopher can avoid addressing such problems, or at least some of them, the critical rereading of the works of philosophers who have come before—in other words, doing history of philosophy—is seen to be an essential part of normal philosophical activity.

This latter perspective is the one that I have chosen, without attempting to hide the fact that such a choice immediately raises two difficulties. The first involves fixing the dates of the period to be studied. Although it will be granted, I take it, that there is nothing surprising about a philosopher showing an interest in his or her own time, it may nonetheless be asked why a century—a perfectly arbitrary unit of measurement, after all—should possess the internal coherence that would justify its being marked off for purposes of analysis. The answer, as one might suspect, becomes clear only in the course of examining the history of a particular century, in this case the twentieth century—even if, as I hope to show at the very outset, the twentieth century actually began in about 1880. Indeed, for the history of philosophy no less than for that of the arts and sciences, the last quarter of the nineteenth century marks a decisive break with what went before, whose consequences we find ourselves caught up in still today.

The second difficulty is this. No rereading of the last one hundred years of Western philosophy, so long as it aims at being critical, can pretend to pass for something neutral or disengaged. While attempting to be as objective as the subject permits, the history (or reconstruction) that I propose here, expressing as it does one way of reading the relevant texts—and therefore of viewing the world—can only be one history among other possible ones. Even though I like to think that my version is not entirely mistaken, I am quite aware that it contains gaps, that in places it is unfair, that—in short—it displays philosophical prejudices. Such defects are inherent in any enterprise of this kind, but there are reasons for mine, which I would like briefly to explain.

LET ME BEGIN with the omissions and injustices, or at least the most glaring ones. In order to preserve as far as possible the integrity of the interpretation I wish to propose, I have limited the scope of this study to philosophy *stricto sensu*. The reader will find no mention of the humanities and social sciences—linguistics, cognitive science, ethology, psychoanalysis, psychology, sociology, political science, history, ethnology, or anthropology—except to the extent that reference to these fields is essential in explaining certain philosophical issues.

I have, moreover, had to abandon the idea of exploring the many philosophical debates that have developed in other fields of knowledge: debates over the determinism of microphysical phenomena, the nature and function of law, the doctrines of Jewish and Christian theology, or the interpretation of literary and artistic works, to name only a few. Forced to be selective—for no one can say everything there is to say—I have restricted myself to remaining inside a "space" of historically determined problems that are common, if not to all, then at least to the majority of the philosophers of the twentieth century.

And because I have been obliged, for the same reasons, to confine myself to the most important philosophers, I have decided to consider only those whose writings have substantially modified the configuration of this common space. If other works, remarkable in themselves, are not mentioned in this book at all, or not often enough, it is not due to any neglect or indifference on my part. It is simply that I have not been able to find a natural way to accommodate them within the limits I have set for myself since, despite their intrinsic interest, such works have remained until now marginal or else deprived of a posterity.

AS FOR MY PREJUDICES, they may be detected not only in the choices I have made of philosophers whom I deem important. They are revealed also by the way in which, in discussing them, I have presented their arguments.

If I had to sum up my method of interpretation in a phrase, I would say that it rests on the conviction that ideas do not fall out of the sky, that they are not the result of a kind of spontaneous generation. The history of ideas is never pure. Embedded in every idea are issues of a scientific, political, or religious nature. Wherever possible I have tried to illuminate these issues, to extract their implicit assumptions from the writings of the philosophers I discuss, to understand whom these philosophers were trying to persuade, or whom they were trying to combat, whenever they advanced a new concept or identified a new problem.

The logic of this position has obliged me in the case of some certain philosophers to go into the details of their biography at some length. Indeed, it seems to me difficult to read certain philosophers correctly without knowing the background, whether personal or sociological, against which their works emerged. More generally, I do not believe that the great philosophical debates of our time can be wholly abstracted from the historical context in which they unfolded. Two world wars, the revolution of 1917, Nazism and Communism, Auschwitz and Hiroshima, the Cold War, the end of the colonial empires, the struggle of oppressed peoples in the Third World and elsewhere, the collapse of the Soviet Union—all these events are too charged with consequence, in every field of learning, for a great part of contemporary philosophy not to have been affected by them in one manner or another.

Let me mention a final, likewise wholly debatable, choice. I have relied in this inquiry on the notions of school and movement, of influence and filiation—concepts customarily employed by the historian of ideas. These notions, although they are unarguably convenient, and although I do not use them here in any thematic way, are nonetheless problematic. No doubt they ought themselves to be the object of critical reflection. This, however, would require a separate book of its own.

THE PRESENT WORK IS, of course, informed not only by constant reading but also, to a degree that I myself am not fully conscious of, by the whole of my own personal experience since I began my apprenticeship in philosophy almost thirty years ago and, in particular, by a great many encounters and conversations with philosophers that, in one way or another, have helped shape my thinking.

It must suffice for the moment to say that some of these encounters left a permanent mark on me. The most decisive was the first, with Édouard Barnoin, who introduced me to philosophy in my final year at the Lycée Louis-le-Grand in Paris in 1966. I would also like to mention a few among the ranks of the great departed whose words are always with me: Jacques Lacan, Louis Althusser, Roman Jakobson, Thomas Kuhn, Herbert Marcuse, Vladimir Jankélévitch, Michel Foucault.

Thanks to them, but also to many others who are still alive—among whom I have at least to cite Jacques Derrida, Jacques Bouveresse, and Stanley Cavell—I have had the exceptional luck of being able to discover, apart from books, some of the many ways in which the verb to think may be conjugated. It has been my wish, too, to share some of this good fortune with my readers, especially with the youngest among them who, like my son, seem doomed to grow up in a world in which the voice of philosophy, threatened by violence of all sorts, will have more and more trouble making itself heard.

Finally, may I thank the two people on account of whom this book exists: Thierry Marchaisse, who inspired it and whose steadfast friendship has greatly assisted me in improving the text, as well as Rose-Marie, whose moral support has been essential to me in arriving at the end of this mad enterprise, which I came close to abandoning more than once.

A History of Philosophy
in the Twentieth Century

The Birth of Modernity

A few more years of various atrocities, in Bosnia, Rwanda, and elsewhere, and our century will draw to a close. It will not have had to cheat in order to win history's grand prize for horror. One would search in vain to find another epoch that has perpetrated so many crimes on so vast a scale: mass crimes rationally organized and committed in cold blood, issued of an unfathomable perversion of thought—a perversion for which the name of Auschwitz will forever stand as the symbol.

Although this century has turned out so badly, it nonetheless got off to a good start. Its beginnings were promising. Indeed, between 1880 and 1914 there were real reasons for optimism, especially in Europe, which was then at the height of its power.

In the thirty years that preceded the First World War, Europe gave every appearance of enjoying a golden age. Militarily and economically, it dominated the rest of the world. Advances in technology, medicine, and education encouraged the belief that the triumph of the Enlightenment was at hand. Moreover, marching behind an avant-garde of radical thinkers and creative artists, Europe was at the same time entering into a new era—modernity—that was heralded by profound changes in the nature of culture.

To appreciate the importance of these changes, one needs to recall that from the Renaissance until the end of the nineteenth century the products of art and learning were regarded not as mental constructions but as faithful *representations* of a preexisting reality. To be sure, the mechanism by which these pictures of reality were generated was the object of quite varied analyses, which sometimes challenged the supposedly natural character of representation in the arts and sciences. Such fits of skepticism remained isolated, however. For the majority of those who inquired into them, human signs were trustworthy, human languages truthful, and human minds fully in accord with the world.

These long-dominant convictions gradually ceased to hold sway after 1880. Tied to a picture of the universe that had scarcely changed for nearly three centuries, they found themselves called into question just as this picture itself came to be contested. Questions that until then had been suppressed now surged forth with great power. Do our signs in fact have a foundation outside of our mind? Are the laws that govern their arrangement the only possible ones? Is it certain that they reflect something other than subjective choices or cultural norms? For a number of reasons, artists, scientists, and philosophers began to have doubts. But even if many of them rejected as illusory the claim that our languages tell the truth, they were fascinated by the signs themselves, which, in losing their transparency, thereby gained in mystery. The same was true for the mechanism of representation, with the result that it, too, soon came to be exposed to devastating criticisms.

It was a moment, then, of crisis—but a crisis experienced as something enriching and, to a large extent, liberating. For if the logic of representation, in the classical sense of the term, were only a construction of the mind and no longer the expression of a natural and immutable structure, other types of construction had to be possible. Other uses of signs could be imagined, other rules of play elaborated that in turn would permit the exploration of new territories, in parallel with the thirst for expansion that seized Europe at this time in every field of endeavor.

These, then, were some of the characteristic preoccupations of the age. In every field in which they found expression, it is possible to discern the emergence between 1880 and 1914 of an unmistakably modern culture.

SUCH PREOCCUPATIONS WERE MANIFEST, for example, among the poets of the period. Rilke, Apollinaire, Saba, Trakl, Cendrars, Pessoa, Ungaretti, and Mayakovsky were not only close in age, they also had in common a certain freedom in handling language that until then had been unthinkable. But words are not without their own powers of resistance: past a certain point, they cannot be toyed with without their meaning being placed in danger. Some—the Russian futurists, for example—were nonetheless willing to run this risk, leading to the invention by Khlebnikov of an unprecedented "trans-mental" language (zaum).

In the universe of sounds, subject to less constraining codes than that of words, experimentation abounded from the end of the nineteenth century. Wagner, Mussorgsky, Mahler, and Debussy succeeded in distending the yoke of harmony, which since Bach had ruled Western music. Arnold Schoenberg ended up ripping it apart. His *Pierrot lunaire* (1912), one of the first thoroughly atonal works (along with the piano piece Opus 11, no. 1), constituted the point of departure for all dodecaphonic and, more broadly, serial music.

But it was pictorial language that more than any other found itself turned upside down by the most spectacular changes. Their immediate cause was the development of photography. What was the point of limiting oneself to the reproduction of appearances now that this task could be carried out by purely mechanical means? Challenged to forge a new legitimacy for their work, painters elected to look within themselves for the laws that would henceforth rule their work rather than allow these to be dictated to them by the eye.

The history of modern painting (a genuinely philosophical adventure in its own right) began with the symbolist movement, on the one hand, and with the reaction of three artists—Cézanne, Van Gogh, and Gaugin—against the optical realism advocated by the impressionists. This trio laid the groundwork for a mental construction of reality that was later systematized by the Fauves, in 1905, and three years later by the Cubists. The symbolists, for their part, whether they claimed to be inspired by Moreau, Redon, or Klimt, chose to turn their back on the sensible world in order to concentrate on the representation of a private mental universe riddled with religious anxieties. Out of this spiritualist rupture emerged what came to be called abstract or nonfigurative painting, first in 1910 under the influence of Kandinsky and Kupka, followed shortly by Malevich and Mondrian.

But there was more to come. If Malevich's painting of a black square on a white ground, *Black on White* (1915), was—to use his term—a "nonobjective" painting, it nonetheless possessed a representative value. Instead of picking out a visible object, it referred to a spiritual absolute. Three years later, his *White on White*—a white square on a white ground—marked the culmination of the nonrepresentational program. Having attained its highest object, supremacist painting supposed itself to have achieved its end. Malevich lay down his brushes.

That he took them up again some years later, however, to compose strange figurative pictures in a "primitive" style proves that the death of painting cannot be decided by decree—no more than that of philosophy can.

FOR SCHOLARS, the advent of modernity was signaled not only by a radical transformation of their image of the world but also by a fresh inquiry into the foundation of the sciences and the establishment of new disciplines concerned with the analysis of representation.

Mathematics was the first field to feel the effects of this rethinking. Dedekind and Cantor, among others, realizing that the basic concepts they employed (in particular, the concepts of arithmetic) were lacking in rigor, embarked upon a bold reappraisal of the language of mathematics in the 1870s. This reassessment was motivated also by new and unparalleled developments in logic, which thereafter came to be considered as the most fundamental of all the sciences.

The physico-chemical sciences likewise found themselves thrown into a period of turmoil in the last years of the nineteenth century. Major discoveries followed. Planck forged the concept of a quantum of action. The ancient hypothesis of the atomic structure of matter came to be definitively confirmed. In 1905 Einstein formulated the theory of relativity. Because it shattered the idea, inherited from Newton, of absolute space and time, Einstein's theory proved to be no less revolutionary for the scientific representation of the world than the invention of abstraction had been for the pictorial representation of the world. Quantum mechanics, the result of research into the structure of the atom, underwent rapid development in the years that followed. In its dominant interpretation, defended by Bohr and reinforced by the publication in 1927 of Heisenberg's uncertainty relation, it ended up calling classical determinism into question—a challenge that in its turn was contested by Einstein, Schrödinger, and de Broglie, whose objections still today lie at the heart of a crucial debate for the future of physics.

The reorientation was not less striking in the biological sciences. On the one hand, the Darwinian theory of evolution had restored nature to history; on the other, the old quarrel between mechanism and vitalism finally died out, giving way to a functionalist approach to the living world. Owing to this change of perspective, physiology and neurology made important advances while the work of Pasteur supplied the basis for modern medicine, and that of Mendel for genetics, or the theory of heredity.

Finally, there were the social sciences. The traditional fields of history, geography, economics, and sociology, devoted to the study of human affairs in space and over time, were enriched after 1880 by the rise of three new disciplines that approached the phenomenon of representation from different angles:

— The principles of a science of language, clearly distinct from those of classical philology, which was more concerned with the historical evolution of languages than with their internal structure, were laid down by the Swiss linguist Ferdinand de Saussure (1857–1913). The full effect of his ideas became apparent only a half-century later.

— Ethnology developed in the wake of the colonial conquests of the nineteenth century while at the same time helping to undermine the ethnocentric ideology that inspired them. Indeed, the discovery of the richness of the customs and "prelogical thought" (to use Lévy-Bruhl's term) of primitive peoples led ethnologists to challenge the supposed superiority of European civilization and to emphasize, beneath the apparent oddity of societies without writing systems, the profound unity of symbolic events and therefore of the human species itself.

— Psychoanalysis, a term coined in 1896 by the Viennese physician Sigmund Freud (1856–1939), though it did not form a science in the usual sense of the term, as Karl Popper was later to point out, did not therefore amount either to a new metaphysics or to a branch of psychology or psychiatry. Far from being merely a romantic notion or nosographic category, the Freudian unconscious provided a name for the universal mental structure that accompanies the appearance of language and, indeed, symbolic expression in general. Exploring the unconscious required a kind of decoding, or deciphering, of neurotic symptoms—as Freud showed in *Studies in Hysteria* (1895), written in collaboration with Josef Breuer; in the normal subject, it required analysis of dreams, slips of the tongue, and jokes—treated by Freud (who seems not, however, to have been aware of the research of his near-contemporary Saussure) in the trilogy constituted by *The Interpretation of Dreams* (1900), *The Psychopathology of Everyday Life* (1901), and *Jokes and Their Relation to the Unconscious* (1905). Common to these last three works is the concept of a psychic stage that serves as the site of a representation, the hidden author of which is the unconscious.

BY CONTRAST WITH THE REVOLUTIONS that took place in the arts and sciences, the rhythm according to which philosophical ideas evolved during the same period may appear to have been rather peaceful. Although they were less spectacular than the transformations we have just looked at, the changes undergone by philosophy between 1880 and 1914 were not therefore less profound. They arose from a concern with the foundations of mathematics, the soundness of which held implications for the whole of human knowledge. If knowledge were to be able to grow under conditions of complete security, it was necessary that basic mathematical principles be formulated in a precise and rigorous language, free from all intuitive assumptions, empirical or metaphysical. In 1880 this was not the case.

Indeed, the manner in which mathematical symbolism was then conceived remained bound up with a doctrine that no longer satisfied the majority of mathematicians. Associated most notably with the Marburg School, led by the neo-Kantian philosopher Hermann Cohen (1842–1918), this doctrine went back in its main contentions to the system of criticism expounded a hundred years earlier by Kant in the *Critique of Pure Reason* (1781). By criticism, Kant meant a theory concerning the foundations and limits of our "faculty of knowing." This rested at bottom on a description and a classification of *judgments*. Every judgment, according to Kant, is an act of the mind that puts a predicate in relation with a subject. It is expressed by a sentence of the form "S is P." It may be either analytic or synthetic. In an analytic judgment, the predicate is contained in the definition of the subject, for example, "All bodies are extended." Since extension constitutes the essence of bodies, such a judgment permits knowledge to be elucidated but not increased. As a consequence, progress in knowledge occurs only by means of synthetic judgments.

Synthetic judgments are, in turn, of two kinds: a priori and a posteriori. In synthetic a posteriori judgments, evidence of the relation between the subject and the predicate must come from outside. It can be apprehended only in an empirical intuition, such as "All bodies have weight"—since weight, unlike extension, does not belong to the essence of bodies. In synthetic a priori judgments, by contrast, the relation between predicate and subject displays a necessary and eternal character. Such judgments depend on a thought experiment independent of all reality—a pure, nonempirical intuition. For Kant, "$7 + 5 = 12$" and "A straight line is the shortest distance between two points" are examples of synthetic a priori judgments.

In the first part of the *Critique*—the "Transcendental Aesthetic"—Kant argued that all mathematical propositions are synthetic a priori judgments. In geometry, pure intuition is of a spatial nature: my mind apprehends the existence of relations between points, lines, and surfaces situated in a mental space. In arithmetic, it is temporal in nature: my mind treats any addition whatever as a succession of numbers unfolding, like thought, in time. All the propositions of physics, by contrast, as well as those of the sciences of nature in general, constitute synthetic a posteriori judgments. They remain, in this respect, indefinitely revisable. Mathematical and physical propositions nonetheless share a common property: they assume that experience may be given in intuition. Whether this intuition is pure or empirical, there can be no knowledge without the help of experience, without the encounter of a concept with an intuition. "Thoughts without content," Kant held, "are empty, intuitions without concepts are blind."[1]

In no case, then, must reason go beyond the bounds of experience. Knowledge is possible only of what presents itself within these bounds—in other words, of phenomena. What things are "in themselves," independently of the way in which they appear to us, cannot be known. This is Kant's first thesis.

Experience does not have the last word, however, for the conditions of its possibility are not themselves empirical. Our intuitions come within the framework, as we have seen, of a priori forms—space and time—that belong to the structure of our sensibility. In the same way, all our concepts derive from a dozen general "categories," which belong to the structure of our understanding. The knowing subject is therefore a "transcendental" subject, prior to all possible experience, by virtue of which the objectivity of science remains independent of the conditions under which science is produced. This is Kant's second thesis.

The two theses are complementary. The first saves us from dogmatism, which is where reason, left to its own devices, is bound to lead (as in the case of Leibniz); the second, from skepticism, which is where a generalized empiricism would land us (along with Hume). Having thus managed to protect knowledge from the two dangers that lay in wait for it, Kant could count himself satisfied. He had succeeded in rescuing philosophy from the battleground (*Kampfplatz*) on which it was pinned down by rival metaphysics and in setting it on "the sure path of science."[2] Henceforth the mission of philosophy was no longer to construct speculative theories, as sterile as they are arbitrary, but to assist the work of science by setting out to clarify its concepts—in other words, to see to it that this work is properly carried out within the framework laid down in the *Critique*.

Kant's system, which amounted to a scientific and (like science itself) cautious philosophy, represents in some sense the highest achievement of the Enlightenment. It is true that its theory of knowledge, when one examines it closely, presents a good many difficulties. But in spite of these, Kantian rationalism nonetheless constituted a model to which all those who followed Kant in holding that the task of philosophy is to provide a ground for science—and that this task could itself be accomplished in a scientific manner—were to continue to refer for more than a hundred years. We know today that these two beliefs are in part illusory. But no philosopher was able to clearly establish this before Wittgenstein and Heidegger finally did so in the 1920s. The anti-Kantian movement that began to gather momentum around 1880 was initially directed less against these grand ideas themselves than against the manner in which Kant tried to apply them, which is to say against the role that his theory assigned to intuition.

Between 1880 and 1914, the two most important attacks came from Frege and Husserl. Frege did away with intuition altogether; Husserl preserved intuition, while giving it a different meaning and purpose. Both of these men shared a common precursor. Kant's first critic, and therefore, in a sense, the first precursor of philosophical modernity, was Bernard Bolzano (1781–1848). A Catholic priest of encyclopedic learning who taught the "science of religion" at Charles University in his native city of Prague—then a provincial capital of the Austro-Hungarian Empire, a vast cultural area in which Kantian thought, henceforth associated with its Prussian origins, had more trouble establishing itself than elsewhere—Bolzano's chief influence was Leibniz. An accomplished mathematician and the author of fundamental theorems in analysis, the branch of mathematics that grew out of Leibniz's invention of the infinitesimal calculus, Bolzano also took a great interest in logic. Here again, long after its emergence during antiquity with Aristotle and the Stoic school, Leibniz—and, before him, the Franciscan philosopher Ramón Llull (1232–1316)—had made important contributions, little appreciated at the time.

Llull (or, in Spanish, Lull), a Catalan who desired to convert Jews and Moslems to Christianity by the force of sound reasoning alone, sought to devise a great Art (ars combinatoria) capable of resolving any theoretical problem—a bit like alchemy, which was supposed to give human beings a sort of omnipotence over matter. Llull survived shipwrecks and imprisonments, but his logico-theological crusades fell far short of meeting with success. Four centuries later they were still regarded with skepticism; Descartes, for one, attached no credit to them. Leibniz, more sensibly, tried to improve upon Llull's art. A seasoned diplomat and ecumenical Christian, he too wished to reestablish the unity of mankind by bringing about the unification of knowledge. But how were the separate branches of learning to be brought together? By translating them into a universal language, accessible to all: the language of mathematics.

Leibniz attempted therefore to devise a formal writing, or *lingua character-istica*, composed of a small number of primitive signs by which all thinkable concepts could be expressed in accordance with combinatorial rules. To this conventional symbolism it would suffice to apply certain operations mechanically in order to obtain through simple calculation the answer to any question. In this quest for a *calculus ratiocinator*, which would long be neglected, Leibniz's contemporaries saw only the effects of a strange propensity to dream. Kant ignored both Llull and Leibniz, and indeed logic in general—a useless discipline, in his view, that had made no progress since Aristotle.[3] This is the main reason why Bolzano, a Leibnizian, rejected Kant.

There was a second reason. Trusting in the virtues of logic, Bolzano thought that its proper use would give a more satisfactory solution to the problem of the foundation of mathematics than the one proposed by Kant. This argument was developed only a few years after Kant's death in his *Contributions to a Well-Founded Account of Mathematics* (1810). Although it went unnoticed at the time, this work was the first to challenge both the notion of synthetic a priori judgment and that of pure intuition, which Bolzano thought "improper" and contradictory. Whether spatial or temporal, intuition, he thought, was always empirical. It might play an accessory role—like the recourse to figures in geometrical demonstrations—of a pedagogical nature; but no theory worthy of the name could be developed on the basis of it. If one wished, as Kant did, to place mathematics on solid foundations, it was necessary that these be conceived in an exclusively logical manner, purged of all intuitive elements.

The desire to succeed where he believed Kant had failed thus led Bolzano to repudiate the doctrine of the Transcendental Aesthetic. Despite the marginal place in the intellectual life of his time to which this ambition condemned him, he nonetheless persevered in his researches and eventually published, to relative indifference, the monumental *Theory of Science* (1837), followed some years later by a posthumous work, *The Paradoxes of the Infinite* (1851). This latter work prefigured the investigations of Richard Dedekind (1831–1916) into the nature of irrational numbers as well as the invention of the theory of sets by another German mathematician, who was also to declare himself vigorously anti-Kantian, Georg Cantor (1845–1916).

Bolzano's *Theory of Science*, for its part, revived the Leibnizian ambition of devising a *mathesis universalis*, which is to say of unifying knowledge by means of purely logical rules. It also introduced the notion of "representation-in-itself" in order to distinguish the conceptual content of a representation from the mental images by which it is expressed. More generally, this work developed the argument—Platonic in origin—that logical laws, being endowed with a "truth-in-itself" independent of our subjectivity, cannot be reduced to the processes accompanying their formulation in our minds.

Bolzano thus appears in retrospect as the pioneer of logicism, a doctrine advocating realism with respect to logical entities that resurfaced at the end of the nineteenth century with Frege and Husserl. But Bolzano's work, exceptionally brilliant and original though it was, began to make its influence felt only long after his death. Nonetheless its effect on philosophers who at the end of the nineteenth century joined him in rejecting Kant, even if they were only reappropriating in their different ways the Kantian injunction to put philosophy on the sure path of science, was substantial.

Bolzano's influence was felt especially in Austria and Poland. In Austria it inspired the work of the Dominican priest and philosopher Franz Brentano (1838–1917), who was born in Germany but taught in Vienna, and that of Alexius von Meinong (1853–1920), a pupil of Brentano who spent the main part of his career in Graz. Brentano and Meinong deepened Bolzano's analysis of the structure of thought and, in particular, of the relation uniting the mental act with the object it aims at. Their insistence on the necessity of protecting the logical content of concepts against all subjective interpretation was later to inspire Frege and Husserl.

The publication in 1894 of a book entitled *On the Content and Object of Representations* by another of Brentano's students, Kasimir Twardowski (1866–1938), helped spread Bolzano's ideas in Poland. At the University of Lvov, where he taught from 1895 to 1930, Twardowski trained a generation of logicians concerned to defend the theory of science against any psychological or empiricist sort of reduction. The investigations of these logicians—Jan Łukasiewicz (1878–1956), Stanislaw Leśniewski (1886–1939), Tadeusz Kotarbiński (1886–1981), and Alfred Tarski (1902–83)—who made up what became known after the First World War as the Warsaw School served to stimulate the later work of Carnap, Popper, and Quine.

Logic, which had known hardly any advance since Leibniz, made considerable progress in the meantime thanks to three other scholars: the Irishman George Boole, the American C. S. Peirce, and the German Gottlob Frege. These men (especially Frege, whose work proved to be the true point of departure for twentieth-century philosophy) proposed novel solutions to the problem of providing mathematics with a sound foundation and, along with Nietzsche, revived interest in the philosophical aspects of language as well.

But in spite of all of this the crisis of representation had not come to an end. It had, however, at least permitted philosophy to free itself from Kantianism and then to discover, by pursuing Kant's project in other directions, that it led to an impasse—a discovery that, together with other considerations, forced thinkers in the twentieth century to call into question the classical conception of reason inherited from Descartes and the Enlightenment.

Chapter One

The Sure Path of Science

Progress in Logic

If one may speak of progress—or, more exactly, of a renaissance—in logic in the nineteenth century, its point of departure is to be found in two great works by George Boole: *The Mathematical Analysis of Logic* (1847), the subtitle of which ("Being an Essay towards a Calculus of Deductive Reasoning") explicitly recalled the Leibnizian notion of a *calculus ratiocinator*, and *An Investigation of the Laws of Thought* (1854).

Boole, a mathematician known for his work in analysis and algebra, followed Leibniz in holding that mathematics constitutes not just the science of number, or of quantity, but a truly formal language of universal import. He believed in the possibility of applying algebraic methods to a great variety of fields or—to use the phrase of his countryman Augustus De Morgan (1806–71)—universes of discourse. In order to test this hypothesis, he undertook to revitalize the Aristotelian theory of the syllogism by translating it into the language of algebra.

Let us suppose that the variables x and y represent classes of any objects whatever. Boole's specific contribution consisted in using 1 to denote the full class (or universe of discourse), 0 the empty class, and the symbol v—which was not yet a quantifier in the precise sense of the term—the notion "some." With the help of this notation, a judgment of the form "All men are mortal" becomes "All y are some x," or $y = vx$. From the corresponding equation $y - vx = 0$ it is easy to derive other formulas by a series of elementary algebraic operations, for example, $y(1 - x) = 0$ ("Nonmortal men do not exist"). The systematic use of such a symbolism made it possible to eliminate the semantic ambiguities inherent in traditional syllogisms, while the mechanical application of the rules of calculation removed all risk of error from the deductive process. Boole thus managed to obtain by a purely formal method all of the results that Aristotle was able to arrive at only in an empirical manner.

Encouraged by this first success, he went on to anticipate the possibility of applying logical technique to the resolution of philosophical problems. His ambition was not (as would later be the case with Carnap) to eliminate philosophy but rather, in the spirit of the grand Leibnizian dream, to facilitate its development. To do this, Boole attempted to formulate algebraically the most general laws of thought—in other words, to construct a global theory of deductive reasoning. Such a huge undertaking, carried out in the first part of his work of 1854, led to difficulties that are in good measure attributable to the imperfections of the notation used. The second part of the *Investigation*, in which Boole tried to deduce by the same procedure the rules of induction—that is, the fundamental laws of the calculus of probabilities —encountered formidable problems as well. In the end, because he remained committed to the idea that it suffices to observe how thought operates in order to know its "natural" laws, Boole did not succeed in detaching his logical calculus from psychological introspection.

Despite its limitations, Boole's algebra nonetheless retained foundational significance. It permitted symbolic logic to accede to the rank of a full-fledged science, making logic an autonomous corpus of knowledge as rigorous as that of mathematics. In doing this, Boole's algebra seemed to open up the way to unlimited future development.

THE DEVELOPMENT OF LOGIC CONTINUED with the work of C. S. (Charles Sanders) Peirce (1839–1914). A philosopher and scholar of many interests, steeped in European culture like all New England intellectuals of his day, Peirce stands also, paradoxically, as the pioneer of a typically American current of thought, pragmatism—although at the end of his career, in order to dissociate himself from the sense given to this term by his pupil William James (1842–1910), he preferred to describe his own doctrine as "pragmaticism."

More than a philosophical system in the classical sense, Peirce's doctrine combined two fundamental theories: a conception of truth that was inseparable from experimental proof together with a method of logic aimed—as he explained in a famous paper published in 1879—at "making our ideas clear."[1] Apart from its undeniable originality, his project was fundamentally therapeutic in character, for it aimed at getting rid of the false problems engendered by a metaphysics that was too far removed from common sense. In this ambition, at least, his work did plainly prefigure that of Carnap.

Pierce was greatly influenced by Kant, from whom he borrowed the term "pragmatic" to describe his own approach, but he was critical of Kantianism, which he reproached, as Bolzano had, for according too important a role to intuition. Peirce situated his logical researches in the context of Boolean algebra. He tried to perfect its notation through simplification, on the one hand, and on the other by introducing (at the suggestion of one of his students in 1883) the universal quantifier ("All . . . ") and the existential quantifier ("Some . . . "). But Peirce was interested less in the technique of calculation than in the philosophy of logic and, in particular, the description of the principal types of signs, which he classed in three families: tokens, indices, and icons. His extensive work in this area makes him the creator—long unrecognized—of a new discipline, semiotics, or the science of signs, and along with Ferdinand de Saussure one of the fathers of modern linguistics.

The leading treatise on logic at the end of the nineteenth century, Ernst Schröder's *Lectures on the Algebra of Logic* (1890), referred mainly to Boole and Peirce, whose influence was subsequently to be felt in the works of the logicians Giuseppe Peano (1858–1932) and Ernst Zermelo (1871–1953). But the great upheaval from which a good part of the philosophy of the twentieth century later emerged was due to an isolated mathematician whose work proceeded from rather different assumptions.

GOTTLOB FREGE (1848–1925), who taught mathematics at the University of Jena for the whole of his professional career, grew up in an intellectual environment dominated by the ideas of Kant and of the mathematician Carl Friedrich Gauss (1777–1855). Like Kant, whose lack of interest in logic he deplored, however, Frege aspired to clarify and so to consolidate the bases of scientific knowledge, beginning with those of mathematics. This last discipline, as Gauss had shown earlier, constituted the common basis for all the experimental sciences. But its own foundations could no longer be conceived at the end of the nineteenth century in terms of Kant's Transcendental Aesthetic.

No matter what orthodox neo-Kantians may have believed, mathematics had in fact greatly evolved since Kant's death. On the one hand, along the path cleared by Gauss, non-Euclidean geometries had been successfully constructed by Lobachevsky (in 1826), Bolyai (1829), and Riemann (1853). Their existence proved that theories that no longer had any connection with Euclidean space could be viable, provided that they rested on coherent systems of axioms. On the other hand, the parallel advances made by analysis and algebra in axiomatization, and therefore in abstraction, little by little emancipated mathematics from its traditional domain of objects—numbers. The theory of sets, anticipated by Bolzano and actually constructed by Cantor, made no appeal to number whatsoever and soon came to be regarded as the simplest and least objectionable of all mathematical theories.

Such is the historical background to Frege's investigations. Early in his career, probably under the influence of the *Logic* (1874) of the philosopher Rudolf Hermann Lotze (1817–81), which was also read by Husserl, he became convinced that arithmetic propositions could not be synthetic a priori judgments but were instead simple analytic judgments, which is to say that their demonstration required no recourse to intuition. If we believe the opposite, this is because we formulate arithmetic statements in our usual language, which possesses neither sufficient precision nor exactitude. In order to eliminate intuition, Frege aimed therefore at freeing arithmetic from the bonds that tied it to natural languages by reformulating it, axiomatically, in terms of a system of conventional signs—logic.

Thanks to Boole, he had at his disposal a first sketch of such a system. Nonetheless, even if Boole had indeed constructed a *calculus ratiocinator*—that is, a technique facilitating the mechanical resolution of certain problems—he had not really demonstrated the validity of the logical laws governing such a procedure. Moreover, Boole's notation was not powerful enough to retranscribe the whole of arithmetic. While recognizing the merits of Boolean algebra, Frege needed therefore to begin by substituting for it a genuine *lingua characteristica*. The principles of this new formalized language of pure thought, as he himself called it, were expounded in his first important work, the *Begriffsschrift* (1879), whose title literally means "writing of concepts" or "ideography."

The symbolism proposed in this slender book—influenced also by the symbolism then employed in algebra, although it was more cumbersome than Boole's and less easily manipulated—effectively permitted Frege to begin to retranslate arithmetic with the help of a limited number of logical terms. The enterprise turned out to be an arduous one. Having published an initial version that still relied on the familiar language of everyday German, *The Foundations of Arithmetic* (1884), Frege now felt the need to modify his approach by generalizing the use of the ideography and taking extreme care to make corrections as he discovered imperfections in it. The task of revision consumed nearly twenty years of unrelenting effort and culminated in a new work, *The Fundamental Laws of Arithmetic*, the first volume of which appeared in 1893 and the second in 1903.

The verdict on this Herculean labor, which must command admiration from an intellectual point of view, remains mixed. Its chief merit is that it achieved a number of important advances in logical, linguistic, and mathematical analysis. On the logical side, Frege's ideography presented a dual advantage. It made possible the predicate calculus by introducing the use of quantifiers (*Begriffsschrift*, §31), four years before Peirce and his students independently hit upon the same idea. It also authorized the reconstruction in axiomatic form of the propositional calculus, unknown to Aristotle and virtually neglected by logicians since its invention by the Stoic school.

Additionally, the revisions that intervened between the *Foundations* and the *Fundamental Laws* led Frege, in an 1892 article entitled "On Sense and Reference," to formulate distinctions that proved to be invaluable not only for logic but also for linguistic analysis. It was necessary, he held, to cease confusing the sense (*Sinn*) of a sign, which is an objective concept, with the subjective representation (*Vorstellung*) that accompanies it in our mind—and, of course, with the object that constitutes its reference (*Bedeutung*). The expressions "Evening Star" and "Morning Star" do not have the same sense although they have the same reference (the planet Venus). These distinctions also apply to propositions. The sense of a proposition—its thought content (*Gedanke*)—is not to be confused with its reference, or truth value, which must be either true or false since, for Frege, there was no third possibility. The interest of this argument lies in its clear break with the "psychologistic error," which consisted in reducing logical concepts to mental contents, and also in showing the formal equivalence of propositions that, though they do not have the same sense, nonetheless possess the same truth value. Frege thus established a fundamental principle of modern logic, the principle of extensionality, according to which every composite proposition is a function of the truth of the propositions of which it is composed.

Finally, on the mathematical side, Frege's contribution was of capital importance for two reasons. First, his ideography permitted arithmetic to be freed at last from its long-standing dependence upon natural languages. Second, the famous definition advanced in the *Foundations* (§68)—that "the Number which belongs to the concept F is the extension of the concept 'equal [*gleichzahlig*] to the concept F'"—constituted an indisputable success for the logicist thesis, for it marked the first time that a cardinal number had been able to be constructed by purely logical methods that owed nothing to intuition.

This was a genuine tour de force and confirmed that the Kantian conception of mathematics had indeed been superseded. One is not therefore obliged, however, to join Frege in upholding the other aspect of the logicist thesis—the belief, shared by both Plato and Cantor, in the actual existence of an intelligible world populated by logico-mathematical entities. On Frege's view, numbers enjoy a reality of their own, their existence being logically prior, now and always, to whatever knowledge we are able to have of them. Although this doctrine continued to be defended by Russell, it was to have difficulty withstanding the criticisms delivered against it after 1920 by Hilbert and Brouwer.

In the meantime, arithmetic as logicized by Frege seemed in the opening years of the present century superior to the logic algebraicized by Boole. It constituted an example, on a far larger scale, of a symbolic system in which the mechanical application of precise rules made it possible to link together the successive steps of a deductive argument until its conclusion is reached. Moreover, given that the meaning of concepts could be fixed at the outset in a conventional manner, it was tempting to suppose that a general method suitable for resolving any problem whatsoever, a *calculus ratiocinator*, had finally been devised—in short, that the true did indeed completely coincide with the demonstrable.

This was not the case, however. Despite its many remarkable aspects, Frege's system was soon to find itself undermined by the discovery of an unsuspected contradiction connected with his use of the notion of concept (or class) extension. This contradiction—which turned out to be, at bottom, identical with certain mathematical antinomies previously detected by Cantor and Burali-Forti—was explicitly identified in June 1902 by one of the first among Frege's few readers, the young Bertrand Russell.

The contradiction may be summarized in terms of the following paradox. Let us consider all the classes that share the property of "not being members of themselves." These must themselves in turn form a class. Is this class a member of itself or not? If it is, then it will have to possess the defining property of this class, which is of not being a member of itself. If it is not, then it cannot possess the property in question and so will have to be a member of itself. Each branch of the alternative therefore logically implies its contrary.

On 16 June 1902 Russell wrote to Frege to inform him of this discovery, which cast doubt upon the entire edifice he had built up. In his response of 22 June, Frege confessed that it "surprised me beyond words and, I should almost like to say, left me thunderstruck." The challenge to his fifth law, he added, was all the more serious because it "seems to undermine not only the foundations of my arithmetic but the only possible foundations of arithmetic as such."[2] Frege's consternation was not without precedent: more than two thousand years earlier, the unforeseen discovery of irrational numbers had likewise led certain Greek philosophers to doubt the very possibility of science itself.

Shortly afterwards, in an appendix added at the last minute to the proofs of the second volume of the Fundamental Laws (1903) with a view to escaping this impasse, Frege proposed a solution that proved to be unsatisfactory on technical grounds. His attempts to improve upon it in the following years were unsuccessful, and he died in 1925 without having managed to consolidate his life's work.

With the Frege-Russell paradox, mathematics saw its foundations shaken by an authentic crisis from which, almost a century later, no real way out has yet been found. One might take the view, however, that this crisis, connected as it is with the problematic conviction that mathematics needs to be provided with foundations in the first place, is less serious than may at first appear since evidently it has not prevented mathematical research from continuing to move forward. Moreover, it did not prevent Frege's own work from playing a philosophically decisive role at the end of the nineteenth century and the beginning of the twentieth. Long before Frege was read by Wittgenstein, Carnap, Quine, Dummett, and others, his work had caused Husserl to experience an intellectual conversion in 1894 and, only a few years later in 1900, inspired a revolution in Russell's thought.

Frege's influence was such that many of the heirs of Husserl and Russell, partisans of phenomenology on the one hand and adherents of logical empiricism on the other, could rightly claim in the person of Frege an ancestor through whom they were linked (although sometimes they denied it) in a single line of descent. For they were all Kantian critics of Kant.

From Logic to Phenomenology

Born in Moravia, then a province of the Austro-Hungarian Empire, Edmund Husserl (1859–1938) displayed when he was still quite young an equal interest in mathematics and philosophy. His choice of a course of study at university confirmed this dual vocation. In 1882 he defended his doctoral thesis, which dealt with the calculus of variations. Around the same time, along with Twardowski, he attended lectures given by Brentano in Vienna and decided to turn in the direction of philosophy—while refusing, like Brentano, to separate this field from science.

From this time forward he devoted himself to the problem of the foundations of mathematics, a subject of great debate since the beginning of the 1880s. In 1887 he obtained his habilitation with an essay on the concept of number (Cantor being among his examiners), out of which four years later came a book that was presented as the first volume of a multivolume Philosophy of Arithmetic. Subtitled "Psychological and Logical Investigations" and dedicated by the author to his teacher Brentano, this work, though it very frequently cites Frege's Foundations, nonetheless challenged the Fregean ambition to reduce all of arithmetic to logic. Husserl thought that it was futile to pretend to explain the basic notions of mathematics (equality, analogy, quantity, unity) in terms of the simplest notions of logic, arguing that it was impossible to eliminate entirely all reference to intuition from the foundation of mathematics. Also in 1891, Husserl published a review of Schröder's Lectures on the Algebra of Logic in which, after having expressed his admiration for formal logic in principle, he criticized it for considering concepts only in terms of extension and not in terms of understanding—in short, for reducing the laws of thought to those of a pure calculus.

Because they did not make a clean break with the empiricist tradition, these arguments could only arouse Frege's disapproval. Frege then believed it both possible and necessary to reconstruct the concept of cardinal number drawing solely upon the resources of logic. Husserl's program, which aimed to make number the product of a mental process of abstraction, seemed to him marred by a useless psychologism. With the publication in 1894 of an article by Frege wholly devoted to the first volume of the Philosophy of Arithmetic,[3] Husserl decided to revise his position.

No doubt his thinking had evolved as a result of a number of convergent factors, and not only in response to Frege's criticisms, by which Husserl actually claimed many years later not to have been at all influenced.[4] Immediately after the appearance of Frege's article, however, Husserl abandoned the idea of bringing out the planned second volume and once again took up the study of logic. Out of this conversion came his best work (an opinion shared even by some of his later disciples), the *Logical Investigations*. Issued in two volumes in 1900 and 1901, the *Investigations* announced the birth of a new discipline, phenomenology, which it defined, using an expression that Husserl was afterwards to renounce, as the "pure ontology of experiences in general."[5]

The first volume, subtitled "Prolegomena to Pure Logic"—no mention of psychology this time—seems to have been written to illustrate a line from Goethe that Husserl not unhumorously cites at the end of his preface: "There is nothing to which one is more severe than the errors that one has just abandoned."[6] Nothing could have been more severe, in fact, than Husserl's condemnation of the associationist psychology that issued from Locke and, more recently, had found expression in the *Logic* (1843) of John Stuart Mill.

Mill, a thoroughgoing empiricist, remains famous for having attempted to reduce the principle of contradiction—the basic principle of logic—to a simple generalization drawn by an observing mind from its own experience. As against such a view—to which Husserl himself never subscribed—and, beyond this, against all forms of empiricism and psychologism, including those advocated in his own time by a number of illustrious scholars (Mach among them), Husserl henceforth set out, following in the footsteps of both Brentano and Frege, to preserve the objective nature of logical concepts as the sole guarantor of the universal validity of mathematics and of science as a whole. Furthermore, he paid tribute to Bolzano's work, in an admirable passage in the first volume of the *Investigations*, ardently proclaiming its philosophical importance.[7]

In the second volume, devoted more particularly to principles of the theory of knowledge, Husserl developed a conception of logic that still contained echoes of Frege—although he hardly cited Frege any longer—but that also revealed the influences, albeit contradictory ones, of Kant and Bolzano. Like Bolzano, he wished to establish logic and the theory of knowledge as autonomous disciplines. These disciplines were to serve in turn, in Husserl's scheme, as the basis for a new, rigorously scientific philosophy. At the same time, here following Kant rather than Frege, he persisted in making the objectivity of logical concepts depend on what he called an "experience" of consciousness.

To use his terms, this experience was plainly "transcendental"—the experience of an obviousness (*Evidenz*), or indubitability, extracted from the jumble of our mental images. Plainly, too, an intellectual "vision" that involved ideal meanings independent of subjective personal experience owed more to Descartes than to either Kant (who rejected its possibility) or the arguments advanced, first in his *Essay on the Immediate Data of Consciousness* (1889) and then in *Matter and Memory* (1896), by the French philosopher Henri Bergson (1859–1941), whose spiritualist and vitalist doctrines were at the time unknown to Husserl. Moreover, if Bergson confided to intuition the mission of embracing reality in its fundamental essence, which for him was the same thing as pure "duration," his elevation of intuition above the intellect (or the conceptual faculty, downgraded in Bergson's scheme to the rank of "inferior" knowledge) was scarcely compatible with the requirement that phenomenological analysis be scientific. It is all the more paradoxical, then, considering this requirement as well as of the antipsychological positions explicitly adopted at the outset of the *Investigations*, to see Husserl hang the whole of his construction on the enigmatic notion of "intuition of essences."

Husserl was by no means unaware of these contradictions, inseparable as they were from the very ambition of the project he had set for himself. Although Husserl thought of the *Investigations*, reasonably enough, as just that—investigations—he nonetheless needed to try to resolve the contradictions. He therefore spent several more years perfecting his method, hoping to locate at last the sources of the clarity and indubitability whose existence he was determined to demonstrate.

The decisive turning point in this regard is to be found in the five lectures that he delivered in April and May 1907 to his students at the University of Göttingen, which he later left in 1916 to go to the University of Freiburg. Now explicitly adopting the Cartesian approach as a model, Husserl affirmed in these lectures (published after his death under the title *The Idea of Phenomenology*) that in order to place philosophy on an unshakable foundation it was necessary to begin by questioning every other source of knowledge. The only reality whose existence imposes itself in an absolute way thus remains that of our thoughts (*cogitationes*), that is, phenomena that appear to our mind—provided, of course, that the mind is defined not as an empirical "I" but as pure consciousness endowed with the capacity of "seeing" essences in themselves, independently of any reference to a "bracketed" world. It is in this difficult text that the transition is made (as Heidegger would later point out)[8] from the metaphysical neutrality of the *Logical Investigations* to a new philosophy of the subject—in other words, to a new transcendental idealism.

Husserl's chief purpose in the years that followed was to develop the main themes of this new idealism. The *Ideas towards a Pure Phenomenology and a Phenomenological Philosophy* (1913) gave a systematic statement of it. *Formal and Transcendental Logic* (1929) took up again, now in a detailed way, the whole of his criticisms of the extensional logic inherited from Frege. Finally, the *Cartesian Meditations*, which grew out of lectures delivered in Paris in 1929, frankly acknowledged his indebtedness to the pre-Kantian tradition in French philosophy.

Can the essential features of Husserlian phenomenology be extracted from this body of texts? Clearly, it does not have much to do with the enterprise pursued by Hegel in the *Phenomenology of Spirit* (1807); it is nearer, by contrast, to the "phaneroscopy," or description of the structure of appearances, imagined by Peirce (although Peirce, like Bergson, was unknown to Husserl). Nonetheless, it cannot easily be reduced to a general schema since it depends on what Husserl called the "obviousnesses," or indubitabilities, of consciousness. To simplify matters, let us distinguish three closely related moments, or stages, of phenomenological investigation.

The first involves *epochē*—at once an act of methodical doubt, suspension of judgment, and bracketing off (*Einklammerung*) of the empirical world in which naive consciousness (including scientific knowledge) remains ensnared. This reflective act of pulling back from the world tears us away from the passivity that characterizes mental life, thereby allowing us to observe not merely brute facts but also the phenomena that are constitutive of consciousness ("this red") and, through these phenomena, the ideal essences ("red") that embody them. *Epochē* thus opens the way to an eidetic reduction (from the Greek *eidos*, "essence") that makes it possible to give a concrete description of the most general structures of being (a description that claims to be more fundamental than the one given by the sciences of nature) and, beyond this, to a "transcendental" reduction that permits access to the modalities of appearing as such. It is, moreover, this return to things themselves (*zu Sachen selbst*)—in other words, to phenomena—that was initially to be responsible for the success of the phenomenological method among philosophers (such as Heidegger and Sartre) who had grown weary of the abstractions circulated by both German neo-Kantians (such as Hermann Cohen) and French neo-Kantians (such as Léon Brunschvicg).

A second stage consists in constitution—that is to say the act by which reflecting subjects, in order to escape solipsism, make a world for themselves, conceiving it as a "horizon of meaning." It is in this context that the intentional function, by re-creating a link between my consciousness and the object that it aims at, comes to be deployed in its full scope. Husserl was inspired here by Brentano's *Psychology from an Empirical Standpoint* (1874), which he credited with reviving the old medieval scholastic notion of intentionality and making it a central concept of modern psychology. All consciousness is consciousness *of* something. For Brentano, however, as for Kant, psychology remained a natural science. Husserl, by contrast, situated intentionality in a transcendental region, independent of and prior to any psychological description. The implications of this move are developed at length in the *Ideas*, which introduces the concept of *noēma*, the indispensable mediator between the mental act (*noēsis*) and its real object.

In a third and final moment, consciousness rediscovers in itself, beneath the culturally produced idealities (or concepts) that arise from scientific thought, the actually experienced or "lived-in" world (*Lebenswelt*). Indeed, this necessarily intersubjective world is the source of such concepts. Even mathematical idealities issue forth from it, since they were intuitions before they were concepts—an argument Husserl made in one of his last books, *The Origin of Geometry* (1936), which bears perhaps some trace of the influence of Heideggerian existentialism on his thought. In any case, by taking up once again the concern with foundations characteristic of the 1880s, this work marks the final flowering of Husserlian phenomenology—and, in a certain sense, its closure upon itself.

ONE SHOULD BE CAREFUL not to judge Husserl's achievement too hastily. Phenomenological theory and practice being closely related, their results are in large measure a function of the skill with which the phenomenologist applies his theory to the concrete analysis of a given phenomenon. The best phenomenological descriptions are often, like those of Sartre, the work of genuinely gifted writers. Even so, was phenomenology really, as Husserl often claimed, an absolutely original project whose realization would at last bring the long odyssey of Western philosophy to an end?

Nothing could be less certain. Indeed, on closer examination it becomes clear that, despite its singular character, phenomenology descended directly from Kantianism and, to a still greater degree, from Cartesianism. For it was Descartes, after all, who first located the foundation of all science in the experience of consciousness as pure thought (*res cogitans*). And it was Kant who located the conditions for the possibility of knowledge—namely, forms of sensibility and categories of understanding—in the structures of the transcendental subject.

Husserl's originality consists ultimately in radicalizing this dual schema. Like both Kant and Descartes, he decided to anchor knowledge in the subject. And like Descartes—but, this time, unlike Kant—he conferred upon the obviousness of subjective experience (known now as intuition of essences) an exorbitant capacity for discerning the truth. Again, like both Descartes and Kant, he was unable to conceive of a better way of founding the sciences than by subordinating them to a philosophy considered more scientific than they themselves were. Husserl thus carries out in his own way the main program of European idealism as though, from Marx to Nietzsche and from Bolzano to Frege, it had never been called into question.

Husserl's approach was, then, a very classical one—too classical, Heidegger said in 1927. In Husserl's judgment, however, it was the only possible one. To grasp the import of such a claim, it is necessary to go back to the text that best stated it, "Philosophy as Rigorous Science" (1911). This article is all the more central to Husserl's work since it was not a mere essay but a genuine manifesto—the manifesto of a phenomenology that, at least until the First World War, felt itself to be borne along on the wings of triumph.

It opens by proclaiming that philosophy, from "its earliest beginnings . . . has claimed to be rigorous science"[9] and that it has never renounced this ideal, no matter what obstacles may have stood in the way of its realization. But these obstacles, Husserl conceded, were serious. On the one hand, the most recent advances in knowledge owed more to progress in scientific experimentation than to the quibbling of philosophers. On the other hand, the importance accorded since Hegel to the notion of history had led to a relativization of the value of knowledge, seen now only as one product of human evolution among others. Primacy was granted, then, to the natural sciences, or naturalism, on the one side, and to history, or historicism, on the other—thus, in 1911, the two dominant forms of a single positivism whose principal effect was to empty the idea of truth of all content and, in so doing, to deprive philosophy of any role for itself.

Husserl resolved to rise up against this positivism. The first part of his manifesto was therefore aimed at refuting naturalism, and the second, historicism. In both he tried to show that the opposing position, taken to its logical extreme, would lead ultimately to incoherence. The first doctrine, associated most notably with the German biologist Ernst Haeckel, champion of a radical materialism, amounted to naturalizing ideas and conscious experience, that is, to treating them as things, which was contrary to what Husserl took to be their essence. By reducing logical laws to simple psychological regularities, and these in turn to physico-chemical processes, it destroyed—without accounting for—the very basis of scientific knowledge, although it pretended to hold this as its supreme value. Naturalism was therefore not the objective method that it claimed to be. It was only a philosophy—and an inconsistent one at that.

As for historicism, which for Husserl was represented by the work of Wilhelm Dilthey (1833–1911), prophet of the sciences of the mind (*Geisteswissenschaften*), or those human sciences in which the historical dimension is central, it likewise rested on an implicit postulate: the assertion that there is no truth as such, independent of human evolution, only ideas that are socially recognized as valid in a definite place and moment in time. The contradiction is blatantly obvious—if there is no truth as such, independent of evolution, then the truth of historicism is no more certain than that of the opposite doctrine. More generally, if everything is relative, the very possibility of knowledge melts away. It should be noted in passing that this argument would frequently be employed by adversaries of relativism who came after Husserl, most recently by Habermas and Putnam, for example, in their debates with Rorty.

In each of its two forms, then, positivism was shown to be dangerous. Against this danger, in which he detected the true cause of the spiritual "distress" of his time[10]—a notion that would later be popularized by Heidegger and his followers—Husserl took up arms, boldly affirming the superiority (both de facto and de jure) of philosophy. To rescue knowledge, to allow reason to flourish in the act of knowing, it was necessary to root this act in a stable, unshifting ground. But such a ground could be furnished only by phenomenological philosophy, understood as the science of essences, itself anchored in a transcendental subject.

In denouncing the impotence of his precursors—Kant included—to set philosophy securely on the sure path of science, Husserl moved to reappropriate their aims while at the same time asserting that he alone was capable of bringing such a project to a successful conclusion. With him, and only him, philosophy would become a rigorous science—not one among others, but the first and most rigorous of them all by virtue of being the "scientific theory of reason" itself.[11] The essay of 1911 announced, in short, a new departure not only for philosophy but also for culture as a whole, of which philosophy was the highest spiritual expression.

In prophesying the (re)birth of philosophy from its own rubble, Husserl was only mimicking the rhetorical gesture made earlier by Descartes, and after him by Kant—the same gesture by which every foundational style of thought establishes itself. Moreover, this act of imitation, by enabling phenomenology to claim a place for itself in the grand tradition of classical metaphysics, helped to confine it within the very model it wished to go beyond. But the archaism that therefore infected phenomenology was not immediately apparent to Husserl and his earliest followers. Indeed, many of those who rallied to the cause of phenomenology from the second decade of the century on—with the notable exception of Heidegger—did so in the belief that they were working to promote the cause of reason, and so of progress tout court. Fortified by their support, Husserl resolutely continued to move forward along the path that he had set for himself, persuaded that the future, if not the present, would eventually prove him right.

Testifying to this perseverance is the paper he delivered twenty-four years after the 1911 essay, as if in echo of it, at the Kulturbund in Vienna on 7 May 1935, "Philosophy and the Crisis of European Man." It took as its point of departure the idea that Europe forms a "family" of nations united together by a "fraternal" bond,[12] a sort of spiritual homeland that Husserl considered to enjoy an obvious superiority over all other cultures, whether those of India or China or, to take his example, that of the Papua New Guineans, whom little separated, in his view, from animality. Husserl held that European superiority was based on its tripart invention of reason, science, and philosophy. But this formidable invention was now in danger, increasingly eaten away by the cancer of positivism, which, by destroying idealities, led to intellectual and moral materialism. The ultimate outcome would be the negation of philosophy, opening the way to every irrationalist excess.

Positivism, then, was the main cause of the distress that characterized the period.[13] On this point, his analysis had not changed since 1911. Nor did it differ with regard to the nature of the remedy. For Husserl, there was only one: to give back to philosophy its primordial place at the foundation of knowledge, to permit philosophy to become the "archon" of humanity,[14] and, simultaneously, to put philosophy back on the right path—that of rigorous science, which is to say, the phenomenological science of essences.

It may seem surprising, in view of the date of this lecture (two years after Hitler's coming to power), that Husserl was not more sensitive to his own ethnocentrism or to the implications of his use of the term archon—unless he deliberately sought to oppose a good to a bad Führer, the two words being practically synonymous. It is equally surprising, given the gravity of his purpose, that he did not succeed in giving it a more politically persuasive formulation. Because he saw barbarism as having its roots in positivism—a vague notion at best—it sufficed for Husserl to restore the science of essences its prerogatives in order to put an end to it. It must be said that there is something disconcerting about such a form of intellectualism.

Did Husserl underestimate the true nature of the danger that threatened the world in 1935? Quite the contrary. For him, the debate over the crisis of European values—a debate that involved Valéry, Rosenzweig, Heidegger, and so many others from 1918 on—was not simply a formal exercise. One needs only to recall that he had lost a son in the First World War and that in 1933 the Nazis barred him from all public activity in Germany on account of his Jewish origins, even though he had freely converted to Protestantism in 1886. If only for these two reasons, Husserl was a profoundly wounded man.

But if the man was wounded, the philosopher, who saw his duty as that of a "civil servant to humanity," felt an obligation to rise above the suffering and contingencies of history. Nothing could force him to doubt himself—not external events, not even, within the academic world, the growing indifference among scientists to his position. For—and this is the main point that needs to be made—the ambition of phenomenology to become the science of sciences had by the middle of the 1930s manifestly failed. Husserl, moreover, was well aware of it. He saw that the sciences, mathematical and experimental alike, went on developing around him with scarcely any regard for his famous eidetic reduction. Indeed, he acknowledged the loss of interest in his work with some melancholy. In this connection one passage is often cited but poorly understood, appendix 28 to paragraph 73 of *The Crisis of European Sciences and Transcendental Phenomenology*, composed during the summer of 1935: "Philosophy as science, as serious, rigorous, indeed apodictically rigorous, science: *the dream is over [der Traum ist ausgetraümt]*."[15]

The meaning of this statement has frequently been misinterpreted. That the dream was finished was indeed the opinion in 1935 of many of those who first believed in phenomenology. Nonetheless, although Husserl took note of their disappointment, he refused to share it; and if he regretted having been deserted along the way, he had no intention of abandoning the journey himself. Once again, phenomenology had to go on, no matter what might happen.

And it did go on, resurfacing after the Second World War in works of the most diverse sort. But now it figured only as a more or less distant point of reference, gradually eclipsed by other currents of thought: the existentialism of Karl Jaspers, the hermeneutics of Hans-Georg Gadamer and Gianni Vattimo, the Marxism of Jean-Paul Sartre, the gestalt psychology of Maurice Merleau-Ponty. Religious, or at least spiritual, concerns were frequently to be mixed together with it as well, some Jewish in origin (as in the work of Martin Buber and Emmanuel Levinas, for instance), others Catholic (Jean-Luc Marion) or Protestant (Paul Ricoeur). Phenomenology, in short, survived less in its pure state than as an element of various alloys, within which its uniqueness—along with its initial ambitions—tended to become blurred.

The reasons for this are not hard to grasp. With his *Logical Investigations*, Husserl rendered an immense service to European philosophy. Coming after Frege and before Russell, he forced it to acknowledge the necessity of utterly rethinking its relation to science and to the theory of knowledge. He saved philosophy from falling into the rut of psychologism and restored its proper purpose as an authentic "thought via concepts"; at the same time, he pulled philosophy down from the heaven of neo-Kantian abstractions in which it had long been laid up in order to call attention to the urgent need of taking into account the world actually lived in by the individual subject.

But Husserl also led philosophy into an impasse, from 1907 on, by gradually confining it within the narrow framework of the *cogito* (even if his was a more comprehensive *cogito* than that of Descartes), by deliberately turning his back upon the evolution of science, and, above all, by haughtily ignoring the constraints of everything—history, language, desire—that threatened to undermine from within the illusory sovereignty of the transcendental subject. "Pure" phenomenology, in the sense the aging Husserl intended, thus found itself condemned little by little, despite its healthy desire to bring about a return to things themselves, to turn away from the real world—a fate his younger followers could escape only by freeing themselves, more or less overtly, from Husserlian orthodoxy.

Let us go a step further. If indeed phenomenology displayed a certain inability to conceive reality in its full complexity, was this not a weakness that from the beginning was built into the dream—grandiose but utopian—of a philosophy defined both as rigorous science and as the founding science of all other sciences? Was not such a dream doomed to failure in advance? The case of Husserl is not the only one that suggests as much. That of Bertrand Russell, who dreamt the same dream during the same years, only in another language—Fregean logic—led in its own way to the same conclusion.

From Logic to Politics

Born into an English aristocratic family of liberal convictions, Bertrand Arthur William Russell (1872–1970) was the grandson of Lord John Russell, a Whig politician who served twice as prime minister. After a solitary childhood, marked early on by a passion for certainty, he found himself being pushed by his family toward an administrative career for which he felt no attraction. At the age of eighteen, however, he discovered Mill's *Logic* and decided to pursue his interest in mathematics at Cambridge. Rapidly disappointed by the conventional manner in which the subject was then taught, he turned instead toward philosophy—more precisely, toward idealism.

English universities during this period were undergoing a phase of reaction against the empiricism that, from Locke through Hume and Mill, had long dominated the British scene. After 1880 this reaction took the form of a return to Kant and, especially, to Hegel. Introduced at Oxford by T. H. (Thomas Hill) Green (1836–82) and Edward Caird (1835–1908), Hegelian doctrines were embraced by Bernard Bosanquet (1848–1923) and F. H. (Francis Herbert) Bradley (1846–1924), whose *Appearance and Reality* (1893) enjoyed a lively success. Cambridge also had its neo-Hegelians, George Stout (1860–1944), editor of the journal *Mind*, and J. M. E. (John McTaggart Ellis) McTaggart (1866–1925), who were to be the young Russell's first teachers. McTaggart, he would later write, "said he could prove by logic that the world is good and the soul immortal. The proof, he admitted, was long and difficult."[16]

Under their supervision, Russell composed for his fellowship dissertation in 1894 an essay, which he later repudiated, on the foundations of geometry. In it he tried, without great success, to defend the Kantian philosophy of mathematics against the refutation implicit in the multiplication of non-Euclidean geometries. At the same time he took up the study of political economy, spending some time the following year in Berlin for this purpose.

Russell's stay in Berlin allowed him to familiarize himself with the doctrines of the German Social Democrats, notably Wilhelm Liebknecht and August Bebel. Derived from Marx (but a Marx freed from all dogmatism and frequently reinterpreted in Kantian terms) and marked by a commitment to social justice and the emancipation of women, these doctrines made a favorable impression upon him. Moreover, the philosophers Hermann Cohen and Paul Natorp, the chief representatives of the neo-Kantian movement whose main seat was located at Marburg, made no attempt to conceal their sympathy for socialist ideas. Owing to these convergences of philosophy and politics, Russell once more took up the study of Kant, which in turn led him back again to mathematics.

His first three published books revealed, significantly as it turned out, the range of his areas of interest. The first, *German Social Democracy* (1896), was drawn from his Berlin experience. The second, *An Essay on the Foundations of Geometry* (1897), developed the themes of his fellowship dissertation. The third, *A Critical Exposition of the Philosophy of Leibniz* (1900)—which was shortly to be echoed by the work of another student of Leibniz, the French logician Louis Couturat (1868–1914)—showed the growing place in his thought occupied by the study of logic. This ability to pass with ease from one subject to another remained until the end one of the most remarkable characteristics of Russell's career. It is explained by the constancy in his thinking of a small number of fundamental preoccupations, foremost among them truth and justice.

On returning to Cambridge from Berlin, Russell was elected a fellow of Trinity College. It was there that in the following years he carried out his revolt against idealism, already anticipated in the work of one of his colleagues, the philosopher G. E. (George Edward) Moore (1873–1958).

Moore had likewise started out as an idealist. Very quickly, however, he began to wonder whether neo-Hegelian metaphysics could be taken seriously. What, he asked, could a theory so far removed from science and common sense really mean? From skepticism, Moore—shortly followed by Russell—passed over into dissent. In April 1899, he announced his change of position by publishing in the journal *Mind* (of which he became the editor in 1921) an article, "The Nature of Judgment," that openly took issue with F. H. Bradley's *Principles of Logic* (1883).

Because he held to a rigorously unitary conception of the absolute, Bradley professed not to believe in the existence of relations. As a result, even though he claimed to be opposed to empiricism, he fell into psychologism by refusing to admit that the meaning of an idea might possess a reality in itself, independent of the subject that thinks it. As against such a doctrine, which leads to a mixed and mystical conception of knowledge, Moore proposed returning to a realist position in respect of concepts and relations. The first he conceived as being endowed with their own existence, independent of our minds, and the second as being quite distinct from the terms that they relate. Although naive in certain respects, this realism had two virtues. On the one hand, it contributed in its own way to finishing off psychologism. On the other hand, it allowed a rational theory of knowledge to be constructed that was analytic, pluralist, and open to the idea of verification.

Four years later, in 1903, Moore published another article, "The Refutation of Idealism," which dealt severely with Berkeley's solipsism, as well as his first great book, *Principia Ethica*, which illustrated the possibility of extending realism to the sphere of moral concepts. Underlying this work, whose influence was to be considerable upon Anglo-American philosophy, is the thesis that the "Good" is not a noun, or the name of a particular "thing," but a predicate used in certain types of judgment—ethical judgments. This predicate is, moreover, undefinable since its meaning, far from being mysterious, is both simple and unique and cannot possibly be mistaken. By relying upon common sense and trusting in ordinary language, correctly analyzed, Moore thus managed to dispel what he called the naturalistic fallacy, that is, the deceptive reasoning by which metaphysicians such as Bentham and Mill believed they were able to "explain" the Good in reducing it to something else—to pleasure, for example, or to utility.

At the time, the method was revolutionary. Filled with enthusiasm by the prospect that it held out for progress in philosophy, Russell came to adopt it as his own. But if he was a convert to Moore's ideas, he chose to apply them to a different domain than ethics, or, more exactly, to start back again along the path that had attracted him at the end of his student career and to renew his inquiry into the foundations of mathematics. This was essentially a Kantian inquiry, only now Russell called into question the doctrine of the Transcendental Aesthetic, as Frege, whose work was still unknown to him, had done earlier. He had, however, already discovered the work of Boole, Peirce, Schröder, and, above all, the Italian logician Giuseppe Peano, whom he met in Paris in July 1900 at an international congress of philosophy.

This turned out to be a decisive encounter, for it provoked a genuine revolution in Russell's thinking; his later changes, as he said afterwards, were the product of simple evolution. Under the joint influence of Moore and Peano, Russell set to work to found mathematics on a purely logical basis—the only one, he believed, capable of guaranteeing its objectivity. A first sketch of this grand project was contained in the *Principles of Mathematics* (published in 1903 but written for the most part at the end of 1900), the definitive form of which was developed in *Principia Mathematica*. Written in close cooperation with the philosopher and mathematician Alfred North Whitehead (1867–1947), the three volumes of the *Principia*—whose title was modeled on that of Moore's book—appeared between 1910 and 1913.

From Moore the *Principles of Mathematics* borrowed both a method—attention to the structures of language—and a philosophy—pluralism and realism of concepts. Denouncing in his own turn the psychologism of both Bradley and Mill, Russell clearly distinguished the proposition, an autonomous logical entity, from the sentence that expresses it in words. He held furthermore that the linguistic analysis of a sentence may serve to illuminate the logical analysis of the corresponding proposition, provided one is careful not to mix up the two levels. Without being a master, grammar could yet be a guide.

As the herald of a linguistic turn in modern thought, this method in its various forms became the common frame of reference during the decades that followed for all practitioners of analytic philosophy, a style of thought—still dominant in Britain and America—that from the point of view of philosophical technique constitutes the major innovation of the century. Its first application in the *Principles of Mathematics* led Russell to make a fundamental distinction between meaning and denotation. Closely related to the one that Frege had introduced in 1892 between sense and reference, this distinction rests on a pair of simple definitions: a name "signifies" a concept—and, by virtue of this, has meaning—while a concept "denotes" an object. By hypothesis, the fact that we understand what a term means implies that it refers, via a concept, to an object endowed with real existence, whether material (a chair, for example) or intelligible (a number). Such a strongly Platonist ontology was soon shown to be excessively rich, however, and in 1905 Russell settled for a less luxuriant version.

In the meantime it offered a convenient framework for the reconstruction of mathematics. Defining the notion of a class on the basis of the purely logical notion of a propositional function (a class being the set of objects by which a function is verified), Russell used the calculus of classes to introduce a theory of orders, and this in turn to construct the concept of cardinal number. Technically, the success of the logicist program was due to Peano. In his *Notations of Mathematical Logic* (1894), and then in the five-volume *Mathematical Compendium* (or "Formulario Completo," which appeared in installments between 1895 and 1908), Peano devised a system of notation called pasigraphy that influenced Russell and others. Capable of "noting everything," as its name suggests, Peano's pasigraphy facilitated the translation of mathematical reasoning into purely logical terms as well as its axiomatization in a less profound but more manageable manner than Frege's ideography, whose partial influence he acknowledged.

It was moreover from Peano, during their meeting in July 1900, that Russell first heard of Frege's work. Working his way through it over the course of the next ten years, Russell discovered with some surprise a good many points of convergence between Frege's thinking and his own. The two men shared, among other things, the same Platonist conception of number, which Russell for his part summarized in this striking formula: "Every one except a philosopher can see the difference between a post and my idea of a post, but few see the difference between the number 2 and my idea of the number 2. Yet the distinction is as necessary in one case as in the other. . . . In short, all knowledge must be recognition . . . ; Arithmetic must be discovered in just the same sense in which Columbus discovered the West Indies, and we no more create numbers than he created the Indians."[17]

Unfortunately, it was not long before the discovery of the foundations of mathematics revealed itself to be as dangerous as that of the New World. The ancient Greeks had examined the problem of what credit should be attached to the sentence "All Cretans are liars" when this sentence is uttered by a Cretan—what came to be called Epimenides' Paradox; nearer our own time, as we have already seen, contradictions of the same kind had been detected by Cantor (in 1895) and Burali-Forti (in 1897). Russell became aware of the existence of these latter difficulties in 1901 on reading Cantor's work. But even though such antinomies, related to the concept of class, threatened to undermine the logicist construction, he did not immediately appreciate their consequences. It was only when he received Frege's despairing reply to his letter pointing out a new contradiction in the first volume of the *Fundamental Laws of Arithmetic* that he understood the importance of what was at stake. If mathematics were to be saved, it was essential that this paradox be resolved. It was no longer a question of a simple mental game, but of the very future of science.

Like Frege in the second volume of the *Fundamental Laws*, Russell added to the *Principles of Mathematics* a passage just prior to publication in which he called attention to his awkward discovery—and, at the same time, paid tribute to Frege's work, which had anticipated his own. The two works both appeared in 1903, a few weeks apart. Frege's work proposed a device for eliminating the contradiction whose precariousness he himself recognized; Russell's, on the other hand, suggested the beginnings of a solution.

Relying on the distinction, introduced by Peano, between membership and inclusion, according to which a set is prohibited from being a member of itself, this solution assumed the form of a theory of logical types, or levels. No more than mortality is itself mortal, a predicate cannot be predicated of itself—only of an individual, that is, of a logically lower type. Indeed, it did seem as though the common source of all such contradictions resided in the appearance of predicative expressions violating this logical hierarchy—as when one speaks, for example, of a class that is a member of itself—and that the formation of such "meaningless," and therefore illegitimate, expressions could be ruled out from the start by appropriate syntactical rules, which is to say by supplementary postulates.

Although Frege was loath to make his system depend on conventions of language, Russell's suggestion was not the less appealing for this. It proceeded from a desire, similar to Moore's, to eliminate false problems. This motivation was to be met with again twenty years later in the doctrines of the Vienna Circle; in the meantime it remained for Russell to give his proposal a precise logical statement, a task that took him several more years to accomplish, and one that obliged him in the process to curtail the overly permissive ontology that formed the basis of the *Principles*.

This reduction in entities was carried out in a brief but crucial article, "On Denotation" (1905). Russell took up once again the thorny problem of denoting expressions—"the father of Charles II," "the author of *Waverley*," and so on—and showed that such expressions could be treated as a formula of the type "the term having the property F," that is, as a simple function $F(x)$ that by itself denotes nothing. The question of denotation could then be resolved by the construction of a sentence containing an existential quantifier: "there exists an x such that $F(x)$." This sentence, in turn, could be verified (or not) by the usual procedures.

The new technique of analysis was conveniently manipulated and allowed substantial ontological economies to be achieved. Breaking with the Platonism he himself had defended two years earlier, following Meinong and Frege, Russell henceforth admitted that certain plainly meaningful expressions—"the current king of France," "the gold mountain"—nonetheless in reality denoted no object whatever. At the same time he turned in the direction of a cautious constructivism. In order to prevent the emergence of problematic entities, every complex notion was now to be redescribed—or reconstructed—on the basis of simpler notions, themselves properly formed, exactly as arithmetic concepts were handled in a correct axiomatic treatment.

The fruits of this new philosophy, the three volumes of *Principia Mathematica*, began to appear five years later, in 1910. This work, due as much to

Whitehead as to Russell, constituted their major contribution to the foundations of mathematics and, still more importantly, the most complete realization of the logicist program, anticipated by Bolzano nearly a century earlier,
which Frege himself had been unable, however, to bring to a successful conclusion. Its superiority over previous attempts was due to three things. First,
unlike Peano, who had restricted himself to translating the formulas of arithmetic into the language of logic, Russell and Whitehead managed to reconstruct these formulas by solely logical means. Moreover, not only was all of
arithmetic and analysis at last reduced to the laws of logic, but these laws
were themselves reconstructed with implacable rigor on the basis of a small
number of primitive notions. As has often been remarked, it is not until the
second theorem of the one hundred tenth chapter of the second volume of
the *Principia* that the formula "$1 + 1 = 2$" is able to be demonstrated.

Second, the solidity of the edifice was now guaranteed by the definitive
exposition—in a much more detailed form than in 1903—of the theory of
types. The contradictions that marred the work of Cantor and Frege had now
disappeared for good. Finally, the use of the theory of descriptions worked
out in 1905 made it possible to replace the anarchic ontology of the *Principles*
with a methodological nominalism inspired by Occam's famous razor, combined now with a vigilant constructivism. The *Principia*—a monument of
pure thought whose formidable success depended ultimately on its agreement with common sense—appeared at first to be an impregnable fortress.

But it was not without its flaws. Let us begin with the technical difficulties, connected with the inevitably endless nature of any search for foundations. To establish the foundations of arithmetic, Russell and Whitehead
had to have recourse to certain doubtful postulates, of which at least one—
asserting the existence of an infinite set—seemed impossible to justify from
a strictly logical point of view. Second, the work remained incomplete since
it ignored geometry. Indeed, in principle, the categorical nature of logical
laws is incompatible with the hypothetical character of systems of geometrical axioms. Russell, who had started out as a Kantian in geometry, came to
realize this in 1910. "It has gradually appeared," he wrote that year, "by the
increase of non-Euclidean systems, that Geometry throws no more light
upon the nature of space than Arithmetic throws upon the population of the
United States. . . . Whether Euclid's axioms are true, is a question as to
which the pure mathematician is indifferent."[18] The long-repressed consequences of this quite unassailable position found expression in the fact that

there is no fourth volume of the *Principia*, which deals exclusively with arithmetic; geometry, if it is only an axiomatic game, must elude the grasp of pure mathematics, and therefore of the logicist reduction as well.

Third, to the question whether the choice of primitive notions made by Russell and Whitehead was the right one, the only possible answer is that it was justified a posteriori, by the fact that it permitted the reconstruction of arithmetic and analysis. In short, it was a matter of the consequences guaranteeing the validity of the premises rather than the other way round, as is usually the case. This situation was a source of frustration to professional mathematicians and explains why over the course of the twentieth century they came to display a certain skepticism with regard to logic and, eventually, indifference to the problem of the foundations of their own discipline. For most mathematicians today, the *Principia* no longer holds anything more than strictly historical interest.

Still worse was to come. Russell, as we have seen, regarded logical laws as categorical principles. He believed in their universality and in their absolute truth—truth residing, for him as for many ancient and medieval philosophers, in the agreement of a statement with an objective reality, in this case an intelligible reality. Indeed, such traces of Platonism as survived in Russell's thinking at the time of the *Principia* are connected with this very belief. But the Platonist conception of truth, which in the last analysis was indispensable to the cohesion of the logicist system, proved unable to withstand the rapid evolution of logico-mathematical investigation in the years that followed.

In 1920, for example, the Polish logician Łukasiewicz elaborated a three-valued calculus in which, between the true and the false, he introduced a third truth value, neither true nor false. Every bit as coherent as two-valued logic, such a calculus proved that the sacrosanct principle of the excluded middle was by no means inviolable. Doubts about this principle had begun to develop as early as 1908 with the early work of the Dutch mathematician L. E. J. Brouwer (1881–1966). Acting on a suggestion made by Henri Poincaré (1854–1912)—one of the most resolute adversaries of Russellian logicism— Brouwer advocated a return to Kantian doctrine as well as a radical nominalism. Holding that the only concepts admissible in mathematics are those whose construction can be carried out within the framework of an intuition, he developed in the 1920s and 1930s a new intuitionist mathematics from which certain types of classical reasoning, such as reduction to the absurd, were excluded.

Another mathematician, the German David Hilbert (1862–1943), who had worked on the question of axiomatization since the appearance of his *Foundations of Geometry* (1899), developed a formalist theory of mathematical reasoning in the 1920s. Opposed to both intuitionism and logicism, it amounted to conceiving not only geometry but also the whole of mathematics as a simple hypothetico-deductive system. Finally, in 1931, the Austrian mathematician Kurt Gödel (1906–78) demonstrated two important theorems—of which we shall have more to say further on—that established once and for all the necessary limits of formalization in mathematics.

All these investigations have one thing in common: they challenged the validity of the logicist enterprise. One of Russell's first disciples, the philosopher Ludwig Wittgenstein, had in fact anticipated their arguments. Of all the readers of the *Principia*, none detected its weaknesses more astutely than Wittgenstein. His objections bore essentially on three points. First, the theory of judgment assumed by this work relied surreptitiously upon the metaphysical notion of the subject. Second, the theory of types, contrary to what was claimed, was not a purely syntactic theory. Finally, if one truly wished to escape Platonist ontology, it was necessary to accept the view that logical and mathematical propositions were trivial tautologies. These criticisms, formulated at Cambridge in 1913 and delivered verbally that summer with the harshness that was sometimes typical of Wittgenstein, despite his immense admiration for Russell, were taken very hard by his teacher. In January of the following year, Russell confided to Ottoline Morrell that the attacks of his young student had reduced him to despair.[19] Two years later he admitted that his philosophical spirit was shattered.

In 1922, however, in the preface that he wrote for Wittgenstein's *Tractatus Logico-Philosophicus*, Russell tried to reconcile the latter's position with his own. A new introduction to the second edition of the *Principia* in 1925— which Whitehead, who had gone to Harvard the year before, refused to join him in signing—together with certain minor corrections show that Russell still believed in the possibility of defusing Wittgenstein's criticisms by partially integrating them. But their points of view were decidedly too opposed, and in any case logicism did not readily lend itself to detailed revisions. Did Russell at this point believe that he could not go any further along the path that he had chosen? Or was it rather that logic, to which he had given so much, had ceased to interest him? However this may be, in the years that followed he scarcely devoted himself either to logic or to philosophy of mathematics in general.

He now turned his attention to problems that raised larger issues of an ontological and epistemological nature. What, for example, were the conceptions of the world and of knowledge that formed the background to the *Principia*? First sketched in *The Problems of Philosophy* (1912), a small book that became a classic of twentieth-century literature, the answer to this question was developed in *Our Knowledge of the External World* (1914) as well as in a series of lectures given in 1918, "The Philosophy of Logical Atomism," in which Russell explicitly acknowledged his debt to certain of Wittgenstein's ideas.

In *Our Knowledge of the External World*, Russell argued that on the basis of the information supplied by sensible experience ("sense data") it is possible in principle—so long as the rules of logic and mathematics are respected—to reconstruct the human mind in its subjective unity as well as the objects of the material world, or, more precisely, to reconstruct the "atomic facts" out of which this world is composed and that are studied by the experimental sciences.

Such a conception amounts to deriving the whole of reality from the contents of our consciousness. The question arises whether it is to be interpreted as a form of idealism or of materialism. Russell—who in 1914 leaned toward a neutral monism that did not distinguish mind from matter—refused to choose between these two systems, which he considered metaphysical, opting instead for a restricted phenomenalism, similar to the pragmatism of William James and the empiricism of Ernst Mach that in turn influenced Wittgenstein and the Vienna Circle. It raised formidable difficulties, however, to which Carnap in particular called attention. Russell himself elected to avoid them by gradually retreating toward a more classical materialism based on the priority of matter in relation to mind.

Reflection upon the philosophical problems of the experimental sciences occupied Russell until the end of his life. This was in any case the only area of philosophy in which he continued to be productive after 1920 on a regular basis. Among other works, *Analysis of Mind* (1921), *Analysis of Matter* (1927), *Determinism and Physics* (1936), *Meaning and Truth* (1940), and *Human Knowledge* (1948) testify to his abiding interest in developments in physics, psychology, and linguistics. The structure of the universe, the nature of space and time, and the functioning of the human brain were now the major topics of his writing. Henceforth they interested him more than the investigations of his youth. The increasingly modest opinion that he came to have of his own role as a philosopher was itself a sign of a profound change in his personality. From 1914 on he seemed to regard the experimental sciences as the sole valid source of knowledge—as though he could no longer see any other mission for philosophy than to humbly assist scientists in overcoming the theoretical obstacles they encountered in their work.

TO UNDERSTAND THIS CHANGE, one must realize that the First World War radically altered the course of Russell's life. The triumph of barbarism on the battlefields caused him to feel intensely the vanity of culture and the hypocrisy of morality, forcing his "retreat from Pythagoras," as he later described the course of his philosophical development.[20]

Fighting in favor of reason—or, more simply, common sense—in the social sphere now displaced pure research as the most important thing in Russell's life. If his own account is to be believed, this battle had nothing to do with philosophy in the strict sense, since philosophy reduced to analysis of the sciences; it had, by contrast, to accommodate itself to the forms of action that were liable to influence public opinion—journalism, the lecture circuit, polemical essays—as though, at bottom, no close connection between theory and practice was possible.

There existed therefore a political Russell who deliberately turned his back upon Russell the philosopher and logician, engaged with his century but regarding himself as at best a pamphleteer, never as a philosopher. This strange dissociation of personalities reached back far in Russell's life; his first published book, it will be recalled, was an essay on socialism. Twenty years later, his need to intervene in the great national and international debates of the day was reawakened by the shock of war. The horror that it inspired in him unleashed a veritable frenzy of words. Four works, appearing within the space of two years, testify to the vigor of his involvement: "War, the Offspring of Fear" (1915), *Justice in War-Time* (1915), *Principles of Social Reconstruction* (1916), and *Political Ideals* (1917). Shortly afterwards, in 1918, he found himself imprisoned for several months for having written an article criticizing certain actions of the American army.

A self-styled freethinker and, by virtue of his internationalist outlook, a pacifist, sympathetic to progressive ideas and deeply concerned with social justice, Russell stood in the left wing of the Labour Party. He was well disposed in principle toward the Bolshevik revolution, and in 1920 he accompanied a British delegation officially invited to visit the Soviet Union. What he discovered during this brief but extremely busy trip—during which he was even received by Lenin for an hour—prompted him, however, to revise his opinions.

It was not so much the new economic system that he rejected—to the contrary, he admitted that the Soviet government had done its best under difficult circumstances to feed the population—as the absence of political liberty. The book that he wrote in the aftermath of this trip, The Practice and Theory of Bolshevism (1920), was ultimately harsh in its judgment of the Soviet Union—a prison run by zealots, as he put it—and of Bolshevism—which he accused of being "a religion, not an ordinary political movement."[21] At the level of detail Russell showed himself to be an excellent observer, noting without prejudice positive as well as negative aspects of the new regime. He did not hate the Bolsheviks. "They are neither angels to be worshipped nor devils to be exterminated," he wrote, "but merely bold and able men attempting with great skill an almost impossible task."[22] His report ended on an optimistic note: "Russian Communism may fail and go under, but Socialism itself will not die."[23] Not such a bad prediction, as it turns out.

During the following decades, Russell took many stands on subjects of all kinds. Stretching out over a half-century, his essays on politics and morals—which won him the Nobel Prize for Literature in 1950—treated the condition of women, marriage, education, happiness, religion (which he saw as the principal brake on the progress of civilization), democracy (which he thought unachievable in Africa),[24] the future of humanity, the impact of science on society, and, above all, the necessity of preserving world peace.

Russell's pacifism was strengthened by the First World War and remained his fundamental conviction until his death. To this two notable exceptions existed, one perhaps more understandable than the other. While it is natural that he should have approved the Allies' commitment to fight Hitler during the Second World War, it may seem surprising that he so fervently advocated mounting a preventive war in the 1950s against the Soviet Union, with the sole aim of preventing it from equipping itself with atomic weapons. But Russell genuinely feared nuclear apocalypse. The force of his convictions in this connection won him a second stay (of a week) in prison in 1961, when he was eighty-nine years old.

Another paradox is that his radical condemnation of American intervention in Vietnam in the 1960s drew him closer to Sartre and various movements of the extreme Left whose political program he did not share. But Lord

Russell—a title he had borne since the death of his elder brother, the Second Earl Russell, in 1931—was nothing if not contradictory, in both his public and his personal life. Such reversals sometimes reflected his own development, sometimes the circumstantial necessities of the various battles that he waged simultaneously. They seem in any case to justify Russell's view that the struggle for social progress, because it cannot be made to conform to the requirements of logic, comes under the head of a type of activity that is not to be confused with philosophy.

Such a view, although it reflects an admirable honesty, nonetheless carries with it serious disadvantages. On the one hand, it restricts philosophers to the analysis of science, excluding all other subjects. On the other hand, it has the effect of abandoning ethics, aesthetics, and politics to the lies of ideologues, the inaccuracies of journalists, and the reveries of poets. It decrees, without really demonstrating, the existence of an unbridgeable gap between knowledge and action—a gap as dangerous, finally, for the one as for the other.

Russell's career therefore leads to conclusions similar to those suggested by Husserl's, despite the obvious differences between the two. Both thinkers, because they had set for themselves the same unrealizable ideal—of placing philosophy on the sure path of science—were for just this reason condemned to philosophize outside the world: Husserl for having gradually cut himself off from the actual work of professional scientists, whom he suspected of positivism; Russell, conversely, for having sealed philosophy off within a parascientific sphere, artificially separated from the social world. Neither one knew how—or wished—to give to reason, their common inheritance from the Enlightenment, the permission to confront the problems of their age.

As a result, the initially radical character of their respective programs was swept away by the winds of history after the First World War, and the basic assumptions of these programs soon came to be called into question by their followers. If certain themes of Husserlian phenomenology have in spite of everything survived the century, they owe it to their having been recycled and transformed by existentialist thought (in the hands of Heidegger and Sartre) and religious philosophy (by Levinas and others). Russell's work, although it remains a major point of reference for contemporary Anglo-American philosophy, was seriously contested during his lifetime—in the first place by the very person whom Russell expected to be its foremost representative,

Ludwig Wittgenstein. This challenge had considerable consequences for all those who, even still today, claim to be inspired by the analytic—or logical and linguistic—tradition of which Frege was the forebear.

Wittgenstein's Dissidence

Ludwig Wittgenstein (1889–1951), the most important philosopher of the twentieth century, published only one book during his lifetime, the *Tractatus Logico-Philosophicus* (1921). From 1929, in his courses, conversations, and letters he began to reject certain of the theses advanced in this work. Two years after his death, an unfinished second book on which he had been working from 1936 to 1949 appeared under the title *Philosophical Investigations*. In this work new lines of thought are sketched that, although they derive from the *Tractatus*, sometimes depart from it in essential respects. Both works proceed nonetheless from a single ambition: to understand what it meant to practice philosophy now that it had become clear that philosophy could not in any way be thought of as a science. This project took various forms over the years, in large part owing to the complex personality of a philosopher for whom intense self-examination was a way of life.

Wittgenstein was born into a wealthy upper-middle-class family in Vienna. His father, an enlightened industrialist, was the patron of the painter Gustav Klimt, who painted a magnificent portrait of one of Ludwig's sisters. Ravel dedicated the *Concerto for the Left Hand* to his brother Paul, a gifted concert pianist who lost an arm during the war. An excellent musician himself, Wittgenstein remained influenced throughout his life by the aesthetics of the Viennese avant-garde. The sober and geometric style of the *Tractatus* evoked that of the architect Adolf Loos, while its attention to language recalled the writer Karl Kraus's critical vigilance against journalistic jargon.

Wittgenstein's family was originally Jewish but had already long been assimilated by the end of the nineteenth century. The young Ludwig, baptized and brought up in the Catholic faith like his seven brothers and sisters, nonetheless wondered from time to time whether he ought to consider himself a Jew—a question that preoccupied him all the more as anti-Semitism continued to grow in Austrian society during this period. No doubt connected with the anxiety that this question aroused in him was the disturbing interest that he showed in *Sex and Character* (1903), a notorious anti-Semitic and antifeminist pamphlet published by the Viennese Jewish and homosexual writer Otto Weininger.

With the completion of his secondary education, having shown himself to be a rather average student, he left for Germany and thence to England. There, in Manchester, from 1908 to 1911 he devoted himself to the study of aeronautics, then a booming field. He was attracted to a technical trade that suited his taste for the concrete, his aptitude for manual work, and his desire to become, like his father, a man of action. Fate decided otherwise—even though, once he had become a philosopher, Wittgenstein stood out for his ability to treat theoretical problems in practical terms, to settle them as one settles a business matter.

In the summer of 1911, however—at least according to Wittgenstein's own account, which has not been satisfactorily confirmed—he went to Jena to meet Frege. His engineering studies had led him in the meantime to take an interest in the foundations of mathematics, and he now found himself unsure which path to choose. Frege advised him to return to England in order to study with Russell at Cambridge. A few weeks later Wittgenstein obediently enrolled at Trinity College.

Meeting Russell, who was seventeen years older and just then finishing the *Principia*, turned out to be the decisive event of Wittgenstein's life. Under Russell's tutelage he threw himself into the study of mathematical logic. It was not long before his intellectual gifts attracted the admiring notice of the dons at Cambridge. Moore, Russell, the economist John Maynard Keynes, and other members of the faculty accepted him as though he were a colleague, treating him as an equal in debate. After having been at first irritated by the fiery temper of the young Austrian, Russell felt tempted to regard him as his spiritual son.

Wittgenstein, for his part, though he was fascinated by the logicist program, very quickly came to have doubts about the scientific character of Russell's philosophy of mathematics and, in particular, about the validity of one of its essential elements, the theory of types. Stormy arguments followed that left Russell profoundly despondent. In 1913 relations between the two men began to deteriorate. They were never to be set right.

It must be said that Wittgenstein combined a naturally mercurial disposition with often unpredictable behavior. His ill temper soon became as well known as his depressions. The years from 1911 to 1914 coincided, moreover, with a particularly acute phase of personal crisis. He was wrestling at the time with the problem of providing foundations for mathematics, which he returned to Jena to discuss with Frege in December 1913; the desire to write a definitive book contended in his mind with the worry that he might not be capable of it. Additionally, the development of his homosexual tendencies threw him into a fit of despair that the rigidity of his moral conscience did nothing to assuage. In 1914 he was haunted by the idea of suicide.

He might actually have gone through with it had the war not suddenly broken out, catching him by surprise in Austria, where he had returned for a summer vacation. He enlisted at once as a volunteer even though he had been exempted from military service for medical reasons. In this he was guided not only by patriotism but also by the need, as he himself said, to atone for his sins—to reassert his worth in his own eyes by giving a clear and simple meaning to his existence. The war brought him a sort of moral redemption, while at the same time allowing him to sublimate his suicidal impulses.

Sent first to the Russian front and then to the Italian front, he deliberately sought danger, giving proof on several occasions of exemplary courage. Despite the difficulties of his daily life, he continued to work. He read Nietzsche, Emerson, and Dostoyevsky. Although his concerns remained centered on logic, they now extended to the whole of philosophy and, in particular, to ethics. Ethics and logic seemed to him, unlike Russell, to be mysteriously linked. Each, he wrote in his notebook on 24 July 1916, must be a "condition of the world."[25] By August 1918 he had managed to finish the manuscript of the book that he had been working on for several years, which he titled *Logisch-philosophische Abhandlung* (Logical-Philosophical Treatise). Rarely has a work been conceived under such dramatic circumstances.

Taken prisoner by the Italian army on 3 November 1918, a few days before the armistice, Wittgenstein was brought to Monte Cassino. He rejected all attempts at intervention on his behalf, including those of his English friends concerned for his fate, and was set free only in August 1919. In the meantime he decided to renounce a university career. Back in Vienna, in September 1919, he gave away to two of his sisters his share of the fortune that he had inherited on their father's death six years earlier. Resolved to make himself useful to society while leading a life in closer agreement with his own aspirations, he chose to become a schoolteacher in a remote Austrian village. His new career began in the fall of 1920 and lasted until 1926.

At the same time that Wittgenstein was embarking upon this ascetic path, he applied himself to the task—a difficult one, as it was to turn out—of finding a publisher for his *Treatise*. In the spring of 1919 he wrote to Frege and Russell for advice. Their responses were scarcely encouraging. Frege, the first to reply, informed him in a letter dated 28 June 1919 that he did not understand what the book meant. Given that all his questions dealt with the first page, it may be wondered whether he had made any attempt to read further. A few weeks later, on 13 August, a letter from Russell showed that although he had read the entire manuscript he was interested only in the remarks on logic, and even there he was far from wholeheartedly approving. Disappointed, Wittgenstein turned next to Viennese publishing houses, where—despite Rilke's support—he met with rejection after rejection. Finally, in December 1919, he went to The Hague to meet again with Russell, whom he had not seen since 1914. Russell agreed to help and even offered to write an introduction. Wittgenstein later said that it showed that Russell had not understood the book any better than Frege had.

The *Treatise* finally appeared in 1921 in a journal published in Leipzig, *Annalen der Naturphilosophie*, but with a great many errors since the proofs had not been corrected. Wittgenstein was horrified. Russell was able to find an English publisher, however, and the work appeared again the following year, this time in a bilingual version. Wittgenstein subsequently regarded the German text of this second edition as the authoritative text; the English translation was the work of a brilliant young Cambridge logician, Frank P. Ramsey (1903–30). In the meantime the book had undergone a change of title and henceforth, on the recommendation of Moore, who was anxious to suggest a parallel between Wittgenstein and Spinoza, was called *Tractatus Logico-Philosophicus*.

THE BOOK IS EXCEPTIONAL in all respects. Written by a young man who, although he was an able logician, took hardly any interest in the history of philosophy and seemed to have read only a few works by Saint Augustine, Schopenhauer, Kierkegaard, and Nietzsche, it nonetheless gives proof of an immense intellectual ambition, manifested by the brief preface Wittgenstein composed to explain the point of his enterprise.

Its object, he asserted, was to show that philosophical problems in general are false problems and that "the reason why these problems are posed is that the logic of our language is misunderstood"[26]—in other words, that they rest upon a vast linguistic misunderstanding. To this first provocation Wittgenstein added a second, declaring himself to be unconcerned whether what he had written might agree or not with what others before him had thought. (He did acknowledge, however, an enormous debt to "Frege's great works" and to "the writings of my friend Mr Bertrand Russell.") He concluded by emphasizing—a third provocation—that the truth of the thoughts expressed in his book seemed to him "unassailable and definitive." Wittgenstein believed himself "to have found, on all essential points, the final solution of the problems"[27]—a claim that he would eventually abandon after 1929.

Short and concise, less than eighty pages long, the *Tractatus* is presented in the form of a succession of propositions numbered according to a simple system (1, 1.1, 1.11, 1.2, 2, etc.) designed to recall the axiomatic presentation of *Principia Mathematica*. This structure is, however, only superficially clear. In fact, Wittgenstein rarely takes the trouble to argue for his claims or to make explicit the links that underlie the transition from one proposition to another. It is rather as though, convinced that logic and philosophy are two distinctly different activities, he meant to challenge in advance any attempt to make the latter a demonstrative science on the model of the former. Moreover this was not, as we shall see, merely a methodological assumption; it constitutes one of the principal theses of the work.

The *Tractatus* rests upon a dual and parallel analysis of reality and language, directly inspired by the theory of the atomic structure of matter. According to the first proposition of the book, the world—which is only another name for reality—is "everything that is the case." It is made up of molecular, or complex, facts, which in turn may be broken down into atomic facts or "states of affairs," which is to say, into configurations of elementary objects. Correspondingly, thought—that is, language—is made up of complex propositions, analyzable into atomic propositions that jointly link up the names, or "simple signs," of objects.

Just as a geographical map represents a physical landscape, the connection of elements within a proposition represents that of objects in the world. What is more, these two types of connection are the same. They are identical with the "form of representation" that the world and the picture of the world given by our language have in common (2.151). As a consequence, this picture may be taken to represent everything—with the exception, however, of its own form of representation. With regard to the latter form, Wittgenstein adds, "A picture cannot . . . depict its pictorial form: it displays it" (2.172). Even if it recalls other similar distinctions—the distinction between phenomenon and the thing-in-itself in Kant, for example, or between representation and will in Schopenhauer—the one introduced here was both new and fundamental. There are objects—objects of the world—that one may speak of, or represent; and there are others—the form itself of representation—about which one can say nothing, that may only be shown. This opposition between *saying* and *showing*, which constitutes the central core of the *Tractatus*, continues to be developed during the course of the book.

Meanwhile Wittgenstein observes that assertion of a structural identity between the world and language carries with it a crucial implication: the totality of true propositions, coinciding with the totality of the natural sciences, must provide a "logical picture of facts" (3) that, by definition, is adequate and complete. Wittgenstein is careful, following the example of scientific empiricists such as Mach, Boltzmann, and Hertz, to emphasize that the laws of science are nothing more than the expression of a logical connection among phenomena—in short, that the experimental sciences do not supply an explanation, only a simple description, of the world. It is nonetheless the case that the natural sciences say everything that can be said about the world and that, in order to do this, they have no need of philosophy.

Another important implication is that if a "well-formed" proposition is equivalent to the correct description of a state of affairs, understanding the meaning of such a proposition amounts to knowing "what is the case if it is true" (4.024). By identifying the meaning of a proposition with the possibility of verifying it "in practice," this thesis involuntarily echoed similar formulations that had appeared earlier in the work of pragmatists such as Peirce (in "How to Make Our Ideas Clear") and even in the Marxist tradition ("The proof of the pudding," as Engels said in 1880, "is in the eating").[28] Wittgenstein's thesis would subsequently be taken over and amplified by the members of the Vienna Circle, though it is not clear that Wittgenstein gave it as radical a sense as Schlick and Carnap were later to do.

For Wittgenstein logico-mathematical propositions are mere "tautologies." They say nothing about the world: "For example, I know nothing about the weather when I know that it is either raining or not raining" (4.461). Logic and mathematics, in other words, describe no preexisting reality, empirical or intelligible. It follows that they have no need of being grounded upon any philosophy whatsoever. This is why Wittgenstein says of logic that it "must look after itself" (5.473)—an injunction that goes for mathematics as well, since a mathematical proposition likewise "does not express a thought" (6.21). Thus were the last traces of the Platonism on which the logicist doctrine rested swept away.

But if logic and philosophy must be clearly distinguished from each other, logic may yet illuminate philosophy. It can help philosophy understand at which point it becomes absurd to try to contravene the rules of ordinary language, since "language itself prevents every logical mistake"

(5.4731) and "all the propositions of our everyday language, just as they stand, are in perfect logical order" (5.5563). At first sight this seems a surprising declaration. Is it to be interpreted as saying that, apart from scientific descriptions of states of affairs, no discourse is possible? Can nothing be said that goes beyond such descriptions, for example, about the meaning of the world in general?

The answer given in the Tractatus is categorical and comes in two parts: if the world has a meaning, this meaning cannot be found inside of it, only outside; and if this meaning exists, it cannot be said (that is, described or represented), only shown, since, being located outside the world, it lies beyond the sphere of what is representable. In short, if one takes ethics to be concerned with the meaning of life and of the world, there cannot in fact be any ethical propositions. Ethics, as discourse, is impossible. The same thing is true of aesthetics, since "ethics and aesthetics are one and the same" (6.421) and both are transcendental to the extent that they aim, through the Good and the Beautiful, at conditions of the world that lie beyond it.

One may say nothing, in particular, about the will as a "subject of ethical attributes" (6.423), unless this amounts to each person giving—through his or her behavior, rather than through words—a meaning to his or her existence. The most that can be asserted is that the "world of the happy man is a different one from that of the unhappy man" (6.43). One can no longer talk of death. "Death is not an event in life: we do not live to experience death" (6.4311). Is the soul immortal? Does God exist? It hardly needs to be emphasized that these questions likewise have no expressible meaning for Wittgenstein.

In short, not only does philosophy have nothing to add to the scientific description of the world, it is just as impotent to deal with problems relating to values. Proposition 6.53 finally settles this matter, one might say, in several definitive sentences. The only correct method in philosophy "would really be the following: to say nothing except what can be said, i.e. propositions of natural science—i.e. something that has nothing to do with philosophy—and then, whenever someone else wanted to say something metaphysical, to demonstrate to him that he had failed to give a meaning to certain signs in his propositions."

The general conclusion of the Tractatus, therefore, is that philosophy has neither an object nor a method of its own, that it "is not a body of doctrine but an activity" (4.112), and that its sole usefulness is in helping to clarify our thoughts—in other words, to clear up metaphysical propositions, which result from a wrong use of language, through analysis of their logical form. But as for the rest, the only thing to do is to stop talking. This, moreover, is what the seventh and final proposition of the book succinctly enjoins: "What we cannot speak about we must pass over in silence."[29]

Contrary, however, to what the members of the Vienna Circle asserted in the 1920s, Wittgenstein nowhere says that metaphysics, as such, is devoid of interest. He simply claims that it is not possible *as discourse*. He does not deny that it might have a sense, only that this could be elucidated *by language*. His purpose is limited to tracing the lines of demarcation between the sayable and the unsayable and to warning against the temptation to pursue a—possibly legitimate—objective using unsuitable means.

Such a doctrine may seem either overly subtle or insufficiently explicit. However this may be, it nevertheless left itself open to a good many misunderstandings, some of which have persisted up until the present day. It must be said, too, that the book's curious mixture of formalism and mysticism did not help to enlarge its audience. What is more, at just the moment when the *Tractatus* appeared, Wittgenstein himself disappeared from the philosophical scene, shutting himself away in a mountain village to work as a schoolteacher. He had ceased to write, just as Malevich some years earlier had ceased to paint.

LIKE MALEVICH, however, Wittgenstein was eventually to take up his brushes again. His desire to blend in with ordinary people proved inadequate to withstand the harsh realities of rural life. The mutual incomprehension that reigned between him and the villagers led to incidents. Accused of having struck a child who was slow to respond to his questions in class, he quit his post in the spring of 1926. For several weeks he held a job as a gardener in a monastery. He then returned to Vienna at the urging of his sister Margarete, who asked him to draw up the plans for her new house, and gradually reintegrated himself into social life. He also returned to doing philosophy.

In February 1927 Margarete put him in contact with the philosopher Moritz Schlick, who had been one of the earliest admirers of the *Tractatus*. While refusing to participate in the gatherings of the Vienna Circle, founded by Schlick, Wittgenstein agreed to meet with him from time to time along with Carnap and Waismann. Their conversations rapidly made it clear that they were not on the same wavelength. The neopositivists had believed that the *Tractatus* announced the end of metaphysics in the sense that they themselves fervently wished. When at last they approached Wittgenstein and, perhaps to provoke them, he read long poems by Rabindranath Tagore, they understood their mistake. They did manage, however, to get him to discuss certain questions relating to the language of science. Waismann even succeeded in persuading him to attend a lecture on intuitionism in mathematics by Brouwer in March 1928.

Brouwer had pushed the critique of Russell's arguments a good deal further than Wittgenstein himself had done up until that point, and it may well be, as many suppose, that this lecture is what convinced the author of the *Tractatus* that there was still a great deal for philosophy to do. In any case his interest in philosophical questions revived at this time, and several months later, in January 1929, he returned to Cambridge.

Trinity College welcomed him back with open arms. In a rather contrived ceremony, in which Moore and Russell acted as his examiners, Wittgenstein obtained his doctorate on 18 June 1929, submitting the *Tractatus*—already a cult book in philosophical circles—as his dissertation. ("It is my personal opinion," Moore noted in his report, "that Mr Wittgenstein's thesis is a work of genius; but, be that as it may, it is certainly well up to the standard required for the Cambridge degree of Doctor of Philosophy.")[30] He also received a research fellowship that helped him get back to work. He immediately composed a brief conference paper entitled "Some Remarks on Logical Form" that was published later the same year in the *Proceedings of the Aristotelian Society*. It was the last work by Wittgenstein to appear during his lifetime. He disowned it shortly after it was published.

Wittgenstein's thought at this time, spurred on by a critical reexamination of the *Tractatus*, was developing at a dizzying pace. Nor did it cease evolving, as his manuscript notes of 1930 (*Philosophical Remarks*) and 1931 (*Philosophical Grammar*) testify, together with the lecture notes he dictated in 1933–34 (the *Blue Book* and *Yellow Book*) and 1934–35 (the *Brown Book*)—all published after his death by his friends and former students. During the academic year 1929–30 he agreed—something quite unprecedented—to deliver a public lecture at Cambridge. His subject was the definition of ethics. At first glance it may appear as though Wittgenstein's intention was merely to elaborate upon the final reflections of the *Tractatus*. Recalling the distinction between scientific judgments (bearing upon the world) and value judgments (expressions of will), he once again stressed the impossibility of ethics finding expression in the form of speech: "This running up against the limits of language is *ethics*," as he restated the point to Waismann on 30 December 1929 during a trip to Vienna.[31] Whereas the *Tractatus* appeared to condemn ethics to eternal silence, Wittgenstein's remarks eight years later attested to an intensification of his moral concerns. He no longer hesitated to enter into grand debates with his colleagues over the meaning of existence. He displayed a growing interest in Schopenhauer and Kierkegaard, even claiming on occasion to understand what Heidegger meant by "being" and "anxiety."[32] In short, he continued to distance himself both from Russell and from the Vienna Circle.

At the same time he began to show a new curiosity about the way in which the social sciences—ethnology, in particular—apprehend their objects. Ethnology, by calling attention to various systems of ethics different from our own, invites us to consider each of them as a system closed in upon itself, drawing its justification solely from the fact of its own existence. Such a perspective could only strengthen Wittgenstein's natural tendency—in the sphere of morals no less than in the philosophy of language or of mathematics—to privilege the practical or pragmatic point of view in relation to the speculative. Indeed, the notes he made in 1931 while reading one of the classic works of ethnology, Frazer's *The Golden Bough* (1890), throw new light on the functionalist conception of metaphysics that he was now developing.

On this view, magico-religious practice, which consists of uttering certain words or making certain gestures under specific circumstances, operates without any need for external justification. Why, Wittgenstein asked, should it not be the same with metaphysics? Strictly speaking, metaphysics—just like magic and religion—is neither true nor false. It is simply a symbolic practice connected with a particular civilization or way of life, namely, ours. This is why Wittgenstein, unlike Carnap, refrained from condemning it, and why, unlike Frazer, he refrained from mocking the belief of primitive peoples in the power of magic. It is also why he did not feel a need to endorse the view of either one.

A course he gave on belief a few years later, in 1938, moreover clearly showed that although Wittgenstein, an agnostic, regarded religious discourse as both unjustifiable and unassailable from the scientific point of view, he nonetheless considered it a perfectly legitimate "form of life"—an existential choice eluding all argument. Like ethical behavior, religious behavior consists in following a set of rules. Attempting to inquire from the outside into the meaning of such a practice, Wittgenstein held, is useless. One better understands, then, why he objected to Russell's militant atheism, another source of friction between the two men.

This growing interest in the "point of view of praxis" may also have been connected with the fact that, as a fellow of Trinity College (to which he was elected in 1930), Wittgenstein made the acquaintance of the Italian economist Piero Sraffa, a Marxist and friend of Gramsci. The intellectual climate of the Cambridge colleges at the beginning of the 1930s was, of course, favorable to socialism—so much so that Wittgenstein, who remained unsatisfied with his situation, decided in 1935 to go to the Soviet Union in the hope of finding work there as a manual laborer. His stay in Leningrad, and afterwards in Moscow, was brief. Living conditions in these cities were so difficult that before long he abandoned his plan, not least because the Soviet authorities, although they were ready to offer him a post as professor of philosophy, did not wish to have him as an unskilled worker. He returned to England, where until 1937 he nonetheless continued to dream of participating in the communist experience, even of training to become a doctor and going back to settle in the Soviet Union. Such aspirations, although they do not come through in his writings, confirm his commitment to socially progressive ideals, just as his well-known taste for movies (especially American Westerns) and detective stories testifies in its own way to his contempt for the values of the British establishment.

Events, however, obliged Wittgenstein to remain in Cambridge. After the *Anschluss* in 1938, there was no longer any question of his returning to Austria, still less of allowing German citizenship to be imposed upon him. The only solution was to become a British citizen and, in 1939, with Moore's retirement, to accept his chair.

This period was also marked by a feverish pace of work. In 1936 he began to compose what became the manuscript of the *Philosophical Investigations*. In 1938 he taught a course at Cambridge that provided him with an opportunity to develop his ideas on aesthetics. At the same time he deepened his acquaintance with psychoanalysis—in which he took a lively, although not uncritical, interest—and of the gestalt approach to perceptual psychology worked out in the 1930s by Wolfgang Köhler (1887–1967). The reflections that the new psychological research inspired him to put down during this period, and also after 1945, were divided up after his death between two volumes entitled *Remarks on the Philosophy of Psychology* (followed by a third volume, *Last Writings on the Philosophy of Psychology*) and a collection called *Zettel* (after the German word for the slips of paper on which the remarks were written).

Finally, he came back in 1939 to the philosophy of mathematics, again using a series of lectures (in the three terms of 1939) to help stimulate his thinking. His manuscript notes on this subject, written between 1937 and 1944, were published posthumously as *Remarks on the Foundations of Mathematics*. The title of this volume may seem to suggest a lingering attachment to the tradition of Frege and Russell, as though Wittgenstein still entertained the possibility of reducing mathematics to logic. But not at all. A careful reading of these remarks shows that the question of foundations had long ceased to have priority for Wittgenstein. Particularly telling, in this connection, was his refusal to endorse any of the principal responses to the question, logicism, formalism, or intuitionism.

His disagreement was clearest in the case of logicism; indeed, it was already explicit in the *Tractatus*. Wittgenstein's chief objection was that to try to ground mathematics upon logic amounts only to displacing the problem since there exists no transcendental knowledge upon which logic itself could be grounded in turn. His rejection of the formalist response was almost as categorical. Developed by Hilbert during the 1920s, it sought to preserve the coherence of mathematics by establishing its noncontradictory character within the framework of a metamathematical theory—that is, of a metalanguage that was itself mathematical, rather than logical, in nature. But since for Wittgenstein discourse admits of no external point of view, no such metalanguage is possible. This thesis, first asserted in the *Tractatus*, was never renounced. As for intuitionism, Wittgenstein dismissed it on account of its psychologistic implications, going so far as to call the whole of intuitionist doctrine "bosh"—utter nonsense.[33] Brouwer's vigorous challenge to the validity of the principle of the excluded middle, did, however, leave a mark on his thinking.[34]

Although Wittgenstein now conceived of mathematical entities as pure constructions of the mind, his refusal to allow a role for intuition ruled out any possibility of a return to Kant. Instead, he advocated a sort of moderate conventionalism, regarding the mathematician not as a discoverer but as an inventor. On this view, mathematical activity does not consist in exploring a preexisting universe, whether of a logical nature (*pace* Russell) or of a psychological nature (*pace* Brouwer), but rather resembles a game played according to rules. These rules, just like the ones that govern the grammar of a language, are unmotivated, in the sense that they have no prior justification, but they are not therefore entirely arbitrary. Thus, mathematics works (indeed, works rather well) because its rules were suitably chosen at the outset.

Comparing mathematics to English grammar or to a game of chess, as Wittgenstein did during the 1930s, amounted therefore to saying that it has no more need than they do of an external guarantee. Mathematics has to find—as, moreover, the Tractatus had already suggested it must—its reason for existing within itself. The propositions of which it is composed may be clarified but not grounded. Their ultimate sense cannot be said, only shown, to the extent that respect for the rules that govern their connection produces results—in short, to the extent that the use that is made of them by the community of mathematicians proves to be, in practice, decisive.

As Wittgenstein put it in a note of 1944, "the application of the concept 'following a rule' presupposes a custom."[35] In other words, it refers to a social practice that is legitimated by its successes. One might almost say that mathematics is nothing more than what mathematicians agree to recognize as the set of statements that are useful to them at a given moment: epistemology could therefore be replaced by sociology of science. Wittgenstein himself did not go so far as to formulate this ultrapragmatist conclusion explicitly, but others would do it for him later, citing him as their authority.

There remains one question to which Wittgenstein's answer may seem disappointing: what to make of the Frege-Russell paradox or of the contradictions that are liable to arise in mathematics in general. This question was all the less avoidable for having been posed once more in 1931 by two celebrated theorems due to Gödel. According to the first theorem, even in a formal system as elementary as the arithmetic axiomatized by Russell it is possible to establish the existence of at least one undecidable proposition, which is to say a proposition whose truth or falsity cannot be demonstrated within the system itself. From our inability to prevent the appearance of such a proposition it follows that the body of axioms on which arithmetic rests is by definition incomplete. Gödel's second theorem, which demonstrates the impossibility of proving the noncontradictory character of arithmetic by arithmetic means alone, initially seemed less disturbing. But it too revealed the existence of absolute limits that imposed themselves from within upon the enterprise of formalization.

Taken together, these two theorems—extended in 1936 by the Church-Turing thesis—sounded the death knell both for logicism and for Hilbert's ambitions. They helped to bring mathematics down from the pedestal it had occupied since the time of the Greeks, and to naturalize it by drawing it nearer to the empirical sciences. But—and this says a great deal about the development of his ideas—these results hardly seemed to move Wittgenstein. His final position on the subject was to say, let us wait until we see a contradiction actually appear. When that happens we will invent an ad hoc procedure to quarantine it, so to speak, so that the pathological statement will not prevent us from continuing to use the healthy part of mathematics—a reassuring position, but one whose pragmatic spirit few mathematicians have approved.

WITTGENSTEIN WAS FIFTY YEARS OLD when the Second World War broke out. Once again he had a desire to become involved, only this time against Germany. His wish to perform a social duty in the service of his new country led him in 1941 to seek a job as a porter in a London hospital.

When he returned, unenthusiastically, to Trinity College in 1944, his relations with Russell had gone from bad to worse. Each reproached the other for having produced nothing of value—in Russell's case since the time of the Principia, in Wittgenstein's since the Tractatus. Even Wittgenstein's friendship with Sraffa went through a difficult phase. Teaching no longer held any interest for him. On 26 October 1946, during a lecture given at Cambridge by Karl Popper, Wittgenstein got into a heated argument with the speaker. According to Popper, who was defending the idea that there exist philosophical problems, Wittgenstein menacingly brandished a poker and then, exasperated by Popper's arguments, stormed out, slamming the door behind him.[36] In 1947 Wittgenstein resigned his chair.

His last years were marked by a certain amount of traveling, as well as by the painful growth of the cancer that was finally to kill him at the age of sixty-two. These were nonetheless years of intense activity so far as writing was concerned. In 1949 Wittgenstein finished a draft version of the Philosophical Investigations, which he could never make up his mind whether to correct or not, despite having many times expressed his willingness to see the book published as it stood. Next he composed the Remarks on Colour and continued to work until shortly before his death on a text that also remained unfinished, On Certainty.

The Philosophical Investigations, which appeared in 1953, two years after his death, aroused much perplexity. Russell claimed to find nothing of interest in it.[37] The neopositivists, from Carnap to Quine, avoided dealing with it. Nevertheless it exercised a profound influence upon the community of professional philosophers, above all in the English-speaking countries, where it was received by some as the manifesto of what came to be called Wittgenstein's later philosophy. This characterization is surely exaggerated, but it is true that the way in which the book is divided up, and the difficulty of grasping its guiding thread, license a number of different readings. It is rather as though, contrary to his past practice, Wittgenstein now took pleasure in giving his thought an antisystematic twist, a form more ironic than assertive. In fact, this work was more the product of a new state of mind—itself the result of an evolution in his thinking that dated back to 1929—than the expression of a new doctrine.

One indication that Wittgenstein's thought had changed direction is that the *Investigations* implicitly abandoned the ontological ambition of the *Tractatus* (to describe the structure of the world) together with the concepts that had allowed him to realize this ambition. Turning his back once and for all on the preoccupations of Frege and Russell, Wittgenstein renounced his earlier logical atomism as well as the picture theory of meaning that derived from it. But he did this in order to put himself in a better position to give a description of actual language practices, and therefore to strengthen the therapeutic effectiveness that the *Tractatus* had originally claimed for philosophy—in sum, a new path for reaching an end that had hardly changed.

The *Investigations*,[38] prefaced by a passage from Saint Augustine's *Confessions* concerning the child's acquisition of language, begins with the question of how we learn that a given name refers to a given object, a given verb to a given action. Wittgenstein's answer takes the form of a simple observation: we learn by means of games—"language games" (§7). It rapidly becomes clear, however, that this notion, which Wittgenstein began to employ in the academic year 1933–34 in the *Blue Book*, is susceptible to far larger application. All language, he holds, is a set of rule-governed games, connected with the situations of life and not at all interchangeable, even if some of them bear "family resemblances" to each other (§67). The list is virtually infinite:

Giving orders, and obeying them—
Describing the appearance of an object, or giving its measurements—
Constructing an object from a description (a drawing)—
Reporting an event—
Speculating about an event—
Forming and testing a hypothesis—
Presenting the results of an experiment in tables and diagrams—
Making up a story; and reading it—
Play-acting—
Singing catches—
Guessing riddles—
Making a joke; telling it—

Solving a problem in practical arithmetic—
Translating from one language into another—
Asking, thanking, cursing, greeting, praying . . . (§23)

In practice, however, we seldom make a mistake. Experience takes it upon itself to teach us, in each situation, what the appropriate language game is. On this view, language is comparable to a vast "tool box" (§11) that we gradually learn to use. For each word, as for each tool, we may say that we know its *meaning* when we know its *use*—in other words, when we know the set of rules that governs its use.

For everything, finally, is a question of rules. Those that govern the use of a word or of an expression constitute what Wittgenstein calls its "grammar." Now, in the case either of a word or of a language, the grammar does not have to be explained. It has simply to be described in order to be understood by its users. And to understand a grammar means understanding "something that is already in plain view" (§89), since it is a question of following a simple model.

The search for a metalinguistic theory of language is therefore a futile quest. The only problem—a purely technical one—is knowing *how* we ought to talk, not of trying to guess *why* we talk as we do. Logic and mathematics, which are only particular forms of language, do not require a different analysis. It is useless to ask what they mean; the only thing that matters is knowing of what use they are. Thus, from the *Tractatus*—which commands us to submit to everyday language—to the *Investigations*—which treats every symbolic activity, including science, as a rule-governed game—Wittgenstein's journey can be seen to have been in the pursuit of a single aim, namely, of imposing upon philosophy a strict respect for the grammars, or codes, that define the legitimate uses of signs in general.

Did this journey wind up committing philosophy, in effect, to a neutralist position, forbidding it to engage in any self-reflective questioning whatsoever? Certain passages of the *Investigations* may give this impression, as, for example, the famous declaration that "Philosophy may in no way interfere with the actual real use of language; it can in the end only describe it. For it cannot give it any foundation either. It leaves everything as it is. It also leaves mathematics as it is, and no mathematical discovery can advance it" (§124). However, the very plan of this long work, in which Wittgenstein converses uninterruptedly with an imaginary interlocutor who seems never to tire of presenting him with new enigmas, suggests that reality is more complex. Indeed, two questions that recur insistently throughout the text signal the presence in Wittgenstein's thought of concerns that grammar, by itself, is not in a position to answer.

The first question has to do with the notion of a rule, which, as one of the best interpreters of Wittgenstein, the American philosopher and logician Saul Kripke, has rightly observed is at the very heart of the book.[39] What is a rule? For everyday language and the language of mathematics alike, Wittgenstein's response is to say that a rule cannot be thought of independently of the social and cultural environment that determines its status. There cannot be a private rule, conceived by an isolated individual for his or her personal use alone: for, otherwise, "thinking one was obeying a rule would be the same thing as obeying it" (§202). It is, of course, possible to think of language as a "form of life" (§19) and to ask that words express "internal experiences" (§243); even so, it is necessary that these words, in order for them to be understood, conform to an established usage.

Here one encounters the trace of a dual influence on Wittgenstein's thought. On the one hand, there is the anthropological perspective that he adopted following his discovery of the *Golden Bough*; but there is also the globalizing approach peculiar to the gestalt school of perceptual psychology, whose assumptions the second part of the *Investigations* tries once again to clarify in a series of arduous arguments. Less often read than the beginning of the book, this second part offers insight into the last stage reached by Wittgenstein in his attempt to devise a new way of philosophizing, nearer to psychology than to logic.

It remained for him to define exactly what was at stake with this new philosophy. This is the second strand of the *Investigations*, likewise the object of sustained reflection throughout the book. "Philosophy," says Wittgenstein, "is a battle against the bewitchment of our intelligence by means of language" (§109). By this we are to understand that it is essentially a struggle with itself, since philosophical puzzles arise "when language *goes on holiday*" (§38), and that philosophy as a whole is only "a dream of our language" (§358). In short, the role of philosophy continues to consist, as it did in the *Tractatus*, in the treatment of those sicknesses to which it has itself given rise. But the treatment proposed by the *Investigations* represented a radical and unprecedented departure. For it was no longer a question of analyzing the logical form of metaphysical propositions, but of understanding (and thereby making disappear) the psychological causes that lead us to formulate such propositions. Wittgenstein wanted now to deliver his readers not only from classical metaphysics—the result of manifestly erroneous distinctions such as the one between mind and body—but also from modern doctrines according to which science somehow explains reality. This is the reason why the *Investigations*, moving from the principle that there is no ultimate explanation, did not seek to substitute one doctrine for another but aimed, more profoundly, at turning philosophers away from the very idea of theory—as though the ambition to "see to the bottom of things" (§89) were itself the root of the problem; as though the sole mission left to philosophy were to "shew the fly the way out of the fly-bottle" (§309).

"So in the end when one is doing philosophy," as Wittgenstein says elsewhere, "one gets to the point where one would like just to emit an inarticulate sound" (§261). His attitude toward civilization in general after 1945 seems dominated by an overwhelming feeling of revulsion, the result of his natural pessimism, no doubt, reinforced by the experience of two world wars. To gauge the depth of this feeling one has only to reread certain pages of the *Vermischte Bemerkungen* ("mixed remarks," published in English under the title *Culture and Value*), dating from 1945–47. Here one finds Wittgenstein expressing a desire to see the atomic bomb soon bring about the complete destruction of humanity and, in particular, of "our disgusting soapy water science," which to his mind was what modern science had finally become.[40]

This disenchantment—the word is scarcely adequate to describe Wittgenstein's state of mind at this time—seems far removed from the confidence he placed in science at the time of the *Tractatus*. Both the *Tractatus* and the *Investigations*, however, despite their different perspectives, have rather similarly been misinterpreted. The first was read by the members of the Vienna Circle as a prophecy of the end of metaphysics, giving hope for the advent of a new "positive" age. The second was made the object of a still more restrictive interpretation on the part of certain Anglo-American authors. In the early 1950s, the British philosopher John Austin gave currency to the notion of a "later" Wittgenstein, distinct from the Wittgenstein of the *Tractatus*, a strategy aimed at limiting philosophy to the meticulous study of ordinary language. Twenty years later, the American Richard Rorty, wishing to combat both the analytic philosophy inherited from Frege and, more generally, any philosophical or scientific pretension to truth, went so far as to make the *Investigations* out to be the death certificate of Western philosophy in all its forms—in other words, of reason in the classical sense of the term.

This is a doubtful conclusion, to say the least. Wittgenstein, as we have seen, continued to write after having finished the *Investigations*, even embarking toward the end of his life upon a new work on certainty. The anguished tone of these last writings does not at all give the impression that, as far as he was concerned, all philosophical problems had been settled. No doubt there was a good bit of the antiphilosopher in Wittgenstein—an antiphilosopher who, in moments of exasperation, implied that he simply wanted to be done with it all. But in Wittgenstein's case, as with Pascal and Nietzsche, it may be wondered whether his vexation amounted to anything other than a search, sustained by anger and irony, for a new way of philosophizing.

The theme of the end of philosophy is certainly not absent from Wittgenstein's thought, but nor can it alone account for his philosophy in its full complexity. And even if this theme has acquired great significance in the philosophy of the twentieth century, it owes less to Wittgenstein than to a series of historical developments of unprecedented horror that began with the First World War—a war that, although unquestionably it left its mark on the author of the *Tractatus*, caused other philosophers, such as Heidegger, to react in far more aggressive ways.

Philosophies of the End

The End of Europe

From 1880 to 1914, as we have seen, European civilization reached a kind of apogee. During these thirty-odd years scientists reshaped man's vision of the world. Artists and writers invented new languages. Philosophers, convinced that they had attained unshakable truths, believed that the Kantian dream was at last being realized. The fall from this height, in 1914, was as sudden as the illusion was grand.

The horror that still attaches to the memory of the First World War in Europe today has to do, first, with its exceptional cruelty: millions of victims, tens of millions of traumatized survivors, generations decimated, whole villages wiped off the map—all this, to say nothing of the first aerial bombardments or of the use of chemical weapons, left indelible traces in the minds of those who lived on.

These things were all the more painful as this was a war that could have been avoided. The indifference of irresponsible politicians ensured that it was not. It could at the very least have been conducted in a way that would have been less costly in human lives. Again, it was not, owing to the stupidity of generals eager for glory. In the trenches, millions of men died for nothing: for a few acres of land that were in turn lost, regained, and lost again, or because, rebelling against the barbarism of their situation, they were gunned down on the orders of their own commanding officers.

The absurdity of such massacres was plain for all to see once the armistice was finally concluded. But the Treaty of Versailles proved incapable of laying the basis for a durable peace. To the contrary, the manner in which it redrew the map of the world had the effect only of exacerbating frustrations and feeding desires for revenge. As Bertrand Russell was one of the first to emphasize, the rise of Nazism, itself the cause of the Second World War, was the consequence in part of the chaotic state in which the Treaty of Versailles left Europe in 1919. A more remote consequence was the reawakening at the end of the 1980s of political and religious fanaticism in the Balkans, with fresh massacres into the bargain.

The war of 1914 was therefore something quite different than a mere violent parenthesis in an otherwise civilized history. It was the first symptom of a suicidal impulse that afterwards devoured Europe, the dramatic beginning—as unexpected and spectacular as the sinking of the Titanic two years earlier—of a process of decline pregnant with menace for the future.

INDEED, this was the opinion of a number of intellectuals at the time. In The Decline of the West (1918), the German essayist Oswald Spengler (1880–1936) proposed an interpretation of European decadence founded on a "vitalist" philosophy that lent itself to the most doubtful generalizations. Colored by a Nietzschean sort of twilight romanticism, Spengler's work enjoyed a lively and long-lasting literary success in spite of its defects, informing the speculations of Arnold Toynbee (1889–1975) about world history as well as the spiritualist aesthetics of André Malraux (1901–76). In the meantime, the doctrine of Prussian socialism advocated by Spengler to stem the rising tide of violence influenced theoreticians of the "conservative revolution" (notably Moeller van den Bruck) who, in adapting the ideology of the German extreme right to the preoccupations of their time, helped to prepare the way during the 1920s for Hitler's coming to power.

More sober but no less pessimistic judgments about the future of Europe were also found in France. Paul Valéry's letters on The Intellectual Crisis (1919) summed up the matter in a few words. "The facts," Valéry wrote, "are plain and merciless: There are the thousands of young writers and young artists who have been killed. There are the lost illusion of a European culture and the demonstrated inability of knowledge to save anything whatsoever; there is science, touched mortally in its ethical ambitions and as if dishonoured by the cruelty of its applications."[1] This analysis of the crisis of the age likewise enjoyed a remarkable reputation in the following decades.

Among artists the revolt was not less fierce. It manifested itself first in Zurich, in 1916, with the explosive emergence of dadaism. An informal movement without respect for national boundaries—among its number were Hugo Ball, Max Ernst, Hans Arp, Tristan Tzara, and Marcel Duchamp— dadaism rebelled not only against the conventions of academic art but also, more generally, against the purported values of a civilization that, despite its worship of the Enlightenment, sent men off to be slaughtered. The subversive spirit of dadaism in turn fueled surrealist painting and literature as well as expressionist cinema, whose vogue between the two world wars betrayed a growing preoccupation in educated circles with the dark forces that were thought to stir up the human unconscious.

Finally, the wave of traumatic neuroses that the war unleashed among survivors of the trenches aroused the interest of psychologists as well. Shell shock and other disorders led Freud to elaborate the notion of a "death wish"— introduced for the first time in a 1920 essay, *Beyond the Pleasure Principle*—and to establish a second "topography" for psychoanalysis, centered on the pathogenic conflicts that set the "id," "ego," and "superego" against one another. Over the following years Freud showed an increasing interest in the role played by unconscious mechanisms in social processes. In *Group Psychology and Analysis of the Ego* (1921) he tried to explain the "desire to submit" that led the masses to entrust themselves to a providential "guide" (he was thinking here of Leninism, but the analysis was largely to apply to European fascisms as well) while his last works—*The Future of an Illusion* (1927) and *Civilization and Its Discontents* (1930)—revealed the extent to which pessimism shaped his view of history.

SIMILAR ANXIETIES SEIZED the philosophical world. Some well-known figures, such as Hermann Cohen, Max Scheler, and Henri Bergson, succumbed during the war to the temptations of patriotism. But the problem was deeper than this: philosophy had been unable either to foresee or to prevent the catastrophe; and once it had passed, it proved incapable of drawing clear lessons from the experience.

Had rationalism also died on the battlefields? Had the Enlightenment been extinguished at Verdun, swallowed up in the mud of the Chemin des Dames? Some feared as much. We have already seen that Russell renounced all work in logical philosophy in order to devote the main part of his energies to political activity. Even Wittgenstein—who was not a pacifist—was shaken by the war. The icy tone of the *Tractatus*, the detachment of its attitude toward life, the view of the world as a "limited totality" that constitutes the background of the book—were not all these things, at least in part, due to a singular experience of death?

For understandable reasons, the malaise was most profoundly felt in German philosophy. Indeed, among the major European nations, the collective identity of the Germans after the war was the most unstable. Not only was German national unity recent, dating only from 1871; it remained incomplete to the extent that the German state—defeated in 1918, ruined, and humiliated by the loss of its colonial possessions—did not yet include within its borders all the German-speaking communities of Europe. Moreover, the Weimar Republic found itself challenged from within by all sorts of extremist movements to which the economic crisis that followed the war lent popular support. The inability of its politicians to safeguard democracy did the rest. It is therefore unsurprising that German philosophy in the 1920s should have echoed these collective anxieties.

There were exceptions, of course. Some German thinkers still remained faithful to the tradition of the *Aufklärung*. They were found for the most part among the neo-Kantians of the Marburg School, though some belonged to the phenomenological movement. At Marburg, the intellectual tradition embodied until 1918 by Hermann Cohen was carried on by his closest disciple, Ernst Cassirer (1874–1945). Appointed in 1919 to the faculty of the University of Hamburg, where his colleagues included Hilbert, Cassirer continued his early studies in the philosophy of science while composing the monumental three-volume *Philosophy of Symbolic Forms* (the first volume appearing in 1923, the second in 1925, and the third in 1929). Informed by a rationalism that was both humanist and classical, this work attempted to extend the Kantian method of criticism to language, myth, and works of art; that is, to the fundamental elements of culture. Its true importance was not recognized until after 1945.

Phenomenology, for its part, had fragmented into a variety of tendencies after 1910. Husserl, the guardian of a temple that he had built himself, became absorbed in ever more speculative researches. His first students went their own separate ways. Max Scheler (1874–1928) devoted a book, *On Resentment and Moral Value Judgments* (1912), to criticizing bourgeois culture and then, after having passed through an intensely nationalist phase during the war, moved in the direction of both the philosophy of religion and the sociology of knowledge. Karl Jaspers was led by his medical training to inquire into psychology and psychiatry in *General Psychopathology* (1913), while at the same time conducting an original inquiry into the philosophical foundations of the grand "conceptions of the world."

Because they appealed in one way or another to the ideals of the Enlightenment, these thinkers are an essential part of the landscape of European philosophy. But however great their interest may be, they were not the ones who best expressed the crisis through which Germany was passing in the aftermath of the war. The most significant works in this regard came from two very different authors. One, The Star of Redemption (1921) by Franz Rosenzweig, reflected the spiritual concerns of a community—the Jewish community—whose intense activity was soon to be interrupted by Nazism. The other, Being and Time (1927) by Martin Heidegger, broke with the phenomenological movement from which it derived in order to call into question once again the very foundations of philosophical activity. These two works, published only a few years apart, laid the basis for a new movement that was soon to be called existentialism.

Both Rosenzweig and Heidegger attempted to sublimate their historical despair through investigation of a messianic and revolutionary "elsewhere." Their approach to philosophy seemed destined to bring them together; history, however, was to draw them apart forever.

FRANZ ROSENZWEIG (1886–1929) was born in Cassel to a family of the assimilated Jewish bourgeoisie that encouraged him to pursue a medical career. After having given up medicine for history, in 1910 he embarked upon a study of Hegel's political thought. Almost entirely finished in 1914, this work did not appear until 1920, under the title Hegel and the State, at a moment when Rosenzweig felt so alienated from Hegel's thought that he had come to regard Hegel as the very symbol of everything he would henceforth abominate.

It must be kept in mind that in the meantime war had intervened. For two years, between 1916 and 1918, Rosenzweig dodged death in the trenches of the Balkans. In July 1918, under the shock of a grave moral crisis, he began to write The Star of Redemption. Having no access to writing paper, he composed the first part of it on postcards sent to his mother from the front. Completed in February 1919, the book finally saw the light of day in 1921—the same year as the first edition of the Tractatus Logico-Philosophicus, likewise born amidst the glow of bursting shells.

Its immediate impact, outside of Jewish circles, remained limited. Moreover, Rosenzweig had hardly any time to come back to it. From 1920 he applied himself to the task of founding (together with Martin Buber) a center of independent Judaic studies in Frankfurt, the Freies Jüdisches Lehrhaus, aimed at counteracting the excesses of assimilation. Among its early participants were Gershom Scholem and Erich Fromm. Then, in 1922, he discovered that he was afflicted with an incurable disease that deprived him of the use of speech as well as of all motor function. From 1923 until his death six years later he was practically paralyzed, devoting the last of his energies to translating (with Buber's help) the great texts of the Hebrew bible into German. With the advent of Nazism his writings were consigned to oblivion—an oblivion from which they have never quite escaped.

The Star of Redemption is a major book, however, whose existentialist flavor recalls both Nietzsche and Kierkegaard. The first sentence—"All knowledge of the Whole originates in death, in the fear of death"[2]—testifies to the authenticity of a meditation directly inspired by the trenches. But if true knowledge can only be acquired in the immediate vicinity of death—one's own or the death of a close friend—such knowledge starts from the observation that death in itself has no meaning. It is the absurd par excellence—an absurd to which philosophy vainly attempts to give various meanings, all of them trivial. The truth of anguish, which the comforts of rational discourse are powerless to oppose, opens a rift that nothing can fill. Rosenzweig's first task, then, was to challenge all of the apparently meaningful and reassuring pretensions of classical metaphysics; that is, to dismiss, in a single stroke, all the systems of the past—in other words, Hegel.

As a total system, Hegelianism aspired to sum up the entire course of European philosophy. By rejecting Hegel, Rosenzweig thus meant to condemn all of European philosophy as well. In 1921, Rosenzweig's motivation could only have been an existential one. Although Hegel can be criticized for many things, it cannot be said that he was mistaken in his predictions. If anything, he anticipated the future too well; he understood too well, and too openly justified, the dialectical—that is, the conflictual—nature of historical events.

What, according to The Star of Redemption, did Hegel say? That conflict is the exclusive motor of history, that all of history culminated with the advent of the nation-state, and that the nation-state is both the highest political form and the one that best accords with the fundamentally Christian essence of Western civilization. On all these points, Rosenzweig held, events have only proved Hegel right. The modern state has indeed come to exercise supreme authority: in its name any individual can be sacrificed at any moment. Relations among states, engaged in a ruthless competition that results in turn from technological advance, can only be belligerent. War henceforth finds itself inseparable from the very logic of Christian civilization. And since nothing is any longer more sacred than the nation, for which each population is prepared to fight to the death, the future threatens to be an age of universal war, as merciless as it will be interminable.

However doubtful this interpretation of Hegel may be, Rosenzweig's position was clear: he was committed to opposing a philosophy that, to his way of thinking, worked only to justify war. He opposed it, first, in the name of the individual and of the individual's right to defend himself against the bloody appetite of states, but also, more generally, in the name of a radically different vision of the world, founded on dialogue, community, and the desire to escape the finitude of human life through the transcendent experience of aesthetic emotion and religious celebration.

For Rosenzweig, individual singularity was to be preferred to abstract totality, the subjective to the objective, the real to the conceptual. He sided with those who keep their distance from history in order to preserve some connection with eternity, rather than with those who aspire only to rush forward into the quotidian battle for material life. As a result, he was led to seek refuge in the philosophical foundations of traditional Judaism, marginalized for two thousand years by the triumph of Christianity.

Rosenzweig's rebellion is hardly reducible, however, to a pure and simple return to Jewish sources. There are two major differences. On the one hand, Rosenzweig did not at all claim to regard Judaism as the right faith for humanity as a whole. He conceded that while Jewish revelation remained best for Jews, Christian revelation—in its most authentic aspects—might be no less satisfactory for Christians: in short, that there exist at least two forms of revelation, both equally legitimate, which rest (as he was fond of stressing) on a common basis. Such an ecumenicism was bound to run into trouble with the guardians of theological orthodoxy in each camp. What is more, the Judeo-Christian dialogue advocated by *The Star of Redemption* had scarcely any philosophical echo at all, even after the Second World War.

The second point on which Rosenzweig departed from the most militant tendencies of the Judaism of his time was his attitude toward Zionism, a movement launched by the publication in 1896 of Theodor Herzl's *The Jewish State*. Unlike Cohen, Rosenzweig was not in favor of total assimilation. But he was not convinced that going back to Palestine—an idea that Scholem and Buber, for their part, were soon to put into practice—was what was called for either. He feared that in reconstituting a state in the Promised Land, the Jewish people in their turn would become merely another people like the rest, left to be devoured by history, by the struggle for life, by nationalist ambition. His Zionism therefore remained, as it were, a spiritual Zionism, implying no need for a literal return to Jerusalem. Rosenzweig wished to remain German, even if he reproached his German co-religionists for having lost sight of the great principles of biblical morality.

One does not have to share Rosenzweig's religious philosophy in order to admire him for basing it on a sincere and intense consideration of human suffering in the face of the absurdity of death, the horror of war, and the injustice of state-imposed oppression. This resolutely individualistic style of thinking—like that of Wittgenstein—made hardly any reference to academic works. It proceeded, on the one hand, from the later philosophy of Schelling—the distant ancestor of all existentialists—and, on the other hand, from Cohen's last book, *Religion of Reason Out of the Sources of Judaism* (1919), in which the neo-Kantian philosopher attempted to show that the grandeur of the Jewish religion was essentially a matter of the richness and universality of its ethical content. But Rosenzweig's work went beyond these influences by integrating them: beyond its strictly religious conclusions, it was fundamentally oriented toward the future, toward the promise of an internal new world and spiritual rebirth.

It was in any case the first work of the twentieth century to rebel, if not against reason itself, at least against the totalitarian pretensions of dialectical *logos*. Six years before Heidegger—who never cited Rosenzweig—it asserted that metaphysics was "finite" and that, in order to "go beyond" it, it was necessary to reestablish the lost bond linking man to Being, by assigning to thought a more authentic horizon than technological domination of the world. It must be said that this vision has an unmistakably Heideggerian quality.

Indeed, another Jewish philosopher, Karl Löwith (1897–1973), published an essay during his American exile in 1942 that explicitly compared the two thinkers.[3] But the comparison by this point had taken on a new dimension by virtue of Heidegger's personal involvement—from 1933—in the ranks of the National Socialist Party. Löwith concluded that, while the primacy of existence in the face of death was indeed the common point of departure for these two philosophers, they diverged utterly with respect to the spirit in which they worked out its implications. Even so, there are some philosophers yet today who, following the late Emmanuel Levinas, think it possible to claim allegiance to both at the same time.

MARTIN HEIDEGGER (1889–1976) was born in Messkirch, in what was then the state of Baden, in the heart of an essentially rural, Catholic, and conservative region. He came from a modest, churchgoing family. His father, a cooper, performed the duties of sacristan in the local parish. The young Martin's brilliant record at school seemed to ordain him for an ecclesiastical career.

His intellectual interests quickly expanded, however, going beyond theology to take in philosophy and literature. In 1907 a priest made him a gift of a book by Franz Brentano, *The Several Senses of Being in Aristotle* (1862), that was to decisively orient his thought. For it was in this book—Brentano's doctoral thesis—that Heidegger discovered the question of the relation between Being (simple and one) and beings (innumerable) that subsequently became the leitmotif of his own work. Brentano's thought, as we have seen, inspired two other major movements in twentieth-century philosophy in addition to existentialism: logical philosophy (via Meinong and Twardowski) and phenomenology (via Husserl).

On completing his secondary studies, Heidegger entered the Society of Jesus as a novice. He lasted fifteen days, at the end of which the Jesuits expelled him, apparently on grounds of physical unfitness. He then enrolled in the faculty of theology at the University of Freiburg. There he pursued his philosophical reading: Saint Thomas and the scholastics for the most part, but also Husserl's *Logical Investigations*, to which he was attracted by the fact that Husserl had been a student of Brentano, to whom the work was dedicated. It was at this moment, in 1910, that Heidegger published his first articles, in a Catholic journal, vigorously taking issue with free thought, modern materialism, and the theories of Nietzsche. From the same year dated a brief occasional piece that he composed to mark the erection of a monument to Abraham a Sancta Clara, a theologian of the Counter-Reformation known for the virulence of his anti-Judaism.

In 1911 heart trouble forced Heidegger to renounce his religious vocation once and for all. Sent back to his family, he experienced several months of depression and at last decided to return to Freiburg, now with the aim of pursuing studies in mathematics and physics. During this period he also attended courses in philosophy and, inspired by his reading of Husserl, began to study modern logic. He finally obtained his doctorate from the faculty of philosophy at Freiburg in July 1913 with a dissertation, *The Doctrine of the Judgment in Psychologism*, that showed Brentano's influence. Two years later, in 1915, under the direction of Heinrich Rickert (1863–1936), the leader of the neo-Kantian school of Bade, he received his habilitation on the strength of a study of Duns Scotus's doctrine of categories and meaning.

In the meantime, in October 1914, Heidegger had been called up to active duty, but, again for reasons of health, he was assigned to the reserve. Called up again in August 1915, he was posted to the office of the postal censor in Freiburg. In his spare time he gave courses in philosophy as a *Privatdozent*. During the summer of 1916, to his great delight, the University of Freiburg recruited a new and prestigious professor: Edmund Husserl. Heidegger, hoping to assure himself of Husserl's support for his candidacy at Freiburg, went to meet him at once. Husserl did not really begin to appreciate Heidegger's talents until the winter of 1917–18, however, and at first paid scarcely any attention to him.

The lack of solid connections was one of the reasons why that summer Heidegger was refused the stable academic position he coveted. He held a group of Catholic professors responsible for the rebuff, which produced a mood of profound disappointment similar to the depressions that his dismissal from the novitiate, and then from the faculty of theology, had aroused previously. The following year, in 1917, he married a young Protestant woman. Together, these events partly explain why from 1918 Heidegger moved away from Catholicism, began to read Luther, and affirmed his independence—as a philosopher—of all religions. His later adherence to National Socialist doctrines was in any case facilitated by his rejection of the Catholic faith.

Chances of obtaining a regular post at Freiburg appearing small for the immediate future, Heidegger presented himself as a candidate for a junior position at the University of Marburg that had opened up with the retirement of Paul Natorp (1854–1924). This time Husserl enthusiastically promoted his candidacy, and Heidegger was hired. He remained at Marburg for five years, from 1923 to 1928. His courses—less conventional than those of his colleagues—attracted many students. During this period he entered into a romantic relationship with one of them, a young Jewish woman named Hannah Arendt. Their relationship was to be long-lasting; both of them tried to hide it throughout their lives. Heidegger was not really happy in the north of Germany, however, and took advantage of every opportunity to go back to his mountain hut at Todtnauberg in the southwest, near Freiburg. It was in this retreat that he wrote most of *Being and Time*, his first book and his first publication since 1916.

Adorned with a warm dedication to Husserl ("in friendship and admiration"), *Being and Time* appeared in 1927. It enjoyed an immediate and lively success, from which Heidegger profited to prepare his return to Freiburg. There he obtained a chair almost at once—the one previously occupied by Husserl, who retired in 1928. He served as rector of the university in 1933–34 and continued to teach there until being removed from his position by the Allies at the end of the Second World War.

Being and Time, unlike Rosenzweig's *Star of Redemption*, owed nothing to the experience of the trenches. Heidegger spent only two months, at the very end of the war, in a combat zone. The anxieties that formed the background of the two books were, nonetheless, the same: war, defeat, the collapse of European values, the impotence of science and technology to satisfy the spiritual needs of the German people. But Heidegger's book seldom mentioned these problems, at least not overtly. Indeed, *Being and Time* was presented as above all a "metaphilosophical" meditation, concerned with the very essence and fate of metaphysics.

The "Question of Being," Heidegger says in the opening line of the book, "has today been forgotten." This question, however, is the most fundamental question there is. "It is one which provided a stimulus for the researches of Plato and Aristotle, only to subside from then on *as a theme for actual investigation*"[4]—hence the necessity of undertaking a reconsideration, or, in Heidegger's phrase, a "plain restating" of this question. But if such a repetition is to be possible, two preliminary tasks must be successfully carried out. The first consists in forging an "analytic" of *Dasein*, or "being there"—a term that here denotes mankind, or human reality in its concrete individual singularity. The second consists in realizing what is variously called in English a "destruction" or, more recently, a "de(con)struction" (the euphemistic French translation of Heidegger's harsh neologism, *Destruktion*, is "disobstruction") of classical ontology; in other words, a radical critique of the history of metaphysics, which stands accused of having lost sight of the fundamental question.

One may wonder why an inquiry into being ought to have to proceed first via an analysis of *Dasein*. Heidegger's reply is to point out that, man being the only animal that thinks, *Dasein* is the only creature for which the question of its own being is indistinguishable from the question of the meaning of Being in general. "Dasein is ontically distinctive"—that is, distinguished from other beings—"in that it *is* ontological."[5] This is the reason why, according to Heidegger, fundamental ontology "must be sought in the *existential analytic of Dasein*,"[6] which is to say in the description of the conditions allowing it to conceive its own existence.

Heidegger goes on to point to "*temporality* as the meaning of the Being of that entity which we call 'Dasein.'"[7] This term refers to the property that man—and man alone—possesses of having the sense and consciousness of time. The task then becomes to give time a "primordial" explanation "as the horizon for the understanding of Being, and in terms of temporality as the Being of Dasein, which understands Being."[8] Such a project implies in its turn the need to confront the classical philosopher who went furthest in exploring what the temporal dimension signifies for man—Kant. It therefore becomes necessary to reconsider the Kantian doctrine of time, to demonstrate its inadequacies, and, finally, to substitute for it an "analytic" nearer to the experience actually lived by *Dasein*, more in keeping with the Husserlian call for a "return to things themselves."

At the end of this process (inspired partly by a course given by Husserl in 1904–5 on the "phenomenology of the intimate consciousness of time"), the central notion of the work, temporality, comes to be defined as a permanent tendency to project oneself "outside of oneself." This is why Heidegger gives the modalities of past, present, and future the name of temporal "ecstases" (*ek-stases*). But these three ecstases are not, existentially, on the same plane. "The primary phenomenon of primordial and authentic temporality"—that is, the most important of the three modalities—"is the future."[9] For care (*Sorge*), which is the constitutive mode of being of *Dasein*, is a concern related to the future: a concern for death. "Care," Heidegger says, "is Being-toward-death."[10]

Anxiety in the face of death is therefore, for *Dasein*, the authentic experience par excellence, the experience that calls its very being into question. Here we are very near Rosenzweig, and, going further back, Kierkegaard. But from this common position Heidegger heads off in a different direction. Turning away from the religious transcendence embraced by his predecessors, he goes on instead to work out the description of the "historiality" of *Dasein* in greater detail.

Dasein is historial to the extent that it knows itself to be finite, condemned to know only a historically limited experience. However, in the common activities of its everyday life, it has a tendency to forget this limitation. It leads, most of the time, an unauthentic existence, bogged down in anonymity. It is not itself, it is a "one"—one being among others, an object, an animal. This forgetfulness of oneself—this ontic "decline," this "forfeiture"—is nothing other than forgetfulness of Being and must be opposed.

It is difficult not to hear an echo in the terms *decline* and *forfeiture* of the Spenglerian theme of decadence. The parallel, though it has its limits, can be pushed further. Just as Spengler urged his younger readers to acknowledge the end of all high culture as a condition of taking part, militarily and technologically, in the "conquest of the world" that in his view remained the last hope of the West, so Heidegger exhorted *Dasein* to react by a historic "decision" (albeit formulated in vaguer terms) to assume its authentic destiny—in other words, the spiritual destiny of the community to which it belongs and that alone can give meaning to its existence. This amounted to a radical and, in some ways, revolutionary decision. For it was indeed a sort of revolution that the end of *Being and Time* called for—even if, quite clearly, the word was intended in this work only to evoke a return to the eternal values of Greek and German high culture.

Neither the necessity nor the meaning of this revolution is made explicit by Heidegger. And with good reason: in affirming what in the final analysis are shown to be the *practical* roots of our *theoretical* choices, Heidegger treats the faculty of choosing as a subjective "resolution," the grounds for which cannot be deduced a priori. As a consequence, the decision that he calls for remains a purely formal one. The thing to which it uniquely refers—the historical community of *Dasein*—is only one empirical fact among others. Nothing, at this stage, tells us in what sense it is to be understood, as though what links the resolution to its consequences were impossible to conceive.

The doctrine of decisionism nonetheless represents the most original advance of *Being and Time*. It constitutes both a major challenge to classical metaphysics and a point of unexpected convergence with the *Tractatus*, which also denied to human beings the possibility of grounding their ethical choices in rational discourse. On the other hand, the difficulties involved in working out a philosophy of history on the basis of an "existential analytic" caused the book to come to an abrupt end. Indeed, not only did the volume published in 1927—advertised as the first part of a larger work—have no successor, but the planned third section of this volume was missing as well. The fact that certain dead ends had been reached did not, however, prevent the book from being read with enthusiasm by the educated youth of the period.

Such enthusiasm was all the more surprising since *Being and Time* is an eminently difficult book, as much for the problems it raises as for its language. The likely explanation of this paradox is that another message—this time a simple one—is implicit in the text. In claiming that no philosopher before him had truly understood the question of Being, Heidegger was not content merely to denounce the "tyranny" of logical thought, to which his predecessors felt themselves obliged to submit; he asserted that rationalism as a whole had been "overcome"—without saying how, but suggesting nonetheless the possibility of a historic "new departure" whose content remained largely undetermined. At the end of the 1920s, such a message could only have exercised a dark fascination upon a certain part of the German intelligentsia, detached by the defeat of 1918 from the (largely French) tradition of the Enlightenment, disappointed by the intellectualist orientation of Husserlian phenomenology, and searching in a confused way for a spiritual revolution that would be both national and conservative.

The message was soon made more explicit. In his inaugural lecture at the University of Freiburg in late 1928, "What Is Metaphysics?" Heidegger returned to the theme of anxiety. Nothingness, he announced, is originally present within Being. The discovery of this "contradiction" led him to declare that "the sovereignty of reason" thus finds itself shattered, and that the very idea of logic dissolves "in the vortex of a more original questioning."[11] "Philosophy," he asserted, now without any ambiguity, "can never be measured with the yard-stick of the idea of science."[12] This warning—once again with unintentionally Wittgensteinian overtones—was uttered in the presence of Husserl, who held exactly the opposite view and who had grave reservations about the anthropologism he saw in the existential analytic of *Being and Time*. With this lecture Heidegger broke once and for all with phenomenology and, beyond this, with the whole Kantian heritage.

The following year saw him take part in a public debate, devoted to the question "What Is Man?" at the second round of Franco-German university meetings held at Davos, Switzerland, from 17 March to 6 April 1929. This debate furnished Heidegger with the opportunity to declare—before an audience that included students from both France and Germany—a sort of open war on the tradition of the *Aufklärung*, personified in the present instance by Ernst Cassirer, a Jew and a neo-Kantian. It began with a discussion of the Kantian interpretation of time. Then, in the middle of the session, Heidegger handed out a summary of his talk that made it clear that something more fundamental than Kant's theory of time was at stake. In this text—the French translation of which he tried unsuccessfully to block forty years later, although its content did not depart in any fundamental way from the doctrines of *Being and Time*—Heidegger peremptorily asserted the necessity of a "destruction" (here the meaning of the German term, *Zerstörung*, is not in doubt) "of all that which until now has been the foundation of Western metaphysics (Mind, Logos, Reason)."[13] In short, whereas Cassirer declared himself open to a critical reexamination of Kantianism, Heidegger proposed purely and simply to turn his back on the rationalist heritage altogether.

Unlike Cassirer, a man of intellectual courage who unfortunately was perceived at the time as a narrow academic, Heidegger appeared to herald a new era of thought. Although the illusion was not long in being dispelled, the Davos meetings nonetheless represent an important moment in the history of contemporary philosophy for two reasons. First, they mark the advent of a debate about the nature and function of reason that has continued to be carried on until the present day in various forms, though the stakes have not changed in the interval. Second, they signaled the return to the intellectual scene of a figure long absent from it, the "master of truth," at once thinker, poet, and prophet, unburdened by any obligation to argue for his theses—a figure most perfectly embodied in the twentieth century by Heidegger himself. Moreover, the audience at Davos—which included a number of young French philosophers, among them Jean Cavaillès, Emmanuel Levinas, and Maurice de Gandillac—could not have failed to remark the violence of Heidegger's attacks against Cassirer, with whom he is said to have refused to shake hands at the end.

Violence had, it is true, already become a daily reality in Germany by 1929. Scarcely recovered from its wounds, Europe as a whole now prepared to sink into a fresh round of convulsions. Mussolini's fascist "revolution" in Italy soon brought in its train other revolts against democracy in the West; while in the east the great gleam of hope that suddenly appeared one morning in 1917 was gradually to fade, carrying off with it the dreams of all the world's oppressed.

The End of Oppression

The war of 1914 did not kill only soldiers. It had in the meantime caused several great empires to crumble—among them the Prussian, Austro-Hungarian, and Ottoman monarchies, of course, but also the tsarist regime in Russia, whose death had been slowly approaching for a quarter of a century.

The seizure of power in October 1917 by a handful of revolutionaries led by Vladimir Ilyich Ulyanov, known as Lenin, caused a new state to be born, the Union of Soviet Socialist Republics. Although it lasted scarcely more than seventy years, during the course of these decades it embodied, for better or for worse, the grand illusion that lay at the heart of the international Communist movement: to break the history of the world in two, to put an end to the enslavement of humanity, and to build a future that would be worthy of human aspirations—in a word, to establish a single, classless society throughout the world.

Precisely because its aims were humanist and universal, this tragic epic—the adventure of European Communism and its ultimate failure—can only really be understood if it is put back in the context of the philosophical movement from which it derived. This means, first, putting it back in the context of the thought of its founder, Karl Marx. Many of the problematic aspects of his thought stand, in their turn, to be illuminated by the later course of events.

Going back to examine Marx's ideas is all the more necessary because they have continued to be distorted for more than a hundred years now, by partisans and detractors alike, and because they are now in danger, having been in effect sentenced without right of appeal since the end of the 1980s, of sinking at least temporarily into oblivion. It is disquieting that already, and in a work such as this, one should have to justify returning to them.

KARL MARX (1818–83) was very much a man of his century. Born into a middle-class German family, his academic training was marked by the dual influence of European romanticism and the philosophy of the Enlightenment. The young Marx followed Kant, Hegel, and Feuerbach, as well as Voltaire, Helvétius, and d'Holbach—and also the ancient materialist philosophers Democritus and Epicurus, to whom he devoted his doctoral thesis in 1841—in assigning to philosophy a progressive, critical, and redemptive mission: to rescue humanity from the shadows of ignorance and to promote the pursuit of happiness in a free and fraternal society.

A utopian task? Not necessarily. During the last quarter of the eighteenth century, the American and French revolutions had proven that oppression was not everywhere and always inevitable. But if feudalism had receded since then, the reign of the bourgeoisie was still far from coinciding with the universal triumph of reason. The bourgeoisie had only confiscated for its own profit what might have been a treasure for all of mankind. It prospered only by exploiting a class much more numerous than itself: the proletariat.

In the nineteenth century, the proletariat was made to pass through the hell of forced industrialization. It is hard to imagine today what the conditions of life then were like. The workers, who paid for the development of European capitalism with their sweat and blood, had every reason to wish to change the world. Coming after Babeuf and Saint-Simon, and the first French and British socialists, Marx could only be sympathetic to the justice of their cause. He identified himself with the new socialist movement and tried to help draw it nearer to its ultimate phase—when the workers, in liberating themselves from their chains, would succeed in liberating humanity as a whole.

At the outset, therefore, Marx's first impulse was ethical in character. Moreover, in becoming a socialist at the beginning of the 1840s he did not thereby cease to belong to the family of idealist moralists. Like Kant and Hegel, he reserved for philosophy a decisive role in achieving human progress. And if he criticized certain of their doctrines, or if he reformulated them to place greater emphasis on social ideals, he nonetheless remained the prisoner of a metaphysics of the "eternal essence" of man. One thinks, for example, of the use made of the Hegelian concept of alienation in his early writings, subsequently published as *Economic and Philosophical Manuscripts of 1844*. Very shortly thereafter, however, two other texts published in 1845, *Theses on Feuerbach* and *The German Ideology*, gave evidence of a sudden turn in his thought. This was a crucial moment—the moment when Marx became Marx.

This turn consisted first in breaking not only with idealism but also with speculative philosophy in all its forms. Although he now declared himself a radical materialist, Marx gave to this term a sense that no longer had anything to do with Helvétius or Feuerbach. To be a materialist, for him, meant asserting the primacy of science over philosophy and of action over reflection. In short, he was resolved to quit wasting his time criticizing other philosophers in order to concentrate his energies on a single end: the transformation of society.

Nothing better sums up this new program than the eleventh thesis on Feuerbach: "Philosophers have only *interpreted* the world in different ways; the point is to *change* it."[14] Let us reread this formidably elliptic sentence with care. In a few words, Marx denounces the ineffectiveness of philosophical speculation, its powerlessness to rid the world of oppression. He dismisses it to affirm the priority of action (praxis). What matters, he says, is changing the world. But he omits to say to *whom* such a mission must fall. This asymmetry—"interpreted" has a subject (philosophers) whereas "to change" does not—gave rise to two misunderstandings.

Many Marxists since have assumed that Marx charged philosophers with changing the world. Some—Platonists in spite of themselves—have even claimed that he invented a philosophy that by its mere existence would be capable of generating such a transformation. Both of these claims are mistaken, at least if one sticks to the letter of the text. For by 1845 Marx had ceased to have faith in philosophy, as his attacks in The German Ideology on left-wing Hegelians (until then close allies) reveal. Now only the workers found grace in his eyes, because they alone were capable of transforming the world. As a result, he found his way entirely laid out before him. He needed first to devise a way to bring about social revolution, relying on the proletariat. A genuinely philosophical revolution, however, would have to wait.

Unfortunately for this second revolution, it had to wait a long time; in the minds of some, it is still waiting to occur. Marx himself, in any case, hardly ever returned to the subject. There were two reasons for this. First, he considered the fundamental problem of philosophy, involving the relation between "being" and "thought," to be a false problem. For him, there was only one reality—nature as transformed by man—and only one valid form of knowledge—science. Second, from the materialist point of view, a new philosophy could in any event appear only as the result of a change in society. From 1845 until his death, Marx therefore devoted himself exclusively to constructing a program of social revolution.

This program was in two parts, one theoretical, the other political. On the theoretical (or "scientific") plane, it was necessary first to provide a rigorous basis for action by the proletariat in order to be in a position to direct it. This in turn required a new conception of history whose emergence itself depended on a radical critique of bourgeois political economy. Briefly sketched in the unfinished manuscript of The German Ideology (which was not published until 1932), the main lines of this part of the program were developed in Capital, the first volume of which appeared in 1867. On the political plane, on the other hand, it was necessary to help the proletariat organize itself—a difficult task that after the creation of the First International in 1864 absorbed an increasing share of Marx's energies. In 1848 he signed the Communist Manifesto with Engels. For more than one hundred and fifty years since, his ideas have shaken the world.

At his death in 1883, Marx left behind a new "science," or theory of revolution, and a guide for the struggle of the workers' movement, the materialist conception of history—what Engels, at the end of his life, called "historical materialism." But he left behind *no* philosophy at all.

IT WILL BE OBJECTED that there is indeed philosophy *in* Marx. Unquestionably so. Contrary to what Marx's own followers have claimed, however, there is no philosophy *of* Marx.

To clarify what is at issue here, let us distinguish the concepts of science, which have an objective reference, from the categories of philosophy, which are instruments of rational analysis. Categories of this kind (causality, totality, contradiction, and so on) were necessary elements of the work that Marx carried out in order to lay the foundations of historical science, particularly in order to criticize the central notions of bourgeois economics (value and wealth) and to substitute for them concepts of his own invention (social formation, mode of production, surplus value, class struggle, and so on). But they remained for the most part implicit, forming a sort of ad hoc philosophy that needed to be reworked, elaborated, and enriched. This was a task that could be fully accomplished only once the revolution had succeeded.

Certainly there are moments when Marx seems to have thought otherwise. If one rereads everything that Marx wrote over the course of his long life, one does indeed come across passages in which he begins to sketch out a critical analysis of concepts that the rest of the time he uses in an uncritical manner. A very few sketches of this sort can be found in the *Grundrisse* (1857–58) as well as in the preface to the *Contribution to a Critique of Political Economy* (1859).

Much ink has been spilled over these passages. With the passing of time, however, one must confess to a certain sense of disappointment. Even when Marx talked of the necessity of "overturning" the Hegelian dialectic in order to "put it back on its feet again," he was only sketching an agenda. Otherwise he was content to develop his ideas within the context of two of the traditions to which he was heir: Hegelian dialectics and the materialism of the Enlightenment. It is not that their categories satisfied him; it is simply that, as imperfect as they were, they sufficed to allow him to formulate the theses that he then attempted to put into effect—which was the only thing that mattered to him.

It bears repeating that these theses do not concern philosophy, but rather two other practices that for him were indissociable: "scientific" practice (concerning history as it is conceived) and political practice (concerning history as it is actually made). Apart from the vague injunction from which both derive—namely, that it is necessary to liberate the proletariat in order to liberate humanity—neither one, strictly speaking, is rooted in an original philosophy. One must therefore limit oneself to acknowledging this negative fact: there is no philosophy due to Marx himself.

It is possible, by contrast, to see a new philosophy being born in the last years of Marx's life and developing independently of him—Marxism. This new philosophy, which grew out of certain remarks made by Marx that were subsequently taken up by Engels and elaborated by their successors, swiftly spread throughout the world. Until 1917 it exhibited a splendid vitality. With the success of the Bolshevik revolution, however, and to a still greater degree after the death of Lenin, it deteriorated into a dogmatic and rigid ideology, Marxism-Leninism. The story of how this happened, though depressing, is nonetheless highly instructive.

MARX'S THOUGHT on almost every subject remained flexible and open to criticism. It was in a state of continual gestation, although it could not remain in such a state indefinitely. Indeed, the practical nature of the objective he had set for himself—revolution—meant that at a certain moment it had to become structured in order itself to be used to structure reality. In short, it had to become a *system* if it was to be able to conquer minds.

This system, subsequently known as Marxism, began to develop in the 1870s without Marx taking any direct part in it. Its first architect was none other than Friedrich Engels (1820–95)—the unfailing friend, the faithful companion in misfortune, the humble executor who out of sincere modesty stood always in the great thinker's shadow. One can hardly reproach Engels (whom it is pointlessly malicious to portray as the idiot of the duo, as some have done) for having been unable to resolve the theoretical problems with which Marx himself wrestled unsuccessfully. To the contrary, he must be credited with having undertaken the impossible mission of giving Marx's ideas the unity of a grand worldview (*Weltanschauung*) in advance of any political transformation that might have brought forth new categories of thought.

Engels therefore attempted to extract the philosophy implicit in Marx's writings, which he summarized, in order to make it generally accessible, in a few inevitably schematic theses that asserted the primacy of a "materialist" conception of the world and of a "dialectic" method of analysis. Engels's fascination with science—he was a great reader of Darwin—led him to try to show that these theses were in every respect consistent with the latest results in physics and biology. Thus, for example, he appealed to the theory of evolution to prove that not only society but also nature itself functions dialectically. Thus, too, using a curious language borrowed both from Darwin and from formal logic, he reformulated the most general laws of dialectics, supposing them to apply equally to being and mind.

These various arguments were expounded in a series of works in which the scientific, the political, and the philosophical are mixed together without great rigor. A number of them—Dialectics of Nature (1875–76), Anti-Dühring (1877–78), Socialism: Utopian and Scientific (1880), Ludwig Feuerbach and the End of Classical German Philosophy (1888)—must be reread today with indulgence. The sketch they give of a Marxist philosophy is highly unsatisfying, it is true; but it was intended to mask the unavoidable incompleteness of the thought of a man who, so long as the revolution had not begun, could not compose the philosophical sequel that the Theses on Feuerbach had called for.

Engels himself died without having published the unfinished manuscript of the Dialectics of Nature (which did not appear until 1925). He had, of course, helped to clarify the political part of the Marxist program, ratified at the Congress of Erfurt in 1891, the principal demands of which—direct and secret universal suffrage, equality before the law for both men and women, education, justice, and medical care free of charge, abolition of the death penalty, an eight-hour work day, exemption of children under the age of fourteen from labor—were later adopted by the German socialist workers' party founded by Wilhelm Liebknecht. But beyond these demands, which were revolutionary at the time, the strictly philosophical part of Marxism remained to be worked out in detail. Various theoreticians tried to fill the gaps in Marxist theory over the next twenty years. It must be said in their defense that they were able, independent-minded, and resistant to all forms of dogma.

THE PERIOD THAT STRETCHES from the founding of the Second International in 1889 until 1914, when it broke up under the pressure of war, was one of intense philosophical vitality for Marxist thought that stimulated keen political debate among the different factions of the workers' movement. This movement continued to be dominated, particularly in Germany, by the orthodox branch led by Karl Kautsky (1854–1938). Inspired by Engels's initial attempt at synthesis, he sought to build a "scientific socialism" that was res-olutely deterministic, naturalistic, and Darwinian. At the same time, how-ever, other conceptions came to the fore that departed more or less from this narrowly positivist vision.

In Italy, Antonio Labriola (1843–1904) revived the concept of praxis found in the writings of the young Marx. He thus stands as the forerunner of a hu-manistic Marxism, closely linked to Hegel, that was later to influence Anto-nio Gramsci and György Lukács.

In Germany itself, Eduard Bernstein (1850–1932), who had served as En-gels's executor, subsequently published The Presuppositions of Socialism and the Task of Social Democracy (1899), which rapidly became the bible of revisionist Marxists. In the name of Kant he attacked both Marx's materialism, which he thought dogmatic, and the belief that history is governed by necessary laws. He thus challenged the notion that revolution was inevitable, for which he was condemned by Kautsky. His doctrine, which advocated a peaceful transi-tion by means of progressive reforms from capitalism to socialism, nonethe-less enjoyed great success until the First World War. After 1918 Bernstein sev-ered all ties with Marxism, becoming one of the leading theoreticians of European social democracy.

In Austria, Max Adler (1873–1937)—who in 1904 launched the journal Marx-Studien—and Otto Bauer (1882–1938) tried to reformulate the philo-sophical principles of Marxism in a still more overtly Kantian sense. Al-though as partisans of the ethical socialism defended by Hermann Cohen they too were hostile to materialism, the Austromarxists (as they were called) nonetheless did not see a place for themselves in Bernstein's revisionist scheme since, unlike him, they admitted the idea of a dictatorship of the pro-letariat. Their movement disappeared in 1914.

In Russia, Georgii Valentinovich Plekhanov (1856–1918) sought to combat the growing influence of the neo-Kantians by putting Marxism back into the tradition of philosophical materialism associated with Spinoza, Helvétius, and d'Holbach. The circumstances of his quarrel with Bernstein led him in the 1890s to emphasize that the materialist explanation of history consti-tuted only a part of the materialist conception of Marx and Engels and to affirm that any study of their system had to begin with that of its philosophi-cal bases: materialism and dialectics. He was, moreover, the first (in 1891) to use the expression "dialectical materialism"—which is found neither in Marx nor in Engels[15]—without realizing that it had already been coined independently (in 1887) by Joseph Dietzgen, a self-taught German worker who attempted to develop Marx's ideas on his own.

It is to Plekhanov, then, who was also the first Marxist to go back and carefully read Hegel, that we owe the famous distinction between Marxist "science" and Marxist "philosophy"; that is, between historical materialism and dialectical materialism. This distinction was later adopted and systematized by Lenin, who regarded Plekhanov as his teacher—although Plekhanov, not being a Bolshevik, did not take part in the revolution of 1917.

Russian Marxism was also the source at the beginning of the present century of a bold conception developed by Alexandr Alexandrovich Bogdanov (1873–1928)—empirio-monism—to which Lenin, however, remained firmly opposed. To grasp its significance one needs first to examine the doctrine that inspired it—empirio-criticism—advanced some years earlier by the German philosopher Richard Avenarius (1843–96) and, in particular, the Austro-Hungarian physicist Ernst Mach (1838–1916), neither one of whom was a Marxist. We have already had occasion to note Mach's influence upon Russell and Wittgenstein; later we will encounter him again in connection with the Vienna Circle. An encyclopedic mind, Mach was an authority on optics, physiology, and experimental psychology as well as a historian of science and philosophy. The term *empirio-criticism*—referring to a theory of knowledge derived from Kantian criticism, only still more resolutely empiricist—was introduced in one of his first works, *Remarks on the Analysis of Sensations* (1886).

An enemy of metaphysics in all its forms, Mach relied on a principle of economy in scientific research (challenged by Husserl[16]) according to which scientists ought to attempt to take into account a maximum of phenomena with the aid of a minimum of hypotheses. Considering sensations to be the only objectively real facts, and so the source of all knowledge, he rejected idealism and materialism as useless hypotheses. The only acceptable position on his view was a strict sensationalism. This amounted to denying any substantive distinction between mind and matter—terms that merely represent different attitudes (or "directions of investigation") toward physical sensations, which alone are real—and to defining human knowledge as "signs" or "hieroglyphs" of these sensations.

At the end of the nineteenth century Bogdanov sought to radicalize this position. He acknowledged a debt to Mach for having shattered the doctrine of mind-body dualism and went on to eliminate all traces of it, affirming that all phenomena, whether mental or physical, are at bottom identical. Pushed to its logical extreme, this version of empirio-monism led to a liquidation not only of materialism, now seen as a metaphysical anachronism, but also of the idea of absolute truth. For Bogdanov, truth was only a way of organizing experience that, by its constant evolution, reinforces the human capacity for adaptation in the struggle for life. It followed from this that the proletariat, the only class capable of leading humanity in the direction of greater mastery over nature, was also the only one capable of advancing it along the path of scientific progress. Indeed, after the revolution Bogdanov became a leading theoretician of "proletarian culture" and the first to campaign on behalf of proletarian (as opposed to bourgeois) science. Similarly, another empirio-monist, Anatoly Vasilyevich Lunacharsky (1875–1933), on becoming the first Soviet commissar for education, argued in favor of a proletarian, radically anti-academic art that was temporarily to rally the forces of the Russian artistic avant-garde, including Malevich and Tatlin as well as the futurists.

Although they are mostly forgotten today, these divergent viewpoints testify to the liberty of expression that reigned within the Marxist constellation, at least until 1914. The October Revolution gradually put an end to it. From 1917 Marxism ceased to be the common property of all the members of the moribund Second International. Little by little it passed into the hands of the Russian revolutionaries, and, more particularly, into those of its leader, Lenin, elevated by the force of events to the position of Marx's legitimate heir and guardian of orthodoxy.

VLADIMIR ILYICH ULYANOV (1870–1924) became a Marxist around 1890. His older brother, accused of conspiring against the tsar, was hanged in 1887. The influence of his reading—Marx, Engels, Plekhanov—did the rest. Henceforth, Ulyanov had only one aim in mind: to seize power with the purpose of bringing about the triumph of socialism in Russia.

A lawyer by training, he was interested at first in the economic aspects of Marxist doctrine, which he used to combat the arguments made by Russian populists. As against the latter, who favored a rural society composed of small landholders, Ulyanov believed both in the mission of the industrial proletariat and in the necessity of passing through capitalism in order to reach socialism. In one of his earliest writings, *What the "Friends of the People" Are and How They Fight the Social Democrats* (1894), he argued that Marxist dialectic was an entirely different proposition than the Hegelian "triad" of thesis, antithesis, and synthesis,[17] although by this time he had not yet read any of Hegel's works.

In 1895 he met Plekhanov. In the years immediately following he took up the study of philosophy, reading Helvétius, d'Holbach, and Kant. In 1901 he adopted the pseudonym Lenin and began gradually to construct a personal vision of Marxism. This vision can be summed up in a simple slogan: everything is political. In the struggle against tsarism as well as in the rivalries that opposed the various socialist movements to each other, the value of ideas was to be measured by their capacity for contributing to the success of revolutionary strategy. Practice thus became the ultimate criterion of truth. Lenin, at bottom, was a radical pragmatist.

As an atheist he was convinced, like Marx, that religion was the "opium of the people," the cement of reactionary ideologies, the most solid guarantee of the bourgeois order. It was for this essentially political reason that he adhered unreservedly to the materialist tradition; and this adherence in turn explains his determination to combat all forms of neo-Kantian Marxism, particularly empirio-monism.

In 1906 he discovered a "danger" concealed in Bogdanov's writings and decided at once to undertake a refutation. He thought the task serious enough to justify devoting an entire year of work to it, including several months spent in London in the library of the British Museum. The result, *Materialism and Empirio-Criticism*, appeared in Moscow in 1909. It was the sole work of philosophy that Lenin published in his lifetime.

As one might expect, the strictly philosophical content of this work, derived directly from Engels (Marx himself is cited only twice), is rather slender. It can be reduced to a single thesis: just as in the struggle between the classes there are only two possible positions and, in politics, only supporters and opponents of revolution, so too the history of philosophy is only the history of the struggle between two hostile and irreconcilable tendencies, materialism and idealism. It is necessary then to choose one's camp, and to choose it clearly. Those without a party, Lenin added, are as hopelessly stupid in philosophy as they are in politics.[18]

Moving from this premise, he went on to take vigorous issue with Mach, Helmholtz, Poincaré, and scientists in general, who stand accused of contradicting themselves when they venture into the domain of philosophy. While they are unavoidably materialists within the domain of science, they feel obliged to abandon this position—embracing instead empiricism, criticism, and idealism in general—when they dare to formulate a theory of knowledge. Of course, for Lenin, to deny that matter is the sole objective reality, to hold that it resides instead in the sensations of the subject, amounted to endorsing (without admitting it) the solipsism of Bishop Berkeley. Against such a metaphysical malady there was only one possible remedy: materialism—more precisely, dialectical materialism. The second term of this expression refers to a conception of the world according to which matter is prior to thought, the latter being only a product of the former. The first term denotes a theory of knowledge, defined as "reflection," that holds that our true ideas are not "hieroglyphs" but "copies" of reality—images modified through an indefinite process of practical verification. On this view, each new discovery is achieved by the negation of previously acquired knowledge.

The exposition of these ideas, unoriginal in themselves, was marred by doubtful prophecies as well. Lenin refused to accept, for example, that physics might one day renounce absolute determinism. In spite of errors in judgment of this sort, his work succeeded in placing empirio-monism in a difficult position from which it never recovered. But outside revolutionary circles, *Materialism and Empirio-Criticism* found hardly any audience. It was not until the end of the 1920s that the book finally achieved the rank of a classic of Marxism.

In his last works, *Imperialism, The Highest Stage of Capitalism* (1916) and *State and Revolution* (1917), Lenin set out to develop the political part of Marx's program. He now paid hardly any attention to philosophy, except to meticulously correct this or that politically dangerous "deviation"—the theory of "proletarian" culture, for example, which he was always to regard with contempt on account of its empirio-monist origins. In September 1914, however, when the war had just broken out, Lenin buried himself in Hegel's *Logic*, presumably in order to better understand what "dialectics" meant. Over the next two years he took dozens of pages of notes, which were published in 1929 under the title *Philosophical Notebooks*. Nothing really novel is to be found in these notes, excepting the rightly celebrated aphorism that Marx's *Capital* cannot be understood if one has not read Hegel's *Logic*.[19]

Otherwise, strictly political tasks soon acquired priority. After 1917 Lenin was no longer a revolutionary hunted by the tsarist police. He had become a statesman. In the end, he was to influence his century more profoundly than all but a very few others.

A NOW-CLASSIC DEBATE divides historians over the question of what Lenin contributed in a general way to Marxism.

To this question three replies may be given: either that Lenin contributed nothing essential because all of Lenin—including the prison system of the Gulag—was already contained in Marx's thought; or that Lenin knowingly betrayed Marx in making Marxism a weapon in the service solely of his own thirst for power, which equally implied the Gulag; or that Lenin took the risk of distorting Marx's theory out of a desire to adapt it to a new reality, the exercise of power in the Soviet Union, adding to it an authoritarian conception of the role of the party in the state from which the Gulag could not help but develop. Each of these conclusions relies, obviously, on a different reading of Soviet history. Given the current state of our knowledge, however, the third interpretation seems the best.

The second one can in any case be dismissed without too much hesitation. Contrary to what certain of his adversaries claimed, Lenin was not an isolated conspirator. What occurred in 1917 was indeed a popular revolution against the tsarist regime. How can one forget that millions of people within the old empire welcomed it with great hope and enthusiasm? Or forget that the Bolshevik government was the first government during World War I to make peace? Or forget the pictures taken by Dzhiga Vertov in the opening days of the revolution showing the joy of Muslim women freed at last from wearing the chador? It must be kept in mind that the revolution did, in fact, almost succeed. Making the revolution succeed was indeed Lenin's objective, even if, very quickly, things began to go wrong.

Nor can the first interpretation be sustained. Seeing the Gulag as necessarily contained within the very idea of revolution no doubt has the advantage of simplifying the problem: if the Gulag is in Marx, then Marx can only be fundamentally bad, and the idea of social transformation radically dangerous. Marx having been made into the devil, the only thing left to do is to burn him, which is what in fact the Nazis did. Nothing is more powerful, nothing has a greater hold on the collective imagination, than the temptation to find scapegoats. But nothing is more illusory either.

For even if the Gulag really were in Marx, the fact remains that millions of people, first in Russia, then in China and elsewhere, embraced the cause of Communism in the belief that they were putting an end to an eternity of oppression. Moreover, one has only to read Marx, and then Lenin, to see that the Gulag is not in Marx, but in Leninism, which is by no means a mere "detail." Lenin did, to be sure, consider himself to be Marx's heir. But

Leninism—the codification of which was completed only under Stalin and therefore after Lenin's death—was something quite different from Marxism and, of course, from Marx's actual thought.

Lenin is not in Marx any more than Marx is in Hegel, or Hegel in Kant. Marx was a philosopher who went off in search of history. Along the way he found politics and abandoned philosophy. Lenin was not a philosopher, but a militant revolutionary who had a need of simple principles to guide his actions, to stir up the people and, ultimately, to take power. Marx was a theoretician; Lenin a strategist. It is not surprising, then, that Lenin took from Marx only those theses that were of use to him or that he reinterpreted them in a way that in his judgment was best adapted to the objective he had set for himself.

Lenin therefore cannot be reproached for having deliberately betrayed Marx. In using Marxist theory as a blueprint for the seizure of power, in making it serve the Bolshevik party in its domination of the former Russian Empire, Lenin was right to suppose that he had taken this theory to its logical conclusion. Marx himself did not wish to see it remain nothing more than a heavenly ideal. In 1845 he had proclaimed the necessity of transforming the world. In order to bring about the transformation of the world, it was necessary to begin by transforming one country. Lenin was therefore not a traitor to Marxism. The problem, of course, lies elsewhere. It resides in the unreadiness of Russian society—rural, feudal, almost entirely lacking in industrial infrastructure and proletariat—to allow itself to be transformed in the sense Marx intended, and in Lenin's insistence on breaking down resistance, hurrying things, forcing the pace of events at any cost. In 1924 illness prematurely removed him from power, and it fell to Stalin to see the process through to its end.

The Moscow trials, the purges, the massacres, the deportations, the Gulag—in short, everything that is associated with the hideous reputation of Stalinism—flowed from just this, from the relentless determination to impose upon a divided people a model of change that had not been conceived for it, in the context of international conflict (until 1922) and in the face of the hatred of the rest of Europe (until 1989) as well as of various sources of internal opposition (the clergy, for example) that, as their reemergence since the late 1980s has made clear, were not themselves always motivated by a pure love of democracy.

The point of recalling these things is not to exculpate Lenin—still less

Stalin—but to show how, under the pressure of events, Marxism as a critical weapon came to be seriously distorted.

LET US GO BACK TO 1917. By this date, under the joint influence of Engels, Kautsky, Plekhanov, and Lenin, Marxism had at last acquired a stable identity. In the eyes of the workers' movement, this vulgar version of Marx's thought—at once scientific, political, and philosophical—represented the best guide for the seizure of power and therefore the best possible philosophy, one that would permit humanity to escape once and for all from its long prehistory. Twenty years later, in 1938, one no longer spoke of Marxism, but of Marxism-Leninism. The essential difference was this: Marxism-Leninism, although it claimed to comprise a philosophy (the only true philosophy, of course), was no longer animated by any vital impulse. It was only a fixed construction, a product of dictatorship, an ideological monstrosity whose dates of birth and death (roughly 1929–89) coincided with those of Stalinism itself. What happened?

Just as Marxism began to take shape following Marx's death, so too Leninism came to be worked out only after Lenin's death. Lenin himself, while he believed he had completed Marxist doctrine in respect of certain practical points (the theory of imperialism, the role of the party and the state in revolution), did nothing to give his ideas the force of law. He was too pragmatic to become trapped by a dogma. And while he perceived the existence of lacunae in Marxism, in particular from the philosophical point of view, he did not consider himself capable of filling them alone. Surely after 1917 he judged it opportune to reinforce the theoretical foundations of Marxist doctrine and therefore sought once again to promote a program of strictly philosophical research within the party. The diversity of views within the party at that time proves that the die was not yet cast, however, and that Lenin was in no great hurry to decide between the discrepant opinions of his comrades.

In 1922, for instance, the Moscow journal Under the Banner of Marxism opened its pages to a debate whose candor indicated that freedom of thought was still alive. Lenin himself contributed an article in which he recalled the necessity of anchoring Marxism in the dual tradition of Enlightenment materialism and Hegelian dialectics. Another writer, a Bolshevik academic named Minin, proclaimed the uselessness of philosophy and urged authentic Marxists to throw it overboard along with religion. Minin was not punished for his statements. Many revolutionaries at the time believed that the old philosophy had outlived its usefulness and that in the new world that had just been born it was destined to disappear, giving way to socially more profitable activities.

In 1924 the tone gradually began to change. A few days after Lenin's death, in January, the formula styling him as the "brilliant upholder of Marx" first appeared. In April *Pravda* began publication of a series of articles entitled "Principles of Leninism." Their author, Joseph Dzugashvili (1879–1953), who had adopted the name Stalin, did not attempt to conceal his purpose. Leninism, he said, could not be considered reductively as the result of "the application of Marxism to the particular conditions of the Russian situation." To the contrary, it had to be regarded as the expression of a universal theory and strategy, that of "proletarian revolution in general and of the dictatorship of the proletariat in particular."[20]

Leninism was therefore a political doctrine. On this point, one can only agree. But Stalin did not stop there. He wished also to make it pass for a philosophical doctrine. Leninism, he added, was "the Marxism of the era of imperialism and of proletarian revolution." It was "Marxism developed more deeply."[21] In short, Stalin was determined to call attention to Leninism's roots in Marxism and to stress the continuity between the two, and also to ensure that he would be seen as their natural successor, the heir not only to Lenin but to Marx himself.

Nonetheless, Stalin was not the only claimant to succeed Lenin. In January 1929 he exiled his rival Leon Trotsky (1879–1940) from the Soviet Union, though Trotsky continued to have a good many followers there. One of them, oddly enough, a former Menshevik and adversary of Lenin named Deborin, managed to have the term *Marxism-Leninism* officially imposed at the second national conference of scientific research institutions held later that year. This term covered both dialectical materialism and historical materialism, which together were said to constitute the common and inalienable heritage of all Communists, regardless of faction.

Finally, in 1931, events took a decisive turn. In the text of a decree concerning the future of the journal *Under the Banner of Marxism*, Stalin appropriated most of Deborin's theses while reproaching him, altogether untruthfully, for having deviated from them. The stakes were quite obviously more political than theoretical. At issue was whether Stalin or Deborin and his allies (suspected of Trotskyism) were to inherit Lenin's legacy, which is to say power—police power, to be sure, but also the power to decide the truth, the latter being the indispensable ideological basis of the former.

By 1931 it was clear that Lenin's heir would be Stalin. Some years later, in 1938, he formally established himself as a philosopher by publishing *Dialectical Materialism and Historical Materialism*, the first of his works to address itself to purely philosophical, rather than political, topics. From this point on Stalin ruled absolutely over a closely monitored realm of theoretical debate, deciding all questions in the name of dialectical materialism—or *diamat*, in the Russian shorthand—of which he was, by definition, the only person capable of stating the orthodox version. Not only, then, did diamat become the official philosophy of the Soviet state; so fiercely was the cosubstantiality of state and philosophy insisted upon at the time that the state actually seemed—at least if its pronouncements were interpreted literally—to be the realization of the philosophy, and therefore the incarnation of absolute truth. In retrospect, the admiration that the philosopher Alexandre Kojève (a Russian émigré to France who, although not a Communist, was a Hegelian) felt toward Stalin, whose death moved him, he said, as much as that of his father,[22] may appear not altogether paradoxical.

Indeed, Stalinism in one sense was nothing other than the ultimate avatar of Hegelian philosophy. It represented the realization of all philosophy, indeed of all rationality, *in and by* the modern state. It was philosophy *made state*, fully achieved by its own triumph. Nonetheless, even if Stalinism corresponded to a historical stage correctly predicted by Hegel, it plainly had little, if any, organic connection with Marx's actual thought, which it seized control of by a series of violent blows, totally emptying it of its original inspiration.

MARXIST PHILOSOPHY, having been suffocated in the Soviet Union, could do no more than attempt to survive, and then only with difficulty, within the margin of tolerance conceded it in Western Europe. Between the two wars it was limited to a few figures: the Hungarian György Lukács, the German Ernst Bloch, the Italian Antonio Gramsci, and the Frenchmen Paul Nizan and Georges Politzer—philosophers who were all, in one way or another, victims of fascism or Nazism.

A drama critic in his youth, György (also Georg) Lukács (1885–1971) lived for some years in Berlin and Heidelberg, during which he published two volumes on aesthetics—*The Soul and the Forms* (1910) and *The Theory of the Novel* (1916)—and became a Marxist at the end of the First World War. In December 1918 he joined the Communist Party and served as Commissar for Culture in the short-lived government of Béla Kun in Budapest. When the Hungarian revolution was crushed in August 1919 he sought refuge in Vienna and Berlin and then, after 1933, in Moscow. In Vienna he published one of the most important Marxist texts of the twentieth century, History and Class Consciousness (1923). Concerned with elucidating the concept of dialectical method, which it equated with the "point of view of totality," this work was immediately attacked by prominent Soviet critics of the Communist movement (including Deborin). Lukács found himself reproached for having reduced Marxist materialism to Hegelian idealism, for having challenged Engels's notion of "dialectics of nature," and for having conceived the role of the proletariat too "humanistically" as the "subject" of history. Lukács agreed to engage in self-criticism. Although during his subsequent stay in Moscow he was not prevented from elaborating a personal conception of realism in art (rather removed from the doctrine of socialist realism), he was obliged to take a more orthodox line, which he tried to escape once more upon his return to Budapest in 1945.

Four years later, however, a sharp Stalinist attack directed against his "bourgeois" and "cosmopolitan" tendencies forced Lukács to undergo a second period of self-criticism. In 1954 he published a detailed inquiry into the ideological antecedents of national socialism, The Destruction of Reason. Appearing in two volumes (From Schelling to Nietzsche and From Dilthey to Toynbee), it denounced Spengler's system, Heideggerian existentialism, and all forms of "vitalism" or philosophical irrationalism. In 1956 an anti-Soviet insurrection broke out in Budapest. Lukács was actively associated with it and served in the first government under Imre Nagy as Minister of Culture, the same post that he had held in the Kun regime almost forty years earlier. When the revolt was put down by the Soviet army, he took refuge first in the Yugoslav Embassy and then went into exile for several months. Permitted to return to Budapest in the spring of the following year, he now refused all self-criticism; although Nagy was executed, in 1958, Lukács resolved to pass the rest of his life in Hungary, despite the close surveillance to which he was subject.

Ernst Bloch (1885–1977), like Lukács a precocious writer, composed his first philosophical essay at the age of thirteen. From 1908 until 1911 Bloch lived in Berlin, where he and Lukács formed a lasting friendship, and then in the following years in Heidelberg and Barmisch. A pacifist, horrified by the war and Prussian militarism, he went into exile in Switzerland in 1917, returning to Berlin afterwards to join the Spartacist movement. The two great books of his youth testify to his gradual conversion to Communism. The more innovative of the two, *The Spirit of Utopia* (1918), resulted from a surprising combination of Jewish messianism with a spiritual interpretation of Marxism, most of its economic aspects having been taken out. The second book, *Thomas Münzer as Theologian of Revolution* (1921), paid homage to this sixteenth-century reformer, who preached revolt to the German peasants in the name of a democratic reading of the gospel.

Bloch was almost fifty years old when the events of 1933 forced him to go into exile, first in Switzerland, then in Austria, France, Czechoslovakia, and the United States. Despite these tribulations, he managed nonetheless to go on building a considerable and unclassifiable body of work, irreducible either to orthodox Marxism or to the Frankfurt School version and marked by a constant concern with ethical questions. From his research into the subversive power of religious mystics and grand utopian visions came three volumes that constitute his major work, *The Principle of Hope* (1954–59). These appeared in East Germany, to which Bloch came back to live in 1948. With the construction of the Berlin Wall in 1961 he sought exile in Western Europe a final time, finishing out his wandering existence in Tübingen.

Still more dramatic was the life of Antonio Gramsci (1891–1937). After having become a socialist in 1916, he participated in the workers' councils movement in Turin in 1919 as well as in the founding of the Italian Communist Party in 1921. Elected a deputy three years later, he was arrested in 1926 on the orders of Mussolini. Jailed for more than ten years, during which he composed his *Prison Notebooks*, he eventually died from the mistreatment he endured in captivity.

Gramsci distanced himself both from materialist monism and metaphysical idealism. His conception of Marxism, following along the path opened up by Labriola, was above all a philosophy of praxis. It saw itself as both humanist—since the existing situation can only be overcome by an effort of human will—and historicist—since all reality, including science and philosophy, is only a product of history. No doubt Gramscian historicism has its roots in a specifically Italian tradition, descending from Machiavelli, Vico, and, nearer our own time, the philosophers Benedetto Croce (1886–1952), who was influenced by Hegel and Nietzsche, and Giovanni Gentile (1875–1944). But it had its own concerns as well. Gramsci was anxious to put politics back into history in order to emphasize—as against Stalin—the transitory character of the revolutionary state. Its disappearance was to be welcomed in the interest of creating new political forms, to which proletarian praxis—in other words, the capacity of the working class for self-organization—could not but help give rise.

The anti-Stalinism of Gramsci's thought exercised considerable influence after the Second World War upon the Italian Communist Party, which, more than the other European parties, was able to preserve its autonomy in relation to Moscow, as well as upon a good number of Marxist intellectuals eager to escape Soviet orthodoxy. Gramsci's humanism is found in Sartre, and his concern for conceptual analysis in Althusser.

Born in Hungary, Georges Politzer (1903–42) emigrated to France with the failure of the revolution in his native country in 1919. An interest in psychoanalysis led him to publish first a *Critique of the Foundations of Psychology* (1928), marked by a "return to the concrete" and reflection upon the "human drama." Upon joining the French Communist Party in 1929 he turned his attention to irrationalism, represented for him by Bergson, whom he criticized in a book entitled *End of a Philosophical Parade: Bergsonianism* (1929); some years later he returned to the attack, this time opposing the existential thought of Heidegger, Jean Wahl, and Gabriel Marcel in an article entitled "Philosophy and Myths" (1939). During the Second World War he took an active part in the Resistance. Arrested by the Vichy government, he was shot by the Nazis.

Paul Nizan (1905–40) had still less time to produce a body of work. The son of a railroad employee and a schoolmate of Sartre, he entered the École Normale Supérieure, became a Marxist, traveled to Aden, joined the Communist Party in 1927, passed the *agrégation* examination in philosophy, and then after a year spent teaching decided to devote himself to journalism. His best work remains *The Watchdogs* (1932), a call for revolt against the spiritualist and reactionary philosophy that dominated French universities at the time in the person of "the four Bs": Henri Bergson, Maurice Blondel, Émile Boutroux, and Léon Brunschvicg. As a partisan of absolute engagement, Nizan conceived of philosophy as a collective undertaking, filled with problems from everyday life, made by and for the people. He died at the front at the beginning of the Second World War.

Neither the writings of these courageous philosophers nor, after 1945, the works of Sartre, Althusser, and the Frankfurt School, nor even the sizable (and not uninteresting) politico-philosophical production of the Chinese revolutionary Mao Zedong (1893–1976) succeeded in checking the progressive decline of Marxist thought. With the crumbling of the major Communist regimes in Eastern Europe in the months following the fall of the Berlin Wall on 9 November 1989, Marxism was dealt a devastating blow, from which it will not soon recover—even if the desire to bring into existence a world from which oppression has been banished still remains, now more than ever, ethically and politically understandable.

The End of Metaphysics

Before 1914 Husserl and Russell had dreamed of setting philosophy securely on the sure path of science. After the First World War, with Wittgenstein, this dream faded and gave way to a new conviction: philosophy, or at least its classic figure, metaphysics, was finished. Did it need to be replaced by something else? If so, by what? By a more fundamental form of thought, the "thought of Being"—Heidegger's answer? Or by a revolutionary project, itself anchored in a vast "conception of the world"—Lenin's answer? In Austria, at the end of the 1920s, the same question received a more cautious answer. For the famous circle of scholars whose mutual affinities drew them together in Vienna, it was up to all the existing sciences—mathematical and experimental—to take over from metaphysics and, in their own special language, to pose questions that metaphysics, because it could not itself become a science, had never been able to answer.

Baptized neopositivism (although it bore hardly any direct relation to the positivism of Auguste Comte)—also logical positivism and, later, logical empiricism—this movement was led by Moritz Schlick, Rudolf Carnap, Hans Hahn, and Otto Neurath. It did not constitute a school in the strict sense. Despite the publication in 1929 of a collective manifesto, great differences of opinion were found among both its followers and its leaders. Two general characteristics, common to all the members of the group, may nonetheless be discerned. The first is their interest in logic; the second, their radical empiricism.

The Vienna Circle was resolutely opposed to German idealism and, especially, to Hegel. Like Leibniz and Bolzano, its members dreamed of creating a universal language into which it would suffice to retranslate a given question in order to give it a definite answer or to show that it involved a false problem. Convinced that this language could be only that of positive science, analyzed in the light of modern logic, they joined in supporting the linguistic turn in philosophy initiated by Frege, Moore, and Russell while assigning it a still more antimetaphysical significance than their predecessors had done. It was, moreover, a neopositivist, Gustav Bergmann, who in 1953 first proposed the expression "linguistic turn," later popularized by the title of a celebrated anthology of analytic writings edited by Richard Rorty.[23]

Although the members of the Vienna Circle moved away from Kant, owing to their professed empiricism, they did nonetheless adopt the Kantian project of founding science on an unshakable basis in another form that drew them nearer to Hume and, in particular, to a more modern current of thought we have already mentioned, Mach's empirio-criticism—born, like the work of Bolzano, in the heart of the old Austro-Hungarian Empire. Mach, the unchallenged master of the neopositivists, taught experimental physics for twenty-eight years at Charles University in Prague before accepting the chair of philosophy (which he renamed "Chair of History and Theory of the Inductive Sciences") at the University of Vienna in 1895, a post he occupied until illness forced him to retire six years later. He advocated a radical and antimetaphysical sensationalism, seeing in the objects treated by the sciences only abstractions constructed by the scientist on the basis of complexes of sensations. These were, moreover, dangerous abstractions since the task of the scientist according to Mach was to describe the world, not to pretend to explain it. On this view, science was at most only a phenomenology.

Accordingly, Mach challenged the notion of causality—which he suggested replacing with that of functional relation among variables—along with Newtonian and Kantian ideas of absolute space and time, thus prefiguring their imminent destruction by Einstein. Any apparently meaningful statement that contained terms to which no empirical significance could be attached was to be rejected. In this way Mach avoided getting caught up in the traditional opposition between idealism and materialism. His sensationalism, which resembled instead the theses defended by William James—who went to Prague in 1882 to meet Mach—inspired the doctrine of neutral monism elaborated by Russell in 1914 as well as Carnap's early philosophy in the *Aufbau* a decade later. Because it allowed the set of concepts belonging to all the empirical sciences to be considered as deriving from one and the same source, sensationalism also justified the thesis of the unity of science, to which the neopositivists, eager to make the sciences of mind a direct extension of the sciences of nature, showed a strong attachment. Their debt to Mach was therefore considerable—even if they did not share his unwavering belief in the physiological origin of logical laws, already criticized earlier by Husserl.

When Mach retired, his chair went to another Austrian physicist, Ludwig Boltzmann, and then, after Boltzmann's suicide, to the philosopher Adolf Stöhr. It was during these decisive years preceding the First World War, between 1907 and 1912, that what is sometimes called the first Vienna Circle came together. At this point it amounted to nothing more than occasional meetings among three young scholars who wished to exchange ideas on the fashionable topic of empirio-criticism. One of them, Hans Hahn, was a mathematician; another, Philipp Frank, a physicist; the third, Otto Neurath, an economist and sociologist. At the heart of their discussions was the philosophy of the sciences. In addition to Mach, all three were disciples of the French physicists and philosophers of science Pierre Duhem (1861–1916) and Abel Rey (1873–1940). Duhem's masterwork, *The Aim and Structure of Physical Theory* (1906), had been translated into German in 1908; Rey's *Theory of Physics* (1907) came out in German the same year. The future neopositivists were also heavily influenced by the conventionalism defended by these authors; that is, the thesis that the basic propositions of scientific theories, always determined by a decision of the scientist, may be revised if necessary. But their debates sometimes went beyond epistemological questions to consider problems of a political, social, or religious nature, to which they were far from being indifferent.

The experience of the war strengthened the weight of these latter concerns in their thinking. Won over by Marx's ideas, Otto Neurath (1882–1945) joined the Social Democratic Party in 1918. The following year he interrupted his academic activities to take charge of planning for the newly installed socialist government in Bavaria. When this government, which in the meantime had become Communist, was toppled by the Right in 1919, Neurath, after escaping an assassination attempt, was arrested and sentenced to eighteen months in prison. On the intervention of the Austrian government his sentence was commuted to expulsion from the country. Neurath then returned to Vienna, where he was named director of the Social and Economic Museum.

During the same period the University of Vienna, acting on Hahn's recommendation, appointed the German philosopher Moritz Schlick to Mach's chair, vacant since Stöhr's death in 1919. Schlick was, at the time, the author of two books, *Space and Time in Contemporary Physics* (1917), which developed the philosophical implications of the theory of relativity, as well as *General Theory of Knowledge* (1918), which adopted Bolzano's critique of the notion of synthetic a priori judgment. Such judgments could not exist since there was no intersection between logico-mathematical propositions, on the one hand, these being analytic a priori, and the synthetic propositions of the empirical sciences on the other. In a single stroke, the possibility of specifically metaphysical statements was ruled out.

Schlick came to Vienna in 1922. Once again Hahn played a decisive role, this time persuading the mathematicians Friedrich Waismann and Kurt Gödel along with his friends Frank and Neurath to meet periodically with Schlick, since otherwise the group lacked a professional philosopher. These informal meetings, which eventually came to be held regularly on Thursday evenings at a Viennese café, provided their participants with the opportunity to jointly discover the work of Frege and Russell—as well as Wittgenstein's *Tractatus*, the definitive version of which appeared in 1922. Four years later, the group was further strengthened by the arrival of a young German, Rudolf Carnap, who had come to the University of Vienna to obtain his habilitation. From this moment the second Vienna Circle entered into its most intense phase of activity, lasting for about three years. These years were notable in particular for the publication of Carnap's most ambitious—and most controversial—book, *Der Logische Aufbau der Welt* (The Logical Construction of the World).

RUDOLF CARNAP (1891–1970) became interested in mathematics, physics, and philosophy at a very young age. In the fall of 1910 he went to Jena to study with Frege. The outbreak of the First World War struck him immediately as an "incomprehensible catastrophe."[24] Called to active duty, he fought on the front until 1917. He received news of the Russian revolution with joy, as later, in 1918–19, of the fleeting victory of the Left in Germany.

In 1919 Carnap earned his doctorate at Jena with a thesis on the concept of space, marked by the influence of the theory of relativity. The same year he immersed himself—on Frege's advice—in the works of Russell, particularly *Our Knowledge of the External World*, which made a profound impression on him, and *Principia Mathematica*, which led him to compose a *Sketch of Mathematical Logic* (written in 1924 but not published until 1929). Along with Wittgenstein's *Tractatus*, this was one of the first works to take the advances of modern logic seriously from a philosophical point of view. In 1923 another encounter that proved decisive for Carnap's development took place, this time with the Hamburg philosopher Hans Reichenbach (1891–1953). Reichenbach had recently published *Relativity Theory and A Priori Knowledge* (1920), whose anti-Kantianism made it clear to Carnap that they were pursuing the same goal of replacing philosophical speculation with a scientific way of thinking that would be faithful to the rules of logic and the constraints of experience.

The *Aufbau* was composed during the years 1922–25 and published in 1928, two years after its author's arrival in Vienna and his first contacts with the Circle. Attracted by the neutral monism that Russell, following in the tradition of Mach and James, had argued for in *Our Knowledge of the External World*, Carnap meant to carry out a project that Russell envisaged only as a theoretical possibility, namely (in Quine's words) "the derivation of our scientific explanation of the physical world on the basis of sensory experience, by logical construction."[25] In other words, the philosophical premises of the project corresponded to those of Mach's sensationalism and Russell's phenomenalism; the formal tool used to attempt it was that of the *Principia*. To Carnap's credit, he had the audacity to try. To claim to be able to reconstruct on the basis of simple rules the set of all those objects in the world that could be treated as objects of science, for the purpose of unifying the structure of knowledge, he needed a great deal of daring indeed.

In the preface to the first edition of the *Aufbau*, Carnap enlisted his project in the battle on behalf of clarity, and therefore of the Enlightenment, against the "irrationalist" philosophies that had recently come back into fashion—an expression that took aim, on the one hand, at Heideggerian existentialism and, on the other, at the Bergsonian metaphysics of intuition. Irrationalism was doomed to lose the battle, in his view, since it represented the forces of the past. By contrast, Carnap noted, deep similarities existed between the scientific way of thinking he called for in philosophy and the modern attitude that sought to express itself at the same time in art and architecture (in the work of the Bauhaus, for instance, which had recently been founded by Gropius, in 1919) and politics (via movements that sought to promote "meaningful forms of personal and collective life, of education, and of external organization in general"—movements that Carnap did not name but that plainly were socialist in orientation). This orientation, he noted, "acknowledges the bonds that tie men together, but at the same time strives for free development of the individual. Our work is carried by the faith that this attitude will win the future."[26]

The book begins with an analysis of our knowledge of the simplest physical objects, which establishes that these objects can be reconstructed out of "basic elements" combined with each other according to rules defined by "basic relations." In keeping with Mach's doctrine, basic elements are the sensible qualities ("this red") that affect our subjectivity when we perceive an object; that is, global and instantaneous experiences, which Carnap calls elementary experiences (*Elementarerlebnisse*). The base of the pyramid of objects needing to be reconstructed, made up of one's own immediate sensations, is therefore self-psychological (*eigenpsychische*). The primary basic relation consisted in what he called a recollection of similarity (*Ähnlichkeitserinnerung*). This relation, which serves to organize structured connections among elementary experiences, was then supplemented by the whole of the formal language of modern logic.

Given this, the plan of the *Aufbau* ineluctably imposed itself. On the basis of elementary statements introducing the content of our sensory experiences, Carnap first reconstructed self-psychological objects (which constitute subjectivity) and then, at a second level, physical objects, resulting from the logical combination of sense data. Next came a third level of "heteropsychological" objects (other persons, which is to say the intersubjective world), and, finally, a fourth level of sociocultural objects (ethics, aesthetics, politics, and so on).

In the event, however, the higher levels of the pyramid were barely sketched. The most difficult part, as it turned out, was to construct the base, that is, the set of self-psychological objects. This is why Carnap devoted the better part of his efforts in the *Aufbau* to showing that qualities such as colors can be defined in a purely logical manner on the basis solely of the elements provided for at the outset. The many criticisms to which this attempt gave rise in the following years showed that he was not altogether successful. It must be said, too, that the possibility of erecting so heavy and complicated a scaffolding on a strictly sensual—not to say solipsistic—base seemed unlikely from the very start.

But this was not the main issue. The important thing, in 1928, was that Carnap's book gave the members of the Vienna Circle the feeling that an immense program of work had now been laid out before them, which would allow them to eliminate—by clarifying once and for all—the problems against which metaphysics ran up, particularly in connection with the nature of reality and the limits of our knowledge of the world. The enthusiasm that now seized hold of the logical positivists gave birth the following year to a collective statement that henceforth was referred to as the "Manifesto of the Vienna Circle."

ALSO KNOWN AS THE "Yellow Pamphlet," from the color of its cover, the manifesto was published anonymously. Only the preface was signed—by Hahn, Neurath, and Carnap. The pamphlet, they explained, was dedicated to Moritz Schlick (who was temporarily on leave, having gone to lecture in the United States for a term, at Stanford) to thank him for having decided to remain in Vienna rather than accept the chair that had been offered to him at Bonn. This pretext allowed the authors to present the outlines of their conception of the world—hence the title of the pamphlet, *Wissenschaftliche Weltauffassung: Der Wiener Kreiss* (The Scientific World View: The Vienna Circle). Their initiative was not without precedent. Earlier, in 1911, Mach had joined Einstein, Freud, and Hilbert in calling for the creation of a society for the diffusion of "positivist" philosophy. However, this first manifesto, which was to have no lasting consequence, went unmentioned by the authors of the Yellow Pamphlet, who were anxious instead to stress the novelty of their own program.

The 1929 manifesto begins with a statement that Lenin would not have disagreed with, namely, that there is a conflict between, on the one hand, metaphysics—associated by the authors with theology—and, on the other hand, the spirit of the Enlightenment, among whose recent defenders Russell, Whitehead, James, and the Marxists are briefly mentioned. Vienna is next described as a propitious place for a new scientific conception of the world to be devised, in view of the heritage of Bolzano (whose *Paradoxes of the Infinite*, edited by Hahn, had appeared in 1920), the influence exerted by Mach, and, last but not least, the elaboration of certain aspects of Marx's thought by the Austromarxists Adler and Bauer. The social sciences are therefore characterized at the outset as belonging to the continuum of natural sciences. As for the pamphlet's authors, they identify themselves as forming around Schlick (along with unnamed others) a group united by the desire to be done with metaphysics while wishing also to emphasize the connection between scientific questions and practical problems. "Endeavours toward a new organization of economic and social relations, toward the unification of mankind, toward a reform of school and education," they declare, "all show an inner link with the scientific world-conception."[27]

The second section opens with a call for a theoretical style similar to the aesthetics being elaborated just then by the members of the Bauhaus, Tatlin and the constructivists, and Mondrian and the neoplasticists. "Neatness and clarity are striven for, and dark distances and unfathomable depths rejected. In science there are no 'depths'; there is surface everywhere."[28] In rejecting "unsolvable riddles," partisans of a scientific conception of the world are committed to the clarification of concepts by means of logical analysis. Moreover, it is this recourse to logic that distinguishes the "recent empiricism and positivism" from "the earlier version," whose orientation was more biological and psychological.

Faced with someone who claims, for example, "There is a God," the logical positivist would not reply, "What you say is false," but "What do you mean by such a statement?" For the logical positivist there is a very clear distinction between two types of sentences: those of science that can be analyzed as reducing to statements about a particular empirical datum, and those of metaphysics, theology, and poetry that, describing no such datum, "merely express a certain mood and spirit"[29]—that is, a certain feeling about life. A further distinction can be made in this connection as well between poetry, the form best adapted to the expression of such feeling, and metaphysics, which, in the last analysis, has neither scientific value nor real poetic qualities.

How, then, is the historical success of metaphysics to be explained? Acknowledging the difficulty of the problem, the authors seek to illuminate it by reference to Freudian psychology and to the theory of the "ideological superstructure"—Marxism—as well as to purely logical approaches. The "aberrations" to which metaphysicians are liable, they argue, come from too narrow a dependence on the logical form of natural languages and a tendency to overestimate the capacities of pure thought. The Kantian theory of the synthetic a priori is denounced in passing, as well as the Bergsonian conception of intuition as the supreme form of knowledge. By contrast with these, the serious work of bringing out the unity of science by showing that its concepts can be reconstructed on the basis of our sensory experience alone—a program that plainly was none other than that of the *Aufbau*—remained to be done.

The third section lays out, and classifies according to their domain, the principal problems "stemming from various branches of science" on which the members of the Circle wished to take a position. With regard to the nature of mathematical propositions, for example, they pronounce themselves in favor of the thesis, defended by Wittgenstein, that such propositions are pure tautologies. In the fourth and final section, it is denied that the program just described in any way amounts to a disguised attempt to raise up philosophy again from its ashes. No matter what term may be used to refer to the investigations of the Circle, they are not intended to re-create a philosophy understood "as a basic or universal science alongside or above the various fields of the one empirical science."[30] Indeed, contrary to what Husserl maintained, the sciences are sufficient unto themselves. They have no need either of being founded or of being judged, but simply of being clarified—as they can be, from within, by the method of logical analysis. The scientific conception of the world leads therefore to a philosophy that is internal, as it were, to scientific practice itself and not to a "philosophy of science" that claims to "stand over or beyond" this practice.

In conclusion, the authors turn to the social and political dimensions of their purpose. As against the practitioners of metaphysics, who are often the defenders of an outdated social order as well, they present themselves as supporting an empiricism shared by "the masses" that goes hand-in-hand with the authors' "socialist attitudes."[31] The scientific view of the world thus finds expression in all areas of private and public life, which it aspires to organize in a rational fashion: "The scientific world-conception serves life, and life receives it."[32]

Widely distributed at a conference held in Prague in September 1929, the Yellow Pamphlet was thereafter seldom referred to within the Circle. There were two reasons for this: first, because it drew upon an interpretation of the Tractatus that Wittgenstein himself challenged; and second, because the theses it upheld were far from meeting with unanimous agreement among the members of the Circle itself. The pro-socialist orientation of the manifesto, although it expressed Carnap's and Neurath's political views, excited rather less enthusiasm among the others. Schlick, in particular, who read the pamphlet on his return from America, disapproved of what he regarded as its overly radical tone. From this point on tensions between him and Neurath were only to intensify. The Circle continued to be active, however, until 1936. In 1930 the group established its own journal, Erkenntnis, jointly edited by Carnap and Reichenbach, which made the work of a number of scientists and philosophers close to the Circle, among them Tarski and the logicians of the Warsaw School, more widely known. Most importantly, its second issue (1931–32) contained a provocative article, signed this time by Carnap alone, that might have passed for the Circle's second manifesto.

ENTITLED "The Overcoming [Überwindung] of Metaphysics through Logical Analysis of Language," this explicitly anti-Heideggerian text constituted a declaration of war against metaphysics in all its forms. To be sure, the inspiration from which it proceeded was not new. Bolzano, Brentano, Peirce, and

Mach (and before them Hobbes and Berkeley) had already denounced the use by metaphysicians of words that are devoid of meaning, incorrect, or otherwise misleading. Wittgenstein, also a reader of Mach, went still further in the Tractatus, characterizing as "nonsensical" (unsinnig) "most of the propositions and questions" bequeathed by philosophical tradition (4.003).

Within the Circle itself, Schlick had earlier published an article, "Experience, Cognition and Metaphysics" (1926), affirming that metaphysics, to the extent that it pretended to knowledge in a transcendent sense, was quite simply impossible since the very claim involved a contradiction in terms. "If the metaphysician," Schlick argued, "was striving only for experience, his demand could be fulfilled, through poetry and art and life itself. But in that he absolutely demands to experience the transcendent, he confuses living and knowing, and, bemused by a double contradiction, chases empty shadows." In the best case, when metaphysical texts evoke the transcendent they enrich life, but not knowledge. "They are to be valued," he concluded, "not as truths, but as works of art. The systems of the metaphysicians sometimes contain science and sometimes poetry, but they never contain metaphysics."[33]

The necessity of "overcoming" the quarrels of the metaphysicians had long preoccupied Carnap. In his youth he had been excited by the recent invention of Esperanto (in 1887), which in turn stimulated Peano's Latino sine flexione (1903) and Couturat's Ido (1907). After the upheaval of the First World War, however, the Leibnizian—and pacifist—dream of a universal language that would enable all people at last to use words in the same sense survived only in anarchist circles and countries advocating proletarian internationalism. Under the influence of Frege and Russell he now came to regard the language of science, unified by the rules of logic, as the most perfect realization of such a dream. The Aufbau, representing a first historic attempt to reconstruct the whole of human knowledge in what amounted to a scientific version of Esperanto, was therefore bound to condemn metaphysics, which, because it could not be reconstructed on a strictly empirical basis, could only be seen as falling into the realm of nonsense.

Carnap's position on this point was developed also in a short monograph, Pseudoproblems in Philosophy, that appeared in 1928, the same year as the Aufbau. Relying on the phenomenalism that he defended at the time, he tried to show that the quarrel between realism and idealism (both of which he dismissed as inadequate) rested on "pseudostatements," or statements that can be neither confirmed nor denied on the basis of empirical experience alone. This quarrel, he wrote, was itself a "pseudoproblem" (Scheinproblem)—the word Schein in this expression implicitly echoing Kant's critique of the transcendental "appearances" of reason.[34]

What, then, was new about the 1931 article? Mainly a way of formulating logical arguments by virtue of which metaphysical propositions, taken as a whole, were to be disqualified. Carnap begins by clarifying the use he makes of the term unsinnig. There are two types of propositions that are "devoid of meaning": those that manifestly contain grammatical errors—which, being easily recognized, are seldom dangerous—and, much more problematically, those that consist of grammatically correct arrangements of words that conceal logical defects.

These defects are in turn of two sorts, semantic and syntactical. Semantic defects arise through the introduction in a statement of a term that lacks empirical reference. A word, Carnap asserts, "is significant only if the statements in which it may occur are reducible to protocol statements,"[35] which is to say to those elementary statements that we use to express our sensory experiences and that are found at the base of the pyramid constructed in the Aufbau. In other words, the meaning of a word is entirely determined "by the relations of deducibility entered into by its elementary sentence-form, by its truth conditions, by the method of its verification."[36] Known since as the principle of verifiability, this thesis, anticipated by Peirce and Engels, was at least implicit in the Tractatus (4.024). Carnap proposed the following application of it: if a metaphysician introduces a new word—teavy, for example—and affirms that there are things that are teavy and others that are not, we must ask what is the empirical criterion for such an assertion. If no criterion can be discovered, the term must be refused. Many metaphysical terms, Carnap added, fall into the same category as teavy—words such as God, idea, I, absolute, non-being, thing-in-itself, and so on. The statements in which they occur have no meaning. They are pseudostatements.

Syntactic defects are more subtle. They are concealed in propositions whose words, taken one at a time, each have a sense but may be juxtaposed in a way that, although apparently correct grammatically, nonetheless violates logical syntax. An example of this type of solecism is the statement "Caesar is a prime number," which asserts a relation of identity between terms belonging to unrelated logical categories.[37] In an ideal language whose grammar conforms to the rules of logic, such expressions would be unconstructible. Unfortunately, the grammars of our natural languages are powerless to prevent their formulation. This is why they proliferate in the discourse of metaphysicians.

Carnap gave an example taken from the work of a thinker who was then in vogue in Germany—Heidegger. It is not difficult, as he showed by examining Heidegger's inaugural lecture at Freiburg three years earlier, "What Is Metaphysics?" to single out doubtful uses of the term nothing and its variants for criticism. Even supposing that this word implies a negative existence proposition and so has a logical meaning, Carnap argued, it is nonetheless not permissible to make it the name of an object as Heideggerian queries and statements typically do ("How is it with Nothingness?" for example, or "Anxiety reveals the Nothing"). Still less acceptable is a pseudostatement of the type "The Nothing itself nothings." In response, finally, to Heidegger's insistence that the "primordial" question of Nothingness could be posed in its full scope only if standard logic were abandoned, Carnap observed that Heidegger had at least the honesty to turn his back openly on all scientific ways of thinking.

Such honesty may incline some to give Heidegger the benefit of the doubt. What if, after all, he were actually to have succeeded in inventing a truly new way of thinking? Carnap did not seriously believe for a moment that such a thing was possible. Nor did he bother to attack metaphysicians who were more rigorous than Heidegger; for him, Heideggerian philosophical language was typical of the whole of classical metaphysics. To accuse an entire philosophical tradition of meaninglessness, as Carnap did, invited the charge of unwarranted generalization. But Carnap brushed all objection aside, advancing two arguments. On the one hand, metaphysics must inevitably be devoid of meaning since it is expressed in natural languages whose grammatical structures are by definition logically imperfect. On the other hand, metaphysicians are collectively "guilty" of deliberately pursuing an inconsistent objective, of discovering and formulating "a kind of knowledge which is not accessible to empirical science."[38]

In the wake of this unqualified condemnation, two questions remained. The first concerned the future of philosophy. What was to become of it once the need to overcome (überwinden) metaphysics had been grasped? This, curiously, was the same question that Heidegger had posed in his 1928 lecture. He too, in his own way, called for metaphysics to be overcome, urging philosophy to embrace a more "truthful" thought, the "thought of Being." But the manner in which he understood this overcoming (Überwindung) consisted in reviving a quite ancient philosophical question—in preserving, at least in part, what was to be overcome. Carnap's position was entirely different. For him, overcoming meant rejecting—eliminating, purely and simply. Metaphysics had no future. It was *finished*, in every sense of the term. As for what was proposed in its place, namely, the method of logical analysis as practiced by Carnap and others, this did not amount to a new philosophical theory. It was a scientific method. For lack of a better name, it might be called logical syntax of the language of science. What Carnap wished to emphasize, in any case, is that there was not the least difference in kind between this method and science.

There remained a second question as well: if metaphysics was only a corpus of false problems, how could so many distinguished thinkers have gone astray? Carnap's response—like that of Schlick in 1926—was to throw metaphysics back on the side of art, for which it provided a cheap substitute (*Ersatz*). Its role, similar to that of art, was to give expression to a general attitude toward life (*Lebenseinstellung* or *Lebensgefühl*). Unfortunately, its success in doing this could in most cases only be considered "inadequate," at least if its results were compared to the masterpieces of music and poetry. Carnap's conclusion was merciless: metaphysicians are, at bottom, only "musicians without musical ability."[39]

This devastating text enjoyed an immediate success throughout Europe. In 1932 the Soviet journal *Under the Banner of Marxism* published a critical review of it, judging Carnap's approach too "formalistic." In 1934 the article was translated into French. In the years that followed Heidegger attempted to refute its arguments. His notes (composed between 1936 and 1946 under the title "Overcoming Metaphysics"[40]), though they made no mention of Carnap, attacked the dual positivistic reduction of philosophy to the theory of knowledge and of the theory of knowledge to logical empiricism, concluding that even if metaphysics—and, indeed, philosophy—was finished, this did not at all imply "the end of thought."

One may imagine Wittgenstein's reaction. Since returning to Cambridge in 1929 he had continued to distance himself from the views of the Vienna Circle. His meetings with Schlick and Waismann between December 1929 and July 1932 showed that he had never unreservedly subscribed to the principle of verifiability, attributed to him by the neopositivists, and that he had ceased to believe in the possibility of making philosophical problems disappear by clarifying their logical form. Owing, finally, to his hostility to Carnap's brand of "scientism," he had hardly any contact with the members of the group after 1932. Moreover, the neopositivists themselves were far from being unanimously in agreement with Carnap, as the rise of new internal debates within the Circle in the first half of the 1930s was to reveal.

AT THE CENTER of these debates was the *Aufbau*, which found itself caught in a crossfire. Its phenomenalist base, derived from the sensationalism of Mach and Schlick, was criticized as unsound by Neurath, who proposed substituting for it a physicalist base. But this substitution supposed, for its part, a conventionalism disapproved by Schlick.

Neurath launched his offensive in the pages of *Erkenntnis* in 1931–32 with an article entitled "Sociology in Physicalism" that attacked the idea that one could readily distinguish protocol statements from other scientific statements. Statements can be compared only with other statements, Neurath declared, never with reality itself. Arguing that scientific theories rest not on subjective experiences but on a determinate set of linguistic conventions, he proposed (here relying on an argument made earlier by Duhem) that the sensationalist base of the *Aufbau* could profitably be replaced by physicalist conventions more in keeping with the familiar notion that actual objects, existing independently of our perception, constitute the basis of empirical science.

Admitting in part the validity of these criticisms, Carnap responded in 1932 with two articles, "Physical Language as Universal Language of Science" (revised and translated into English two years later as *The Unity of Science*) and "Psychology in Physical Language." Although he now abandoned the attempt to deduce protocol statements from primitive sensory experience, he held nonetheless that the former could be put into relation to the latter by means of a confirmation procedure more liberal than the principle of verifiability described in the *Aufbau*. This was not enough for Neurath. He replied immediately with an article entitled "Protocol Statements," characterizing such statements as "metaphysical fictions" and denouncing the solipsistic temptation that, on his view, lurked behind the belief in their possibility.

Whether or not he was entirely convinced, Carnap ended up accepting—in a final article, "On Protocol Statements"—that while such statements serve as a convenient reminder that science depends ultimately on data obtained from observation, one could nonetheless replace them, without doing serious harm, by statements of another sort. He thus agreed to exchange phenomenalism for physicalism, substituting for Mach's doctrine of sensationalism a Duhemian conventionalism. In short, Carnap now abandoned a theory of truth according to which truth is determined by the correspondence of statements with reality in favor of one that made it reside instead in the internal coherence of statements with each other.

Schlick regarded such a shift in the direction of what he considered to be a form of relativism with misgiving. Was one obliged to accept any fable whatsoever so long as its internal coherence could be demonstrated? Carnap was not ready to admit as much, but neither was he prepared to turn back, as the last of his books published in Vienna, The Logical Syntax of Language (1934), attests. This exceptionally complex work attempted to carry out the positive part of the program sketched in "The Overcoming of Metaphysics by the Logical Analysis of Language." Metaphysics having been eliminated, and the very word philosophy having been gotten rid of (as Neurath wished), it remained to reconstruct the "logic of science"—the syntax of scientific language—that was to replace metaphysics. Because syntactic propositions, no less than logical propositions, needed to be rigorously analyzed, the syntax had to be elaborated in terms of the language of science itself. This, at any rate, is the task Carnap sets for himself at the beginning of the book.[41]

Later on, however, serious problems were encountered. To try to resolve them, Carnap drew upon the metamathematics devised by Hilbert to demonstrate the noncontradictory character of mathematics, the metalogic worked out for the same purpose in logic by Tarski, and Gödel's results on the arithmetization of syntax—a strategy that, from the outset, was implicitly to lead him further and further away from the logicism defended by his teacher Frege. On finally reaching the end of a road strewn with obstacles, Carnap found himself forced to recognize that the ideal of syntactic analyticity was inevitably subject to certain limitations. Indeed, for any language S, the syntax of S can be formulated in S only if the vocabulary of S is sufficiently rich to permit its formulation. As it turns out, the formalization Carnap sought "requires an infinite series of ever richer languages."[42]

Without being catastrophic for logic itself, this result helped to show—as Gödel's theorems had three years earlier—that the initial ambitions of the logicist program were in part unrealizable. This had two effects. On the one hand it led Carnap, in "Testability and Meaning" (1936–37), to liberalize—and in the end to abandon—the more radical aspects of neopositivist doctrine; on the other hand it led him, in Introduction to Semantics (1942) and Meaning and Necessity (1947), to complete the syntax of scientific language by a semantics that was increasingly elaborate and, by virtue of this, also increasingly less faithful to the Fregean ideal of logical extensionality. His American disciples, beginning with Quine, observed these developments with very great concern.

IN THE MEANTIME, Carnap found himself under attack again—this time by a young, practically unknown secondary school teacher of mathematics and physics named Karl Popper (1902–94).

Popper was not a member of the Circle. He was nonetheless Viennese by birth and as a student at the University of Vienna had attended Hahn's lectures on mathematics. He met Neurath at a socialist meeting and was on friendly terms with Carnap and other members of the Circle, whose writings he read assiduously. While he shared their fascination with the logic of science, neither Carnap's arguments nor those of Wittgenstein managed to convince him. Moreover, as an avowed Kantian who defended a thoroughgoing realism, more concerned with objects than with words, he rejected both Neurath's conventionalism and Mach's sensationalism, in which he saw only two different forms of a single fundamental solipsism.

If metaphysics, to his way of thinking, was obviously not a science, it did not seem to him for all that to be devoid of meaning. Rather than challenge it altogether, he thought a better course was to try to dismantle it piece by piece. Nor did he subscribe to the principle of verifiability, which seemed to him doubly absurd: first, because there are certain disciplines—such as quantum mechanics, which deals by definition with the infinitely small—to which it cannot be applied; second, because this principle rests on the idea that scientific theories are constructed on the basis of the repeated accumulation of identical observations—in other words, on an inductivist conception of discovery that had already been broadly criticized by Kant.

Unlike the neopositivists, Popper did not believe that a universal law—at least one that assumes the world is infinite in both space and time—could ever be authenticated by a series of observations: no matter how large this might be, it would always remain finite. To Popper's mind this was enough to prove that the validity of a law is not an inductive process but, more simply, arises from the fact that in spite of systematic attempts not a single counterexample has been able to be adduced against it. Experience does indeed have a role to play, but this role consists in eliminating bad hypotheses by "falsifying" them rather than by "confirming" good ones. Popper therefore proposed replacing the principle of verifiability by a principle of falsifiability that, among other things, would make it possible to reconcile the neopositivist conception of science with what he, for his part, continued to call "objective" reality.

These arguments were expounded in his first book, The Logic of Scientific Discovery, which appeared in Vienna at the end of 1934 in a series edited, ironically enough, by Schlick and Frank. The following year, in the pages of Erkenntnis, Neurath attacked the book while Carnap defended it. Carnap may at that point have had hopes of making an ally of Popper; if so, they were swiftly disappointed.

Popper was firmly resolved to preserve his independence in the matter. On the one hand, he had no intention of treating Carnap's principle of confirmability with greater indulgence than the principle of verifiability, both resting on the same (in his view, erroneous) belief in the powers of induction—a belief that Carnap, for his part, was never to renounce, as his later works on the logic of probability show. On the other hand, Popper dismissed as utopian both the ambition of The Logical Syntax of Language to incorporate the syntax of science within science itself and, more generally, any attempt to reconstruct within an artificial language the whole of unified science: first, because Gödel's theorems seemed to him to establish that such a language, if one existed, would not even be adequate to answer the needs of elementary arithmetic; second, because he regarded Tarski's work on semantics (which he first discovered in German translation in 1936) as definitively demonstrating the impossibility of translating, for any given language, the whole of the metalanguage expressing the logic of this language. Popper even went so far—here somewhat forcing the conclusions reached in Tarski's 1931 article "The Concept of Truth in Formalized Languages"— to congratulate him for having rehabilitated the classical definition of truth as a "correspondence" between our statements and reality.

In an essay written in 1955 (but not published until 1964), entitled "The Demarcation between Science and Metaphysics,"[43] Popper summed up his irreconcilable differences with Carnap. Then, twenty years later, in his autobiography Unended Quest (1974), he made himself out to be the real "murderer"[44] of logical positivism—whose principal weaknesses, he felt, his book of 1934 had already succeeded in rigorously exposing. No doubt this retrospective view contained an element of exaggeration. But the fact remains that by the middle of the 1930s neopositivism had indeed entered into a difficult phase. The troubles it faced were not related solely to disagreements among the members of the Circle or to Popper's criticisms; they were also a product of the harshness of the time.

FROM THE END of the 1920s, the extreme Right continued to gain ground in Austria. The members of the Vienna Circle—left-wing atheists, some of them Jewish—now became the special target of increasingly violent attacks.

In 1931 Herbert Feigl decided to settle in the United States. The same year Carnap and Frank, without breaking with the Circle, moved to Prague. In 1932 the Austrian elections revealed a surge in Nazi support. At the end of January 1933, Hitler came to power in Germany. Several weeks later the Austrian chancellor, Dollfuss, dissolved the parliament and installed a fascist-style regime. The Communist Party was outlawed. In 1934, the year of Hahn's death, a warrant was issued for Neurath's arrest. As it happened, he was away on a trip to Moscow and instead of returning to Austria made his way to the Netherlands, and from there to England.

Then, in 1936, tragedy struck. On 22 June Moritz Schlick was assassinated, shot on the steps of the University of Vienna by a deranged student. The reactionary press in the capital seized upon the event to emphasize that the philosopher's ideas could not have led to any other outcome. The atmosphere in Austria by this time had become intolerable for anyone who wished to think freely. Throughout Europe the danger of another war was now widely felt.

The great exodus began the same year. Carnap left Prague in 1936, like Feigl going to the United States, where he finished out his career. He was soon rejoined there by Reichenbach, Hempel, Gödel, Tarski, Bergmann, and Frank. At the beginning of 1937, Popper—whose parents were Jewish converts to Protestantism—likewise chose exile. He passed the whole of the war in New Zealand before settling permanently in England, where, thanks to his friend Friedrich von Hayek, the economist, he was able to obtain a post at the London School of Economics. Some months after Popper's departure, finally, Friedrich Waismann left to take up residence in Oxford. When Hitler invaded Austria, in March 1938, none of the members of the Vienna Circle was left in Vienna.

But if the Circle as such was dead—the victim of its own internal contradictions as well as of the blows of history—the spirit of logical positivism lived on. Following the war it spread throughout the English-speaking world, where it has exercised a lasting influence until the present day.

After the End

Between the two wars, then, four philosophical movements—associated with the names of Rosenzweig, Heidegger, Lenin, and Carnap—proposed the overcoming of metaphysics as their primary objective. None of them, it is clear, fully succeeded in carrying out its program. Rosenzweig's philosophy ended up putting its trust in religious faith. Heidegger's sank after 1933 to the level of endorsing National Socialist ideology. Lenin's became immobilized for fifty years in Stalinist dogma. Startling as these outcomes may seem, unquestionably the most surprising destiny of the four turned out to be that of logical positivism.

Contrary to its ambitions, logical positivism did not succeed in putting an end to metaphysics or even to the idea of philosophy as something separate from science. It was to have the opposite and unforeseen effect of reanimating the Kantian (and Russellian) project of a scientific philosophy, convinced of its continuing advance along the sure path of science while yet nonetheless remaining a distinct field. This was particularly true in Great Britain and the United States, where increasingly from the end of the 1930s philosophy came to be conceived as but one of a number of scientific disciplines, reserved for technical specialists and promising slow, but ineluctable, progress.

The renaissance of an autonomous and self-confident form of philosophical activity, although at variance with the ideas of the Vienna Circle and even with those of the later Wittgenstein, nonetheless was not the result of chance. It is explained by the fact that the new positivist doctrine, issuing from a tradition that went back to Frege, found in both England and the United States ground that was favorable to its flowering; and that the local traditions upon which neopositivism was able to graft itself, by giving it renewed vitality, allowed it to blossom in a flurry of new researches. The habit that has taken root since of referring to these researches by the general name of analytic philosophy risks, however, giving the mistaken impression that their inspiration was in all cases the same. For although philosophy in the English-speaking world during the past fifty years does indeed proceed from the "linguistic turn" of the beginning of the century, and although English-speaking philosophers share the belief that the chief problems with which they are concerned may be illuminated by the analysis of the words used to express them, they frequently diverge with regard to the choice of a suitable language into which these problems are to be retranslated in order, finally, to be solved. One might even argue—once again simplifying somewhat—that from the 1940s to the 1970s the dominant school in England placed its trust in a return to "ordinary" language, rather in the spirit of the later Wittgenstein, while the majority of American philosophers, situating themselves more in the line of the *Tractatus* and Carnap, continued in various ways to insist upon the requirement of an "ideal" language, which for them coincided with that of science.

IN GREAT BRITAIN the ground favorable to the positivist graft had been prepared around 1900 by Moore and Russell. Moore wished to make philosophy submit to the constraints of common sense, a thesis to which he gave deliberately provocative expression in an article of 1925 appropriately entitled, "A Defence of Common Sense."[45] Russell discouraged philosophers from exceeding the limits of what he regarded as their proper domain, that of reflection upon the sciences. Moreover, Wittgenstein's return to Cambridge in 1929, and the classes he gave there over the next twenty years, familiarized his friends and students with the idea that a good many philosophical puzzles arise simply from transgressions against the rules of ordinary grammar.

In the 1930s, then, an analytic current existed in British philosophy. But it was at Oxford, rather than at Cambridge, that this current enjoyed its first breakthrough thanks to the decisive influence of Gilbert Ryle (1900–1976). In his youth, Ryle showed an interest in German philosophy, particularly in Husserl's *Logical Investigations*, which he criticized for having neglected the question of logico-mathematical paradoxes, and Heidegger's *Being and Time*, to which he gave a frankly critical review in 1929. In the following years he got to know Wittgenstein and published an article, "Systematically Misleading Expressions" (1932), that showed him still influenced by the search for a logically ideal language, an ambition inherited from Russell and the *Tractatus* that shortly thereafter he gave up.

The same year, in 1932, Ryle suggested to one of his students, A. J. (Alfred Jules) Ayer (1910–89), that he go to Vienna in order to become acquainted with neopositivist doctrine. Some months later Ayer returned full of enthusiasm for the new teaching, to which he devoted the first book to appear on the subject in English, *Language, Truth, and Logic* (1936). Ryle reacted strongly against the radically antimetaphysical theses advanced in this work and thereafter worked to block Ayer's appointment to Oxford, which was to occur only in 1959. Ayer himself was henceforth—very much like Carnap—to modify his initial positions, but he nonetheless remained until his death the official representative of British neopositivism. His *Philosophy in the 20th Century*, which appeared in 1982 when his reputation was at its height, well testifies to the constancy of his commitments. Most of this work is given over to discussions of Russell, Moore, Wittgenstein, and Carnap as well as of various American philosophers and the Oxford don R. G. (Robin George) Collingwood (1889–1943), whose historicism was close to that of Croce, while Heidegger, Sartre, and Merleau-Ponty are rapidly disposed of as representatives of a nonscientific movement, namely phenomenology—Marxism, hermeneutics, and structuralism being conspicuous by their absence.

For his part, Ryle, who in 1947 succeeded Moore as editor of *Mind*, did not remain inactive. While he rejected the new form of positivism, he did not refrain from putting metaphysical discourse to the test of analysis, as both his 1938 article on logical categories and his most important book, *The Concept of Mind* (1949), attest. The latter attempted to refute the Cartesian distinction between body and mind, characterized as a "myth" engendered by the persistent error of treating mental phenomena as an autonomous conceptual category. For Ryle, the mind is not "in" the body, as though it were a sort of ghost in a machine. It stands in the same relation to the body as Oxford University does to the set of buildings of which it is composed: there is no difference between the two, in fact, except so far as it is a question of a point of view—in other words, of language.

Rejecting dualism, Ryle was equally opposed to materialism, which he judged reductive. As against these conceptions, he defended a view of human behavior that was at once behaviorist and nominalist. Human behavior he thought had to be considered as a whole and explained from the outside in the most objective and economical manner possible. The application of this principle entails that the intellect cannot be separated from the actions in which it manifests itself; that the will is not distinct from volitions, or individual acts of will; and that, finally, feelings can be described as global "events" of personality.

This work—which aroused lively opposition in the French phenomenological camp, still attached to its Cartesian heritage—was not without affinities with the investigations of the later Wittgenstein, in particular with the writings that had been circulating in manuscript form since the end of the 1930s. Indirectly, then, a problem arises to which Ryle's subsequent works— given that he refused to consider himself a disciple of Wittgenstein—do not really give an answer: how can the Wittgensteinian injunction to place our trust in the categories of natural language be reconciled with the fact that natural language teems with expressions that themselves oblige us to assume the duality of mind and body? Notwithstanding this difficulty, reference to everyday grammar was soon to become absolutely de rigueur among Ryle's younger colleagues. One group—in whose meetings Ryle did not participate—came to be known independently at the beginning of the 1950s as the Oxford School. Its most eminent members, the originators of so-called ordinary language philosophy, were J. L. (John Langshaw) Austin (1911–60) and P. F. (Peter Frederick) Strawson (b. 1919).

Austin, the founder of the group, was led by his study of philology to take an interest in questions of linguistic precision. He set himself the task, at the beginning of the Second World War, of promoting clarity and rigor in the use of words. Distancing himself as much from Ryle as from the later Wittgenstein—of whom he is often reminiscent, although he hardly ever cites Wittgenstein, and then never without a hint of irony—he was wary both of the scientistic jargon of the neopositivists and the obscurities of classical metaphysics. And although he was the first English translator of Frege's *Foundations of Arithmetic*, he utterly rejected the longing for an ideal, artificially reconstructed language. Every conceivable nuance of human thought having been inscribed in ordinary language over the course of centuries, how could any scholar, working in isolation, in a matter of a few weeks, even years, create a better one?

The philosopher must therefore, according to Austin, seek the solution to the questions that he poses—not all of which, by the way, are illegitimate—through a meticulous analysis of the meaning of sentences. For this he has no need to burden himself with historical learning, still less to resort to the pointless subtleties of logico-mathematical analysis. It suffices that he rely on a good dictionary, the depository of all possible knowledge relating to the correct use of language, and that he verify, by checking with other speakers, that this use indeed corresponds to the actual practice of his own linguistic community.

Austin's teaching was essentially oral; skeptical of all existing theories, he published only a few articles during his lifetime. These were collected after his premature death, together with his principal lectures, in three books that left a lasting mark on the landscape of English philosophy: *Philosophical Papers* (1961), *Sense and Sensibilia* (1962), and *How to Do Things with Words* (1962).

This last work, based on lectures delivered at Harvard in 1955, had as its point of departure the observation—aimed against neopositivist theories of language—that the function of speech is less to describe states of affairs ("constative" statements) than to carry out an action by means of them: this is the case, in particular, with sentences expressing requests, promises, permission, and so forth ("performative" statements). Neither true nor false, these sentences may or may not elicit a response depending on the manner in which they are interpreted by the person who utters them and by the person to whom they are directed. On the basis of this insight Austin went on to develop an original theory of utterances that divided "speech acts" into three categories: "locutionary," "illocutionary," and "perlocutionary." *How to Do Things with Words* thus opened up, alongside phonology, syntax, and semantics, a new field for linguistics known as pragmatics (a term coined in 1938 by the American philosopher Charles Morris), the object of which was no longer language considered as a closed system but as the set of uses to which it could be put in this or that particular context. Since then it has undergone considerable development, due in part to the work of one of Austin's American followers, John R. Searle (b. 1932)—who tried to show in *Speech Acts* (1969) that these uses are governed by implicit but precise rules—as well as by that of a number of semioticians. We will later find traces of its influence on Paul Ricoeur, Karl-Otto Apel, and Jürgen Habermas.

At least one English philosopher, Bertrand Russell, from the beginning openly rejected this style of research, which seemed to him too narrowly focused on linguistic analysis. Russell (whose attacks in this connection were supported by Popper) judged the views of Austin and his students to be as uninteresting as the theses of the later Wittgenstein, with which he rather briskly identified them. Popper, for his part, went further, seeing their concentration on "*minutiae* (upon 'puzzles') and especially upon the meaning of words" as evidence of a new "scholasticism."[46] Nonetheless, ordinary language philosophy was not the enemy of philosophy altogether, as Strawson's work showed.

More of a theoretician than Austin, and in this sense nearer to Ryle—whose chair at Oxford he took over in 1968, teaching there until 1987—Strawson first became known for an article, "On Referring" (1950),[47] devoted to a critical reexamination of Russell's analysis of denoting expressions. But his main service was to give Austin's largely empirical technique the methodological justifications that it lacked. These were subsequently developed in *Individuals* (1959), a book that described itself, not unprovocatively, as an "Essay in Descriptive Metaphysics."

The reappearance here of the term *metaphysics* well illustrates the oblivion into which the theses of the Vienna Circle had fallen in the meantime. It was not a matter simply of going back to Kant—even if, in quite Kantian fashion, Strawson declared that he was interested not only in ordinary language but also in the conditions of its possibility, which is to say in the conceptual schemes underlying our ways of speaking of the world. In fact, the book's conclusion takes a rather behaviorist line, arguing that only material bodies and physical persons really exist. A quarter-century later, another of his essays, "Analysis and Metaphysics" (1985), confirmed that the Austinian method of linguistic clarification of concepts, though it remained for him an irreplaceable instrument of analysis, could also be put to the service of an ontological project that did not shrink from renewing ties with the central tradition of classical philosophy.

Faithful to the heritage of Moore, the philosophy of ordinary language was also interested in the study of the ethical questions raised by daily life. In 1952 a book by Richard M. Hare (b. 1919), The Language of Morals, paved the way for research into the logic of moral choices, later given a further boost with the publication of Strawson's Freedom and Resentment (1974) and, from a different perspective, the studies of Bernard Williams (b. 1929) in such works as Moral Luck (1981) and Ethics and the Limits of Philosophy (1985). Another Oxford philosopher, Michael Dummett (b. 1925), convinced that the analytic method could be profitably applied to political and social problems, became personally involved in the struggle against racism as one of the founders of the Joint Council for the Welfare of Immigrants, writing also on voting procedures in addition to his work on Frege's philosophy of language.

Such concerns suggest that in due course a dialogue might have developed with Sartre or Foucault. One of the outstanding characteristics of British philosophy for a half-century, however, has been its relative indifference to the rest of European thought and, especially, to French philosophy—no representative of which, or almost none, has met with its approval. Reinforced by a corresponding lack of interest on the part of French philosophers in the work of their counterparts in Great Britain, this attitude, owing to intransigence on both sides, has ended up creating a philosophical gulf between the two countries as well—consider the dialogue of the deaf that took place at the memorable 1958 meeting at Royaumont between analytic and phenomenological philosophers, or, more recently, the uproar at Cambridge caused by the offer of a doctorate honoris causa to Jacques Derrida in 1992.

The existence of such a gulf is not merely regrettable but paradoxical, all the more so since, as Dummett has rightly emphasized,[48] Frege is not only the common ancestor of English-language analytic philosophy and continental neopositivism; he is also, on account of the influence his thinking exerted upon Husserl in the *Logical Investigations*, one of the principal sources of inspiration for phenomenology, whose followers remain numerous in France and the other Latin countries. Clearly still more time is needed before the chief tendencies of contemporary philosophy can be put in historical perspective in a way that will be generally accepted on both sides of the Channel.

IN THE UNITED STATES, the diffusion of logical positivism—known there instead as logical empiricism, on the suggestion of Carnap himself in "Testability and Meaning," his first paper to be published originally in English—was facilitated by the largely pragmatist orientation of American philosophy since the beginning of the century.

The pragmatist tradition founded by James (who died in 1910) and Peirce (who died in 1914) remained until the Second World War the dominant movement in universities across the Atlantic. It inspired in differing degrees both the "new realism" propounded in a volume of essays appearing under that title in 1912 by a group of young philosophers that included Ralph Barton Perry (1876–1957) and William Pepperell Montague (1873–1953) and the "critical realism" developed in response to it and laid out in another collection of essays in 1920 by Arthur O. Lovejoy (1873–1962), George Santayana (1863–1952), and others. It also influenced—more than one might suppose—the "communitarian" ideal of the philosopher and logician Josiah Royce (1855–1916), a friend of James and Peirce and the champion of an absolute and profoundly religious idealism. But pragmatism flourished most completely in the work of John Dewey (1859–1952), the most important American philosopher of the first half-century, and that of C. I. (Clarence Irving) Lewis (1883–1964), who, having been Royce's student and assistant at Harvard, later became one of Quine's teachers.

Dewey, who considered knowledge as an instrument by which human beings are able both to adapt themselves to the world and transform it, preferred to call his own doctrine "instrumentalism." At the University of Chicago—where he worked from 1894 to 1904, leaving to join the faculty of Columbia, where he taught from 1905 until his retirement in 1930—he founded an experimental school that allowed him to elaborate a new pedagogy as well as to undertake original research of a logical and psychological character into the nature of intelligence. Although this research was from the very beginning centered upon the relationship between thought and experience, it was by no means cut off from the great currents of European idealism. Influenced in his youth by his reading of Kant and Hegel, Dewey shared Hegel's aspiration to a totalizing vision of reality. Traces of this speculative ambition can still be found in Art as Experience (1934) and above all in his last great work, Logic: The Theory of Inquiry (1938), an imposing epistemological summa that attempted to formulate the most general rules of scientific discovery.

At the same time, his indefatigable dynamism as well as the intensity of his convictions made Dewey the perfect embodiment of a typically American conception of philosophy, steeped in humanism and optimism. Nothing better sums up this conception than the celebrated formula by which, in Democracy and Education (1916), he affirmed the duty of philosophy to become the "generalized theory of education,"[49] emphasizing that its development was itself intrinsically tied to the progress of democracy. Like the neopositivists—from whom, however, he dissociated himself on a number of points—Dewey insisted that the social sciences could not be separated from the natural sciences. Nor was he content merely to extend to the former his thinking about the methodology of the so-called exact sciences. His work as a whole, based on the belief that society in general is the "laboratory" in which all thought occurs, amounted to an attempt to show that the principle of respect for experience was absolutely inseparable from a concern for individual liberty and collective solidarity, particularly with regard to the most disadvantaged members of society. Seen in this way, it constituted the first original attempt to construct a pragmatist politics, closely related to an experimental and utilitarian conception of knowledge that was itself derived from Peirce and James.

Finally, Dewey insisted on putting his most deeply held convictions into practice as fully as possible. Over the course of a long life he did not hesitate to commit himself to any number of partisan causes—like Russell in one sense but, unlike Russell, all the while maintaining a profound coherence between these positions and the rest of his philosophy. He was attracted to regions of the world where new forms of social organization were being invented, traveling during the 1920s to Turkey, Mexico, and the Soviet Union—countries whose educational initiatives he studied with interest without, however, unlike his disciple and friend Sidney Hook (1902–89), subscribing even temporarily to Marxist theories.[50] In 1937, it is worth noting, he presided over a commission of inquiry in Mexico charged with examining the validity of the accusations brought against Trotsky during the Moscow trials (the verdict delivered by the commission was not guilty).

Dewey's work, as vast and varied as that of Russell, thus appears in retrospect to have been the victim to some degree of its own range and versatility—one of the reasons why, although it has lost none of its topicality, it suffers today from a relative and unjust neglect.[51] Lewis's work, by contrast, gives a greater impression of unity, being concerned mainly with elaborating a pragmatist conception of formal logic that was influenced by both Peirce and Russell. In 1910, on Royce's advice, Lewis read the first volume of *Principia Mathematica* and eight years later published the first history of formal logic, devoting himself in the meantime to the analysis of the problems associated with implication. His entire career was spent at Harvard, where he was joined by Whitehead in 1924. Whitehead finished out his own career there following the publication of his most important work, *Process and Reality* (1929), a monumental treatment of cosmology based on the apprehension of reality as a process of becoming. Together they made Harvard the first institution where the study of philosophy was chiefly concerned with logic and the theory of science—a model that was gradually to be imitated after the war by the majority of American universities.

It was under Lewis and Whitehead, moreover, that the young W. V. (Willard Van Orman) Quine (b. 1908) pursued his graduate studies, subsequently joining the faculty at Harvard himself. Attracted at an early age to a precise and rigorous view of the world, Quine read *Principia Mathematica* when he was twenty and devoted his first published article in 1930 to the work of the French mathematician Jean Nicod. Then, at the urging of Herbert Feigl, he took advantage of a travel grant awarded him in the fall of 1932 to go—like Ayer and at the same time—to Central Europe. In Vienna he attended Schlick's lectures and in January 1933 he read a paper to the members of the Circle. In March of that year he traveled to Prague to meet Carnap—whose friend and disciple he later became—and thence to Warsaw to make the acquaintance of Łukasiewicz, Leśniewski, and Tarski. Upon returning at the end of this tour to the United States, he considered himself a supporter of logical positivism. He remained one his whole life, in a sense, even if after 1939 he no longer felt himself wholly in agreement with the development of Carnap's thinking, marked by a growing interest in semantics and the logic of probability that gradually led Carnap away from the initial program of the *Aufbau*. Quine himself admitted that the program needed to be relaxed, but it was only in a lastingly influential article published in 1951, "Two Dogmas of Empiricism,"[52] that he proposed a new formulation of it.

Carnap's philosophy, Quine held, relied on two dogmas that had to be abandoned if empiricism were to be saved and, ultimately, made invulnerable to criticism. The first consisted in asserting the existence of a fundamental cleavage between language and facts, between analytic truths and synthetic truths. For Quine, purely analytic truths do not exist: all truth depends on both language and facts. Even logic and mathematics are, in the last analysis, sciences of empirical origin. Certain experimental discoveries may, moreover, force us to revise logical laws long held to be obvious: thus quantum mechanics, for example, had demonstrated the fragility of the law of excluded middle, challenged earlier by Brouwer. In general terms, knowledge is nothing other than a psycho-physiological process having its seat in an empirical structure, the human brain, that attempts to construct theories on the basis of the sensible information it receives from the outside world that permit it to account for reality—in other words, to act upon itself. This is why Quine proposed to naturalize epistemology; that is, to consider it as a branch of psychology and therefore of the natural sciences generally. It may be wondered, however, whether mind can be reduced to brain without eliminating a property possessed by mental states, intentionality—in other words, the property of being *about* something—that no purely physical state of matter possesses.[53]

The second dogma to be rejected, no less prejudicial to a radical empiricism, was reductionism. It is illusory to hope, as Carnap did in the *Aufbau*, that every scientific statement can be reduced to an immediate experience that verifies it. Considered separately and individually, our statements are not verifiable: only science in its totality can be confronted with the totality of our experience, which it attempts to reconstruct in a language that is itself determined by our mental structures. Known as holism (from the Greek *holos*, meaning "whole"), Quine's doctrine explicitly drew upon the work of Duhem and Émile Meyerson. It went further, however, since it applied not only to physics (as Duhem had intended) but to all of the sciences, the logical and mathematical sciences included.

This doctrine had two important consequences. The first is the thesis that theories are underdetermined by experience. Because several different theories may offer equally satisfactory accounts of the same experimental facts, it is illegitimate to suppose that scientific progress will infallibly draw us ever nearer to a unique and definitive truth. The second is the principle of the indeterminacy of translation. No statement of our language, scientific or not, possesses a fixed and immutable translation into another language. Translation is, of course, possible, but only from one language into another considered in its totality; moreover, it can be carried out only in relation to a corpus of translation rules chosen by the translator that is always subject to revision. It follows from this that meaning "in itself" does not exist, meaning being itself only a function of the entire set of rules adopted to apprehend it.

Quine's holism plainly exhibited aspects both of the conventionalism denounced by Schlick and of certain forms of psychologism rejected by Frege and Russell. It amounted, in effect, to reorienting logical empiricism in a pragmatist direction. A similar reorientation was being proposed at the same time by another American philosopher, Wilfred Sellars (1912–89), whose important essay "Empiricism and the Philosophy of Mind" (1956) likewise undertook to criticize the "myth of the given," which is to say the traditional sense-data empiricism defended by Russell, Carnap, and Ayer. One might argue further that this reorientation corresponded to the general tendency already outlined in Wittgenstein's later writings. Quine, however, never commented personally on the *Philosophical Investigations* and preferred to keep his distance from both Wittgenstein and the ordinary language philosophers.

Like Lewis's work, Quine's writings—notably *From a Logical Point of View* (1953), *Word and Object* (1960), and *Philosophy of Logic* (1970)—have concerned themselves principally with logic and the theory of knowledge. But the empiricism and rigorous nominalism that animate them (as well as the writings of his Harvard colleague Nelson Goodman) go beyond this strict framework. If, following Carnap's example, Quine is inclined to erase the distinction between science and philosophy, if he thinks that "good" philosophy must be a specialized practice of a scientific and experimental kind, and if, as a result, he regards its history as being less important than its results—or, as he himself has said, the errors of past philosophers as less interesting than the arguments currently held to be true[54]—he does not for all that believe that philosophy as such is finished. Nor does he intend to limit it to the analysis of logico-mathematical language, even though this has remained his own preferred domain of investigation. Convinced that the mission of philosophy is to explore the fundamental features of reality, he considers that ontology— which the neopositivists would have nothing to do with—can be treated in a rigorous manner and accepts that ethics can also make progress by means of logical analysis. By contrast, he leaves responsibility for resolving aesthetic problems to psychology and responsibility for settling political questions to sociology. Although this position is consistent with the spirit of Carnap's thought in one sense, it had the effect—given the complete hold over American philosophy enjoyed by logical empiricism in the 1950s and 1960s—of temporarily turning philosophy in America away from reflection upon history and society. It should not come as a surprise in any case that Quine's conservative style of thought, whose high point coincided with that of the Cold War, shows no traces of the sympathy Carnap felt for socialist ideals.

For his part, Nelson Goodman (1906–98) adopted the project of the *Aufbau*—abandoned by Carnap himself—in his doctoral thesis, published as *A Study of Qualities* (1940). His work led him, in *The Structure of Appearance* (1951), to reelaborate this project in a form that was both more modest and more logically satisfying. Unlike Carnap's constructivism, which remained the prisoner of its solipsistic base, Goodman's rests on the idea that it is impossible to give a sense to the notion of basic elements, unless by reference to a given, necessarily arbitrary criterion. Later, in *Ways of Worldmaking* (1978), he argued that science, art, and philosophy are only languages, which is to say rule-governed ways of manipulating symbols in order to "manufacture facts" and reconstruct "worlds." Goodman was nonetheless not a relativist: he held that certain languages are more correct than others (in terms of coherence or adaptation to empirical context) and that there is a distinction between fact and convention, even though this distinction may itself be conventional. He is also one of the first to have applied, within the framework of a "general theory of symbols," the analytic method to the study of the formal structures peculiar to works of art, regarded as systems of signs whose internal rules of composition alone matter—a position he defended in *Languages of Art* (1968), and later in *Reconceptions in Philosophy and Other Arts and Sciences* (1988), that links his aesthetics in a distinctive way with the aesthetic theory developed independently of him at the same time by the European structuralists.[55]

With Donald Davidson (b. 1917), finally, one sees the resurgence of the thesis that a real boundary—albeit a shifting one—separates philosophy from the rest of the sciences, philosophy having to take responsibility for problems to which the sciences provide no answer. Davidson's thought, strongly colored by the influence of Quine's work while departing from it in important respects, is developed in a series of articles on topics in philosophy of mind and ethics of which the most important have been collected in two volumes, *Essays on Actions and Events* (1980) and *Inquiries into Truth and In-*

terpretation (1984). He reintroduced the idea, common to Popper and Quine but contrary to the central thesis of the *Aufbau* (to whose spirit Goodman, for his part, remained faithful), that reality is not a logico-linguistic construction but has instead an objective basis in the world, the most general features of which are revealed to us by the structure of our language. Neither he nor Quine, however, has been able to give a satisfactory account of this mysterious correspondence between our brain and the world. Like both Carnap and Ryle, Davidson is persuaded that materialism is as mistaken as idealism, but, unlike them, he holds that the relation between mind and body can be conceived only in terms of an "anomalous" monism—a position that led him to disapprove of the physicalist pretention of the cognitive sciences to elucidate the mechanism of our mental acts by reducing them to physical states.

It is true that these sciences, situated at the promising crossroads of computer science, neurobiology, philosophy, and psycholinguistics, are still young. Their origins may be traced to the work done in the 1930s by Alan Turing (1912–54)[56] on the automatization of calculation procedures (out of which came the first computers) as well as to cybernetics, popularized by the mathematician Norbert Wiener (1894–1964) in his 1948 book of the same title (treating the theory of "control and communication in the animal and the machine"), and information theory, pioneered by the mathematician Claude Shannon (b. 1916). Systematic research along these lines began to develop in the 1950s, and it is only recently that genuine attempts at synthesis have emerged with the work of the philosophers Jerry A. Fodor (b. 1935), in *The Language of Thought* (1975), and Daniel C. Dennett (b. 1942), in *Consciousness Explained* (1991). Firm conclusions, if any are possible, clearly lie far in the future. For the moment, however, Davidson's dissenting views have found support in the work of a number of other philosophers, notably Saul A. Kripke (b. 1940), whose influential doctrines concerning the "rigidity" of names and the necessity of identity statements—first laid out in a long paper on modal logic, "Naming and Necessity" (1972)—together with his rejection of the traditional association of necessary and a priori truths, led him to attack mind-brain identity theories as inadequate and mistaken.

In this respect Kripke's thinking is not unrelated to that of another contemporary philosopher of mind and language whom we have already mentioned, John Searle, which, although it derives from the rather different speech-act tradition pioneered by Austin, is likewise concerned to combat the orthodox claim of cognitive science that the mind is simply "what the brain does."[57] Searle's famous (and endlessly disputed) "Chinese room argument" illustrates the contrary thesis that the mind, though it indisputably has a material basis, nonetheless possesses an irreducibly subjective dimension that is utterly closed to neurobiological investigation. This notion of "mentality"—that being in a certain material or functional state *feels* like something—and the relevance of lived experience (once again, the echo of Husserl) to attempts at scientific explanation have been much insisted upon also by Thomas Nagel (b. 1937) in a number of incisive yet unusually accessible works, *The View from Nowhere* (1986) being perhaps the best known.[58]

And so, despite their many differences, Quine, Goodman, and Davidson—along with Kripke, Nagel, and, despite his British training, Searle—may be said to represent a single movement. One of the remarkable peculiarities of the American version of analytic philosophy, clearly distinguished from its British counterpart by its faithfulness to the pragmatist heritage, is that it never totally cut its ties to the continental philosophy from which it derived, or at least to certain tendencies of this philosophy, which it helped to introduce to the United States beginning in the late 1930s. Significantly, however, it was only with the entrance onto the American university scene in the 1940s and 1950s of a small number of defectors from the tradition of logical empiricism that a renewed Euro-American dialogue, comparable in scope to the one that existed in the period between 1880 and 1939 (at the beginning of which James was in close contact with Mach and Bergson, and at the end the young Quine with the Vienna Circle), became possible.

The history of this dissidence itself consists of two overlapping phases. One is associated with the work, to which we shall return later, of Thomas Kuhn—whose philosophy of science, reaching back beyond Carnap and Popper, revived the anti-empiricist orientation of Bachelard and Koyré—as well as with that of the linguist Noam Chomsky (b. 1928). Chomsky's work, rationalist in the Cartesian sense of the term and therefore anti-empiricist as well, proceeded from the conviction that the child's acquisition of language could not be explained from the strictly behaviorist perspective of Quine or, more generally, of analytic philosophy. Drawing instead upon the notion of "general grammar" forged in the seventeenth century by the linguists of Port-Royal, Chomsky sought to construct a formal model of "innate" syntactic structures that could account for the evolution in human beings of a capacity for speech. His writings, particularly *Cartesian Linguistics* (1966), immediately enjoyed a great success in Europe, where, unlike the United States, the reputation his many controversial political stands had won him as a committed intellectual—indeed as a leftist—did not seem at all foreign. In

America, Chomsky's antibehaviorism has been even more influential in the development of cognitive science, contributing among other things to the ongoing revival of interest noted earlier in the old scholastic—later Brentanian and Husserlian—theme of intentionality. Philosophers such as Fodor have since followed Chomsky in holding that our mental representations, even though they may be reduced to neurobiological processes, nonetheless possess a specific (or "autonomous") reality; those who join Dennett in rejecting this form of intentional realism remain opposed to Chomskyan doctrines, preferring the so-called eliminative materialism elaborated by Paul Churchland (b. 1942) and other defenders of a strong version of artificial intelligence.[59]

At the same time a second phase of the anti-empiricist dissidence had begun developing in the work of a quite different group of thinkers—Richard Rorty, Hilary Putnam, John Rawls, and Stanley Cavell—who gradually came to consider the analytic tradition too confining and turned their attention instead, from the 1970s onward, to topics (particularly in ethics and politics) that until then had been almost entirely neglected by Quine and his followers. What is more, they have shown themselves to be considerably less averse to entering into debate with European philosophers such as Habermas, Foucault, and Derrida. Their work has continued to be marked, however, by a certain resistance to philosophy of history of any kind as well as by a notable reluctance to tackle contemporary social issues. In this connection one cannot fail to detect the lingering influence of logical empiricism, with its contempt for all forms of dialectical thought derived from Hegel and its deliberate practice of privileging facts in relation to values.

Such inhibitions will surely be overcome in time. The emergence of a new interest in Husserlian phenomenology on the part of some American philosophers, who find its analysis of the structures of the mind useful in evaluating the implications of current research in cognitive science and artificial intelligence, is an encouraging sign.[60] And yet still today in the United States neither Marxism nor existentialism is really considered worthy of serious examination, or even worth attacking; and as for the theories of Foucault and the Frankfurt School, these are regarded by most American philosophers as belonging to cultural and literary theory rather than to philosophy. Yet another gulf remains therefore to be bridged.

Conceiving Auschwitz

Paths of Exile

The *Anschluss* in 1938 marked the end of basic freedoms in Austria, forcing the emigration of those who, like Freud and Schrödinger, had not been able to make up their minds until that point. But this had been the situation in Germany for more than five years.

From the moment when the NSDAP—the National Socialist Party—won fourteen million votes in the elections of 31 July 1932 and obtained 230 of the 600 seats in the Reichstag, the days of the Weimar Republic were numbered. On 30 January 1933, President Hindenburg named Adolf Hitler chancellor. On 14 April one of the first laws of the new regime ordered the removal of Jewish, Communist, and Social Democrat officials. Many academics found themselves dismissed from their posts without any protest by university authorities, except in a few cases. The Jewish community now understood the threat that now faced it, but not all German Jews immediately chose exile.

To gauge the scope of the disaster—followed by a still more terrible catastrophe, the extermination of those who were not able to get out in time—it needs to be kept in mind that on the eve of the Second World War the Jewish community in Germany was one of the best assimilated in all of Europe, as much from the cultural as from the social point of view. Highly educated, and committed to progressive ideals that had enjoyed widespread support since the time of Moses Mendelssohn (1729–86), Jews played a major role in the life of the country. From Heine to Marx and Einstein, some of the greatest figures in German arts, letters, and sciences in the nineteenth and twentieth centuries were Jewish.

German Jewish philosophers, in particular, constituted a complex intellectual family of exceptional brilliance whose integration with the surrounding society seemed so complete in the first third of the twentieth century that the majority of its members believed themselves to be sheltered from all serious danger in Germany, for centuries their homeland—a homeland that many of them had served in the First World War with exemplary devotion. Leaving aside Hermann Cohen and Franz Rosenzweig, both of whom died well before the triumph of National Socialism, the fact that no Jewish intellectual of note seriously contemplated leaving Germany before 1933 is further evidence of the optimism that prevailed at the time. This last remark admits, it is true, of at least one exception—Gershom Scholem (1897–1982). But Scholem's departure for Jerusalem in 1923 was not a forced exile; it was motivated instead by the despairing conviction, as the young philosopher put it in his private journal on 1 August 1916, that the First World War signaled the death and "entombment" of Europe.[1]

Born in Berlin to a fully assimilated family—one of his brothers became a Communist while the other associated with nationalist groups on the extreme Right—Scholem first turned to mathematics. Along with Carnap he belonged to an elite group of students who regularly attended Frege's courses at Jena. Rather quickly, however, he came to see that his true interests lay rather in the Jewish Kabbalah, a mystic form of thought in which numerological speculations play an important role; his attraction to it was, moreover, intellectual rather than religious. A convert to Zionism—at the time a minority view in the Jewish communities of Central Europe—he freely chose at the age of twenty-six to move to Jerusalem, then a largely Arab city. Two years later, in 1925, he participated in the creation of the Hebrew University, where he spent his entire career. His work, devoted to the historical and structural analysis of the major currents of Jewish mysticism, illustrated the possibility of a scientific approach to religious texts while contributing to the moral edification of the new state of Israel following its founding in 1948.

If one also puts aside the case of Scholem, then, it is plain that German Jewish philosophers decided upon exile only when they found themselves directly affected by Hitler's coming to power. No doubt many of them regretted the failure in 1919 of the socialist revolution in November of the previous year, crushed by reactionary and clerical forces. No doubt they also sensed that the crisis of identity that ensued after the end of the war risked rekindling the fires of anti-Semitism, whose remote origins were both Protestant (with Luther) and Catholic (with the Counter-Reformation) and which had never really died out in Germany. Indeed, since the massacres provoked by the First Crusade in 1096, the Jews had often served as scapegoats for the internal problems of a German nation that was slow to unify. But if in the 1920s they foresaw having to pass through a disagreeable phase, they were far—very far—from imagining that the worst was still to come: that the greater part of the German people—one of the most civilized in the world—was soon to give to Hitler the means by which to realize the program of extermination that had been more or less overtly announced in his *Mein Kampf* (1925).

THEIR FORCED DEPARTURE, from 1933 on, came therefore as a cruel shock and brought in its train all sorts of material hardship and psychological suffering. For Cassirer, for example, the downfall was sudden. A renowned scholar, rector of the University of Hamburg, and one of the most respected liberal intellectuals of the Weimar Republic, he found himself immediately relieved of all responsibilities. He left for Oxford, going on to Sweden in 1935. In 1941 he settled in New York, dying there a few days before the end of the war in 1945. His last years, darkened by the news of genocide that reached the United States and the loss of members of his family, were given over to reflection upon the tragic end of German idealism, as well as the uncertain future of humanity, in *Essay on Man* (1944).

Cassirer's student and colleague at the University of Hamburg, the art historian Erwin Panofsky (1892–1968), emigrated to the United States in 1934. Some years previously he had published a short article, "Perspective as 'Symbolic Form'" (1927), that gave a new theoretical impetus to the study of art history. It was now no longer possible to study aesthetic revolutions without placing them within the framework of the great transformations—religious, philosophical, and scientific—of our view of the world in which they participate and help, in part, to explain them. Another of Cassirer's students, Eric Weil (1904–77), left for France in 1933. Drafted into the French army in 1940 and subsequently captured by the Germans, he survived four years' imprisonment in Germany—saved by an assumed name—and returned after the war to France, where he carried on the Kantian tradition in moral and political philosophy.

Martin Buber, born like Cassirer in 1878, was likewise a well-known and respected philosopher when the Nazis took power. Moreover, he was one of the foremost figures of European Judaism. Professor of Jewish philosophy and religion at the University of Frankfurt since 1923, he had published studies in the history of Hassidism—a mystical movement that emerged from the ghettos of Eastern Europe—as well as a book influenced by phenomenology, *I and Thou* (1923), on the ethical meaning of personal dialogue. An advocate of reconciliation with Christianity as well as of Judeo-Arab entente in Palestine, he represented (along with Rosenzweig) the so-called spiritual wing of Zionism that attracted Jews anxious to rediscover the sources of Jewish culture while at the same time remaining German. Although he was forced to give up his chair in 1933, he nonetheless chose initially to remain in Germany in order to lead a sort of internal resistance to Nazism, creating a Central Office for Jewish Education that he managed to keep in operation for five years. It was only in 1938, at the age of sixty, that he found himself obliged to flee. He arrived safely in Palestine where he was reunited with Scholem and where he died in 1965, having taken part in the founding of the state of Israel.

ANOTHER GROUP LASTINGLY AFFECTED by exile was the one assembled at Frankfurt by the philosopher Max Horkheimer (1895–1973). Born in Stuttgart to a family of conservative and religious industrialists, Horkheimer began his career working in his father's firm. In Munich, where he was living in 1919, he supported the revolution. When it was crushed he was briefly detained and then went to Frankfurt to devote himself to the study of philosophy, taking courses on gestalt psychology with Wolfgang Köhler and Max Wertheimer as well. He also spent two semesters at Freiburg, where Husserl's teaching impressed him less than the existentialism then being worked out by Heidegger.

After having obtained his habilitation in 1925 he was appointed to an assistant professorship at Frankfurt. Before long he was in a position to lecture on the authors who really interested him: Hegel, Marx, and the French philosophers of the Enlightenment. His first article in 1930 was devoted to a critique of idealist arguments developed in the sociology of knowledge by his colleague Karl Mannheim (1893–1947), a disciple of the sociologist Max Weber (1864–1920). The same year he was offered a chair in the philosophy of society and, more importantly, the directorship of a laboratory attached to the university, the Institut für Sozialforschung (Institute of Social Research). The institute had been founded in 1923 by a wealthy Jewish businessman, Felix Weil, who, shocked by the events of 1918, was converted to revolutionary ideas and thereafter worked to help left-wing artists and writers. From

1924 to 1930 it was directed by Carl Grünberg, under whom research was concentrated on the history of socialism, workers' movements, and economic theory. Through its journal *Zeitschrift für Sozialforschung* the institute helped make available a number of previously unpublished works by Marx and Engels, the manuscripts of which were then scattered throughout Germany and the Soviet Union.

From 1931 on Horkheimer breathed new life into the institute—the only one of its kind and the birthplace of what later was called the Frankfurt School—and into the journal, which soon became the favored publication outlet for its members. He reformulated the institute's research agenda, proclaiming the necessity of adopting an interdisciplinary approach if social phenomena were to be satisfactorily explained. At the time Horkheimer was convinced that the old philosophy was destined to be replaced by the social sciences, understood in a materialist sense. But though there was scarcely any doubt where his own sympathies lay, he carefully avoided openly declaring himself a Marxist. His choice of collaborators, on the other hand, clearly indicated how he saw the institute's mission. The ones closest to him—Erich Fromm, Theodor W. Adorno, and Herbert Marcuse—were not only young scholars with bright futures ahead of them; they were also politically committed intellectuals.

Raised in an orthodox Jewish family, Erich Fromm (1900–1980) had been associated with Scholem in the early twenties in the independent center for Jewish studies founded by Rosenzweig and Buber at Frankfurt. In 1924 he discovered psychoanalysis and began practicing three years later. In 1929 he founded along with his wife a psychoanalytic institute that operated, thanks to Horkheimer's enthusiastic support, under the auspices of the Institut für Sozialforschung—a historic event, since it amounted to nothing less than the first official recognition of psychoanalysis by a university. Henceforth the theoreticians of the Frankfurt School were frequently to blend Marxism and psychoanalysis in proposing hypotheses for research. Fromm, though his politics were less radical than those of the Austro-Hungarian psychiatrist Wilhelm Reich (1897–1957)—who at the beginning of the 1930s launched a movement in Berlin calling for a proletarian sexual politics that was considered proof of Trotskyite deviationism by Stalinists—was nonetheless at this time a left-wing Freudian concerned to link the theory of instincts with that of class struggle and to put both of them in the service of human liberation. *The Dogma of Christ* (1930) marked the beginning of his voluminous output, which after the war took a more conservative direction.

Theodor W. Adorno (1903–69), born in Frankfurt, bore a double name originally, Wiesengrund-Adorno, composed of the family name of his father, a Jew converted to Christianity who had his son baptized as a Protestant, and that of his mother, a Catholic of Corsican origins. At the end of a comfortable and sheltered childhood in which music played a major role—as it had in the case of Wittgenstein—he discovered aesthetics from Lukác's *Theory of the Novel* and revolution from Bloch's *Spirit of Utopia*. From 1921 to 1932 he devoted himself to musical criticism. Adorno was fascinated by the atonal music of the Austrian school and in 1925 went to Vienna with the intention of studying piano and composition under Arnold Schoenberg. Rapidly convinced that he lacked sufficient ability, he returned after a few months to Frankfurt, settling finally for a university career concerned chiefly with aesthetics.

In 1929 he published an article on the dodecaphonic technique and obtained his habilitation two years later with a thesis that appeared at the beginning of 1933 under the title *Kierkegaard: Construction of the Aesthetic*. In the meantime Adorno grew closer to Horkheimer, whom he had known for several years, and embraced Marxist materialism, which he interpreted in a personal sense similar to that given it by Bloch. In 1932 he became a contributor to the *Zeitschrift für Sozialforschung*, which four years later published an article he had written on jazz—the first attempt by a philosopher to make sense of this new art form. There was only one cloud on the horizon. In 1934 he published an article in another German journal praising certain songs whose lyrics were taken from a collection of poems dedicated to Hitler. He publicly expressed his remorse after the war.

Herbert Marcuse (1898–1979) was born in Berlin to a bourgeois family whose values he repudiated at a very young age. In 1917 he joined the Social Democratic Party. Called up in 1918, he was elected at the beginning of the November revolution to a soviet, or council, of Berlin soldiers. The failure of the revolution the following year led him to quit the party, however, convinced that its leaders had taken part in the assassination of the Spartacist leaders Karl Liebknecht and Rosa Luxemburg. He then turned away from politics to take up the study of literature, completing his doctoral thesis in 1922. A few years later he obtained an assistant professorship at Freiburg under Heidegger, from whom he began to dissociate himself in 1932. It was only in the course of the following year that he met Horkheimer, however; he subsequently joined the Frankfurt group in exile.

For these four men—Horkheimer, Fromm, Adorno, and Marcuse—

Hitler's coming to power changed the course of the world. On 13 March 1933 the institute was closed by the Nazi police on the ground that its activities were hostile to the state. By this time Horkheimer had already quit Frankfurt for Geneva, while arranging with the French publisher Félix Alcan for the institute's journal to continue to appear in Paris, in German, with the help of Raymond Aron. During his brief stay in Geneva, where Bloch had also temporarily taken refuge, Horkheimer found time to organize an ambitious sociological inquiry into the evolution of authority within the modern family, the results of which were published in 1936. Sensing that the rise of fascism threatened the peace of all of Europe, he embarked for the United States in April 1934. Two months later he concluded an agreement with Columbia University that allowed the institute to be housed there. At the end of the year he was rejoined by Fromm and Marcuse. As for Adorno, he moved first to Oxford before finally, at Horkheimer's urging, coming to New York in 1938.

A new page in the history of the institute began, then, in the New World. Emigration to America saved many other German Jewish intellectuals as well, among them Karl Löwith and Hannah Arendt (both of them former students of Heidegger) and Leo Strauss. Despite its hardships, exile for these victims of persecution was synonymous with survival. One philosopher, however—and not the least of them—missed the opportunity to escape: Walter Benjamin. To retrace Benjamin's journey is also to understand the tragic fate that awaited Jews who, whether owing to an excess of optimism or an error of judgment, hesitated too long before making the painful decision to leave.

BORN IN BERLIN, Walter Benjamin (1892–1940) was a sensitive, tormented soul of stunning intellectual precocity. Equally drawn to literature and philosophy, he met Gershom Scholem in 1915. Scholem, five years his junior, remained his confidant until the end and many years later, in 1975, devoted a moving book to the story of their friendship.[2] In 1921 Benjamin rediscovered the richness of Jewish culture in reading, at Scholem's insistence, Rosenzweig's *Star of Redemption*. Two years earlier he had made the acquaintance of Bloch, whom he admired, and shortly afterwards of Adorno, whom he fascinated. His first writings revealed at once his interest in aesthetics and history, his sympathy for progressive causes, his affinities with romanticism and expressionism, his curiosity about psychoanalysis, modern painting, popular art, and occult sciences, but also the difficulties he experienced in giving organized expression to the outpouring of his ideas in a way that conformed to academic norms.

Despite completing a doctoral thesis, "The Concept of Art Criticism in German Romanticism" (1919), and then a habilitation thesis, "The Origin of German Baroque Drama" (1928)—the latter ultimately rejected by the University of Frankfurt but, like the earlier thesis, subsequently published as a book—he was unable to find a teaching post in Germany. Forced to live by his pen, he devoted part of his energies to journalism in order to support himself while nonetheless managing to publish a number of books, including *Goethe's Elective Affinities* (1925) and *One-Way Street* (1928). At the end of the 1920s Scholem tried without success to get him to come to the Hebrew University of Jerusalem. Benjamin was taken briefly with the prospect of moving to Palestine, then abandoned the idea. Earlier, in 1924, he had met a young Russian revolutionary, Asja Lacis, whom he could not bring himself to leave.

Lacis, a stage director, introduced him to Brecht, made him read Lukács, and convinced him to make a trip in December 1926 to Moscow. On his return to Berlin in January 1927 Benjamin turned more and more resolutely in the direction of historical materialism, which, like Bloch, he interpreted in a messianic sense, more theological than sociological. He nonetheless continued to pursue aesthetic investigations. His acute sense of modernity, his poetic sensibility, and his aptitude for deciphering the signs of reality as one would read a book led him to compose a series of difficult, unclassifiable texts—*The Work of Art in the Age of Mechanical Reproduction* (1936) and an unfinished collection of writings published posthumously under the title *Book of Passages* (1982)—that were to receive their just due only after the war.

Henceforth history was at the center of his thinking, the source of its secret unity. Hostile to positivist philosophy as well as to evolutionism in all its forms—and therefore to certain aspects of Marxism—Benjamin now embraced a political reading of history, past and future, based on an analysis of the contradictions that constituted its present. He challenged both the idea of mechanical causality and the belief in the ineluctable character of progress, developing over the course of the following years a discontinuist conception of time similar in spirit to that of Rosenzweig, Bloch, and Scholem. Time he saw as the site par excellence of utopia—obviously a fragile utopia, but nonetheless one that was realizable if the oppressed, on becoming aware of their situation, could regain the powers of speech and artistic expression of which they had so long been deprived and put humanity back on the longed-for path of redemption. This complicated argument, in which Marxism was reappropriated and "overcome," was more fully developed in his last work, the unfinished *Theses on the Concept of History* (written in 1939–40 and first published in Los Angeles, in German, in 1942).

An indefatigable traveler, in love with French literature, an admirer of Baudelaire, Proust, and Aragon and the surrealists, Benjamin moved to Paris in 1933. Owing to the intercession of Adorno, who pleaded his case to Horkheimer, he was henceforth closely associated with the exiled members of the Institut für Sozialforschung. But he was less convinced than they were that disaster was imminent: not because he was unaware of the danger that with the rise of fascism now hung over Europe but because, like many intellectuals on the Left, he had difficulty imagining the possibility of an open war between capitalist countries. History itself would shortly take it upon itself to contradict this illusion.

Worn down by anxieties as well as by material hardships, Benjamin finally decided in the fall of 1940 to quit Europe to rejoin his Frankfurt friends in New York. By now it was too late. France had fallen to the Germans. In order to find a boat going to the United States it was necessary for him to get to Spain. On the evening of 26 September he was arrested by Franco's police attempting to cross the Spanish border at Port-Bou in Catalonia. He was allowed to spend the night in a hotel. Knowing that he would be sent back the next day to a French concentration camp, he resolved at dawn on 27 September to take his life by swallowing morphine tablets.

This desperate act strikingly illustrated the dramatic atmosphere in which German Jews had lived since 1933—without it even yet being known that of those members of the community who remained only a few thousand would survive the Holocaust.[3] For them life would never be the same.

Heidegger's Choice

The year 1933 was tragic for another reason as well. A few weeks after Hitler's coming into power, the most celebrated German philosopher of the day, Martin Heidegger, assumed the rectorship of the University of Freiburg and, at the same time, became a member of the National Socialist Party.

Heidegger was forty-four when he joined the NSDAP. It was not a question, therefore, of a youthful mistake. Moreover, he remained a member of the party until 1945. Nor, then, was it a matter of a brief involvement. Nor was it by inadvertence, but rather through the active connivance of pro-Nazi colleagues and the support of administrative authorities, that he was placed in charge of his university—a position he held for a year, from April 1933 until March 1934. The rectorship was neither a neutral nor a purely honorific position. It conferred real power while requiring total political commitment. The bringing to heel (*Gleischhaltung*) of the university sector was an essential part of the Nazis' effort to control civil society. Confiding responsibility for carrying out this task to disobedient or indecisive persons was unthinkable.

Furthermore, Heidegger's appointment as rector was directly related to the central theme of the Nazi program: the elimination of the Jews. His appointment came after the resignation of his predecessor, the biologist Wilhelm von Möllendorf, who had refused—quite exceptionally—to apply a new law passed by the *Landtag* of the province of Baden that imposed automatic and indefinite leaves of absence on professors judged to be "non-Aryan." In spite of von Möllendorf the law was applied: of the ninety-three electors charged with choosing his successor, thirteen were forbidden to vote for "racial" reasons. This apparently did not pose the least moral dilemma for Heidegger, any more than did the public burning of "Jewish and Marxist books" that took place in various cities on 10 May 1933, only a few days after his election.

The new rector took up his duties with unmistakable zeal. On 20 May 1933 he addressed a telegram to Hitler to advise him against receiving the officers of the Association of German University Professors so long as this body did not show itself to be more cooperative with the new regime—in short, so long as the association had not been brought to heel. One week later, on 27 May, the investiture ceremony took place at Freiburg. Between martial anthems Heidegger delivered a speech in Party jargon laying out his program for "Nazifying" the University of Freiburg. There is not much to be said with regard to the rather meager substance of this offensive address, pompously entitled "The Self-affirmation of the German University"; at all events one would search in vain for the least trace of intellectual independence in it. Tellingly, its author took care from 1945 until his death to prevent it from being reprinted—so successfully, in fact, that it was to reappear, first in France and then in Germany, only in 1982.

Upon assuming his new post the philosopher devoted himself mainly to reforming the university statutes on the model of the *Führerprinzip* system. Having achieved this reform, which was later to be applied in other institutions, he was himself named Führer of the University of Freiburg on 1 October 1933. With the awarding of this title his powers were strengthened as well. The rectorship had now become a major channel of communication between the National Socialist state and the nation's youth. The consequences of Heidegger's initiative proved catastrophic, no less for students, who now found themselves deprived of all intellectual freedom, than for the universities themselves, whose scholarly standards were not long in falling into decline.

At the same time Heidegger applied himself to his new role as philosopher-propagandist with energy and enthusiasm. His lectures and articles in the press became more frequent.[4] On the eve of the plebiscite of 12 November, he called for voters to cast their ballots for Hitler. On 30 November he gave a speech at Tübingen on the mission of the university in the National Socialist state. Neither his public nor private statements during this period left any doubt about the ideology that inspired them, a mixture of nationalism, anti-Marxism, and anti-Christianity. As for anti-Semitism in the strict sense, if Heidegger did not make an open show of it, this was only because everyone else around him had already undertaken to do so. Anti-Semitism was widespread in Europe during the 1930s, particularly in the part of Germany where Heidegger grew up, and constituted the cornerstone of the Nazi program. As an intellectual Heidegger therefore had no need to emphasize it, above all if he aspired to set himself apart in his public statements from ordinary party officials.

This does not mean that he dissociated himself from anti-Semitism. Not only is there no factual basis for such a conclusion, but at least one piece of evidence can be adduced to the contrary: the secret report that he made in December 1933 to the Göttingen League of National Socialist Lecturers, in which he denounced one of his former colleagues for maintaining "close ties" with Jews.[5] This report, which was meant to be damning for the person concerned, seems today still more damning for Heidegger himself. In the meantime the philosopher's activism, combined with his combative rhetoric, had aroused misgivings among those within the Nazi party who advocated a more pragmatic line. The party itself was divided into rival factions competing for control. Thus, for example, Hitler's entourage and the Schutzstaffel (SS) distrusted the revolutionary ardor of the Sturmabteilung (SA), whose leaders were assassinated on the "Night of the Long Knives" (30 June 1934). At the level of university administration, many of Heidegger's colleagues—beginning with the influential rector at Frankfurt, Ernst Krieck—were irritated by his prophetic zeal, his obscurantist style, and his obvious ambition. Blunders in his handling of university affairs caused opposition to grow in the fall of 1933. Eventually he gave in, quietly resigning his duties as rector in March 1934 on the pretext of wishing to devote more time to his "scientific" work. But he did not quit the Party, nor did he openly renounce any of his convictions between then and 1945—or indeed at any point afterwards.

The philosopher Hans-Georg Gadamer, who was Heidegger's student at Marburg and who never ceased to defend his former teacher, asserts that he was known after 1934 to criticize the regime privately while publicly continuing to support it. There is nothing improbable about this. Humiliated by the failure of his rectorship, which he attributed to the jealousy of others who conspired to have him removed from office, Heidegger must have indeed been tempted to speak ill of a government that did not give him its full support as well as of colleagues who, by outmaneuvering him, were able to remain close to those in power. It would not be at all surprising, then, if from 1934 to 1945 he gradually created a quite personal conception of what National Socialism *should have been*; nor if on occasion, in the company of intimates, he angrily pointed out its failure to live up to this vision.

These shows of temper, attested by Gadamer and explainable by the deep disappointment he suffered in 1934, must, however, not be interpreted as the expression of a rejection of Nazism or of its excesses. They betrayed, to the contrary, a regret that Hitler did not go far enough—or quickly enough—in putting into effect the most revolutionary aspects of the National Socialist program for social and cultural reform. Alarmed by the pragmatism that reigned in official circles, Heidegger seems to have aspired to set himself up as the guardian of doctrinal purity, particularly with respect to what he took at the time to be the necessity of waging an energetic battle against the moderating influence of Christian elements.

Evidence of such an aspiration is supplied by a famous passage in the lectures he gave in the summer semester course of 1935 (published in their original form only in 1953, under the title *An Introduction to Metaphysics*, but without the necessary context later provided by Hugo Ott[6]). Heidegger here attacked the views of a courageous defender of moral values, the Catholic Theodor Haecker (whom he does not cite by name), attacking also the *Frankfurter Zeitung*, the last major newspaper not yet to have been brought to heel, perceived by the Nazis as being favorable to Jews for supporting Haecker. After urging that such views be permanently banned (as they were soon to be), he concluded by resolutely condemning the "works that are being peddled about nowadays as the philosophy of National Socialism but have nothing whatever to do with the inner truth and greatness of this movement."[7] This was a fairly clear way of indicating, more than a year after resigning his rectorship, in which camp he stood.

It should be recalled too that in 1936, when, on a trip to Rome, Heidegger happened to run into his former student Karl Löwith, then living in exile in the Italian capital, he reiterated his support for the National Socialist program (despite certain criticisms aimed at Hitler's entourage), stressing to Löwith the vital link between this political attitude and the rest of his thought.[8] At no time, not even after the anti-Semitic violence of the Kristallnacht ("Crystal Night" or "Night of the Broken Glass," 9–10 November 1938), did Heidegger protest against the turn taken by events. Moreover, a number of accounts confirm that he persisted until 1945 in wearing the Party insignia in his lapel on various public occasions.

It needs to be remembered, finally, that Heidegger—who, it will be recalled, had harshly treated Cassirer, a Jew, at the Davos meetings in 1929— remained until the end of his life incapable of the least gesture of kindness, even privately, toward all former teachers and fellow students who were Jewish. He abruptly broke off relations with Husserl—a convert to Protestantism—in 1930. Heidegger did not visit Husserl during his final illness, nor did he attend the funeral services of the man to whom he had dedicated the first edition of *Being and Time*. When the fourth edition of this work appeared in 1941, Heidegger went to the trouble of removing the dedication to his mentor, who had died three years earlier.

This inglorious era came to a close with the end of the war. On 25 April 1945, French troops entered Freiburg. Heidegger, who was considered an ordinary Nazi, saw his house placed on the list of buildings to be requisitioned for the use of the occupying forces in the middle of May. Shortly afterwards, steps were taken to determine the fate of the former rector. A decision was finally reached in October 1946: Heidegger was made to take early retirement and forbidden to teach publicly. He was not slow to find a way of getting around this restriction. He was giving private lectures already by the following year .

IN THE FALL SEMESTER OF 1945, Heidegger undertook to set down in writing the main lines of the defense that he would adopt until the end of his life,[9] as an interview he granted in September 1966 to the weekly magazine

Der Spiegel—which, in keeping with his wishes, was not published until after his death—attests.[10]

Heidegger had left to him at the end of 1945 a choice between two opposed strategies, each one coherent: either to unrepentently accept responsibility for the whole of his Nazi past, even if it meant condemning himself to isolation and silence; or to admit that he was grievously mistaken, not only in 1933 but during the twelve years that followed, even if it meant publicly acknowledging his error. Each of these two positions, it is true, required courage. No doubt this is why Heidegger chose a third course. This course, both reassuring and deliberately misleading, consisted in minimizing the duration of his membership in the Nazi Party, pretending that he had seriously supported the Party only during the year of his rectorship. Heidegger was thus led to retroactively reorganize his life into three periods—before 1933, 1933–34, and 1934–45—and then to picture himself as having been apolitical during the first period, the victim of events during the second, and fully cognizant of his "mistake" from the beginning of the third.

This version of things is difficult to sustain. Heidegger was far from having been apolitical before 1933. Brought up in an atmosphere of pronounced moral and social conservatism, he looked very early on to the Right—then to the extreme Right—for the means of professional advancement that he felt the Weimar Republic did not offer him quickly enough. As for *Being and Time*, although it is not directly a political book, the ideas found in it are often, as we have seen, only the philosophical transposition of certain themes dear to Spengler and the theoreticians of the conservative revolution. With regard to the year 1933–34, the interpretation that Heidegger gave after 1945—in particular, before the young (and not always very well informed) French students whom he enjoyed receiving on a regular basis—quite simply does not hang together. Sometimes he characterized his behavior as a momentary lapse into stupidity ("eine grosse Dummheit")—a regrettable error in judgment, nothing more; sometimes, however, he asserted that he had accepted the rectorship only in order to be in a stronger position to oppose the control of the Party over the university—which is contrary to the facts of the matter.

It remains to mention the most painful aspect of the affair. If Heidegger had actually been, as he claimed, an opponent of the regime in 1934, he would have had no reason after 1945 not to openly condemn the horror of the Nazi crimes. But he did no such thing. Not once did he utter a word that might have suggested he was outraged by the extermination of the Jews, if only after the fact, nor even that he disapproved of it. This silence, which shocked the poet Paul Celan deeply, weighs all the more heavily since Heidegger knew, better than anyone, that to be silent is not the same as saying nothing.

Did Heidegger go on—like so many other Nazis—ignoring the barbarism of the Holocaust until the day he died? There exists, alas, no reason to suppose otherwise. Indeed, at least two pieces of information seem to support such a conclusion. The first is found in a letter addressed on 20 January 1948 to Herbert Marcuse. Urged by his former student to admit he was wrong, Heidegger refused, downplaying his actions once more and, finally, trivializing the Holocaust by comparing it to the dictatorship that since 1945 had held sway in the popular democracies of Eastern Europe. "If you substitute 'East Germans' for 'Jews,'" he wrote to Marcuse, "then exactly the same charge can be leveled against one of the Allies, the only difference being that the international public knows very well what has been going on since 1945, whereas the Nazis' bloody reign of terror was actually kept secret from the German people."[11] No matter that Jews may find this statement offensive, it is doubly false. On the one hand, it suggests that nothing about Nazism was worse than Communism by eliding the fact that official anti-Semitism was inherent in the one case but not in the other, which makes it impossible to conflate the two types of regime. On the other hand, it passes over the fact that the persecution of the Jews began in 1933 and that from Crystal Night onward a great part of the bloody terror, far from being hidden from the German people, was carried out in the streets. Lies die hard, however; these two, in particular, continue to animate the attacks of revisionist historians in Germany and elsewhere still today.

The second piece of information concerns the only known text—at least until now—in which Heidegger explicitly mentions the gas chambers. The passage in question comes from an unpublished lecture on technology delivered at Bremen in 1949. "Agriculture is now a motorized food industry," Heidegger said, "the same thing in its essence as the production of corpses in the gas chambers and the extermination camps, the same thing as blockades and the reduction of countries to famine, the same thing as the manufacture of hydrogen bombs."[12] One wonders whether such an appalling comparison was the product of utter insensitivity or whether, to the contrary, it was a calculated provocation. Blindness or belligerence? Neither interpretation, it will be admitted, is to Heidegger's credit.

Such are the facts. Unflattering though they are, they remain secondary to this question of principle: is Heidegger's political involvement to be considered as intrinsically connected with his philosophy or instead as an eccentricity unrelated to it? In France, where the Heidegger cult has taken on disturbing proportions over the last forty years, the second option is more commonly favored. It is also, for different reasons, the solution adopted by Gadamer.[13] It runs up against two objections, however: one a matter of theoretical justification, the other a matter of fact.

On the one hand, it is hard to see how the separation of philosophy from politics can be justified in the case of a thinker for whom—as Heidegger himself said to Karl Löwith and as his disciple Jean Beaufret repeated—"everything hangs together."[14] On the other hand, there is nothing to indicate that in joining the Nazi Party Heidegger had the sense that he was breaking somehow with the inspiration of his previous work. Plainly the political implications of *Being and Time* ran in the direction advocated by the extreme German nationalist Right. To be sure, Heidegger changed, but only by remaining remarkably faithful to himself. And if in 1934, and then again after 1945, he distanced himself somewhat from the reality of Nazism, at no moment did he feel the need to renounce the basic convictions—philosophical *and* political—he had held since the late 1920s. On closer examination, the unity of these convictions makes it clear that Heidegger's allegiance to National Socialism was in no way external to the rest of his thought.

Being and Time is an unfinished work. As with all works of philosophy, there are deep reasons for this incompleteness—reasons that Heidegger himself stated in a letter addressed in April 1962 to the American philosopher William Richardson, a Jesuit who currently teaches at Boston College.

If we are to believe Heidegger's own account, the question that is placed at the heart of the book—the question of Being—had concerned him ever since he discovered Brentano's dissertation on Aristotle in 1907. Shortly afterwards, his reading of Husserl's *Logical Investigations* suggested a new way of approaching this ancient question via the phenomenological method, which made it possible to rediscover the very essence of things. Phenomenology then very quickly turned away in the direction of a new transcendental idealism, which Heidegger rejected because he wished instead to conceive Being in its temporality—in its "historiality." Husserl, however, in "Philosophy as Rigorous Science," had turned his back on both history and historicism.[15] Heidegger's thought, as it was first expressed in *Being and Time*, therefore found itself caught in a bind.

To resolve this conflict, so that he could analyze the question of Being in all of its aspects, Heidegger needed to separate the central problem of the 1927 book from whatever metaphysical connotation still attached to it. The analysis of the meaning of the metaphysical enterprise itself and the means for overcoming it, only sketched in *Being and Time*, had to be pushed to its furthest possible extreme—an attempt that was to occupy Heidegger until the end of his life. This is why there is no break in his work but simply, after 1927, an increasingly personal—and anti-Husserlian—interpretation of what phenomenology involves.

The best way to see what it involves may be to connect phenomenology with the intuition from which it originally stemmed, and which Heidegger often said constituted the principle around which his whole thought revolved. In certain contexts he used the term *twofoldness* to express this intuition.[16] It refers to the difference, imperceptible but absolute, that separates Being and being. Although they are closely related, since there cannot be being without Being, nor Being without being, they are nonetheless distinct from each other. The term *being* poses no problem here. The domain of beings is none other than the world to which we belong. Man is a being. God may be considered as the supreme being, theology amounting only to a branch of ontology—the science of being. By contrast, determining how the Being of being is distinguished from being—and, above all, why this distinction ought to be taken as fundamental—remains obscure.

What is Being? Despite its central importance in Heidegger's thought, the reader who seeks an answer in good faith is bound to be disappointed. For Heidegger says repeatedly it is a question that in principle cannot be given an answer. Being is not what metaphysicians call substance, mind, or matter. Nothing can be said about it since it is devoid of attributes; or, more exactly, the only thing that can be said is a tautology: Being is It itself ("Was ist das Sein? Es ist Es selbst").[17] Being, in other words, is irreducible to a concept, ungraspable by *logos*.

This, Heidegger claims, is why Western philosophy as a whole has overlooked it. *Philosophy, metaphysics, onto-theo-logy* are only synonyms—different names for a single failure, a single "forgetfulness," a single "veiling" of Being. All philosophers have failed in the same way, with the possible exception of the pre-Socratics, on the one hand, and Nietzsche, on the other.

They alone might conceivably have caught a *glimpse* of Being for a brief moment. But they lost it again in the very process of glimpsing it: the pre-Socratics, because they were at once retaken prisoner by *logos*; Nietzsche, because in making life the supreme value he committed himself to what Heidegger called—although Nietzsche himself rejected the term—a metaphysics of values.

The main point that emerges from this is that *logos*, or conceptual and demonstrative thinking, although it is indispensable for understanding beings, proves to be inadequate for the task of conceiving what "goes beyond" them (a claim that recalls the attack on "logocentrism" mounted in the 1930s by another pro-Nazi philosopher, Ludwig Klages [1872–1956]). *Logos*, which the pre-Socratics had helped to establish, achieved absolute supremacy over thought only with Plato. Accordingly, when one has understood Plato's error, one has understood the error of all philosophy. For all philosophy is Platonic—even that of Marx, Nietzsche, and Carnap, each of which amounted to a mere "reversal" or inversion of Platonism: to invert Platonism is to stand it on its head, not to escape it.[18] Such a view of the history of philosophy, which does away with materialism by reducing it to a simple variant of idealism, is rather schematic, to say the least. But it has the virtue of being clear, and of entailing consequences that are no less so. To the question, then, what is one to do if one wishes to avoid falling back into the classic philosophical error, the answer is that one must give up doing philosophy.

Being and Time was therefore to remain unfinished since it remained—as the homage to Husserl indicated—a work of philosophy. After 1927 Heidegger was no longer to write books in the usual sense. He was also to make it a point of honor, rather childishly, to decline the title of philosopher. Henceforth he wished to be known as a thinker.

IT WAS NOT ENOUGH for Heidegger to declare philosophy finished, however, to prove that he had in fact found an exit from it. It was still necessary, if the way out were to begin to become visible, that "thought" resolutely distance itself from the rationalist and humanist tradition that ever since its origin in ancient Greece had characterized philosophical discourse. In the aftermath of the First World War, the three dominant forms of this tradition were Christian rationalism, Marxist rationalism, and the liberal and secular rationalism embodied by Husserl, Russell, Cassirer, and Valéry, all of whom were deeply shaken by a conflict that for four years had ravaged Europe during the previous decade. It is hardly coincidental that these were the three currents of thought that from 1927 on Heidegger relentlessly attacked.

Marxism, as one might suspect, seemed to him to represent the most serious threat. So deeply did he abhor it that after the Second World War he pointed to the division of his country and the stationing of Soviet troops in Berlin in order to suggest that Hitler's campaign had been, at bottom, only a campaign against Communism—in other words, in retrospect, a "good" war.

Catholicism, the faith in which he himself had been raised, Heidegger abandoned in 1918. Afterwards he let no opportunity pass for combatting Christianity in general. In his summer semester lectures of 1935, subsequently published as *Introduction to Metaphysics*, or in the 1936 article devoted to elucidating Nietzsche's notion that "God is dead," for example, it is clear that the differences between Christianity and Judaism were less important to him than what they shared in common: he rejected both of them in the name of a German neopaganism that came straight out of the *Sturm und Drang* movement of the late eighteenth century.

Heidegger broke definitively with liberal rationalism—the rationalism of the *Aufklärung* and of phenomenology—following the appearance of *Being and Time*. An essential part of his later work was devoted to denouncing what he regarded as the evil empire of the three great idols of modern reason: science, technology, and the idea of progress. Whereas for Husserl science had its foundation in philosophy, itself conceived as rigorous science, Heidegger transferred the foundational function from philosophy to "thought" while asserting its incommensurability with science. Repeatedly he stressed that "science does not think."[19] This provocative formula, anti-Kantian and anti-Husserlian in spirit, is not dissimilar to proposition 6.21 of the *Tractatus*. The intentions of the two authors, however, were quite different. In declaring that a mathematical proposition "expresses no thought," Wittgenstein meant simply to detach mathematics from the Platonic base on which Frege had grounded it. Heidegger, by contrast, had a more subversive purpose in mind, for in affirming that science does not think he aimed at nothing less than depriving it of all intellectual dignity.

Technology seemed to Heidegger essentially no different than metaphysics, which he accused of wallowing in a state of dependence upon *logos* and, more specifically, *Logistik* (the term used by Heidegger to refer to the whole tradition of research issuing from Frege and Russell), holding it responsible—without adducing the least proof—for everything that was wrong with the world. "The desolation of the earth," he wrote in a series of notes composed in response to Carnap's attacks, was to be understood as "stemming from metaphysics,"[20] of which Carnap himself remained prisoner. In the same peremptory manner Heidegger asserted in 1935 that "Russia and America . . . are metaphysically the same, namely in regard to their world character and their relation to the spirit."[21] Thus after 1945 he assailed both these adversaries of the Third Reich, whose defeat had removed all possibility of checking the spiritual decadence of Europe.

As for the idea of progress, spread both by Communism and the "American Way of Life," unsurprisingly it found hardly any place in Heidegger's thought. As a faithful supporter of the conservative revolution, he sought salvation in the distant past rather than the future. This salvation could only take the form of a deliberate return to the past: a return to the sources of philosophy (the pre-Socratics) on the one hand, but also to the sources of Germanness, to the "purity" of unspoiled origins, prior to the dubious mixtures of later times; a return to the "homeland of Being," which was indistinguishable from the homeland (Heimat) itself; a return to the people (Volk), thought of as representing the warm, reassuring intimacy of a rural and protective family, the clearing in the forest and the path (Holzweg) through it, the mountain hut—in short, to all those archetypes that since the Romantic period, and even from the time of the Lutheran Reformation, had sung the plaintive song of the German soul and its nostalgia for a lost unity (or, more precisely, for one that had never been attained), to say nothing of its episodic and fantastic resentment of the Jew, archetype of an "inauthentic," "aberrant," and, above all, "anti-German" way of life.

To this threefold aversion to science, technology, and progress came also to be added Heidegger's well-known suspicion of ethics, which led him to decree that ethics had no place in a "thought of Being." Here again one observes a superficial convergence with the Wittgensteinian idea that ethics is impossible. But the underlying motivations are, once again, quite different. Although Wittgenstein limited himself to observing that one cannot express judgments about values in a language of facts, Heidegger challenged the very notion of a hierarchy of values since it could only operate within a rational— and, therefore, in his terms, metaphysical—discourse. The point of such a strategy will be readily grasped: absent any concern for values, there is no longer any need to furnish a justification for ethical choices. What better way to make a clean sweep of things, the indispensable condition of ushering in a system founded on force rather than law?

The recourse to force derived in turn from a fundamental conservatism. Because might makes right only so long as one remains stronger than everyone else, the important thing is to remain the strongest of all for as long a time as possible. This is the source of the "discourse of authority" dear to Heidegger and practiced long after the end of his rectorship, at once an oracular style of pronouncement (a statement's very utterance by the master serving as its own proof—"He said it, therefore it must be true") and a magical one, conferring upon citation (provided that this was to another unchallengeable "guide"—Hitler in 1933, Heraclitus in the 1940s, Hölderlin in the later years) the role normally assigned in philosophy to argumentation. And if such a discourse had no room for demonstrative reason, so much the worse; it was reason, obviously, that was in the wrong.

It scarcely comes as a surprise, then, even after so rapid a summary as this, that one of the first texts Heidegger published after the war was the *Letter on Humanism* (addressed to Jean Beaufret in 1946), in which he mercilessly denounced the "misdeeds" of European humanism, embodied at that moment by Sartre; nor that in the brief interview he gave in 1966, clearly intended for posterity, he was still capable of issuing a stinging rebuke to democratic ideals, the fruits of the rationalism of the Enlightenment.

A WAY OF THINKING so deliberately oriented toward a mythical beginning in the remote past could only be inclined to ignore actual history—to empty it of all content, indeed to rewrite it to suit the author's own interests. Heidegger was unable, in the event, to avoid either of these temptations.

It may be objected that the problem of historicity occupies a central place in *Being and Time* and that it was exactly this that attracted Sartre to Heidegger in the late 1930s. But the interpretation of this work that Sartre (whose command of German was poor) developed between 1938 and 1943 rested in fact on a misunderstanding, which Heidegger's hostility toward him was later to bring out clearly. For the historiality of *Dasein*, as the thinker of Freiburg conceived it, was to be taken in an "abyssal" sense that has nothing to do with what common mortals understand by history.

To gauge the extent of the discrepancy between reality and discourse in Heidegger, it suffices to consider the account he proposed after 1935 of the history of Western philosophy. This account, puzzling at first sight, can be explained by putting it back—as Jean-Pierre Faye has done[22]—in the political context that generated it: an internal Party debate over National Socialist philosophy that emerged in the spring of 1934. In April of that year, the rector of the University of Frankfurt, Ernst Krieck, the leading representative of the school of "racial" anthropology and a candidate for the role of the regime's official ideologist (he later became an Obersturmbannführer SS), unleashed a campaign aimed at thoroughly discrediting the former Freiburg rector by publishing in the Nazi journal *Volk im Werden* (People in Transformation) an article in which Heidegger's philosophy was characterized as "metaphysical nihilism" (no doubt because there was much talk of "nothingness" in "What Is Metaphysics?") and compared to the "ratiocinations" of "Jewish scribblers" (presumably Husserl).

To this most dangerous of all charges Heidegger responded by skillfully reversing the terms of the equation. The following year, in his summer term lectures (published as *Introduction to Metaphysics*), he affirmed that nihilism consists in "getting bogged down" in being rather than aiming upwards at Being, and that the thought of Being as Being (which includes the thought of nothingness) remained the only way of freeing oneself of it. In other words, it was not Heidegger, but the adversaries of Being (read: Krieck and the anti-Heideggerian Nazis) who were the real nihilists.

This response did not constitute the turn (*die Kehre*) that Heidegger later spoke of in describing the change of direction required in order to move on from *Being and Time*; his writings from the period between 1927 and 1929 had already announced the need for a "destruction" of metaphysics. It amounted instead to a new strategy, which obliged Heidegger to rewrite the history of metaphysics as the history of nihilism—a very effective strategy, all things considered, since from 1935 to 1945 it permitted him to reply to accusations coming from within the Party and after the war enabled him to establish retroactively the fiction that he had been an opponent of Nazism.

Three particularly significant texts punctuated this laborious enterprise. In an epilogue added in 1943 to *What Is Metaphysics?* that, without mentioning Krieck by name, referred to the accusations brought by him against Heidegger in 1934 (and again in a second article published in *Volk im Werden* in October 1940), Heidegger explained that the famous lecture reprinted in this book already had the secret purpose of overcoming nihilism. An introduction tacked on to the same book in 1949 asserted that nihilism coincided with the entire history of metaphysics, "from Anaximander to Nietzsche." Finally, a 1955 piece composed in homage to the nationalist writer Ernst Jünger (1895–1998)—whose pamphlet *Total Mobilization* (1930) inspired the concept "total state" later devised by the political theorist Carl Schmidt

(1888–1985), an obligatory point of reference for all fascist ideologists of the period—advanced the thesis that the overcoming (*Überwindung*) of nihilism (considered as equivalent to metaphysics) could be carried out only by means of its appropriation (*Verwindung*),[23] which is to say, once again, by its destruction or, more exactly, its deconstruction by the abandonment (*Abbau*)[24] of its constitutive representations.

The point of such claims may seem today rather obscure. To understand what was at issue, let us pause to reflect for a moment upon their most enigmatic aspect: the very doubtful version Heidegger gave of Nietzsche's thought in his course lectures of 1936–40,[25] characterizing it as the supreme form of Western nihilism. It needs to be recalled, first, that Nietzsche's critique of values, directed against Platonism, Christianity, and socialism but also against bourgeois stupidity and anti-Semitism—all summed up in the "German spirit" incarnated for him by Wagner—likewise rested on a thoroughgoing denunciation of European philosophy. On the one hand, Nietzsche had already characterized metaphysics in a pejorative sense; on the other, he reproached it for having led to "nihilism," a term borrowed from the *Essays in Contemporary Psychology* (1883) by the French writer Paul Bourget. Bourget diagnosed nihilism as the disease of modern Europe and ascribed it to the "weariness" that a "too thoughtful humanity" had come to feel for its own thought. It amounted, then, to a will to self-annihilation, which Nietzsche could only detest since for him life was the sole authentic value. By contrast, he saw his own "active" nihilism, which is to say the ambition to destroy all values opposed to life, as the indispensable prelude to the glorious "transmutation" announced by Zarathustra.

Nietzsche's critique came to be severely distorted after his death in 1900, first by his sister—married to a notorious anti-Semite for whom he had only contempt—then by the extreme German nationalist Right during the First World War and, finally, by the Nazis in the 1930s. The Nazis attempted to appropriate the theme of "will to power," in particular, looking to turn it to their advantage by dressing it up in a pseudo-biological language based on the exaltation of "race" and of brute force. It would have been easy for Heidegger, in 1935, to show that such a reading was falsely reductive. But he was interested less, politically speaking, in rectifying a misinterpretation (and a crude one at that) than in denouncing as metaphysics the biologizing philosophy of Krieck, who, through his worship of life, unwittingly continued to express himself in the nihilistic language of a philosophy of values.

Heidegger's main interest in his lectures on Nietzsche's philosophy, then, was to show it to be inadequate—and this for the sole purpose of appearing more revolutionary than the official party ideologues. Nietzsche did indeed speak of overturning the usual assumptions of metaphysics by rehabilitating the sensible in relation to the intelligible. But, Heidegger held, although one may change the meaning of a system—any system—by overturning it, one does not thereby manage to escape it. Nietzsche therefore remained, in spite of himself, a prisoner of nihilism. In this he was only the latest representative of that long and harmful "epoch" whose history had begun with Anaximander and, by the same token, the first to show the necessity, if nihilism were to be escaped, of inventing a truly new way out, far bolder than any mere transmutation of values. Heidegger pretended, first to the Nazis and then, after 1945, to their conquerors, that only "thought of Being"—as the true "homeland" of man—could lead the way out from nihilism.

As vague as they were arbitrary, these arguments nonetheless had the advantage of allowing Heidegger not to be overly worried about his fate either before or after 1945. In the end, the philosopher was able to escape the criticisms of both the Nazis and the anti-Nazis—a disquieting double game. For all sorts of reasons, however, the simple truth of the matter—namely, that the interpretation of Nietzsche constituted a decisive issue in the factional struggles within the Nazi party—is still not accepted in Heideggerian circles.

Furthermore, from 1945 onward Heidegger took ever greater precautions to frustrate any inquiry into the true nature of his prior positions that probed too deeply. The *Letter on Humanism*, for example, is evidence of the attempt to demonstrate that his antihumanism actually was a product of a higher humanism, to clear his use of the words *homeland* and *the West* of all suspicion, and to deflect the accusation of having favored barbarism in advocating the destruction of values. In a lecture dating from the same year, "What Are Poets For?" (1946), he characterized the present epoch, whose outstanding event was the American-Soviet victory, as a "destitute time" and the "world's night."[26] Later, in the 1950s, he wound up taking refuge in a purely speculative sphere, as though his "meditations" were now too profound to sustain the least contact with the real history of human beings or with the mundane events of this world. Abandoning humanity to the pernicious reign of technology, he spent the rest of his life sculpting for posterity his reputation as a great thinker, misunderstood, condemned to internal exile, having virtually no one worthwhile to talk with apart from Heraclitus and Hölderlin. The Heidegger-Hölderlin dialogue, in particular, marked by the final transformation of the question of Being into a poetico-mystical search for the "sacred"—primordial, "tautological," and ineffable—came to exercise a peculiar sort of cultural fascination. The fascination, it is true, remained rather limited within Germany itself. In the Latin countries, however, and above all in France, it wreaked havoc.

THERE IS A CURIOUS CHAPTER in the recent history of ideas that might be entitled "How the French Left, to Avoid Marx, Saved Heidegger from Oblivion."

Heidegger's thought had come into fashion very early, having by the beginning of the 1930s already been well received in Paris. Georges Gurvitch devoted a part of his book on *Current Tendencies in German Philosophy* (1930) to it. The young Emmanuel Levinas, who in 1927 was filled with enthusiasm for *Being and Time*, published an article in 1932 on "Martin Heidegger and Ontology." The association of the rector of Freiburg with National Socialism, if it was known in France as early as 1933—Alexandre Koyré, among others, spoke of it to Levinas[27]—did not yet arouse the revulsion that the war, and with it the revelation of the Holocaust, were later to inspire. Sartre could therefore allow himself to be seduced without undue qualms by the dialectic of "being" and "nothingness" he discovered in 1938 through the French translation of *What Is Metaphysics?* made by Henry Corbin (Koyré's assistant at the École Pratique des Hautes Études and later a specialist on Iranian Shiism).

With the Liberation, the success of Sartrian existentialism brought Heidegger's work back into the media spotlight. But in the meantime the burden of Heidegger's political allegiances had begun to weigh on his reputation. The true nature of Nazism having become clear, Sartre now decided to dissociate himself from Heidegger by publishing in his journal *Les Temps modernes*, in 1946–47, five articles that added most of the available pieces of information to the file. Three of these articles—by Maurice de Gandillac, Karl Löwith, and Eric Weil—condemned Heidegger; only Alphonse de Waelhens and Frédéric de Towarnicki tried to absolve him. From that point the debate was on. Can philosophy be separated from politics? Can a boundary be fixed between, on the one hand, the theoretical condemnation of humanism and, on the other, admiration for National Socialism? Sartre, for his part, replied in the negative. He did make a brief visit in 1952 to Heidegger, marked by mutual incomprehension, but afterwards ceased to refer to his thought, which was rejected more clearly still by the Marxists. Among those who challenged both Marx and the *marxisant* Sartre of the 1950s, various more or less ambiguous attitudes toward Heidegger began to emerge.

The first of these resembled a sort of religious fascination. Its leading representative, Jean Beaufret (1907–82), was a former member of the Resistance. One finds it difficult to fathom the motives that years later led him to write friendly letters (recently published) to the French revisionist Robert Faurisson, the man who believed he had dispelled the "myth" of the gas chambers. But, frankly, one scarcely understands any better why Beaufret, who hastened to go to see Heidegger immediately after the war, in 1946, sought to clear his name by pretending that politics did not interest the self-styled thinker and worked to establish a fervent cult around him—a cult of which he, Beaufret, became the high priest.

A variant of this pious attitude consisted in conceding—as did, for example, François Fédier, one of the principal French translators of Heidegger—that the philosopher had indeed committed some mistakes in 1933, but that the weight of these errors remained negligible by comparison with the body of his work. What is awkward about this position is that it undermines the coherence of the work as a whole, since many writings have to be excluded from it in order for it to be made beyond reproach. The thought of any such editing ran counter to the wishes of Heidegger himself, who until the end of his life refused utterly and completely to engage in self-criticism.

More surprising still was the behavior of a group of intellectuals who, despite the trials and tribulations of recent history, were intent on giving absolute priority to Franco-German dialogue. A similar tendency had worked to ensure the success of Schopenhauer in France around 1880 and, toward 1930, of Hegel. In the 1950s this group included, among others, Alexandre Kojève, Jean Hyppolite, and Jean Wahl. These three were at once anti-Nazi and anti-Communist (Kojève himself emphasized that his admiration for Stalin owed nothing to Marx), readers of Hegel (whose *Phenomenology of Spirit* Hyppolite had translated in 1941), and interested in Nietzsche, Husserl, and Heidegger. Despite Heidegger's errors, they resolved to honor him with a place in the great Germanic tradition, which for them—despite three wars in less than a century—still retained all of its former prestige.

Why should they have chosen to do such a thing? Out of a desire for reconciliation, a wish to be done with Franco-German contention, and perhaps also an urge to erase the trauma experienced by convinced Germanophiles with the revelation of the Holocaust. Above all, however, it was because the French intelligentsia of the 1950s, having refused Sartre and Marx, no longer knew which philosophical saint to swear by. Heidegger thus appeared as a possible savior—all the more as his thought, portrayed as apolitical by his eulogists, answered directly to the prayers of intellectuals who, after Auschwitz and Hiroshima, saw their last political illusions consumed in the blaze of colonial conflict in Algeria and Indochina.

Heidegger's success in France began in earnest in 1955 with the famous ten-day conference at Cerisy-la-Salle organized in his honor by Beaufret and Kostas Axelos (b. 1924). Sartre and Merleau-Ponty refused to attend, but Heidegger made the acquaintance of the poet René Char and, outside the event, passed a few days in the company of the psychoanalyst Jacques Lacan. Lacan saw in Heideggerian existentialism a tragic dimension lacking in Sartre that also made it possible to give an added dimension of philosophical soul to Freud's positivist doctrines. As for Char, like Beaufret a former member of the Resistance, he felt flattered by the interest shown in him by the German thinker. The two men got along famously. Another important writer, who was absent from Cerisy but who had mixed with the extreme Right in the 1930s, Maurice Blanchot, also helped spread the thought of the later Heidegger—the one whose career was restarted in 1946—in avant-garde circles. Heidegger, for his part, was delighted. He could only agree wholeheartedly with his new friends. After all, he had everything to gain: at the very moment when young philosophers in Germany (for example, Habermas) were moving away from him, France now took it upon itself to assure him of a new fame.

Three seminars given by Heidegger at Thor, near Avignon, at the invitation of René Char in 1966, 1968, and 1969 raised this celebrity to its full height. Little by little the circle of Heideggerians became enlarged. Among the philosophers adding their names to the list of those already mentioned were Paul Ricoeur, Michel Foucault, and Jacques Derrida. Ricoeur was developing—at the same time as Gadamer—a "hermeneutic" conception of phenomenology colored by Christianity, existentialism, and psychoanalysis. Foucault used Heidegger to reread Nietzsche. And Derrida, under the influence of Blanchot, situated his own enterprise—"deconstructing" metaphysics—in a direct line of descent from the Heideggerian *Abbau*. Even Louis Althusser, a Marxist, was temporarily caught up in the fashion of the day.

How is the rapidity with which this fashion spread in intellectual circles to be explained? To the concern of some with forgiveness, and the Germanophilia and anti-Communism of others, a new factor was added at the end of the 1960s: the vogue of structuralism in the social sciences. To be sure, these sciences were not interested in Heidegger, but their theoretical antihumanism—elaborated by Lévi-Strauss, Lacan, Althusser, and Foucault—fit well with the antihumanism that had characterized Heidegger's thought since 1927. Furthermore, the renewed interest in language and signs in general brought about by structuralism explains why Blanchot, Foucault, and Derrida, given their attentiveness to problems associated with writing, should have been attracted by the daring style of the master of Freiburg, by his way of deliberately transgressing the accepted limits of philosophical expression—even if their aestheticizing reading of his work meant forgetting its political implications.

By 1961 the only discordant voice left to be heard was that of Jean-Pierre Faye. His various articles did not, however, succeed in turning back the current of fashion, any more than the excellent analysis by the sociologist Pierre Bourdieu in The Political Ontology of Martin Heidegger (1988) would do later. As for the critical biographies by Victor Farias (marred by a good many errors) and Hugo Ott (a very solid piece of scholarship) that appeared in 1987 and 1988, respectively, they provoked such hostile reactions in France—perhaps because they confirmed what those who wished to know already knew, the bulk of the Heidegger file having always been open to inspection—that to recount the history of this episode would require a separate study of its own.[28]

No doubt Ott's work came too late since Heidegger had in the meantime been admitted to the official list of authors whom the French Ministry of Education recommends be studied by students preparing for the baccalauréat—a list that includes, by contrast, neither Russell, nor Wittgenstein, nor Carnap, nor Marcuse.

IN THE 1966 INTERVIEW with Der Spiegel, Heidegger stated that his French friends (possibly only Beaufret) had admitted to him that when they wished to think—to "really philosophize"—they had to abandon their own language for German, so great did its intellectual superiority to French seem to them.

The naïveté of this remark merits no comment. By contrast, it is worth the trouble to take a look, as Henri Meschonnic has done,[29] at Heidegger's language. Metaphors and puns abound in it, as well as those neologisms that the plasticity of German favors more than does French. If Heidegger, who both used and abused the special possibilities of his native tongue, had aspired only to the noble title of poet, there would have been no great problem.

But because he claimed to speak of the true, even of Being itself, his verbal acrobatics came to be elevated to the rank of "thought"—to the detriment, of course, of conceptual language as well as of the demonstrative procedures normally required of philosophy.

It is impossible in a few sentences to describe the pernicious influence that Heidegger's example has had upon generations of students—above all in France, where translators and commentators did not hesitate to add to it, overlaying the master's gibberish with their own jargon and threatening with reprisals anyone who dared criticize them for it. But what is the point of complaining, when Heidegger himself had warned against the dangers of reason? Indeed, in 1943 he wrote that reason was "the most stiff-necked adversary of thought."[30] Here we have a frank declaration of antirationalist faith, unburdened by nuance. If one takes it literally, it must be concluded that Heidegger's thought, by locating itself outside the field of conventional philosophy, escapes all philosophical criticism. There would appear to be no alternative, then, but to adopt one of the following three positions:

— One accepts Heidegger's thought as true and therefore abandons philosophy altogether;

— One regards it as belonging to a literary genre having no relation to philosophy, which makes it possible to go on practicing philosophy as though nothing had happened;

— One redefines the practice of philosophy (as Richard Rorty has suggested) broadly enough to be able to include in it Heidegger's thought, among others. In this case one would have to hold that, far from being a method of conceptual analysis making it possible to determine, by means of rational argument, the relative correctness of certain intellectual choices, philosophy is only a mode of subjective expression endowed with complete autonomy regarding the definition of its own codes of practice—in short, a sort of quasi-private language whose purpose is to increase the happiness of its author and, possibly, of his readers as well.

It must be said that none of these solutions is fully satisfactory. The first is purely religious, requiring belief without understanding. The second leaves unexplained the definite—and hardly negligible—impact that Heidegger has had upon many professional philosophers. The third amounts to depriving philosophy of its special character and, what is more serious, undermines its very basis in rational argument.

The situation is not without a way out, however. On closer inspection it becomes clear that the question that produced these three replies—what is one to make of Heidegger's thought if it lies outside the field of reason?—is not the right question, at least to the extent that it derives from a mistaken premise. It is plain that Heidegger, contrary to his own claim, never abandoned the rationalism that he ceaselessly denounced: first, because he spent a large part of his career reading and commenting (sometimes with great verve) on philosophical texts; second, because even in his most obscure writings he nonetheless relied (although not always explicitly) on concepts and argumentation—as indeed he had to do if his thought was not to be condemned to total unintelligibility. Finally, by virtue of the fact that his thought also had a political side, closely related to a particular ideology, it depended on another form of rationality—one that for twelve years enabled National Socialism to hold German society utterly in its sway, underlying the organization of the Nazi war effort and even the Final Solution itself.

The real problem is therefore, paradoxically, the following. Heidegger's thought, if it were only pure thought, would be no more embarrassing than if it were pure poetry. Unfortunately it is neither one nor the other. It is, in the last analysis, only a philosophy—but a philosophy of the most dubious kind, since it rests on antirationalist premises and yet nonetheless manages to express itself in a sufficiently rational language to convince certain readers. And if Heidegger's philosophy is both problematic and dangerous, this is because reason and unreason are united in it in a unique and particularly troubling way—exactly as the horror peculiar to Auschwitz itself also involved an unprecedented combination of madness, in its purpose, and rationality, in the means used to achieve it.

In the aftermath of the Second World War it became necessary to inquire into the origins of this combination in order to understand how, in the space of two centuries, the Enlightenment could have lost its way as it did. This meant having to treat reason itself as a case to be opened up for investigation.

Preliminary Inquiries

The survivors of the Nazi camps long remained silent, until the appearance in the 1960s of a revisionist movement aimed at denying the very existence of the Holocaust[31] reawakened in them the desire to talk, to bear witness while there was still time. As a result, the reasons for their earlier silence came to light as well.

The first of these reasons was that words did not exist to express the horror of what they had survived. Words did not exist to conceive of Auschwitz—to the extent that it was still possible to "think after Auschwitz," to "surmount the unsurmountable."[32] Indeed, the mere utterance of this latter phrase rekindled a painful debate. Is there a uniqueness to the crime of the Holocaust or not? One sometimes fears that answering this question in the affirmative amounts to minimizing the atrocity of other massacres, such as Hiroshima, or indeed of offending against the memory of other peoples— especially the Armenians and the Tutsis of Rwanda, who have also been the victims of attempts at genocide during the course of the present century. However, there is no choice but to accord the Holocaust the sad privilege of a distinct singularity, due to the manner—at once massive and methodical, cold and rational—in which the extermination of the Jews was carried out between 1941 and 1945 along with the extermination, during the same period and in the same revolting way, of the Gypsies.

Awareness of the Nazi program of "racial purification"—implicitly stated in 1925 in a book, *Mein Kampf*, that was widely translated and accessible to all—did not prevent the Western democracies from supporting the Third Reich for several years (here one thinks of their regular participation in the Olympic Games of 1936) or the Vatican and the Soviet Union from concluding treaties with it. After the Crystal Night of November 1938, nothing seemed capable of checking the escalation of violence. Moreover, the intention to annihilate the Jews was made explicit in a speech delivered by Hitler in January 1939. Although historians still dispute the exact date on which the decision was made to go forward with the Final Solution, it was likely prior to the attack on the Soviet Union. It very probably dated, as Hannah Arendt and Léon Poliakov have argued, from the end of 1940. The first organized massacres of Jewish populations were committed in late June 1941 by the Einsatzgruppen in the wake of the German invasion of the Soviet Union. The first gassings took place in a van at Chelmno, in Poland, on 8 December 1941. Never had the enterprise of collective assassination been planned—and carried through to the end—with such sangfroid and singleness of purpose.

Nor in the course of history had any enterprise of this kind benefited from the combined and irresistible support of science, technology, and a perfectly organized bureaucracy: three resources that National Socialism knew how to exploit to the fullest, leading in 1942–43 to the proliferation of actual killing factories—the death camps. These would not have been possible without the collaboration of many technicians, the planned production of toxic gases in industrial quantities, and the efficiency shown at all levels of the German government in arresting Jews and rounding them up in camps—in short, without the complicity of a non-negligible part of the German population, as Daniel J. Goldhagen has recently shown.[33]

It needs once again to be emphasized that the National Socialist government of Germany—and no other regime—invented this monstrous thing, the extermination camp, and that it also remains the only regime to have carried out extermination on such a scale. To be sure, both work and deportation camps had been set up in the Soviet Union at the end of the 1920s. But while their existence was in and of itself reprehensible, the possibility at least of getting out of them alive was not ruled out in advance. Hitler's Germany was the first country to establish *death camps*: camps exclusively conceived for the killing of all those who were brought to them, women and children included, to say nothing of the medical "experiments" and other tortures inflicted there upon powerless victims, none of whom, it had been decided beforehand, would be allowed to escape.

There is indeed, then, a difference between deportation camps and extermination camps, and one that it would be wrong to try to erase. There are some today who, whether out of hatred for Communism or from anti-Semitism, claim that Hitler's crimes were not worse than those of Stalin—a familiar allegation since the time of the Nuremburg trials in the discourse of old and new Nazis alike. To dispose of this claim it is enough to remember, as Poliakov has rightly observed, that Hitler assassinated children whereas Stalin contented himself with "reeducating" them[34]—a detail that, out of respect for the victims, it is important not to lose sight of.

It is understandable that prior to Auschwitz no one could have imagined how far the Nazi horror would go; that no anti-Nazi could have foreseen that it would reach its height right in the heart of Europe, in the middle of the twentieth century; and that, even if this horror—a horror without precedent—were to be revealed to the world, it would not readily be accepted. In 1945, of course, there was no longer any question of reacting to the news with skepticism, since the evidence already available by that point was sufficient to dispel disbelief at once. But there was a more profound problem. Confronted with the scale of the Holocaust, the Western world experienced a feeling of guilt so intense that, finding itself incapable of actually assuming this guilt, it moved to reject it altogether. It chose to repress the memory of the crime rather than to try to analyze its causes; and, to protect itself against a possible recurrence of what it had repressed, it adopted for more than a quarter-century a strategy founded on indifference: what had actually occurred in the camps was not something worthy of curiosity, not even of strictly scientific curiosity.

This was the second reason why the survivors hesitated so long to speak. They felt themselves surrounded by a wall of indifference, never very far removed from silent hostility and unconscious reproach. They were silent not only because words were lacking to them; they were silent also because we did not wish to hear them.

WAS THE SUBJECT OF AUSCHWITZ taboo after the war? The great works of the postwar period, whether philosophical, literary, or artistic, had little in any case to say about it. When they did, they evoked the "unnameable"—to quote Beckett's term—in a metaphorical way, as if this "thing" could not be spoken of directly, having been pushed back beyond the limits of the representable.

The shortcomings of even the best-intentioned filmmakers are instructive in this regard. Alain Resnais's Night and Fog (1955) constituted the first attempt to deal with the subject but hardly stressed the Jewishness of the victims of the genocide. Holocaust (1978) was an unfortunate television "docudrama," utterly devoid of the tragic reality of death. As for Schindler's List (1993), the naive optimism that suffuses Spielberg's screenplay is not likely to give the uninformed viewer a true sense of the actual drama. The only film, finally, that has been equal to the challenge of the Holocaust remains Claude Lanzmann's Shoah (1985), no doubt because it is not a fictional treatment but a scrupulous collection of firsthand accounts.

Did philosophers succeed any better? Most of them, to tell the truth, went on again with their lives after 1945 as if Auschwitz had never happened. Particularly telling in this connection was the attitude of Hans-Georg Gadamer. Although there was no doubt of his moral disapproval of anti-Semitism, Gadamer continued throughout the Third Reich to exercise his academic functions within the new framework imposed by the Nazis. He admitted, moreover, in his autobiography (published in 1977)[35] that during this period he did not show the least sign of courage. And if his major work, Truth and Method (1960), laid the basis for a hermeneutic philosophy aimed at deciphering the meaning of human events from a perspective that was at once phenomenological and existentialist, one finds in it no real reflection on contemporary history or any attempt to understand—even after the fact—by what torturous detours the glorious heritage of German idealism could have been placed in the service of genocidal barbarism.

In France the attitude of the philosophical community as a whole in the years that followed the end of the war was likewise discreet. It is true that two exceptions stand out against this background of silence and neglect. The first is Jean-Paul Sartre, whose *Reflections on the Jewish Question* (1946) directly confronted anti-Semitism. The book failed, however, to propose an original analysis of the phenomenon; written in haste, it lacked serious documentation. An unwitting consumer of anti-Semitic clichés, common in prewar France, and—like Raymond Aron—the prisoner of assimilationist conceptions still prevalent among French Jews themselves, Sartre did not recognize at the time the cultural uniqueness of Judaism: the Jew, for him, was only an "object" created by the regard of the other and therefore almost did not exist. It was only twenty years later, with his first visit to Israel in 1967, that Sartre was able to remedy his ignorance and overcome the prejudices of his past.

The second exception is Vladimir Jankélévitch (1903–85). Although he was the son of a translator who had helped introduce certain of the works of Hegel and Freud to French readers before the war, and although in 1933 he himself had defended a doctoral thesis on the later philosophy of Schelling, Jankélévitch decided in 1945 to break all ties linking him with German language and culture. His refusal to pardon Nazi officials extended as a result to all German citizens, whom he saw as necessarily complicitous, and even to their descendants. This radical attitude—to which he gave expression in two fine books, *In Honor and Dignity* (1948) and *To Pardon?* (1971)—was honorable and yet nonetheless inadequate to the extent that it rested on the highly questionable notion of collective guilt, and to the extent also that it misunderstood an essential aspect of Nazi barbarism in reducing it to the dimensions of an exclusively German problem.

Very few philosophers, then, tried in the aftermath of the Second World War to understand how Auschwitz could have become possible. The most important attempts remain those of Hannah Arendt (1906–75) and Karl Jaspers (1883–1969)—in particular the course of lectures given by Jaspers at the University of Heidelberg at the beginning of 1946, published later the same year as *The Question of Guilt*.

LIKE OTHER GERMANS of his generation, Jaspers was briefly tempted in his youth by nationalism, passing subsequently through an existentialist phase in the 1920s that led him to move away from Husserl and closer to Heidegger, with whom he became friendly. Because Jaspers was a Protestant married to a Jew, however, Hitler's triumph shattered his career. From 1933 on he was nonetheless one of the very few Christian intellectuals in Germany to resolutely oppose Nazism with the full weight of his reputation. In 1937 he was removed from the chair he occupied at Heidelberg and then, the following year, forbidden to publish. At this point he broke with Heidegger. Reinstated to his post at Heidelberg in January 1946, he was the first German to address—with courageous lucidity—the question of guilt: that of Germany, obviously, but also that of humanity, the whole of which was implicated by the cruelty of the Holocaust.

In *The Question of Guilt* Jaspers refrained from explicitly evoking memories of this event. But it was clearly with reference to the fact of the Holocaust, which could no longer be ignored, that he organized his analysis of the spiritual condition of Germany following its defeat—this at the time of the first Nuremburg trial, when the notion of a crime against humanity was beginning to take hold in individual consciences as well as in international law.

Jaspers argued that the concept of guilt needed to be examined in four senses: criminal, political, moral, and metaphysical. From the criminal (or judicial) point of view, only individuals having actually committed acts judged to be crimes are guilty. From the political point of view, all the citizens of a state—at least those whose government is the result of democratic elections, as was the case with Hitler's regime—share responsibility for the acts, and therefore the crimes, carried out by this state. From the moral point of view, all who witness such crimes must ask themselves if they have always done their best to behave honorably, even under the most difficult conditions. From the metaphysical point of view, finally, which is to say from the point of view of universal brotherhood, each of us is affected by what happens to others, even if apparently we can do nothing about it—for no one can seriously declare himself or herself indifferent to the mistreatment of others, whether next door or the other side of the planet.

From these definitions Jaspers drew two series of conclusions. First, he observed, caution must be exercised in assigning collective responsibility since, strictly speaking, this notion has no sense from either the judicial, moral, or metaphysical point of view. It does have a sense, by contrast, from the political point of view. All German citizens, in fact, whether they were Nazis or not, had an obligation to ask themselves how a National Socialist state, the product of free elections, could have established itself in 1933 and carried on without any real opposition for twelve years.

Was this an accident of German history? Jaspers's answer, though it is only briefly sketched, is one of remarkable firmness: National Socialism was the last avatar of a Germanic nationalism that, from the Reformation to the Treaty of Versailles, assumed increasingly aggressive forms in response to the difficulties experienced by the German nation in achieving political unity. With Hitler, this nationalism had become openly criminal. Germany thus could not turn the page of National Socialism in its history as one closes up a parenthesis. If it wished to be reborn spiritually, it would have to draw the appropriate lessons from its past. That is, the German people had to resolve to regard Auschwitz as representing a turning point in their history. In this regard Jaspers was disappointed by the subsequent course of events in the Federal Republic, whose government seemed to him more concerned at the end of the 1940s with forgetting than reflecting. In 1948 he accepted a chair at the University of Basel and eventually applied for Swiss citizenship.

A second series of conclusions concerned the notions of moral and metaphysical responsibility. These could have only an individual sense, not a collective one. But with respect to the question of moral responsibility, it had to be posed to all Germans who remained in Germany under the Third Reich, and, with respect to metaphysical responsibility, to humanity as a whole. In underlining this last point, it is to Jaspers's credit that he succeeded at last in placing the problem in its proper perspective. Jewish organizations that escaped Nazi control, in Palestine as in Switzerland and the United States, had very quickly alerted Western governments to the implementation of the Final Solution. News of the first massacres carried out by the Einsatzgruppen appeared in a small article in the 26 October 1941 edition of the *New York Times*.[36] The following year, on 26 June 1942, the *Boston Globe* reported that these massacres had already accounted for the death of seven hundred thousand Jews. Two months later, in August, evidence of the existence of the gas chambers reached the United States. The *National Jewish Monthly* made it public in its October issue of that year. By the end of 1942, no doubt remained about the reality of the genocide that was taking place in Europe.

Neither the American government, however, nor any of the other Allied powers, nor the Vatican took any specific steps in response to the news. No plan for rescuing the Jews was devised. When Allied bombers reached Auschwitz in 1944, only industrial sites were targeted: the extermination camp a few kilometers away was ignored. As for the Red Army, it dithered for several days after arriving in the immediate vicinity of the camp before finally occupying it. These delays, these proofs of indifference—which historians generally omit to mention—are not to be dismissed as mere details. Indeed, they have a metaphysical meaning, at least to the extent that they force us to reflect upon the tragic consequences to which an absence of solidarity among peoples may give rise. The present international situation renders such reflection no less necessary today than it was a half-century ago.

WHEREAS JASPERS INQUIRED as a moralist into the many meanings of Auschwitz, eternal symbol of the Nazi extermination of the Jews, Hannah Arendt tried to understand its genesis on the basis of the political and social history of Europe in the nineteenth and twentieth centuries.

Born in Hannover in 1906, Arendt studied philosophy at Marburg, Freiburg, and Heidelberg. Her teachers were Heidegger—with whom she had a lasting and complex relationship,[37] to which the homage that she paid him on his eightieth birthday testifies—and then Jaspers—a lifelong friend whose literary executor she became on his death in 1969. She managed to complete a thesis, "The Concept of Love in Saint Augustine," written under Jaspers's direction and published in 1929, and to begin a biography of Rahel Varnhagen (which appeared only in 1958) before the events of 1933 forced her to leave Germany, going first to Prague and then to Paris. Attracted to Zionism, she participated while in France in the activities of L'Aliya des Jeunes, an organization that helped arrange the emigration of young Jews to Palestine, and in this capacity made a trip to Jerusalem in 1935. She came back with mixed emotions. Although she admired the socialist ideals of the *kibbutzim*, she criticized the Jewish settlers for their tendency to cut themselves off from what was happening in the rest of the world. She rejoiced in the creation of the state of Israel after the war but often felt it necessary to remind its leaders of the necessity for Judeo-Arab cooperation.

In 1940 Arendt was temporarily interned in a camp at Gurs, in the French department of Pyrénées-Atlantiques, from which she managed to cross over into Spain—only several weeks after the failed attempt of her friend Walter Benjamin, whose last manuscripts she helped save. In 1941 she settled in the United States, where she earned her living writing for newspapers and lecturing. Shortly before the end of the war, she began to work on a book provisionally called "Elements of Shame: Anti-Semitism, Imperialism, and Racism, or the Three Columns of Hell." Finished in the fall of 1949, it appeared in 1951 as *The Origins of Totalitarianism*.

In the meantime Arendt had renewed contact with friends in Germany. Like Jaspers, with whom she kept up a considerable correspondence, she was disappointed by the relative ease with which the German people seemed to accept the idea that there might be many unpunished murderers in their midst, while their new leaders devoted themselves mainly to the struggle against Communism. She therefore took American citizenship in 1951, after eighteen years of stateless existence, choosing to spend the rest of her life on the other side of the Atlantic. There she published the rest of her works, in both philosophy and political theory, two fields that she insisted on keeping separate.

Returning after the war to philosophy, which she had almost wholly neglected for fifteen years, she published two articles in 1946, "What Is Existenz Philosophy?" and "French Existentialism," that introduced the ideas of Heidegger and Sartre to the United States. Two later books, *The Human Condition* (1958) and the unfinished *Life of the Mind* (1978), represented an attempt to work out a new anthropology from a phenomenological perspective. Her many works in the field of political theory dealt with the Jewish problem, the crisis of culture, and the concepts of violence and revolution. She closely followed the course of current events abroad, alert to the changes that were transforming the world; at home, in her adopted country, she was an astute observer of American society who valued its democratic institutions while deploring its inability to resolve the problem of racism and what she regarded as its ill-considered involvement in Vietnam. Her fine piece of reporting on the Eichmann trial, *Eichmann in Jerusalem* (1963), aroused sharp controversy in the Jewish community; anxious to dispel any romantic aura that might yet attach to the National Socialist experience, she rightly called attention to the "banality" of evil—perfectly embodied by Eichmann himself, one of the principal Nazi criminals and yet an altogether ordinary man, mediocre in every sense of the word.

Arendt's most lasting contribution to political theory remains, however, her analysis of the "monstrous" evolution of certain European states in the first half of the twentieth century in the *Origins of Totalitarianism*. The book is divided into three parts that attempt to trace the histories of anti-Semitism, imperialism, and totalitarianism back to the French Revolution; but it is mainly concerned with the harmful role played by the great totalitarian ideologies of our time.

Anti-Semitism Arendt interprets as an effect of the decline of the nation-state in the early twentieth century and also of the change in status of Jews themselves, who since 1800 had increasingly become assimilated with the rest of society. This raises two questions. Can anti-Semitism be reduced to political motivations? Is it legitimate to regard anti-Semitism as an exclusively modern phenomenon bearing no relation to the anti-Judaism encouraged for almost two thousand years by Christian tradition? One may disagree with Arendt's arguments on these points while acknowledging that her analysis, based on careful historical research, has in any case the great merit of posing such questions.

The second part of the book contains interesting sections on the genesis of various imperialistic ideologies—pan-Germanism in the German-speaking countries, pan-Slavism in Russia—that since the nineteenth century had sought to undermine the European nation-state from within, then to bring about its destruction by throwing it into ruinous wars abroad. Arendt seems, however, to underestimate the influence of Marx's thought—indeed of all doctrines of social progress—when she asserts the proposition that Bolshevism owed more to pan-Slavism than to any other political or ideological movement.[38]

As for the organization of modern totalitarian societies—the term came into fashion only after the Second World War but derived from the Jünger-Schmitt concept of the total state—Arendt was the first to describe its outstanding characteristics precisely: the preponderance of party over state and of force over law, the complementary functions of police terror internally and ideological propaganda externally, and the illusory pretention to wipe out in a single stroke all differences among social classes. It is to her credit also that she insists from the outset on a fact that liberal political theorists sometimes have trouble admitting, namely, that totalitarian regimes often benefit—at least for a certain time—from the spontaneous support of the greater part of the population that they oppress, without this support being the effect of an absolute ignorance of reality or of any collective brainwashing.[39]

The argument in *Origins of Totalitarianism* nonetheless suffers from certain weaknesses. Her primary concern being to elaborate a theoretical model of totalitarianism, Arendt lays undue stress on Nazism and Stalinism as the only two fully realized instances of the phenomenon in its pure form. The formalism of her approach prevented her from giving fascism proper—incarnated by the regimes of Mussolini, Salazar, and Franco—the attention it deserves, on the one hand, and, on the other, from describing the totalitarian tendencies that are liable to emerge in democratic states in times of crisis. Because she was struck as well by the structural resemblances between Stalinist Russia and Hitlerite Germany, she tends to encourage the belief that these two regimes were at bottom identical. Arendt knew perfectly well, of course, that beyond their superficial similarities a fundamental difference separated the two systems: only one of them produced the Holocaust. But the importance of this distinction is not sufficiently emphasized in her book. If only because of the place and timing of its publication—in the United States during the Korean War—its general outlook seems in retrospect to have been one of anti-Communism at least as much as of anti-Nazism.

Everything considered, it must be said that Arendt's political thought, although morally impeccable, lacks philosophical rigor. She remained the captive of a framework restricted to the technical analysis of state structures, just as Jaspers remained trapped within one of moral idealism. Within these limits, however, she helped open up a number of paths for historical research that afterwards proved to be fertile.

IT IS TEMPTING TO DELIVER a similar judgment with regard to a body of work that in many respects was close to hers, that of her compatriot Leo Strauss (1899–1973). Unlike Arendt, with whom he frequently disagreed, Strauss refused to separate political theory from philosophy. He was educated at Marburg. There, in 1922, after having briefly fallen under the influence of neo-Kantianism, he met Heidegger. Despite the events that led Strauss to emigrate ten years later to France (where he got to know Alexandre Kojève, with whom he kept up a lively correspondence until his death), then to England and, finally, to the United States, where he settled for good in 1938, his work reflected the lifelong fascination that he felt for Heidegger's thought. Although he was one of the first to denounce the National Socialist leanings implicit in *Being and Time*, and though he rejected Heidegger's historicism, he commended Heidegger for pointing out that the First World War had shown the failure of the naive faith in progress on which neo-Kantian philosophy rested and from which both Soviet Communism and American free-market capitalism (or liberalism in the traditional sense) proceeded in their different ways.

Strauss was acutely aware of the crisis afflicting modernity since the 1920s and accepted that the rationalism of the Enlightenment that defined modernity had to be completely rethought. What he refused to accept, unlike Heidegger, was that the only alternative was antirationalist nihilism. How, then, could reason be rescued from its current impasse? Strauss's solution was to try to reconstruct reason within the framework of the nation-state and to put it in the service of a democracy that renounced the ambition of saving the world as well as the illusion of indefinite social progress.

Without abandoning a fundamental pessimism—counterbalanced, however, by a confidence in the moral values of Judaism acquired in his youth—Strauss therefore proposed to reconceive political theory by reexamining the great texts in which it had its source. This meant rereading Machiavelli, Hobbes, Locke, Montesquieu, Rousseau, and Kant, but especially Plato and Aristotle, since for him the ancients retained their superiority over the moderns. The originality of Strauss's interpretation of these authors consisted in its resolute antihistoricism. His refusal to treat the philosophies of the past in terms of the cultural context in which they arose was based on a belief that the great problems facing humanity have always been the same and that the ideas of Socrates, in particular, have lost none of their timeliness. Strauss therefore approached classical texts as though they existed outside of time, drawing on them to build his own system, elitist and conservative but nonetheless respectful of natural law and concerned above all to protect the citizen against tyranny in all its forms, not least the tyranny of the majority characteristic of mass democracy, denounced earlier by Tocqueville.

Strauss's work, critical of modernity (in the broad sense of the term) and hostile to the social sciences, Marxism, and left-wing Hegelianism (as his disagreements with Kojève attested), contributed after 1945 to the rebirth of philosophico-political thought in the West, exercising a considerable influence in the 1960s on a part of the right-wing intelligentsia in the United States that proved decisive in the case of scholars such as Allan Bloom (b. 1930). The path cleared by Strauss was nonetheless a narrow one. It is hard to see how the Socratic ideal of an "aristocratic republic" or "universal aristocracy"[40] that inspired his thought could resolve at once all the contradictions that are characteristic of liberal democracy today; and whatever may be the interest of his interpretation of modern political philosophy, Strauss was no more successful than either Jaspers or Arendt in giving an answer to the question of when and why Western reason began to go astray—how, starting from the Enlightenment, it ended up in ruins in the middle of the twentieth century at Auschwitz.

This question, the formulation of which required not only merciless lucidity but also a genuinely critical theory of history and society, was only really to be posed in its full depth and extent by two other German exiles whom we have already briefly discussed, Max Horkheimer and Theodor W. Adorno.

Investigation of the Case

It will be recalled that *Authority and Family* (1936), published in Paris by the exiled members of the Institut für Sozialforschung in Frankfurt, constituted the first work by this group of scholars that was a truly collaborative effort based on empirical research. For two decades it remained the only one.

Despite their own claims to the contrary, the members of the Frankfurt School were more philosophers than sociologists, more inclined to theory than to fieldwork. Moreover, they had been disconcerted by the conclusions of their own research, which indicated a weakening in the authority of the bourgeois family at a moment when throughout Europe the advance of fascism revealed a generalized reinforcement of authoritarian structures. It is worth observing in this connection that for several years the institute's members, though they were Jews and students of Marx, had no real answer to the question why National Socialism triumphed in Germany. Certainly they did not underestimate the seriousness of the phenomenon, since they emigrated; but just this, combined with the horrible novelty of Nazi barbarism, forced them to acknowledge the inadequacy of their usual instruments of analysis.

This basic difficulty, aggravated by disagreements among the exiles—Fromm began to move away from the group upon his arrival in the United States, finally breaking with it in 1939, while Marcuse gradually dissociated himself from it as well—explains why the Frankfurt School published hardly any important works during the late 1930s and early 1940s. Marcuse composed his first essay on the theory of culture in 1937. Adorno wrote an article on jazz in 1936, mentioned earlier, and another on the music of Wagner three years later. Horkheimer, for his part, continued to dream of writing a great work on dialectical logic; but he hesitated to undertake it alone, fearing he did not possess the requisite philosophical background, and so likewise limited himself to articles. In two of these, "The Dispute over Rationalism in Contemporary Philosophy" (1934) and "Traditional and Critical Theory" (1937), Horkheimer made clear his opposition not only to the Vienna Circle but also to positivism in general, which he saw as promoting an indefensibly narrow conception of rationality. On his own view, reason was to be used as the instrument of a critique of the "established disorder"—hence the term *critical theory*, after 1937 the banner under which the members of the Frankfurt School henceforth presented their philosophical program.

No doubt the philosophy of history being developed by Walter Benjamin, whose collaboration the institute had actively invited since 1936, would have given it a second wind had Benjamin ever made it to New York. Although the romantic tendencies of his writings had at first repelled Horkheimer, his ideas ended up (thanks to Adorno's influence) stimulating a gradual evolution in Horkheimer's own thinking, helping to detach him from both the thoroughgoing Marxism of his youth and the idea that the social sciences could take over from philosophy. This evolution had the effect also of drawing Horkheimer closer to Adorno, whom he particularly valued for his "maliciously sharp eye for existing conditions"[41]—in other words, his critical but unsystematic spirit, his aptitude for discovering the hidden side of things. In April 1941, when Horkheimer left New York for Los Angeles, Adorno quickly followed him. This marked the beginning of a close collaboration between the two men, the like of which is seldom encountered in the history of philosophy, and that the test of wartime was only to strengthen.

News of the first large-scale massacres of the Jews in 1941 made it plainly impossible to avoid the question of anti-Semitism any longer. Reading Benjamin had made Adorno realize that the real problem at this point was no longer the failure of the Marxist revolution but the failure of civilization itself and the triumph of barbarism. Not only did Horkheimer become convinced of the rightness of this way of looking at things, he decided to begin work on a book together with Adorno, who proposed giving it the title *Dialektik der Aufklärung* (Dialectic of Enlightenment). Completed in California in 1944, the work was published in German three years later in Amsterdam.

Aufklärung here referred not only to the century of the Enlightenment, marked by the great forward march of reason, but also more generally to the movement by which reason since the time of ancient Greece had tended increasingly to govern the whole of the social and cultural life of the West. What the authors proposed, then, was a history of reason from Plato to Auschwitz, or, more precisely, elements of such a history, for the book, candidly subtitled "Philosophical Fragments," was neither systematically constructed nor completely finished and even displayed certain internal discrepancies, the first fragment seeming to owe more to Horkheimer and the second more to Adorno.

The reader is confronted at once with the fundamental problem: now that material development has placed ever more powerful means for attaining happiness at our disposal, how have we managed to slide back into barbarism over the last two centuries? How has progress been turned into regress, and reason into its contrary? In the first fragment, "The Concept of Enlightenment," the authors reply that reason and its opposite, myth, far from being external to one another or incommensurable, have always supported a dialectical relationship of mutual identification. For if reason was born in freeing itself from myth—as we know from analysis of the Homeric epics, contemporaneous with the birth of reason—afterwards, in order to combat myth, it had to turn itself into its opposite. Thus was born that formidable ambiguity, the "rational myth."

In the modern period the foremost such myth is the belief in the omnipotence of science and technology and their unlimited capacity for progress. This belief underlies the effort of men since the Renaissance to make themselves masters of nature. Their success has only led, however, to their alienation from it. Science not only determines the relations of men with the world but also their relations with each other; embodied in the modern state, it has brought about the reification of social existence and the colonization of daily life, public and private, by a totalitarian and anonymous administration. On this view, the difference between American democracy and Hitlerite fascism is only one of degree. The latter regime merely raised to a hitherto unknown level of horror the tendency to annihilate thought and "massify" individuals that exists, at least in a latent state, in every system of the capitalist type. This tyrannical reign of "objective" science—which Horkheimer and Adorno call positivism—is held to be ultimately responsible for the catastrophic decadence or, more exactly, drift into barbarism experienced by the Western world in the twentieth century.

A critique that identifies positivism with an important part of European philosophy from Descartes to Russell cannot help but recall the one that Heidegger, relying on Spengler, had developed twenty years earlier. Its theoretical roots, however, are to be sought elsewhere—not only in the thought of Benjamin but also in the reflections of Nietzsche and Freud on the harshness of the civilizing process, and indeed in the humanism of the young Marx. Furthermore, unlike Heidegger, Horkheimer and Adorno had in the meantime renounced the ambition of overcoming philosophy. They now described their purpose as developing "a critique of philosophy [that] therefore refuses to abandon philosophy."[42] From the fact that positivism—in the sense that they gave this term—constituted a "perversion" of reason it did not follow that it was necessary to abandon reason, but instead—what demanded more courage and clear-sightedness—that it was urgent to separate elements of rational knowledge from mythic residues. This is the mission of a genuinely critical theory of society.

The second fragment of the Dialektik, devoted to the "industrial production of cultural goods," is a good example of the way in which Horkheimer and Adorno used the "microsociology" of daily life as support—or pretext—for their philosophy of history. The burden of their analysis of popular American culture in the 1940s was that radio, films, magazines, and other cultural goods, mass-produced according to rationally devised norms, aimed only at mystifying the masses in order to perpetuate their subjection. These pages—animated by an anti-Americanism typical of the European Left during the period—claimed to reveal by means of specific examples the condition of spiritual deprivation in which the most developed country in the world found itself. For Horkheimer and Adorno, so long as the "massification" of culture and society were to continue in the United States, the defeat of fascism in Europe would not resolve all problems facing the West.

Together with Hannah Arendt's 1951 work on the origins of totalitarianism, the third and final major fragment of the Dialektik, "Elements of Anti-Semitism," represented one of the first attempts in contemporary philosophy to expose the roots of the persistent nonsense that down through the ages has constituted the usual foundation of all Jew-hatred. From the standpoint of reason, therefore, making sense of anti-Semitism amounts to trying to conceive the limits of reason itself. The authors had scarcely any illusions about the success of their efforts in this regard. They knew that anti-Semitism could not be explained either by biological considerations, or on economic grounds, or even—despite ancient Christian resentment—by purely theological motives. They held that only an inquiry resting upon psychoanalysis, on the one hand, and, on the other, a history of the social and cultural transformations undergone by the West since late antiquity could disclose the sources of anti-Judaism.

These sources were to be sought in the Jewish conception of happiness, in the absolute value that Judaism places upon respect for the Law, understood as an end in itself, and in the habit of messianic detachment, or withdrawal, from the course of world history that resulted from such obedience. Judaism could be seen, on this view, as the last stronghold of spiritual resistance to the otherwise omnipotent domination of civilized society by positivism. One possible explanation for modern anti-Semitism, then, is that civilized people who have been ground down and left behind by a society that has lost all sense of values feel the need, in order to withstand their own suffering, to be consumed by hatred for the last minority capable of testifying, by its very existence, to the metaphysical failure of the capitalist system. By way of conclusion, Horkheimer and Adorno observed that Nazism, in making anti-Semitism the cornerstone of its program, had involuntarily realized one of the oldest anti-Jewish fantasies. Precisely because it constitutes the ultimate scandal of modern reason, the Nazi genocide forces us today to consider the Jewish question as the "turning point of history."[43]

Thanks to the financial assistance of the American Jewish Committee, the theory of anti-Semitism sketched in the *Dialectic of Enlightenment* gave rise after 1945 to new and more detailed empirical investigations, in which sociologists and psychologists such as Bruno Bettelheim (1903–90) would take part, into the sources of racial prejudice. This research led in its turn to the publication of a series of jointly authored volumes under the general title *Studies in Prejudice*. The third book to appear in the series, *The Authoritarian Personality* (1950), laid out the results of a project directed by Adorno bearing upon the complexes—in the Freudian sense of the term—liable to favor adherence to ideologies of a fascist type. Various psychoanalysts pursued this style of investigation in the years that followed.

IN THE MEANTIME the war had come to an end. Not without apprehension, Horkheimer and Adorno decided to return to Germany. Horkheimer resumed his chair at the University of Frankfurt, where he became rector in 1951. The same year he solemnly reinstated the Institut für Sozialforschung in its native city. Its activities gradually picked up, and, on retiring in 1958, Horkheimer's last official act was to turn over the direction of the institute to Adorno. Because Horkheimer published little new writing during this period, it was necessary to await the posthumous appearance of his *Notizen* (1974) in order to have a proper appreciation of his philosophy of history in its final form.

The Schopenhauerian tone of these notes—recorded on a daily basis between 1949 and 1969—attests to a deepening of Horkheimer's natural pessimism over the last two decades of his life. The end of the war had, of course, sounded the death knell of National Socialism; but barbarism only continued to develop in other forms. While he went on using the categories of historical materialism to understand the functioning of contemporary societies, Horkheimer dismissed both the dictatorships brutally administered in the name of Communism and the more insidious techniques of stupefying the masses that hid behind the liberal veneer of the Western democracies, showing not the least leniency toward either one. "West and east," he suggested, "might ultimately not be the antinomy they want to make us believe in."[44]

Nonetheless, if he despaired of the possibility of effective action, whether in the name of a particular class or nation, Horkheimer did not manage to resign himself completely to the world as it was. As a true partisan of the Enlightenment, he continued at least to believe in the possibility that individuals might act in such a way as to diminish the suffering of other individuals—even if, to refer to this pragmatic attitude, he regretted not being able to find a better term than *humanism*, which seemed to him the "poor, provincial slogan of a half-educated European."[45] Hardly understood at the time, this slogan was once again to enjoy a certain topicality with the end of the Cold War.

ADORNO, having attempted to extend the argument sketched by the *Dialectic of Enlightenment* in a collection of short fragments, *Minima Moralia* (1951), next devoted himself upon his return to Frankfurt to teaching at the university, which offered him a chair, as well as to work on sociology and aesthetics. Literature and music continued to be at the center of his interests. Even if his personal preferences ran toward Schoenberg and the dodecaphonic school, as *Philosophy of Modern Music* (1949) had once more testified, he closely followed the development of Stockhausen's aleatory music in the 1950s.

In 1961 a conference organized at Tübingen by the Deutsche Gesellschaft für Soziologie provided Adorno and Jürgen Habermas—his assistant at Frankfurt since 1956—with the occasion to debate in person with Karl Popper and the German philosopher Hans Albert, leading representatives of the positivism denounced by *Dialectic of Enlightenment*. Out of these encounters came a book, *The Positivist Dispute in German Sociology* (1969), that reprinted the exchanges of the participants. Although the "German quarrel," as it was called at the time, was not quite as serious as the title of the book seemed to suggest, it is nevertheless true that there was a basic incompatibility between Popper's and Adorno's points of view.

Opposed to the dialectic of both Hegel and Marx, Popper sought to guarantee the objectivity and political neutrality of sociological analysis: the social sciences were not to be considered in a different light than the sciences of nature. This position, it will be remembered, was Carnap's as well—although Popper had always refused to be identified with the Vienna Circle and although Carnap, for his part, felt a sympathy for Marxism that Popper hardly shared. Adorno, by contrast, persisted in seeking to connect sociological research with a critical theory of society, which is to say with a vast project aiming at its transformation. In retrospect what stands out about this disagreement, which was to remain unresolved, is the harshness of Popper's attacks on Adorno, particularly against his use of language, which Popper characterized as "obscure" and "trivial." It should be noted that these same criticisms were later made by Adorno himself, in The Jargon of Authenticity (1964), with regard to the language employed by Heidegger.

Shortly afterwards Adorno came back to fundamental philosophy with a major book, Negative Dialectics (1966), the fruit of ten years of work. Devoid, as its title indicates, of all positive content, and written in a magnificent but nonetheless quite difficult style, this atypical text may be considered as a sequel to the cultural history of the West begun in the Dialectic of Enlightenment. It did not rely, however, on the social sciences, bogged down in the morass of "positivity," nor indeed on any empirical research whatever, even if concrete analyses illuminate every page. No doubt this was the result of Adorno's desire to avoid having to develop a full-blown theory of society, too complicated to be worked out in detail; and to draw instead, from personal experience, the broad lines of a philosophy designed to overcome all previous metaphysics in a single stroke—the metaphysics of Hegel, of course, guilty of having dissolved the negative in the final triumph of absolute spirit, but also that of Heidegger, which stood condemned for its political implications among others.

The book opens with a paradox: if philosophy is still alive, this is because it has yet to inquire into the reasons for its failure, that is, its inability to transform the world by freeing man from the hold of alienation. A thorough critique of Heidegger's thought follows, directed not only against its irrationalism but also against the manner in which Being and Time "ontologizes" history,[46] considering the status quo—whatever it may be—to depend on Being itself. This attitude, Adorno argues, explains Heidegger's defense of the established order and his subsequent embrace of Nazism. As against the political "positivism" represented by Heidegger's philosophy and, more generally, the tradition of German idealism from which it proceeded, Adorno places his faith less in Marx than in a "logic of disintegration,"[47] or pure negativity—in other words, in a style of thought that renounces the techniques of Hegelian synthesis and, by virtue of this, rejects the illusion of reconciling opposites while proclaiming their ultimate identity.

Indeed, no synthesis whatsoever is possible as long as a single man suffers at the hands of other men. "The smallest trace of senseless suffering in the empirical world belies all the identitarian philosophy that would talk us out of that suffering,"[48] Adorno writes, as if echoing Georg Simmel's remark that the history of philosophy "shows amazingly few indications of the sufferings of humankind."[49] Pain, being identical with negativity, therefore constitutes the driving force of Adorno's dialectic. The three final chapters of the book give a detailed picture of how it operates: the first of these redefines liberty on the basis of a critique of the formulation given it by Kant; the second takes issue with the Hegelian philosophy of history, and particularly with the notion of the "spirit of a people" (Volksgeist), the foundation of all nationalist and reactionary mysticisms; the third, finally, leads back to an inquiry into the possibility of metaphysics today—in other words, after Auschwitz.

After Auschwitz, Adorno says, "any claim of the positivity of existence" can only be "sanctimonious."[50] "Auschwitz demonstrated irrefutably that culture has failed. . . . All post-Auschwitz culture, including its urgent critique, is garbage."[51] Auschwitz destroyed, in sum, all hope of reconciling philosophy with experience. After Auschwitz, we are all guilty—at least in the metaphysical sense of guilt evoked by Jaspers. At the same time, Adorno asserts that this guilt—and it alone—is what obliges us to go on philosophizing. Philosophy must, in fact, be measured against the existence of absolute evil. It must attempt, if not actually to conceive it (for can absolute evil really be conceived?), then at least to confront it. If it does not do this, if through impotence or cowardice it refuses this confrontation, then it is of no use whatsoever: there would be no difference between it and "the musical accompaniment with which the SS liked to drown out the screams of its victims."[52]

The outcome of this dark combat remains uncertain. However, the materialist nihilism of the later Adorno—who refused as a matter of principle to countenance any attempt to give meaning to death—does not lead to resignation any more than did the pessimism of the later Horkheimer. Despite its essential incompleteness, negative dialectics provides grounds for two forms of salvation.

The first is ethical in nature. Like Horkheimer, Adorno believed in the individual, and in the individual alone. He admitted therefore that individual action was not, a priori, useless. "To arrange [one's] thoughts and actions so that Auschwitz will not repeat itself, so that nothing similar will happen"[53]— since Hitler this had become the new categorical imperative, an imperative no less constraining than Kant's even if, owing to Adorno's rejection of all metaphysical or religious transcendence, finding an absolute foundation for it is difficult. Ethics, in order to press its claims, must be seen to have no need either of God or police: it is up to each one of us, if we wish to give meaning to our existence, to be vigilant.

The second form of salvation, subordinate to the first, falls under the head of aesthetics. As against Schopenhauer's attempt to erect despair into an absolute, Adorno insisted on recalling that the "world's course is not absolutely conclusive. . . . However void every trace of otherness in it, however much all happiness is marred by revocability . . . [being] is still pervaded by the ever-broken pledges of that otherness"[54]—pledges betrayed but also revealed, in spite of themselves, by the "fine appearances" of works of art and by the emotions that these appearances arouse, these "promises of happiness" that no one can resist.

Like Nietzsche, Adorno therefore invited philosophy to become an artist, to sense the mysterious proximity of concept and intuition, of truth and folly. This call for imminent transcendence, demanded by the eye of the philosopher-aesthete "that does not want the colors of the world to fade,"[55] constitutes the final enigma of a book that, thirty years after it first appeared, has yet to yield all of its secrets. It must be said in defense of Adorno—who died three years after the publication of Negative Dialectics, in 1969, at the height of the student revolt—that he hardly had time to explain himself. However, his last book, Aesthetic Theory, published posthumously a year later, in effect completed the argument of Negative Dialectics by asserting the convergence of art and philosophy in their joint production, each by its own means, of a critique of capitalist society in the age of its "decomposition."

Aesthetic Theory is a considerable piece of work on account of both the ambition that animates it and the learning that supports it. It goes back once more to the question that since 1945 had tormented Adorno: "Today it goes without saying that nothing concerning art goes without saying . . . even its right to exist. . . . The place and function of art in society have become uncertain."[56] Lengthy discussions follow, marked again by Benjamin's influence, on the "truth content" of a work of art, its relations with social reality, and the transformations which it has undergone in the technocratic age—an era characterized by the rule of money, the media, and government.

Nonetheless, there also emerges the idea that art, like philosophy, must survive Auschwitz, since it too is a means of political vigilance against the miscarriages of reason. In order to fulfill this function, it has only to cease regarding itself as a purely narcissistic game and to recall that its mission is to preserve the traces of the pain that man has inflicted upon his fellow man and to bear witness against it.

What, Adorno asks, "would become of art as historiography if it wiped out the memory of accumulated suffering"?[57] With this new question, addressed to philosophers as well as to artists and, beyond them, to all men and women, ends the anguished work of a thinker who went as far as he was able to go in investigating the case of reason and the Enlightenment—a case that National Socialism, by its very existence, required to be opened, and whose investigation, a half-century after the end of the war, is yet far from being closed.

In the Cold War

Partisans of Liberalism

Nineteen forty-five was a strange year. In the space of six months, one world war that had lasted six years came to an end, while a second one began that lasted for another forty-four years. At their intersection, two fateful dates: 6 and 9 August.

On those days American bombers, using atomic weapons for the first time, destroyed the Japanese cities of Hiroshima and Nagasaki. In a few moments, one hundred twenty thousand people were killed and many more injured. The bombing caused irreparable damage to the immediate environment and psychological trauma throughout the world. Henceforth humanity lived in the shadow of a new threat: nuclear apocalypse.

Was such an act of mass murder indispensable for assuring the victory of the Allies over the Axis powers? The Germans had already surrendered three months earlier. The Japanese were condemned to capitulate in their turn. A few weeks more and their will to resist would surely have come to an end. But the real problem, for the United States, lay elsewhere. Since May, everything had changed.

On learning of Hitler's suicide, America believed it was finished with Nazism. Owing to a peculiar error of judgment, itself due to a desire to forget their share of the blame for the Holocaust, most Western nations chose at that point to minimize the importance of the National Socialist phenomenon. Instead of recognizing it for what it really was—the political expression, intensified by the bureaucratic and technological organization of the modern state, of an obsession with racial purity (in this case, anti-Semitism) that was deeply rooted in Western culture—they preferred to see it as the product either of an exceptional pathology involving a single individual, Hitler, or of a local history, namely, that of Germany in the 1920s.

Since May 1945, then, Nazism—which no one wished to imagine might not have actually disappeared with Hitler—abruptly ceased to be the chief enemy of the "free" world. It was replaced by a new enemy, Communism, embodied by the Soviet Union and, farther to the east, by the revolutionary forces that were stirring in China. Faced with the growing Maoist insurrection there, and with the advance of Soviet troops in Eastern Europe, the American administration resolved to react swiftly. It decided to launch a massive strike in order not only to put an end to the fighting in the Pacific but also to issue a warning to the Soviets. Thus, the bombing of Hiroshima was both the final act of the war against the Axis and the first one of a new conflict, soon to be called the Cold War.

Like the Second World War, the new one was planetary in scale. It ended without warning, however, on 9 November 1989, with the crumbling of the Berlin Wall, the symbol of the division of Germany, Europe, and the rest of the world into two camps, capitalist and communist. One consequence of this dividing up of the world was that Europe knew a sort of armed peace for a half-century since the two superpowers, American and Soviet, had tacitly agreed to avoid military confrontation on this sensitive territory. They would not hesitate to do battle, by contrast, in Korea, Vietnam, Africa, and Latin America. The new war was hardly cold everywhere. It killed a great many people in developing countries in local conflicts of uncertain outcome that in the end served no purpose, unless by keeping up pressure on the enemy, on the one hand, and, on the other, in working to ruin these countries by depriving them of the means to achieve economic growth. Although it guaranteed peace and security for Europe, the Cold War was a genuine tragedy for the rest of the globe, abandoned to absurd political rivalries, misery, and dictatorship.

In the West, which saw the triumph of the consumer society in the 1960s, this tragedy was scarcely recognized. Among philosophers, some chose to ignore it, either because it did not affect them or because they felt that philosophy ought not let itself get mixed up with history. In pulling off the triple feat of forgetting Auschwitz, turning their back on the Iron Curtain, and blinding themselves to the quotidian dramas of the Third World, they behaved as though reason were of no use for action, and philosophy without social consequence—as though the only possible future for philosophy resided in exploring the maze of subjectivity or the formal procedures of scientific discourse. The age seemed a very peaceful one to many, perhaps most, of the heirs to phenomenology and adepts of logico-linguistic philosophy. Although occasionally they argued with one other, they agreed on at least the necessity of protecting their professional duties from all contact with the world.

A few, by contrast, took sides. They chose their camp not only as men of action but also as philosophers sincerely convinced that their theoretical positions—on the nature of mind or the method of science—compelled definite commitments of an ethical and political kind. Among these figures one finds two defenders of the classical liberal tradition, Karl Popper and Raymond Aron; a thinker for whom liberty was ultimately more important than liberalism, Jean-Paul Sartre; another, Herbert Marcuse, who devoted his life to the search for a "third way"; and, finally, one who believed that Marxism could be saved if it were given a new meaning, Louis Althusser. All of them, however, at one moment or another, had to face up to the refutation that reality was ready to administer—in greater or lesser degree—to their hopes and their theories.

BY A CURIOUS IRONY, the leading thinker on the Western side during the Cold War, Karl Popper, was himself a former Communist—the archetype, in a way, of the sort of repentant Communist more and more frequently encountered among intellectuals in the aftermath of the Hungarian revolt of 1956.

To understand his political development, it is instructive to consult the accounts that he himself left in his autobiography, *Unended Quest* (1974), and in the opening pages of *The Lesson of This Century*, the published version of an interview he gave two years before his death to the Italian journalist Giancarlo Bosetti. According to his own version of events, Popper grew up in an established Viennese family of left-wing sympathies. His father, a lawyer fascinated by social history, had in his library the works of Marx, Lassalle, Kautsky, and Bernstein. The young Karl was barely twelve years old when, in 1914, he first read a book on socialism. When the First World War broke out, he immediately sided with Germany's enemies: for him, as for the rest of the family, the aims of the Austro-German alliance were altogether indefensible.

Following the collapse of the Austrian Empire in early 1919, he began to attend the meetings of a Communist group whose pacifist convictions appealed to him. The Bolsheviks had after all been the first, with the Treaty of Brest-Litovsk, to quit fighting. For several months Popper considered himself a Communist. Then in July 1919, while taking part in a left-wing demonstration, six of his comrades were killed when the Austrian army fired into the crowd. Popper was profoundly affected by this event. Suddenly realizing that the idea of revolution was inseparable from the use of violence, which he hated, he resolved to break all ties with Communism. He therefore became an anti-Marxist via pacifism—a pacifism to which, like Russell, he remained forever firmly attached.

Shortly afterwards he made a careful study of *Capital* and discovered two fundamental propositions whose significance he had not fully grasped until then. According to the first, capitalism could not be improved by reforms but had instead to be destroyed before being replaced by a wholly different system; according to the second, this destruction is inevitable by virtue of the very laws that govern the development of the capitalist economy. Convinced that these two propositions constituted the ultimate justification for the use of violence by the Communist movement, Popper henceforth devoted the rest of his life to combatting them, at least in such periods of leisure as his extensive work on science and the theory of knowledge permitted—for, once again like Russell, he was able to move back and forth between political advocacy and epistemological research with ease.

Looking back over the course of this anti-Marxist crusade, two books stand out. The first, *The Poverty of Historicism* (originally composed in 1935, rewritten in 1944 and published first as a pair of articles in the journal *Economica* in 1944–45, then finally as a book in 1957), contains in its title the name of the doctrine that became his bête noire. Historicism, for Popper, referred not so much—as it did in Husserl's work—to the tendency to reduce the content of a concept to what the study of its historical origins revealed about it as, more fundamentally, to the theory that history itself obeyed laws that, correctly understood, allowed the future to be at least in part anticipated.

Popper saw in this belief—shared not only by Hegel and Marx but also by many professional historians, some of them unmistakably liberal in outlook—the expression of an irrationalist faith incompatible with an authentically scientific attitude. History, he held, could not obey laws; the very idea of a historical law seemed to him, in fact, to be a contradiction in terms. The arguments advanced to justify this claim were unconvincing, however, and the attempt he made some years later, in an article called "Indeterminism in

Quantum Physics and in Classical Physics" (1950), to deduce them from the indeterminacy of quantum physics was still less persuasive (as Popper himself admitted in the foreword to the 1957 edition of The Poverty of Historicism). Whatever may be the difficulties of applying the notion of law to social phenomena, the justification for declaring its application impossible in principle, and so denying history any chance of becoming a scientific discipline, is far from clear.

The second book, published in two volumes as The Open Society and Its Enemies (1945), represented an enterprise of considerably greater scope. Despite the considerable success that it subsequently enjoyed, it too has become dated. Popper begins by adopting Bergson's distinction between "closed" morality (founded on obligation) and "open" morality (tied to the ideal aspirations of the individual) with a view to applying it to societies.[1] Moving then from the rather questionable assumption that historicism, the core of all dialectical thought, necessarily goes together with the will to return to a closed, "tribal" society and therefore implies a contempt for all demands for individual liberty, he attempts to establish the actual existence of such a link in the work of a number of major philosophers—Heraclitus, Plato, Aristotle, Hegel, and Marx—all of them dialectical thinkers.

We may pass over in silence the caricature that is given of the first four of these philosophers. Heraclitus is disfigured, Plato oversimplified in the extreme, and Aristotle dismissed as a mediocre intellect. Indeed, the critique of Heraclitus's "tribalism" is so cavalier that, after having tried to retouch it in the fifth chapter of Conjectures and Refutations (1963), Popper finally admitted to abandoning it in a note to the French translation of The Open Society.[2] Hegel, for his part, is disqualified from the start, on the basis of the claim (taken over from Moore, Russell, and Carnap) that his books are unintelligible—"bombastic and mystifying cant."[3] Throughout the Cold War, analytic philosophers were almost unanimous in approving this judgment.

Popper's analysis of the dangers of German nationalism—exemplified by Fichte—turns out to be more sensible. Finally he comes to Marx, who, by comparison with the others, is accorded preferential treatment. Popper recognizes at the outset that Marx deserves to be ranked "among the liberators of mankind."[4] He salutes Marx for having bequeathed to future generations, in the eighth chapter of the first book of Capital, devoted to the proletarian working day, "a truly imperishable document of human suffering"[5] in the hell of nascent capitalism. Admitting without reservation the correctness of Marx's protest against social injustice, Popper even goes so far as to say that "moral" Marxism—with its "feeling of social responsibility" and "love for freedom"—must survive.[6] This does not by any means prevent him, however, from trying to tear down "scientific" Marxism all the way to its base.

In his view, the claim of Marxism to found a science of history does not stand up to examination. Not only does history have no direction—that is, no inevitable tendency toward progress—but it does not obey any specific law and cannot become the object of science. In claiming the opposite, Marx confounded scientific prediction and prophecy and in so doing set himself up as a false prophet. Any attempt to transform capitalist society with the purpose of realizing his prophecies can only end up leading backwards— Marxist collectivism being only, at best, a form of neotribalism.

The rational attitude, by contrast, consists in recognizing liberal democracy as the best possible regime and in attempting to improve the capitalist system one step at a time, by means of "piecemeal social engineering,"[7] in order gradually and peacefully to make it more fair. This position—social democratic in spirit—was fairly close to the political program of Russell and Schlick. But Popper moved away from it in the 1950s, embracing an unbridled liberalism, fiercely antibureaucratic and antistatist, which led him to advocate the privatization of public services and of higher education. At the end of his life he came back to a more qualified view, entrusting the liberal state with the mission of seeing to it that the laws are obeyed and that citizens are protected against violence.

The Open Society concludes with a tribute to rationalism, accompanied by a warning against the dangers of "mystical intellectualism"[8] that one can hardly disagree with. From time to time Popper is apt to take refuge, for want of any better justification, in a sort of eternal popular wisdom; thus he observes, for example, with an air of apparent disillusionment, that "of all political ideals, that of making the people happy is perhaps the most dangerous one."[9] While truisms of this sort are equally unlikely to arouse controversy, another aspect of the book merits discussion.

Although Popper claimed (in a preface specially written in 1978 for the French edition of The Open Society) that he made the decision to write a defense of liberty the day Hitler invaded Austria, and although the book was published the same year the war ended, the three enemies of the open society—fascism, Nazism, and Communism—are not treated equally. Contrary to what one might reasonably have expected after Auschwitz, the uniqueness of Nazism, implicitly reduced to a simple variant of fascism, goes unrecognized. Racism and anti-Semitism, denounced in a few vague phrases, occasion no analysis. More seriously still, the modern doctrines of fascism, which owe little to Plato, are neither discussed in detail nor even briefly described in this ample work, the second volume of which, by contrast, is wholly devoted to a critique of Marx. In certain passages, where Marxism—assumed to be identical with Stalinism—is explicitly compared with fascism,[10] Popper gives the distinct impression that Marxism is more dangerous than fascism. Marx is the enemy. Next to Marx, Hitler was nothing.

Popper's supporters, when they take the trouble to reply to this kind of criticism, hesitate between two different arguments. Either they assert that in 1945, with the death of Hitler, the principal enemy of the open society was no longer vanquished Nazism but conquering Communism—a shortsighted view since now, fewer than fifty years later, it is once more racist nationalism and not Communism that appears, in Europe and elsewhere, as the most serious threat to democratic values; or they dispose of the debate by claiming that Popper himself wished to transcend it—in other words, that his purpose was not to denounce this or that form of totalitarianism, but rather totalitarianism in general, whether of the Right or of the Left.

It remains to inquire into the pertinence of the second argument, which seems to imply that the opposition of Left and Right no longer has any political significance today. Leaving aside this suggestion—a presumptuous one, to say the least—there is a more troubling question, for the argument seems also to imply that Nazism, fascism, and Communism are to be regarded as absolutely equivalent regimes. This would be to forget that Communism— or, more exactly, socialism, which was responsible for preparing the way for Communism—differed from Nazism and fascism in that it conferred upon a future ideal classless society the mission of encouraging the individual development of all people. There are, moreover, several possible forms that socialism can take in practice—not only a single, Stalinist form—just as there have historically been several forms of fascism. Finally, Nazism is distinguished from both fascism and socialism by the central place occupied in its program by the policy of racial extermination. It is therefore pointless to use the same term to designate realities that are so far removed from one other.

This was, however, what Popper attempted to do. His whole political theory rests in the last analysis on the disconcertingly Manichaean idea that there exist, in effect, only two types of regimes: good (democratic regimes) and bad (totalitarian regimes, also called dictatorships or tyrannies). The criterion for distinguishing them is extremely general. Dictatorial regimes are those "which the ruled cannot get rid of except by way of a successful revolution,"[11] whereas a simple electoral mechanism permits the citizens of a democratic state to change governments peaceably. This distinction may provoke a smile. Had Popper managed to forget during the course of his exile in New Zealand, where from 1938 to 1944 he composed The Open Society, that Nazism was established in Germany precisely as a result of democratic elections and that it almost always took pains to respect—at least superficially—the forms of law?

Later, during the Cold War, both the phenomenon of McCarthyism in the United States and the behavior of certain Latin American client regimes showed that fascism—as Lenin well knew—was perfectly compatible with democracy in the formal sense. And Stalinism, in its final stages of collapse, ended up revealing—if one accepts the Popperian criterion—a mysteriously democratic nature. For socialism, whether in the Soviet Union or in Eastern Europe, did not succumb to the blows of foreign intervention, nor did it fall (with the very problematic exception of Romania) in the aftermath of a bloody insurrection. It died by itself, as a result of its own deficiencies, self-destructing in a deliberate, almost consensual way.

From July 1919 until his death, however, Popper remained a determined anti-Marxist. After the appearance of The Open Society he reaffirmed on many occasions his hostility to any radical critique of capitalism, particularly the one brought by the Frankfurt School. After sharply attacking Adorno during the Tübingen debates in 1961, he went back on the offensive nine years later in an article entitled "Reason or Revolution?"[12] and once more pressed his reformist line in an encounter with Marcuse published in 1971 as "Reason or Reform?"[13] None of these texts contains any substantial modification of his views. Only in one of his last interviews, published posthumously in English as The Lesson of This Century (1996), is there evidence of a belated concern for certain forms of violence endemic to so-called liberal democracies—beginning with the kind insidiously practiced upon the minds of citizens by the audiovisual media.

Despite a certain superficiality, Popper's political thought is nonetheless forceful. Its clarity, and the conviction with which it is expressed, have won it a wide audience, if not in America, where liberalism (in its original sense) is in any case firmly established in the popular mind, then in Western Europe, where it became the bible not only of the traditional Right but of anti-Communist intellectuals in general.

POPPER'S INFLUENCE, as well as that of Leo Strauss and Hannah Arendt, may be seen most notably perhaps in the work of the French philosopher and sociologist Raymond Aron (1905–83). After having passed his examinations at the École Normale Supérieure in 1924, and those for the philosophy *agrégation* in 1928, Aron went to Germany as a research student from 1930–33 at the universities of Cologne and Berlin. There he discovered Husserlian phenomenology, Heideggerian existentialism, the sociological thought of Max Weber, and the harsh reality of Nazism. Back in France he attended Alexandre Kojève's graduate seminar and completed his doctoral thesis, published in 1938 as *Introduction to the Philosophy of History*, which drew upon recent work in German sociology to try to reinterpret the concept of humanity in terms of a plural historicity, at once open and tragic, while combatting both relativistic doctrines and deterministic theories of historical development.

The fall of France in 1940 led Aron to join General de Gaulle in London. He spent the following five years in England. On returning to Paris, after a short stint as a member of André Malraux's personal staff during the brief period Malraux served as a minister in the provisional government created by de Gaulle after the Liberation, he took up political journalism. Although he helped put out the first issues of *Les Temps modernes*, the tensions of the Cold War caused him to break with Sartre, his classmate at the École Normale, in 1946. The same year he joined the staff of the conservative daily *Le Figaro* as an editorial writer. Henceforth he was a tireless opponent of socialist ideas.

One of the high points in this struggle, *The Opium of the Intellectuals* (1955), in which Aron denounced what he regarded as the harmful influence of Sartre and other left-wing intellectuals, is a typically Popperian text, even though Popper himself is never mentioned. Written in a deliberately acerbic style, the work was intended mainly to declare the traditional opposition of the Right and Left obsolete, and to lambaste the Marxist "myths" of revolution and historical determinism. It ought to be added, however, that Aron did not need to wait for Popper's work to appear in order to condemn all forms of dialectical thought, having already in his doctoral thesis firmly challenged Hegelianism and those doctrines—Marx's among them—that issued from it.

Twenty years after the *Opium of the Intellectuals* appeared, the internal dissolution of the Stalinist regimes, the spread of dissidence in Eastern Europe, and the revelations of Alexander Solzhenitsyn about the atrocities of the Gulag provided anti-Marxists with additional arguments. Popper's and Aron's books in turn inspired the antisocialist offensive of 1977 led by the so-called new philosophers in France, most prominently André Glucksmann

(b. 1937) and Bernard-Henri Lévy (b. 1948). The fall of the Berlin Wall, twelve years later, seemed to prove the Popperians right once and for all.

INDEED, for much of the 1990s economic liberalism was wildly successful. But at what price, measured in terms of unemployment, social exclusion, underdevelopment, and waste of planetary resources? Since the end of the Cold War, the validity of democratic ideals is no longer seriously questioned by anyone—leading one commentator, the American political theorist Francis Fukuyama (b. 1952), to feel justified in concluding from this fact, and from a superficial reading of Kojève's interpretation of Hegel, the "end of history."[14] But in how many countries are these ideals actually respected? Popper, alas, had no answer to give to such embarrassing questions.

Nor did Popper realize—although he lived until 1994—that for a half-century he had exaggerated the reality of the Communist threat while dangerously underestimating the threat to world peace associated with the resurgence of doctrines similar to those of National Socialism. We are witnessing just such a resurgence today, both in the form of nationalist movements strongly tinged with racist hatred—consider the recent emergence of xenophobic parties in both Russia and the West as well as the practice of "ethnic cleansing" that has been visited upon the Bosnian Muslims in the former Yugoslavia—and, in other countries, of Christian and Islamic fundamentalisms that once again poorly conceal their anti-Semitic tendencies.

For fifty years, then, Sir Karl Popper (as he was known from 1965—having subsequently been made a Companion of Honour in 1982 on the recommendation of Margaret Thatcher) was mistaken about the true enemy. The end of the Cold War, in rendering his political thought obsolete for the most part, has made this mistake plain for all to see. There is nothing to indicate, however, that the author of *The Open Society* ever acknowledged the fact, or that his followers, who remain numerous, at least in Europe, are prepared to do it for him.

Defender of Liberty

Although he was often considered to be a supporter of the Soviet camp, Jean-Paul Sartre (1905–80) cannot fairly be characterized in such simplistic terms. He was not the exact opposite of Popper, even though certain of his political stands, particularly at the beginning of the 1950s, sometimes made him seem the exact opposite of Aron. Neither a pure Marxist nor anti-Marxist, he was first and foremost a philosopher of liberty, for whom liberty itself was far more important than any of the ideologies that claimed to defend it. He is, for just this reason, politically unclassifiable.

That does not mean he was an isolated figure. He enjoyed the support of a number of close associates and contemporaries—particularly Paul Nizan, Maurice Merleau-Ponty, Albert Camus, and Simone de Beauvoir—even if they did not always agree with him. But Sartre's voice dominated the others. Philosopher and novelist, polemicist and dramatist, leader of the existentialist movement, Sartre was the total intellectual—that mythical figure of French letters that only Voltaire, Hugo, and Zola before him had managed to embody with comparable passion. For this reason he remains, no matter what his detractors may say, the most important French philosopher of the century.

But his detractors are legion. Sartre upset everyone, on the Left as well as on the Right. He disturbed the intellectual comfort of some, ridiculed the cant of others. In France, despite his immense fame, Sartre has never really been appreciated. Still today secondary school students read only his autobiographical essay *Words*, a brief account of a boring childhood. Conventional opinion holds him to have been a bad writer, a mediocre philosopher, and an irresponsible agitator. Even the less aggressive among his detractors did not wait for him to die before piling on, inventing the legend of Sartre's premature senility in order to abruptly dismiss his last ten or twelve years of intellectual activity. In order to understand why he should have aroused such animosity, it is indispensable to retrace the course of his life, which coincided, more or less, with that of the century itself.

Sartre was, like Marx, the product of a bourgeois education. From his birth until the Second World War, he led a sheltered existence, a brilliant student who dreamed of becoming a great writer—which meant, according to the standards of his class and background, a novelist. It was only in his *khâgne*, or second year, at the Lycée Louis-le-Grand preparing to compete for entrance to the École Normale Supérieure that he really acquired a taste for philosophy, having first taken an interest in psychology. In 1924 he entered the École Normale along with Paul Nizan, Raymond Aron, and Georges Canguilhem. In this privileged environment his personality was not slow to assert itself. His originality caused him to be noticed by his classmates and, in 1928, led to his failure in the philosophy *agrégation*. The following year, by contrast, he finished first in the competition. Simone de Beauvoir (1908–86), with whom he prepared for the oral examination, came in second. From that point on they were inseparable. Nothing is more moving, nor more exact, than the portrait of the young Sartre drawn by de Beauvoir thirty years later:

> His mind was always alert. Torpor, somnolence, escapism, intellectual dodges and truces, prudence, and respect were all unknown to him. He was interested in everything and never took anything for granted. Confronted with an object, he would look at it straight in the face instead of trying to explain it away with a myth, a word, an impression, or a preconceived idea: he wouldn't let it go until he had grasped all its ins and outs and all its multiple significations. He didn't ask himself what he ought to think about it, or what it would have been amusing or intelligent to think about it: he simply thought about it. . . . He certainly had no intention of leading the life of a professional literary man; he detested formalities and literary hierarchies, literary "movements," careers, the rights and duties of the man of letters, and all the stuffy pompousness of life. He couldn't reconcile himself to the idea of having a profession, colleagues, superiors, of having to observe and impose rules; he would never be a family man, and would never even marry. . . . The work of art or literature was, in his view, an absolute end in itself. . . . He shrugged disdainful shoulders at all metaphysical disputes. He was interested in social and political questions . . . ; but as far as he was concerned, the main thing was to write and the rest would come later. Besides, at that period he was much more of an anarchist than a revolutionary.[15]

One is tempted to add that Sartre remained more of an anarchist than a revolutionary his whole life. In the meantime, because in any case he had to make a living, he taught philosophy as a secondary school teacher, first at a lycée in Le Havre, then in Laon and Paris. At the same time, thanks to a book by Emmanuel Levinas (1906–95), he made a fundamental discovery: phenomenology.

Born into a Jewish family in Kovno, in Lithuania, Levinas emigrated first to Ukraine before taking up studies in philosophy in France, at Strasbourg. During the academic year 1928–29 he spent some months in Freiburg, where he attended Husserl's last lectures and gave French lessons to Husserl's wife. In 1929, at Davos, he was seduced—as were so many others—by the verve of Heidegger's language, which he found more exalting than Cassirer's rationalism. He devoted the following year to his doctoral thesis, "The Theory of Intuition in Husserl's Phenomenology," which was published immediately.

This was the book that Sartre discovered, a few months after it first appeared, in a bookstore on the Boulevard Saint-Michel in Paris. De Beauvoir, who recounts the story in The Prime of Life, notes that as he leafed through the book, Sartre's "heart missed a beat."[16] And with good reason: Husserl's insistence on the need to come back to the concrete experiences of conscious life in order to give philosophy an unshakable basis corresponded precisely to the ideas that, although he had not yet worked them out, Sartre was wrestling with himself. He did not attempt, however, to meet Levinas, who, for his part, later showed a certain aloofness toward Sartre's philosophy, declining to share in the fashion of existentialism after the Liberation. There was therefore hardly any contact between the two men, and it was in relative isolation that Levinas built up his own philosophy after the war at the intersection of phenomenology, Heideggerian thought, and the Jewish religious tradition.

At the beginning of the 1930s, then, Sartre saw that he had no choice but to throw himself into the study of Husserl. For this purpose he obtained a research grant that allowed him to succeed Aron at the French Institute in Berlin in the fall of 1933. He stayed there for the academic year, embarrassed by his poor knowledge of German. He seems scarcely to have noticed the tumultuous events surrounding him nor, on returning to France in the summer of 1934, to have been aware of the danger posed by National Socialism. He had, on the other hand, succeeded in acquainting himself with Husserl's project, which he attempted to extend in his first philosophical work, a short essay entitled "The Transcendence of the Ego," written in the fall of 1934 and published in 1936 in the journal Recherches philosophiques edited by Alexandre Koyré.

Far from being a simple recapitulation of Husserlian ideas, this essay proposed a radical critique of the notion of the transcendental subject developed a few years previously in Husserl's Cartesian Meditations. In expelling the Ego from the "transcendental field" in order to make it a "being of the world" on the same level with the Ego of the Other, Sartre tried to ground the autonomy of unreflective consciousness, which is to say the mind, in objective reality—this in order to rescue phenomenology from the trap of solipsism against which, in his judgment, Husserl had not protected himself.

Sartre makes the purpose of such a strategy clear in the final pages of the essay. Contrary to the opinion of certain "theorists of the extreme Left"—he no doubt had in mind his friend Nizan, a Communist since 1927, who had sharply attacked spiritualism in his pamphlet The Watchdogs (1932)—

phenomenology could be something other than an idealism unacquainted with "suffering, hunger, and war." If it were to agree to make "the *me* an existent, strictly contemporaneous with the world," phenomenology could in fact produce a "positive" ethics and a "positive" politics, both of them having solid foundations in reality. Sartre goes on to add, "It has always seemed to me that a working hypothesis as fruitful as historical materialism never needed for a foundation the absurdity which is metaphysical materialism."[17] The concern for engagement, the interest in the Marxist conception of history, the refusal to sacrifice human liberty for any determinism whatever—the essential ingredients of Sartre's thought are all found united in these few pages from 1934.

But his thought needed time to mature. In the following years, Sartre developed his ideas about "being in the world," dedicating an enthusiastic article to "A Fundamental Idea of Husserl's Phenomenology: Intentionality" (published in the *Nouvelle Revue Française* in January 1939) and drawing inspiration from the Husserlian method in order to explore the great questions of psychology, which were, for him, inseparable from reflection about art in general and literature in particular. *Imagination* (1936), *Sketch for a Theory of the Emotions* (1939), and *The Imaginary* (1940) were the fruits of this labor. During the same period he composed his first works of fiction: a novel, *Nausea* (1938), and a collection of short stories, *The Wall* (1939). *Nausea* inaugurated a concern with the "contingency" and "facticity" of existence, which led after the war to a "philosophy of the absurd." With "The Childhood of a Leader," the last of the stories collected in *The Wall*, Sartre inquired into the psychological motives for support of fascism. Real history, once more, loomed on the horizon. Sartre still limited himself to observing from afar, however, without seeking to reduce the distance from the world that writing gave him.

In 1936 he refrained from taking part in the elections that brought the victory of the Popular Front. Although he rejoiced in this victory, and was distressed by the military coup d'état in Spain the same year, he continued to remain at the periphery of events. He read widely, however, particularly works in French that helped him improve his knowledge of German philosophy. A book by Jean Wahl (1888–1974), *The Misfortune of Consciousness in Hegel's Philosophy* (1929), gave him access to the *Phenomenology of Spirit*, a work still ignored in most French universities at the time. Similarly, during the winter of 1938–39, through two texts already mentioned, Gurvitch's *Current Tendencies in German Philosophy* (1930) and an article by Levinas, "Martin Heidegger and Ontology" (1932), he discovered the thought of Heidegger in French translation.

Sartre's infatuation was immediate. Heidegger spoke of man, of history, of the dread of death, of the meaning of existence. These themes were all the more fascinating to him since, as we have seen, the political ideas of the former rector of Freiburg did not yet seem as objectionable in France as they later appeared after the war. Even so, the most one can say is that this sudden enthusiasm for Heidegger's work signaled the awakening in Sartre of a new interest in the problem of historicity and, beyond that, in actual history. But this interest would not have developed, perhaps would never have become conscious of itself, were it not for the shock he experienced personally as a result of war.

Still, the war did not alter Sartre's thinking on society and politics right away. The process unfolded in several stages. First, there was the mobilization of September 1939 and the "phony war" of the winter 1939–40—the beginning of a transitional period in which Sartre noted day-to-day events in a private journal (published posthumously as *Carnets de la drôle de guerre*). In these diaries he emphasized the need for an ethics appropriate to the "times of distress" all people now faced. There followed a brief period of captivity in Germany in 1940. On his return to Paris the following year, Sartre founded a politico-intellectual circle with Maurice Merleau-Ponty (1908–61), Socialism and Liberty, that quickly fell apart. Shortly thereafter, in 1943, he contacted the National Writers' Committee of the Resistance, met Albert Camus (1913–60), and contributed to underground publications such as *Lettres françaises* and *Combat*. The same year, moreover, he published *Being and Nothingness* and made his debut in the theater with *The Flies*.

Neither of these last two works supplies evidence of any softness whatsoever toward the occupying regime. But Sartre was not regarded by the authorities as really dangerous, proof of which is found in the fact that his writings got past the censor without incident. He has been much criticized for this. The war did, in fact, come to an end without his having attempted to become part of any real resistance network. History, however, had caught up with him. He was now resolved to devote all his energies to reflecting upon the age in which he lived, having remained at its margins until the age of forty.

The years that followed the Liberation seem also to have been marked by a slight ambiguity on Sartre's part. Although he moved away from the speculative philosophy of his youth to commit himself more and more to political struggle, the general public, carried away perhaps by the thrill of enjoying peace once more, assured *Being and Nothingness* a success that was all the more surprising in view of the work's length and complexity. Following the example of Husserl and Heidegger, Sartre's book—whose title was directly inspired by *Being and Time*—revealed not so much new concepts as a new style of thought, a tone of voice that was unfamiliar to French philosophy of the period. The idea that existence precedes essence, the problem of contingency, the analysis of "bad faith" (the name later given by Sartre to the unconscious), the play upon the Hegelian notions of the "in-itself" and the "for-itself," the acrobatic analyses of experienced temporality (nicely summed up in the famous phrase about the "glass-drunk-from" that "haunts the full glass as its possible and constitutes it as a glass to be drunk from")[18]—all these things no doubt held the attention of the few professional philosophers who read the book from beginning to end. But what the general reading public admired, in 1945, was above all the way in which Sartre, a playwright of genius, dramatized his thought, the way he staged his ideas, setting them in the street or the cafe—in short, the way he managed to confer a universal dimension upon the most ordinary situations of everyday life.

A series of memorable scenes—the one-man play of the waiter in a café, the motorcycle accident, the scene of the woman who finally consents to give her hand to a suitor—exemplified a new and concrete psychology, freed from the clichés of introspection. It is this existentialism, this manner of handling reality—of raising subjective experience to the level of philosophy—that, combined with the effervescent atmosphere of Saint-Germain-des-Prés after the war, explains the vogue of *Being and Nothingness*. This popularity was accompanied, unfortunately, by a fairly general indifference to the strictly philosophical content of the work. Rarely has a best-seller been so little read—by, among others, in the first instance, the censors under the command of the German occupation.

Even if Sartre was not a *résistant* who wrote but rather a writer who resisted—in short, if he did not pose any threat to the regime—*Being and Nothingness* nonetheless constituted a formidable hymn to liberty. In this respect the fourth part of the book, the final and most important part, entitled "Having, Doing, and Being," gives it its full meaning. Sartre recalls here that *Dasein* is defined first by its capacity to modify the surrounding world, by its power to act. Whether it accepts it or not, it *has* this power. Even the slave in chains is free: free to risk death by breaking them. This, Sartre adds, means "that the very meaning of his chains will appear to him in the light of the end which he will have chosen: to remain a slave or to risk the worst in order to get rid of his slavery."[19] In other words, "man being condemned to be free carries the weight of the whole world on his shoulders; he is responsible for the world and for himself as a way of being."[20]

From this analysis a single question follows for each person: what am I to do with my freedom, for the world and for myself? In 1943, this question had a quite particular resonance. The answer, as one may expect, is not to be found in the book. Sartre intended to treat separately—or to save for another, better time—the problem of morality and related questions. "We shall devote to them a future work," concludes the final sentence of *Being and Nothingness*.[21] Unfortunately, the *Notebooks for an Ethics*, begun in 1947–48, remained unfinished.

The book contains many other arguments that at the time were surprising for their boldness. Thus Sartre asserts that, in the Spanish civil war, the Communists had the clearest conception of what had to be done[22]; taking up the problem of the relation between crowd and leader, he explains situations in which "the collectivity rushes into servitude and asks to be treated as an object" in terms of "masochism"[23]; with regard to the notion of race, he explicitly dismisses it as "purely and simply a collective fiction"[24] and says that being Jewish, far from being an objective (read: biological) fact, is at most only one existential project among many others.[25]

Not less unexpected than these statements is the veiled polemic against Heidegger that runs throughout the book. Sartre, it is true, seldom cites Heidegger. But when he does, it is almost always to dissociate himself from him. Thus Sartre speaks ironically of the "abrupt, rather barbaric" fashion in which Heidegger cuts through knotty problems rather than trying to "untie" them, and reproaches Heidegger for not having avoided the trap of solipsism any more than Husserl had[26]—which Sartre sidesteps by asserting the original joint presence, the existential interlocking, of one's own consciousness with that of the Other. Elsewhere, Heidegger is blamed for not having recognized sexuality as a fundamental dimension of *Dasein*[27] and for having ignored the fact that the latter must be defined, first, by its capacity to act upon the world.[28] Finally, the two philosophers entertain diametrically opposed conceptions of death. For Heidegger, *Dasein* is essentially a "being-for-death" (*Sein-zum-Tode*), whereas for Sartre, death—like birth, a contingent fact—comes to man from the outside without his even being aware of it.[29]

Why, then, has it so often been said that French existentialism derives from Heidegger? Because, once again, Sartre was not read—and, what is more, this did not matter to him. The two men, as we have already noted, met only briefly one time, in 1952. Heidegger himself refused, not without reason, to consider Sartre as a disciple. After Sartre had delivered his famous lecture on existentialism and humanism in 1945, Heidegger replied the following year with the *Letter on Humanism*. In this text he maintained that Sartre, in according priority to existence over essence, had only reversed the terms of one metaphysical proposition in order to replace it with another, and that he therefore had not managed to escape the traditional framework of a philosophy of values.[30] As for Sartre, debating with Heidegger mattered to him after 1945 less than politics. That year he founded a new journal, *Les Temps modernes*, whose sympathies lay openly with the Left. Looking back fifteen years later, however, Sartre summed up the project in a more detached fashion, saying that he and his friends aimed at being "anthropologists" and "discover[ing] the ethnography of French society."[31]

Among these anthropologists was Maurice Merleau-Ponty. A 1926 graduate of the École Normale Supérieure—where later, from 1935 to 1939, he held the post of *agrégé-répétiteur* (or examination tutor)—he had known Sartre for many years; but it was only at the end of the war that close ties developed between the two. An imperceptible rivalry undermined their relations, which were never simple, least of all when Sartre saw himself as being further to the left. For the moment, in the euphoria of the Liberation, political differences between the two seemed minimal. Merleau-Ponty, having abandoned the Christian convictions of his youth, had just published a major book, *Phenomenology of Perception* (1945), that sought to reconcile consciousness, the authoritative source of all meaning, with the subjective experience of one's own body, traditionally neglected by transcendental idealism as well as by intellectualist psychology. Like *Being and Nothingness*, this work stood in a direct line of descent from Husserlian phenomenology. It gave new life to the problem of intentionality, however, by bringing insights from gestalt psychology to bear on it; at the same time it harkened back to a style of thinking about the relationship between the sensible and the intelligible that from Descartes and Malebranche to Bergson, via Maine de Biran, had always been influential in French philosophy.

In 1953 Merleau-Ponty entered the Collège de France, delivering an inaugural lecture entitled "In Praise of Philosophy." In the years that followed he moved still further away from a Husserlian science of essences, preferring instead to contemplate one's manner of being in the world and the complex "intertwining" of one's body with the external world. *Eye and Mind*, a fine essay on modern painting written in 1960, and a last unfinished book, *The Visible and the Invisible* (published in 1964, three years after his death), summarize his reflection on these topics. But he was also, like Sartre, acutely sensitive to the practical side of life and fascinated by the events of his time. In the immediate aftermath of the war, in 1945, in any case, there was no higher priority for them than *engagement*.

With Sartre, this willingness to commit himself politically took the form of an impassioned, and at times aggressive, defense of the oppressed. The great struggle of his life was the struggle against injustice in all its forms. We have already noticed that in 1946 his *Reflections on the Jewish Question* gave proof of his indignation in the face of anti-Semitism. A number of anticolonialist writings soon followed. Sartre was opposed, as were others, to the wars being waged by France in Indochina and later in Algeria; but, more than this, he was one of the first European intellectuals to take an interest in what was going on in the countries of the Third World and to understand the necessity of helping these countries develop in an autonomous fashion. It was this awareness of history in the making that led him to be concerned with the condition of blacks in the United States, Franz Fanon's campaign for Algerian independence, the course of events in China and Cuba, Israeli-Palestinian relations—calling upon the two peoples in 1948 to respect each other's incontestable right to exist—and the war in Vietnam, in connection with which he took part in the international tribunal convened in 1966 by Bertrand Russell to judge American war crimes.

At the height of the Cold War, however, one could not take the side of the "wretched of the earth," as a European, without asking oneself how far the commitment extended: in other words, whether or not one subscribed to the Communist view of the world. It is remarkable to observe that on this point, as on others, Sartre's thought, although it has been accused of inconsistency, hardly varied for forty years. Sartre never hid his admiration for Marx's writings, which he read at a rather young age—above all for the early writings and the first book of *Capital*. In his 1934 essay, as we have seen, he expressed the view that historical materialism was the most "fruitful hypothesis" for interpreting history. On the other hand, he distrusted "metaphysical materialism," or what the Marxists of his time called dialectical materialism. This scientific metaphysics, he asserted in a postwar article, "Materialism and Revolution" (1946),[32] had nothing in common with the authentic dialectical evolution of Marx's thought; for him, it was only a fixed, unphilosophical ideology, erected for a purely didactic purpose.

Sartre was viscerally opposed to all dogmatisms, too attached to his own freedom to be able to back any authoritarian regime whatsoever. He was never a Stalinist. While he recognized the achievements of the Soviet revolution, and selectively approved this or that position taken by the Communists, he declined to follow Nizan's example and never joined the Party. To his adversaries, he was a crypto-Communist. But for the Communists, who were clearer on this point, he remained a petit-bourgeois anarchist. This was a difficult situation to manage, and one that provoked immense criticism on all sides.

Several phases mark the development of Sartre's stormy relations with the Communists. The first was characterized by a respectful but distant sympathy for the *parti des fusillés*—that is, the party that had been the soul of the Resistance during the war. It began in October 1945 with the founding of *Les Temps modernes* and a series of statements that soon led Sartre to break with Raymond Aron. In 1947 Merleau-Ponty attempted in *Humanism and Terror* to define toward Communism "a practical stance of comprehension without adherence, of free study without disparagement."[33] This led Sartre, who wholeheartedly endorsed the book's open-mindedness, to fall out momentarily with Camus, who for his part went over into the anti-Communist camp.

Very quickly, however, tensions also appeared between Sartre and the French Communist Party, which passed a severe judgment on the morality of one of his plays, *Dirty Hands* (1948). The same year, Sartre and Merleau-Ponty joined the Rassemblement Démocratique Révolutionnaire, a new movement dedicated to opening up a "third way" between capitalism and communism. In the spring of 1949 they broke away from the group, convinced that the third way in question—discredited, moreover, by the revelation of American financial backing—was only another way of camouflaging the capitalist option. They did not embrace the opposite option, however, as proved by the publication in the January 1950 issue of *Les Temps modernes* of an article by Merleau-Ponty, "The Days of Our Lives," vigorously denouncing—with Sartre's full support—the existence of work camps in the Soviet Union. Annoyed by this gesture, as well as by the support given by the journal to the Titoist experiment in Yugoslavia, Communist intellectuals did not miss an opportunity in the years ahead to attack existentialism, sometimes confusing it for polemical purposes with the "personalism" of the Christian philosopher Emmanuel Mounier (1905–50) and his disciples, associated since 1932 with the periodical *Esprit*.

On 25 June 1950, North Korea invaded South Korea. Merleau-Ponty, who saw this attack as evidence of Stalinist imperialism, definitively broke with Communism and at the same time moved away from Sartre. Sartre reacted just oppositely. Convinced that the Soviet government, faced with the threat of a third world war, remained a supporter of peace, and disgusted by the surge of anti-Communist hatred that shook the West at the time, he decided to choose sides more clearly than he had done up until that point. From that moment on, he wrote later, "I swore to the bourgeoisie a hatred which would only die with me."[34] Thus Sartre became a "fellow traveler" of the French Communist Party, explaining his reasons in a two-part article, "The Communists and Peace," which appeared in the July and October-November 1952 issues of *Les Temps modernes*.[35]

This article brought a reply, "Marxism and Sartre," from a young philosopher close to Merleau-Ponty named Claude Lefort (b. 1924), the founder, along with Cornelius Castoriadis (1922–1997), of a revolutionary but anti-Stalinist journal of political theory, *Socialisme ou barbarie*, which was published from 1949 to 1966. Sartre gave a spirited response and Lefort answered back with a piece entitled "On the Response to the Question." Sartre once more riposted, in the April 1954 issue of *Les Temps modernes*, with a third installment of "The Communists and Peace." In this heated exchange between two men whose allegiance to Marxism was, in each case, quite unorthodox, Sartre appeared less concerned with the theme of "objective" class struggle than with the voluntaristic thesis that it was up to the party, come what may, to embody the legitimate revolt of the workers. Lefort accused Sartre of being guilty of "subjectivism." The criticism was justified, but the attitude in question, far from being the result of a misunderstanding, represented a deliberate political choice, one that was dictated both by Sartre's convictions and by his temperament.

In 1952 Sartre once more had a falling out—this time never to be repaired—with Camus. Then, in 1955, two books appeared that called Sartre's political sympathies into question from different perspectives. In *Adventures of the Dialectic*, Merleau-Ponty devoted an entire chapter, "Sartre and Ultrabolshevism," to criticizing what he supposed to be Sartre's support for Leninism, in effect explaining the reasons for his own decision to cease contributing to *Les Temps modernes*. With *The Opium of the Intellectuals*, Aron provided the Right with a Cold War manifesto while trying to prove, in the tradition not only of Popper but also of Spengler's popularizer, Arnold Toynbee, that the class struggle was a "myth" and that the "end of the age of ideology" was at hand. The recent revival of racist nationalism and religious fundamentalism has shown, in retrospect, how premature this prophecy was. At the time, however, *The Opium of the Intellectuals* enjoyed a great success in the media. Ultimately it led to the fashionable, typically Parisian view that throughout their debate, which lasted until they died, Sartre was wrong and Aron right. The formula is facile but without foundation. On closer examination, it must be admitted that Sartre was not mistaken all that often.

Even in the middle of the 1950s, Sartre's basic position showed few signs of opportunism. He was committed to defending the oppressed—whether of the West, East, or Third World—without showing the least indulgence toward the oppressors, whoever they might be. Moreover, this position resembled that of the Frankfurt School, while differing from it in one important respect, namely, that Sartre's criticism of the dictatorships of the Eastern bloc was a criticism from the pro-Communist Left: it denounced the absence of democracy behind the Iron Curtain in the name of a more authentic conception of Communism. In this regard it displayed similarities with Trotskyite and, more generally, libertarian critiques.

In 1956 Sartre condemned the Soviet invasion of Hungary. In January 1957 he took issue directly with the French Communist Party in an article entitled "The Ghost of Stalin,"[36] which marks the moment when he ceased to be a fellow traveler. A rapprochement then began to develop between Sartre and Merleau-Ponty, favored by their common opposition to the war in Algeria and, later, to Gaullism. Belatedly renewed, the dialogue between the two men was to be interrupted in 1961, however, by Merleau-Ponty's premature death, following which Sartre, devastated by the loss of a dear friend, wrote a splendid essay in his memory.

During these same years, Sartre also found time to compose the *Critique of Dialectical Reason* (1960). This book, in trying to go beyond the vicissitudes of current events, constituted his great argument with Marx. In fact, only the first volume ever appeared. A passionate *livre-fleuve*, which Raymond Aron called a "baroque, crushing, monstrous monument," it was prefaced by an essay written three years earlier, *Search for a Method*, that amounted more to a tentative conclusion than a preface. There would be no definite conclusion— no more than history itself has one. The additional text that was published posthumously in 1985 as the second part of the *Critique* does not really deserve this title since it was taken from a manuscript written between 1958 and 1962, at the same time as the first part and then deliberately abandoned by its author.

The reason the *Critique* was left unfinished is not hard to see. While Sartre and Marx were in agreement in defining history as the place where human praxis is played out, individual praxis remained for Sartre the only thing that mattered, even if inevitably it creeps into collective structures; Marx, because he knew only social praxis, saw no other possible subject in history than classes, mechanically defined by the role that they play in the mode of economic production. Oversimplifying, one might say that Marx knew only "objective" processes while Sartre, faithful to the phenomenological ideals of his youth, persisted in wanting to reconstruct the logic of history on the basis of what for him was the sole reality: actual human beings, the individual subjects of their actions. Marxism and existentialism can therefore be seen to be fundamentally incompatible, even if Sartre did assert that they were complementary, the purpose of existentialism being to restore to Marxism a sense of concrete experience—in other words, to propose a viable way of linking up the theoretical framework furnished by historical materialism with all the work done since Marx's death in the fields of history, sociology, and psychoanalysis. Nonetheless, the obvious ambiguity of a project that aimed to "reconquer man within Marxism"[37] explains why Sartre had the feeling midway through of having reached an impasse.

There remains the book he did complete, which is valuable on its own account. It proposes an original analysis of contemporary society and tries to elaborate a kind of "structural [and] historical anthropology."[38] Although Sartre does not pretend to have discovered dialectic—credit for this goes to Hegel—he wishes to inquire into the foundation and limits of its application to the study of "human objects," or "philosophical anthropology."[39] To the Kantian-style question "Under what conditions is knowledge of history possible?" he replies by laying out all the ways in which individual praxis, shaped and at the same time deflected from its end by social institutions, manages to undo existing syntheses (the "practico-inert") in order to create new ones, which in their turn are undone and then replaced, and so on indefinitely. This process of "detotalization" through "retotalization" implies that no revolution can fundamentally change the nature of history. For even if the oppressed take power, Sartre observes (once more departing from Marx's view), the cycle of alienation/revolt will nevertheless continue to operate. Nor will the oppressed ever take power in the usual sense of the term *take*. Power, therefore, is not in itself either an end or a stake. Here one sees the reappearance of the libertarian, antibureaucratic temptation that always haunted Sartre but that would fully reveal itself only in the last years of his life.

Economics hardly figures at all in the *Critique*. Sartre was uninterested in technical questions, considering Marx's economic theory to be on the whole sound for his purposes. Moreover, he regarded historical materialism—the only part of Marxism that he retained as an essential element of the argument developed in the *Critique*—not as a science but as a philosophy, "the one philosophy of our time which we cannot go beyond."[40] It was, in his view, the only great philosophy of the twentieth century, next to which existentialism itself stood only as an "ideology," having to find its place within the broader framework of Marxism.

But this homage to Marx—for which classical liberals such as Aron would never forgive him—did not prevent Sartre from working out at the edges of Marxist theory his own conception of social reality, or, more exactly, a sort of hyperempiricist sociology that focused on "serial" phenomena. Earlier, in the opening sentence of *Being and Nothingness*, he had praised Husserlian phenomenology for having shown that the existent reduces to "the series of appearances that manifest it." Twenty years later, the *Critique* only transferred this notion from the individual subject to collective modes of being. Always more comfortable with concrete analysis than pure theory, Sartre was at his best in describing serial phenomena such as the queue, the assembly line, and bureaucracy—phenomena that persist until a fused group (*groupe en fusion*) manages to undo the fixed structures underlying them.

Because it appeared at a moment when Gaullism and economic growth had largely succeeded in depoliticizing public debate in France, this analysis—whose attention to the details of real life was unmatched, unless by the theorists of the Frankfurt School, then unknown to Sartre—was scarcely understood at the time. Orthodox Marxists, unanimous in their loathing for Sartre since 1956, rejected the *Critique*; more interestingly, it was picked up a few years later by two British intellectuals, Ronald Laing and David Cooper, who borrowed its philosophical vocabulary to formulate a radical critique of psychiatric institutions and, in particular, of the reductive concept of mental illness. Sartre's analysis also provided one of the most illuminating explanations of the 1968 revolt, which in France (where it was jointly carried out by workers and students), as in other Western countries, laid bare the existing pattern of social relations.

With the events of 1968—a vast process of detotalization led by a fused group similar to the ones described in the *Critique*—the last phase of Sartre's journey began. Challenged by students who preferred the countercultural ideology associated with Marcuse that had been imported from America, accused by workers of being an intellectual cut off from the masses, Sartre nonetheless sided with the Left, which he saw as the victim both of state repression and of the French Communist Party's resistance to change. He condemned the Soviet invasion of Czechoslovakia, which by August had snuffed out the short-lived "Prague spring," and proclaimed once more his opposition to Stalinism in an article published in the summer of 1968, "The Communists Are Afraid of Revolution."[41] Henceforth, his sole point of political reference was the obvious longing of peoples—in the East and the West alike—for a change in the conditions of their existence. From this moment until his death, Sartre positioned himself on the extreme Left, oscillating between its libertarian and Maoist poles. In the highly charged atmosphere of the time, his attraction to Maoism drew criticism; he justified it by his hostility to Moscow, on the one hand, and, on the other, by his sympathy for the utopianism of the Chinese cultural revolution, whose crimes, then little known in Europe, were revealed in detail only later.

At the beginning of the 1970s, while he refused to found or to lead a movement, Sartre selectively supported specific initiatives that seemed to him likely to stir things up—new newspapers, for example, such as *La Cause du peuple* in 1970 and *Révolution* in 1971, and *Libération*, a news agency that would be independent of political parties, which he helped establish in 1971. Two years later Libération launched an alternative daily paper of the same name that Sartre edited for a brief time; always distrustful of power, he resigned his position in 1974. This period was marred, however, by two serious blunders: his approval of the massacre of Israeli athletes by Palestinian terrorists at the Olympic Games in Munich in 1972 and his moral support for another group of terrorists, the German Red Army Faction, in 1974. Such errors in judgment attest to the persistence in him of an old romantic streak, nihilistic and anarchistic, that inclined him sometimes to celebrate political violence in its least acceptable aspects.

With these two inexcusable exceptions, the development of Sartre's thought in the last years of his life does not deserve the opprobrium that since then has been abundantly heaped upon it. To the contrary, the leftism of this period was characterized by a kind of extreme lucidity. The authentic revolutionary inspiration of Marx's thought having been sacrificed by Communist parties everywhere in their bid for power, Sartre concluded that movements of collective emancipation could only end up, by their very logic, creating new and repressive bureaucratic institutions. He therefore gradually abandoned the idea of social revolution, while nonetheless remaining convinced of the necessity of individual revolt against all forms of political power that threatened to suffocate human freedom.

A book of taped conversations, It Is Right to Revolt (1974), conducted with two friends, Philippe Gavi and Pierre Victor (the pseudonym of a young philosopher named Benny Lévy, who entered the École Normale Supérieure in 1965 and shortly afterwards became the leader of the Proletarian Left, a Maoist group), is evidence of the change in Sartre's thinking. The collapse of the leftist movement that was then underway hinted at its final failure. It was now clear that changing the world was an unrealizable dream. The personal revolt—an existential and, in many respects, spiritual revolt—advocated by Sartre in these conversations can be expressed in this way: even if the world cannot be changed, all of us can attempt to change our own lives by refusing to obey laws other than those that we have fixed for ourselves. Freed, finally, from attachment to political parties of any kind, his thinking thus renewed its ties to a partly forgotten philosophical tradition of moral individualism as well as to certain personalist aspects of the Jewish ethical tradition.

Sartre was now elderly and threatened with blindness, unable any longer to read or write. But in talking with Benny Lévy, who from 1973 was his secretary, and with friends and family members (particularly his adopted daughter, herself Jewish), he belatedly discovered the main concepts of Judaism. And it was with Lévy, who at this time sought to return to his roots through study of the Jewish religion, that he recorded a final interview a few weeks before his death (later published as Hope Now) in which the phenomenological question of transcendence reemerged in the context of a tranquil agnosticism. "Rereading this interview," Lévy noted later, "Sartre's voice resonated in such a way that I was able to say in French what had revealed itself to me in Hebrew"[42]—biblical Hebrew, that is.

Immediately disavowed by some of Sartre's close friends, who, failing to understand the course of his intellectual development, mistakenly spoke of him as being "senile," this final interview poses more questions than it provides answers. As disconcerting as this may seem, it nonetheless testifies to a last effort on Sartre's part—perfectly in accord with his original purpose in Being and Nothingness—to establish a philosophy of liberty. The meditation in two voices that unfolds in this book remains, of course, incomplete. But, after all, the Critique of Dialectical Reason and the Notebooks for an Ethics remained unfinished as well. Surely, by definition, the work of this indefatigable activist and raging, insatiable writer—an immense and ongoing construction project, in effect, perpetually in a state of flux—was doomed never to be finished. And surely this is exactly what today makes it more stimulating than so many philosophical systems, satisfied with their own inertia.

In Search of a Third Way

Herbert Marcuse's career, which overlapped with that of Sartre, displays the same critical attitude toward capitalism, the same need to draw upon the dialectical tradition of Hegel and Marx in trying to build a better society. Marcuse's thought, again like that of Sartre, was a negative one. Owing to their "distance from history," both philosophers were able to escape the positivity of "genuine" socialism—in other words, neither one was a Communist, whatever positions their adversaries may have lumped together to give this impression in attacking them.

There are, however, certain dissimilarities between their careers. Whereas Marcuse read Sartre's works closely, the reverse was not true. Sartre, on the other hand, lost some of his credibility among the young after 1968—at least outside Maoist and libertarian circles—whereas Marcuse's reputation was never greater than during this period. Despite its lack of originality and old-fashioned academicism, Marcuse's philosophy was destined, surprisingly enough, to become the major source of inspiration for progressive youth in the West for a number of years.

To understand the development of Marcuse's thought, it must be remembered that the event that marked his life most deeply was the failure of the German revolution of November 1918. The following month, the Spartacists—led by Rosa Luxemburg (1870–1919), the author of a work of economic theory, *The Accumulation of Capital* (1913), and Karl Liebknecht (1871–1919), the son of Wilhelm Liebknecht—founded the German Communist Party. Committed to the program of the October 1917 Revolution in Russia and hostile to the social democratic government headed by Friedrich Ebert, they aimed at making a pro-Bolshevik orientation prevail within the revolution in Germany. Ebert, dependent on the support of the army and conservative forces to remain in power, resolved to crush all attempts at subversion, leading to the "bloody week" in January 1919 at the end of which, on 15 January, Liebknecht and Luxemburg were assassinated in Berlin.

Outraged by Ebert's opportunism, Marcuse quit the Social Democratic

Party, of which he had been a member since 1917. Although he did not reject Marxism as such, he now recognized the need to protect the revolutionary impulse from party machinations and the tactical maneuverings of politicians. For the moment, however, he stood apart from events, devoting himself to his doctoral thesis, "The German 'Kunstlerroman,'" which he finished in 1922, working in the antiquarian book trade, and socializing with Benjamin, Lukács, and likeminded artists.

The thrill he felt on reading *Being and Time* in 1927 led him back from aesthetics to ontology. The "concrete" content of Heidegger's existentialism—the problems of *Dasein*, care, and death—responded to his deepest aspirations. At the same time, the radical tone of the book appealed to Marcuse's revolutionary inclinations. That it was a question in this case of a conservative revolution does not seem to have bothered him, at least not at first. For the moment Marcuse believed in the possibility of a synthesis between existentialism and Marxism. This idea was to be taken up again thirty years later by Sartre, only with quite different political implications.

Hired in 1928 as Heidegger's assistant at Freiburg, Marcuse sought over the next four years to pioneer a "third way," distinct from both the path followed by Heidegger and that of orthodox Marxism, writing essays on the phenomenology of historical materialism, "concrete" philosophy, and transcendental Marxism. Despite his admiration for Heidegger's intellectual abilities, Marcuse realized finally that he was drifting toward National Socialism. As the left-wing follower of an extreme right-wing thinker, the time had come to dissociate himself from the master. Moreover, in 1932 his habilitation thesis, *Hegel's Ontology and the Theory of Historicity*, was rejected by Heidegger. Although the reading of Hegel he proposed was a fairly classical one, already there were signs that Marcuse's real interest lay less in understanding Being than being, less in fundamental ontology than in historical reflection. The same year, Marcuse devoted a study to the young Marx's *Economic and Philosophical Manuscripts* (1844), which had just been published for the first time. The humanistic and revolutionary ontology that inspired them, a sort of left-wing Hegelianism, henceforth seemed to him more concrete than Heideggerian existentialism.

Some weeks later, just before Hitler's coming to power at the end of January 1933, Marcuse left Germany. Almost at once, on the strength of a recommendation from Husserl (who had been one of his thesis examiners in 1922), he joined Horkheimer's group. A complete break with Heidegger was therefore inevitable. It came with the first article he published in the *Zeitschrift für Sozialforschung*, "The Struggle against Liberalism in the Totalitarian Conception of the State" (1934). Although Marcuse was now a member of the Frankfurt School in exile in the United States, he nonetheless preserved his independence within the group. In 1941 he signaled his intention to go it alone with the publication of *Reason and Revolution*, in which he explicitly associated the origins of Frankfurt social theory with Hegelianism. Unlike the 1932 thesis, this new book proposed a deliberately political interpretation of Hegel, at once Marxist and anti-authoritarian. Marcuse saw the critical spirit that symbolized the Enlightenment as the chief component of the dialectical theory founded by Hegel and later developed by Marx. Conceptions of society that considered it possible to ignore this theory he rejected, dismissing all those who condemned Marx and scorned Hegel as positivists. Adopting Bloch's slogan in *The Spirit of Utopia* that "what is cannot be true," he reproached the positivists for having killed the true spirit of the Enlightenment by stifling its fundamentally negative dimension. This argument anticipated the one that Horkheimer and Adorno made six years later—without citing Marcuse—in *Dialectic of Enlightenment*. Marcuse himself developed it further in his later books, replacing the term *positivism* in the 1960s by *one-dimensional thought*.

In order to support himself, Marcuse accepted a job in 1942 with the Office of Strategic Services (OSS), which charged him with identifying Nazi and anti-Nazi movements as part of a planned postwar de-Nazification program. This assignment took him in 1946 to Germany, where he visited Heidegger in the hope of helping him arrange an honorable way out for himself. The renewal of contact proved to be disappointing. Heidegger dug in his heels, refusing to condemn the Holocaust. An exchange of letters at the beginning of 1948 marked the end of their relationship, as we have seen. In the meantime the Cold War had begun. Marcuse continued nonetheless to work for the OSS (and its successor agency, the CIA), contributing in 1949 to a report on "prospects for world Communism," seemingly untroubled by the awkwardness of his position as a Marxist in the service of the U.S. government. Marcuse's differences with Soviet-style socialism were not purely verbal, however, and the search for a third way preoccupied him no less than it had at the beginning of the 1920s. He eventually resigned his position in counterintelligence in 1951. Three years later he went back to academia, teaching first at Brandeis University and then moving to the University of California at San Diego. It was during this period that he composed the works that were to make him known as the philosopher of the "Great Refusal."

This refusal, as we have noted, was not without similarities to Sartre's critique of the capitalist system. For even if Marcuse was skeptical of the subjectivism that inspired *Being and Nothingness*,[43] he sought nonetheless, in a way that offers a striking parallel with Sartre's approach, to reinvigorate the conceptual power of Marxism by freeing it from Stalinist interpretations and bringing to bear upon it the most recent results of research in the social sciences. In each case, theoretical reflection was constantly nourished by an acute sense of the metamorphoses of daily existence as well as of the subversive potential of artistic creation, which gave it its particular richness.

Thus, for example, *Eros and Civilization* (1955), the first of Marcuse's major works published after the war, opens with a denunciation of neo-Freudian revisionism in the form of Fromm's writings since his arrival in the United States, which Marcuse accused of aiming at the "normalization" of the individual—that is, the coercive adaptation of the individual to the repressive structures of society—and of eliminating the metaphysical inspiration of the later Freud in *Civilization and Its Discontents*. Following Freud, Marcuse wished to restore the ontological value expressed by the opposition between instincts of life (*eros*) and of death (*thanatos*). Considering life as a reservoir of urges, which is to say the sum of the energies invested in history, he argued that modern techniques of production, by their capacity to satisfy the needs of all humanity, now rendered useless a large part of the repression imposed upon the individual by the capitalist system in the name of assumed imperatives of social rationalization. Marcuse therefore held out hope for a world in which *eros* (desire) would be freed from *logos* (repressive reason) and *thanatos* (the suicidal impulse, transformed by repression into aggression toward others) would be channeled into symbolic ends in such a way as to reduce the conflicting tensions that weighed upon society. A world pacified in this manner would at last allow the full development of human artistic and sexual potential—the dream that inspired the beat generation of the 1950s and then the hippies in the next decade.

In *Soviet Marxism: A Critical Analysis* (1958), Marcuse clarified what the quest for a third way entailed and explained his reasons for rejecting both "genuine" socialism and capitalism. What made Soviet Communism objectionable was the same thing that, to his mind, made American capitalism objectionable: both are variants of a single type of repressive organization, aiming at subjecting the individual to the primacy of a disfiguring technological rationality whose institutional facade is the tyranny exercised by the state. If the Soviet revolution was a failed, or a betrayed, revolution, this was not because it had failed economically. On the contrary, its failure was due to the fact that Stalinism had been careful not to change any aspect of the relation between the worker and his tools. Whether capitalist or communist, the worker remained the slave of his tools. For Marcuse, altering this relationship, liberating man from his fundamental alienation—that is, from his enslavement to the instruments of production, from his subjection to the economic sphere—was the only authentically revolutionary program.

The broad lines of this program, similar in their motivation to the humanistic writings of the young Marx, were developed in *One-Dimensional Man* (1964). In the first part of the book Marcuse denounces the technique of "repressive desublimation" by which industrial societies in the technocratic age exploit the illusion of individual liberty in order to enslave their citizens. The second part takes issue with the dominant ideology of the Anglo-American world—"one-dimensional thought"—characterized by its rejection of all negative criticism and linked with logical positivism, analytic philosophy (derided for its "artificial and jargonic worries"[44]), and even Wittgenstein himself, charged with the classic positivist error of wanting to "leave things as they are" (*Philosophical Investigations*, §124).

The third part, entitled "The Chance of the Alternatives," lays out Marcuse's main contentions. Taken together, they are intended to trigger a liberating "catastrophe" (the term is used ironically) capable of reversing the current direction of technological progress—in short, of replacing the oppressive conception of reason dominant in the present-day world by a genuinely emancipating conception, summed up by a formula borrowed from Alfred North Whitehead: "The function of Reason is to promote the art of life."[45] Adopting the idea—advanced some thirty years earlier by Horkheimer[46]—that sufficient material means now exist for realizing justice on earth, which therefore no longer appears as a utopian dream, Marcuse advocates a revolutionary reconciliation of technological rationality with individual aspirations to happiness. Such a reconciliation can only occur, on his view, through a reappropriation of private space, which in turn entails the rejection of all authoritarian attempts at colonizing daily life.

The strategic problem—which, in spite of Marcuse, brings us back to Lenin—remained the same, however; namely, identifying those social actors whose intervention could bring about such a revolution. The ease with which the working class had been integrated into the capitalist system disqualified it as a candidate in Marcuse's view. This left the possibility that a demand for change might emerge instead among outsiders to the system—the young, the unemployed and others at the fringes of society, oppressed minorities, and the peoples of the Third World—although, as he admitted, the cohesion of such a mixed alliance as well as its determination and ability to transform the system were problematic. Were outsiders naturally inclined, by the fact of their condition, to rise up? How far would any "spontaneous" revolution triumph without the competition of political parties? How could one be sure this triumph would not reestablish new repressive structures?

Marcuse was well aware that the answers to these questions remained uncertain and that no good result was guaranteed. In closing, while he cited Benjamin ("It is only for the sake of those without hope that hope is given to us"[47]), he acknowledged that the capitalist system was still strong enough to succeed in assimilating all attempts at opposition for a long period of time; that a critical theory of society was not in a position to make promises; and that prudence counseled such a theory to remain purely negative.[48] Indeed, although this work together with Marcuse's next books—Critique of Pure Tolerance (1965), The End of Utopia (1967), and Essay on Liberation (1969)—enjoyed a lively success on university campuses, and although the spread of the student revolt throughout Europe and the United States between 1967 and 1969 seemed at the time to justify hopes for change, the brutal repression of the movement and its subsequent collapse show in retrospect that Marcuse was right to be cautious.

The 1970s, marked by the decline of revolutionary ideologies, were years of great disillusionment. Marcuse's last writings added no new elements to his theory but accepted instead that the present conjunction of circumstances was unfavorable to the "Great Refusal" he had called for. Tellingly, his last book, The Aesthetic Dimension (1977), published two years before his death, represented a return to reflection upon the function of the artistic imagination—as if, for him as for Adorno, in a world in which oppression seemed destined to go on forever individual creation remained the only way to salvation; and as if, in place of politics, art remained the sole form of redemption possible.

From the failure of the German revolution in 1919 to that of the student movement fifty years later, Marcuse's work thus came between two moments of ebbing tide, each of which justified a certain historical pessimism. Marcuse never lost hope, however. Until the end he left a window open in the direction of that final emancipation for which he hoped and prayed, no matter that from 1919 until his death sixty years later the forms in which he tried to imagine it varied little. At the same time the fluctuations and ambiguities of Marcuse's thought can scarcely be denied. They explain, in part, the decline in his influence over the last twenty years or so. It is true that the end of the Cold War, which has seemed to fatally contradict all thought that claims to one degree or another to be inspired by Marx, has played a part as well. Today, the triumph of capitalism appears unchallengeable. In the West, through skillful reforms, it has managed to improve the quality of workers' lives; and in certain developing countries it has been responsible for a number of non-negligible advances. Communism, on the other hand, where it survives (in China, for example), has in the meantime become an object of universal condemnation, suggesting its eventual—and complete— disappearance.

These are the very things, however, that ought to prevent us from forgetting Marcuse. For if the new world that is now taking shape turns out to be still more one-dimensional than the one he denounced thirty years ago, his critique may indeed acquire new relevance in the future. Capitalist technocracy has not fundamentally changed. It remains just as authoritarian, just as impotent to assure the happiness of the greater part of humanity, as before. Indeed, as we have already noticed, in some parts of the world its periodic crises favor the development of certain related—and thinly veiled—forms of the racist and nationalist ideology that took hold in Hitler's Germany. Under such circumstances, who can say that the Marcusian critique may not yet have a future?

Avatars of Marxism

Sartre, although he was a fellow traveler for a short period, from 1950 to 1956, was never a Communist. Nor was Marcuse. Although Marcuse in his youth had sympathized as an outsider with the short-lived Spartacist movement, he spent the rest of his life searching for a third way between capitalism and communism. These two thinkers therefore stood apart from the philosopher Louis Althusser (1918–90), who, having joined the French Communist Party (or PCF) in 1948, remained a member until his retirement from the public scene in 1980.

But there were many ways during the Cold War to be both a philosopher and a Communist. If Althusser had been a philosopher and a Communist in the way that official ideologues were in Eastern bloc countries during the Stalinist period, his work would scarcely deserve to be remembered. This was not the case. To the contrary, the interest of his thinking derives from the fact that quite early, within the PCF itself, it revealed itself to be a dissident style of thought. As a resolute opponent of diamat, Althusser embodied for a quarter-century a historic opportunity for Marxist thought—indeed for the revolutionary movement in general—at least in the field of theory.

During the three decades following the end of the Second World War, Althusser tried to reconceive the relationship between Marxism, science, and philosophy in an entirely original manner. Despite the position of conflict with official party authorities in which he placed himself as a result, his work enjoyed immense influence in France as well as in the rest of the world. Then two quite distinct events occurred in succession that helped extinguish this influence and discredit his work.

The first took place in 1980. On 16 November of that year, in a fit of mad despair, Althusser killed his wife, Hélène Rytmann. Committed to a psychiatric hospital for observation, criminal charges were subsequently dismissed on grounds of insanity, and he was released the following February. From then on, until his death, he lived a quiet, secluded existence.

The second event—the fall of Communist regimes in Eastern Europe, and then in the Soviet Union, after 1989—was only the result, foreseeable since the beginning of the 1970s, of a global process of internal disintegration. At the same time Western Communist parties saw their electoral base shrink substantially, even when, in order to combat this tendency, they chose to change their name and their program.

These two events, although they lacked any common basis for comparison, were nonetheless amalgamated in a singular way by Althusser's adversaries. The end of the Cold War, by assuring the virtually universal triumph of anti-Communist ideologies, seemed to condemn Marx to oblivion. To have been a Marxist for several decades was now considered to be not only a mistake but actually a sin: a moral error, a crime against the human spirit, and an insult to democratic ideals—in a word, proof, or at least a symptom, of mental derangement. Now Althusser was indeed mentally deranged. The murder of his wife—coming after years of depression and psychiatric troubles—was obviously evidence of this. Hence the amalgamation: if Althusser was a Marxist, if he believed in the possibility of breathing new life into Marx's thought, this is because he was mad. Consequently, nothing he may have said is at all worth listening to.

This sophistry needs to be rejected. Whatever personal difficulties—in the event, quite real difficulties—Althusser may have experienced, his published works do not show signs of them. To the contrary, one has only to read these works to see a rigorous, coherent, and clearly articulated project taking shape. If reading Althusser is difficult, indeed sometimes problematic, it is for other, strictly theoretical reasons.

The first reason has to do with the fragmentary nature of Althusser's writings. Faced with an immense task—to rediscover the Marx behind (and opposed to) institutional Marxism—Althusser could only carry it out by proceeding slowly and in stages. He therefore never published an actual book, only brief—typically occasional—pieces: articles, prefaces, lectures. Moreover, a large part of these writings—abandoned manuscripts, course outlines and lecture notes, correspondence—remain unpublished. The odds are that their eventual publication will considerably enrich our understanding of his philosophy.

A second difficulty has to do with the fact that Althusser's writings are part of a process of intellectual and political development that had to be invented each step of the way. Instead of conforming his thought to a prefabricated mold, as so many others had done, Althusser found himself obliged to construct the norms of his own discourse as he went along. This explains why not every aspect of this construction is perfectly linear. On occasion he had to modify his positions, to reconsider theses that had previously been advanced, while attempting in each case to explain his reasons for doing so. Such a concern for clarity was not possible without a certain courage—the courage to challenge the comfortable ideas of the established order (whether that of academic philosophy or of the PCF), but also the courage (much less common) to recognize his own inadequacies.

LOUIS ALTHUSSER WAS BORN in 1918 at Birmandreis, in Algeria, to a conservative bourgeois family. A devout Catholic, he prepared for the entrance examination to the École Supérieure Normale in France, at the Lycée du Parc in Lyons. Among his teachers were two philosophers who were themselves Catholic—Jean Guitton (b. 1901) and Jean Lacroix (1900–1986), both of whom remained lifelong friends. Admitted to the rue d'Ulm in July 1939, the outbreak of the war prevented him from pursuing his studies. Immediately he was called up and shortly thereafter, in June 1940, taken prisoner by the Germans. Thus began a captivity that lasted almost five years.

Thrown suddenly into the world of the prison camps, Althusser managed to cope by teaching himself German and writing his journal. It was in the camps that he experienced his first bouts of depression and his first religious crisis. It was there, too, through several of his fellow prisoners, that he discovered the meaning of Communist engagement. Returning to the rue d'Ulm in October 1945, he resumed his studies in a climate that was slightly unreal by comparison with his experience of the preceding years. He attended Merleau-Ponty's lectures and, in 1947, wrote a master's thesis under the direction of the philosopher and historian of science Gaston Bachelard on the notion of "content" in the thought of Hegel.

In July 1948 he was admitted to the philosophy *agrégation* and in September of the same year took up his new duties as a tutor at the École Normale— duties he fulfilled, as long as his health would permit, with the greatest care—responsible for preparing future examination candidates. This post allowed him to live at the École, of which he became the deputy director some years later; he resided there without interruption until November 1980. While the physical circumstances of this situation were conducive to doing philosophical work, he found them psychologically taxing. Althusser occasionally, and not unhumorously, compared his life at the École to his time in the stalag. However, though it is true that the École can engender among those who rarely leave it the sense of being imprisoned, Althusser was far from being a hermit. Throughout his years there he lived and worked as part of a group, maintaining friendly relations with his many students and receiving visitors from all over the world.

It was also in 1948, in November, that he joined the Communist Party. In this he was motivated by the same spirit of generosity that before the war had attracted him to a social interpretation of Catholicism. A mixture of idealism and altruism inspired in him a sense of obligation to come to the aid of the proletariat in concert with a great fraternity of comrades. Moreover, he did not break at once with the Church. It was only at the beginning of the 1950s that he lost his faith, perhaps permanently. The influence of Hélène Rytmann, who became his companion in 1947—also played a role in his joining the PCF. Eight years older than Althusser, raised in modest circumstances, a former member of the Resistance and a veteran activist, Rytmann was for him the very personification of the authentic Communist. Although she too had serious differences with the Party, her example was one that Althusser, an intellectual from a bourgeois background, was desperate to emulate.

Their relations were stormy from the beginning and only grew worse over the years. His occasional infidelities aroused feelings of guilt that in turn re-inforced his depressive tendencies. In 1949 he underwent analysis. Psycho-analysis thereafter became, along with politics, his major area of interest and led him to read in rapid succession not only Freud but also Lacan, then little known. Althusser was, together with Hyppolite and Merleau-Ponty (in *The Visible and the Invisible*), one of the first philosophers to recognize the theoreti-cal importance of Lacan's researches, devoting an article to the subject that appeared in the June-July 1963 issue of the *Revue de l'enseignement philosophique*; a second article, "Freud and Lacan," appeared in *La Nouvelle Critique* in De-cember 1964.[49] In the interval the two men became acquainted, in December 1963, and the following month Althusser invited the psychoanalyst—whose weekly seminar at the Hôpital Sainte-Anne in Paris had just been canceled—to give it at the École Normale. Lacan taught there in complete freedom for almost six years before being ousted, in June 1969, having once more in-curred the wrath of a reactionary director.

Let us go back to the period just after the war. The complex relationship between Marx's thought and that of Hegel already occupied a central place in Althusser's thinking. In 1947 and 1950 he published two articles directed against the idealist interpretation of Hegel that in France, under Heidegger's influence, had been given by Kojève and Hyppolite. Then in 1953 he pub-lished two other programmatic texts in the *Revue de l'enseignement philos-ophique*, "On Marxism" and a "Note on Dialectical Materialism." Although these last two articles opened up a relatively original line of research by com-parison with the familiar party line of the period, they aroused a violent reac-tion on the part of Merleau-Ponty two years later. In *Adventures of the Dialectic* he denounced "Leninist" philosophy, criticizing its naturalism and its failure to understand the dialectic, and specifically citing Althusser's articles as rep-resentative of these defects.[50] Merleau-Ponty, himself a former Catholic who had been attracted by Marxism in 1945, clearly felt the need, ten years later, to express his disagreement with Sartre and with the PCF—and this at the very moment when Althusser insisted on giving evidence of his own commit-ment in joining the Communist ranks. From then on, any possibility of dia-logue between the two men disappeared. Althusser later was to have very harsh words for his former teacher, whom he condemned in violent terms—in his 1968 lecture on Lenin—along with the whole idealist tradition in French philosophy.

In the course of making this first approach to Marx, Althusser deepened his knowledge of classical political thought from Machiavelli—whom he always held in high esteem, going so far as to call him the true precursor of Marx and Freud—to Rousseau, as well as Hobbes, Spinoza, and Montesquieu. In 1959 he devoted a penetrating essay to Montesquieu, published in a series edited by Jean Lacroix. What Althusser admired most of all in Montesquieu, as in Machiavelli, was the clearness with which he advanced a materialist view of history and politics. The originality of Althusser's conception of materialism comes through in this essay at once: no longer does one find the commonplaces about the priority of matter over mind, conventional since Lenin, but instead a genuine theory of "discourse" that is developed on the basis of two closely related theses. The first, Freudian in inspiration, asserts the necessity of going "beneath" the surface content of a given statement to discover its latent meaning. The second, which derives directly from Marx, affirms that philosophical discourse, far from enjoying some kind of autonomy, is itself only the effect of a process of production determined—indeed, overdetermined—by various structural constraints of an ideological nature that must be taken into account if they are to be escaped. Establishing these two claims required, as Althusser understood, the sort of uncommon lucidity he found in Machiavelli, Montesquieu, and Marx—three philosophers united in their suspicion of all ideologies. He therefore read them together, and with a special intensity.[51]

This new materialism quickly aroused the interest of the young philosophers who entered the École Normale at the end of the 1950s, among them Alain Badiou (b. 1937), Étienne Balibar (b. 1939), Roger Establet (b. 1939), Pierre Macherey (b. 1938), and Jacques Rancière (b. 1940). Attracted to Marxism, they were also fascinated by psychoanalysis, logic, history of science, and structuralism in general. At the intersection of these fields, Althusser's thought now opened upon new horizons. There followed a period of great intellectual creativity, in the course of which—between 1960 and 1964— Althusser published his principal papers on Marx. These appeared first in journals and subsequently were collected in 1965 in a volume entitled *For Marx*. The same year two volumes came out containing papers delivered by Althusser, Balibar, Establet, Macherey, and Rancière at a seminar held in 1964–65, the theme of which gave the work its name: *Reading "Capital"*. The immediate success of these writings may seem as surprising as the oblivion into which they have now fallen, even in France. To appreciate their true value, it must be kept in mind that at the time they were quite revolutionary—not only, of course, in relation to official Marxism but also in relation to the dominant tradition of French philosophy itself.

FOLLOWING THE BONAPARTIST REACTION, the materialist philosophy that had taken root in France during the eighteenth century was abruptly abandoned. Throughout most of the nineteenth century, under the close supervision of conservative regimes, the majority of French academics— with the exception of a handful of adventurous thinkers attracted to Buddhism and Hinduism—confined themselves to a timid spiritualism, as far removed from history and politics as it was from the growth of scientific ideas. Hegel and Marx were systematically ignored. In the first half of the twentieth century, Nietzsche and Freud suffered the same fate. The idealism of Émile Chartier, who wrote under the name of Alain (1868–1951), the neo-Kantianism of Léon Brunschvicg (1869–1944), and the vitalist metaphysics of Henri Bergson defined the dominant mode of thought between the two world wars. At the time only two Marxist philosophers—Paul Nizan and Georges Politzer—protested against this oppressive atmosphere, without really managing to bring about greater openness.

Nonetheless French philosophy received fresh impetus at the beginning of the twentieth century from the innovative work of a number of scholars, including the sociologists Émile Durkheim and Marcel Mauss, the logician Louis Couturat, and the mathematicians Henri Poincaré, Émile Borel, Jean Nicod, and Jacques Herbrand. But the new spirit in French philosophy at this time owed a special debt to two specialists in the history and philosophy of science, Émile Meyerson and Pierre Duhem, and in the decades that followed to their successors, who included Gaston Bachelard, Jean Cavaillès, Alexandre Koyré, Hélène Metzger, Georges Canguilhem, and Michel Foucault.

The works of Gaston Bachelard (1884–1962) and Jean Cavaillès (1903–44) achieved particular prominence in the 1930s. Bachelard, an autodidact, was interested mainly in physics and chemistry. He sought to give an exact account of the mechanisms that, in allowing science to break free of its ideological "prehistory," had permitted human knowledge to advance. In The New Scientific Spirit (1934) and The Philosophy of No (1940) he identified the will to epistemological "rupture"—the readiness to call into question accepted arguments—as the hallmark of scientific research while also drawing on the resources of psychoanalysis, in The Formation of the Scientific Spirit (1938) and The Psychoanalysis of Fire (1938), to detect the affective "obstacles" in the minds of researchers that delay, and sometimes prevent, acceptance of a new theory.

Cavaillès entered the École Normale Supérieure in 1923 and from 1931 to 1935 held the position, like Merleau-Ponty and Althusser after him, of agrégé-répétiteur. His concern for rigor led him to study logic and do work on the foundations of mathematics, becoming the first French philosopher to publish an article, in 1935, on the doctrines of the Vienna Circle. Unfortunately, he was able to produce only two books during his short life, both important—*Remarks on the Development of the Abstract Theory of Sets* (1938) and a posthumously published work, *On the Logic and Theory of Science* (1947), marked by the influence of Bolzano—in addition to editing the correspondence of Cantor and Dedekind, which appeared in 1937. At the beginning of the war he joined the Resistance, in which he played a major role; later, like Politzer, he was captured by the Nazis and shot.

Neither Bachelard nor Cavaillès, however, nor even Kojève, who in the 1930s gave public lectures on Hegel, made much of an impression outside the academy; within the academy, spiritualism made a reappearance after 1945. Bergson remained the favored author on secondary school reading lists, and in the meantime phenomenology had become the fashionable philosophy in higher education. But university professors paid little attention to the interpretation of Husserl proposed by Sartre, whose libertarian philosophy they found disturbing, preferring instead to embrace the thought of Heidegger, which soon gave rise in France to innumerable imitations displaying, as always, the same willful ignorance of history and science.

In an academic atmosphere of such outstanding mediocrity, Althusser's thought inevitably came as a bombshell. Like Cavaillès, to whom he owed more than is generally acknowledged, Althusser took as his point of departure the idea that philosophy, without itself being a science, must try to conform to the norms of scientific discourse. Philosophy resembles science, he held, in being a form of intellectual labor, a result of theoretical "production" that has meaning only insofar as it respects certain rules. On this view, then, it falls to philosophy to forge *concepts*—that is, definable notions—with clarity and precision and to join them together to form *theses*—propositions capable of being justified, if not by formal demonstrations, then at least by coherent arguments.

Conceived in this way—and here Althusser challenged Sartre's reading of Marx with a vigor that is sometimes surprising—philosophy can only be antihumanist. Less surprisingly, the "theoretical" antihumanism he defended (which is not at all incompatible with a certain "practical" humanism, provided that the two levels are carefully distinguished) had little to do with the principles underlying Heidegger's antihumanism. Althusser's doctrine, to the contrary, was the expression of a radical rationalism. In the tradition of Cavaillès, who had earlier called for the replacement of the "philosophy of consciousness" by a "philosophy of the concept,"[52] Althusser considered the point of view of the subject as simply an "ideological" point of view, either imaginary or the product of deception. Philosophy, he believed, had to move not from "man" but from the objective social and unconscious forces that determine his behavior, often without his knowing it.

Rigorous argumentation, long undervalued by French philosophy, now with Althusser became an essential element of philosophical method. Suddenly a convergence seemed to develop between his approach and that which the structuralists, led by Lévi-Strauss and Lacan, were promoting at this time in anthropology and psychoanalysis. But Althusser, though he was saddled with the label at one point, cannot be considered a structuralist: first, because the use he made of the concept of structure was far removed from that of Lévi-Strauss; second, because he was before everything else a Marxist, and structures interested him less, finally, than their transformation—in other words, than history.

AT THE SAME TIME, Althusser's philosophy, founded on a completely new reading of Marx, upset all received ideas within the international Communist movement. Here again it is necessary to review briefly the history of this movement to have a sense of how badly Marx was misinterpreted between 1890 and 1960.

The Marxists of the Second International undertook to associate Marxism with the Kantianism that was then dominant in German universities. The Russian Marxists adapted themselves, after Lenin's death, to the ideological dictatorship of diamat. Those who emulated them in the Western Communist parties—with a few exceptions like Lukács, Gramsci, and Bloch—developed more or less skillful variants of this fixed ideology. In short, no one within the Marxist movement cared any longer to know what Marx had actually said. Althusser realized very early that this amounted to a form of intellectual abdication on the part of the Communists. Moreover, he was convinced that this abdication was at the root of the impasse in which Stalinism found itself. Inspired by the effort that Lacan was making at the same moment to go back to the letter of Freudian texts, with a view to correcting all the "deviations" to which psychoanalysis had constantly been subject since its birth, he therefore felt the need to go back to the very letter of Marx's writings.

Althusser's main objective, then, was to reread Marx. To this task he brought not only the rigor of the philologist who returns to the original texts, casting aside the commentaries beneath which tradition has buried them, scrutinizes their language, and attempts to grasp once again their internal coherence; he also brought the rigor of the psychoanalyst (for Althusser this is always Lacan) who knows how to hear, behind what the texts say, what they are silent about or try to hide. Althusser thus aimed at a "symptomatic" reading of Marx, sensitive to his silences, to what is left unsaid—to what is left unthought, as it were—in his writings.

This long and patient labor of interpretation allowed Althusser to reveal—even to those who thought they knew him—a new, revitalized Marx; or rather two Marxes, for Althusser was the first to seriously study the passage between two distinct periods in the development of Marx's thought separated by what he called (following Bachelard) an epistemological rupture, similar to the one that separated chemistry from alchemy, and, more generally, science from ideology. In the early period, associated with the *Economic and Philosophical Manuscripts* of 1844, Marx adopted a humanist viewpoint in proclaiming man's need to recover his alienated essence. Marx's protest, ethical rather than scientific in character, remained centered on the notion of the subject. Borrowing the language of Kant, Fichte, and the left-wing Hegelians (most notably, Feuerbach), it saw itself as revolutionary and at the same time humanist in spirit. In any case, it was not yet materialist—and therefore not yet Marxist.

The rupture occurred in 1845, anticipated in the *Theses on Feuerbach* and accomplished in *The German Ideology*. It was in this latter work—a text of central importance to Marx's intellectual development but unknown until 1932—that Marx became himself in becoming a materialist. This difficult transformation, which ushered in the later period of his thought, was comprised in its turn of two aspects that need to be considered together. On the one hand, Marx maintained that the motor of history was neither Spirit (or Mind), as Hegel had held, nor the human subject, as Kant and Fichte had maintained, but the objective (although not apparent—in the empirical sense of the term) whole of productive forces and relations of production. He thus succeeded in opening up to science a new continent, history, whose exploration had to be conducted within the framework of historical materialism. On the other hand, the conflictual nature of history as the record of struggle among social classes led Marx to preserve the Hegelian notion of dialectic while at the same time giving it a new theoretical content. He saw, in effect, as Heidegger might have said, that it was not enough to invert the old idealist dialectic to obtain a materialist dialectic; this new dialectic had to be provided with a precise sense of its own if it were to yield a satisfactory theory of the various ways in which an invisible causality (the ensemble of productive forces and relations of production) produces visible effects in social, political, and ideological life (broadly understood to include science, philosophy, and religion).

This theory was scarcely even sketched by Marx during his lifetime. He lacked the leisure necessary for such a task, having assigned priority to bringing another mission to a successful conclusion, namely, the elaboration of a materialist science of history. Working out the details of a specifically Marxist philosophy therefore in 1965 still remained a matter of unfinished business. This is why Althusser dared to claim at the height of the Cold War, contrary to the opinion of allies and adversaries alike, that Marxist philosophy did not exist—or, at least, did not yet exist. Three years later, on 24 February 1968, invited by Jean Wahl to address the Societé Française de Philosophie at the Sorbonne and, perhaps, inspired by a premonition of the revolts that were soon to shake France, he went further. Adapting the Hegelian metaphor of Minerva's owl, which flew only at the end of day, he declared, "The day is always long, but as luck would have it, it is already far advanced, look: dusk will soon fall. Marxist philosophy will take wing."[53]

How did Althusser expect to be able to make such a prophecy come true? By going back—*really* going back—to *Capital*. For it is in this difficult work, which remains the most detailed statement Marx gave of historical materialism, that the categories of materialist dialectic, or invisible causality, are to be found in their "practical state." To make these categories explicit, Althusser looked to two other thinkers who had both tried to conceive a causal structure of this type: Spinoza, who affirmed that God—or nature—is the cause of itself and of all things, and Freud, who made the unconscious the hidden cause of all mental phenomena. The materialist models proposed by these authors had long fascinated Althusser. For years it was rumored he would be bringing out a book on Spinoza; this appears to have been begun but never finished.[54]

Despite the startling swiftness with which the student revolt of May–June 1968 followed upon the declaration made at the Sorbonne the preceding February, the Marxist philosophy promised by Althusser in the end never took wing. Of the thousand reasons that might be given for such a failure, let us mention two that suffice to explain it. The first is that the possibility of freely developing his ideas was, as a practical matter, ruled out in Althusser's case. Instead of pressing forward with the program of research he had set for himself, even if this meant losing his way from time to time, Althusser felt a moral duty toward his Party to assert nothing of which he was not certain. He was aware, too, that any statement he made had political implications, and so he spent a considerable amount of time formulating, modifying, and sometimes repudiating his positions. Thus it was that in 1967, in the preface to the Italian edition of Reading "Capital", he disavowed the "theoricist" error that he now saw as infecting this work.

Althusser had come to feel that Reading "Capital" was based on an overly simplified opposition between (Marxist) science and (bourgeois) ideology. It assigned to philosophy the mission of elaborating the theory of this opposition, which he sometimes called the "theory of theoretical practices." Such a view was not dissimilar to that of logical positivism—from which it derived, in fact, via Cavaillès—and had the effect of obscuring the properly political dimension of the philosophical task. Once aware of the problem, Althusser set about correcting it. This took him quite a while. Finally, in a series of programmatic texts—two separately published essays, Reply to John Lewis (1973) and Elements of Self-criticism (1974), and a lecture delivered in Amiens in 1975 and published the following year, the last of Althusser's philosophical papers to appear in his lifetime[55]—he managed to redefine philosophy as "class struggle in the field of theory"[56] while recognizing that philosophy has the peculiar property of producing effects without having (as Wittgenstein put it) an object of its own.

The second reason his original project remained incomplete was historical in a quite immediate way. The French revolt of May–June 1968 was not directed by the PCF. It was born outside of the Party and developed in opposition to it. A vast movement of collective exasperation supported by five million strikers, it was led at the beginning by elements on the extreme Left—Maoists, Trotskyites, and anarchists for the most part—who looked to challenge the Party's leadership. Their defeat, plain by July, was a source of satisfaction to the PCF, which in the following years embarked upon a strategy of rapprochement with the Socialist Party, crowned in 1981 with Mitterand's victory at the head of a "united Left" in the presidential elections.

For Althusser, this was a difficult period to live through. As a loyal Communist, albeit a quite unorthodox one, he could not publicly approve the pro-Chinese faction in 1968, though it included a number of his students and he was sympathetic to its aims. What is more, the day after the first night on the barricades in May he fell into depression and spent the ensuing

weeks in a psychiatric clinic. With the decline of the revolutionary ideal during the 1970s, the dream of a revival of Marxist philosophy vanished. The
PCF, moreover, had no wish whatever to see such a revival. Although he
knew this, Althusser could not bring himself to leave the party, preferring to
go on challenging it from within. His weariness is evident in a letter that he
addressed on 16 January 1978 to a Georgian friend, the philosopher Merab
Mamardachvili, in which he reproached himself for having done nothing
more than manufacture "a small, very French *justification*" of Marxism's
claim to be a science[57] and doubted that he had succeeded even in this. The
articles that he published in *Le Monde* in April of the same year under the title
"What Can No Longer Go on in the Communist Party" earned him a last
flurry of media attention.[58] The party could not have cared less: it had long
ago renounced, on Moscow's orders, any revolutionary ambitions it might
have had. Like so many other activists, Althusser could only feel that he had
been betrayed, causing him to sink further still into depression. Then, two
years later, tragedy.

IN JULY 1982, in a private clinic (and later also at home), Althusser began to
write again. Only a few fragments of these texts, which echo as if with a voice
from beyond the grave, have been published: a strange piece devoted to the
"materialism of the encounter" and influenced by the work of his friend
Jacques Derrida, in which Althusser tried to deconstruct the classical concept
of materialism in such a way as to be able to link it up with the Heideggerian
conception of nothingness as primordial "void,"[59] and a lengthy autobiographical essay composed in 1985, *The Future Lasts a Long Time*, which, despite
(or perhaps because of) the narcissism to which it testifies, casts an interesting light on certain aspects of his tormented personality.[60]

Other unpublished writings will no doubt come to enrich our sense of Althusser's work still further. Will they succeed in restoring him to the important place that he once occupied and that he seems now to have lost? Nothing could be less certain. But even if it is difficult after the Cold War to reread
Althusser's works without finding them oddly dated, they nonetheless represent an attempt to answer a question in two parts that continues to exist for
us as it did for their author. Is the revolutionary hope (or, if one prefers, the
hope for a transformation of society in the direction of greater justice—a
hope that appeared in the twentieth century chiefly in the form of Commu-

nism) now condemned to oblivion once and for all? If not, how must one proceed today in order to draw from Marx's thought the philosophy that it announced but did not supply and that for more than a century now has yet to take wing?

Althusser never agreed to reply in the affirmative to the first part of this question. Nonetheless he did not deceive himself with regard to the capacity of the proletariat—insofar as this term still had any sense—to transform, peacefully or otherwise, industrial societies in the technocratic age. Although he continued to sincerely believe in the moral (if not historical) necessity of such a transformation, he did not see, any more than did Marcuse, which social group could bring it about. Hence his political hesitations, which persist today. Hence, too, his desire to found a new philosophy by going back to the actual writings of Marx, but by rereading them in the light of everything that history and the development of the social sciences have revealed over the last century. Althusser felt sure that these texts have something to say to us still today. That Marxism—or at least a certain form of Marxism—was dead he was well aware. But he did not doubt that Marx's thought would remain very much alive for anyone who could decipher it, and on this point, no doubt, he was not completely mistaken.

It remains to be determined how Marx is to be reread in these last years of the twentieth century. Faced with a long and arduous journey—on which others, notably Cornelius Castoriadis[61] and Jacques Derrida, have made a start—Althusser has suggested paths to follow that, without being the only imaginable ones, will go on being of interest for many years to come.[62] For this reason alone it would be presumptuous to suppose that his work has already been superseded. Nonetheless it probably will come to be seen, along with that of Marcuse and Sartre, as one of those glorious failures whose lessons will need to be contemplated if we are to succeed in devising a political theory well adapted to present-day problems—that is, if we really want (as the French philosopher Manuel de Diéguez has put it) to stop thinking about politics in religious terms and to renounce all forms of secular "idolatry."[63]

Chapter Five

Reason in Question

Structure versus Subject

Torn between Auschwitz and Hiroshima—between the impossible memory of the Holocaust and the unbearable terror of nuclear apocalypse—split into two by the Cold War, and skeptical about the feasibility of building a Community along the lines proposed by technocrats and politicians, Europe in the 1950s had almost ceased to believe in its own future.

Under these circumstances it comes as no surprise that intellectuals found themselves in severe disarray. Some of them reacted, as we have seen, by embracing engagement—siding either with the American model, the Marxist model, or an improbable third way. But others were far from sharing such ideological enthusiasms. Pessimism raged among artists and writers. The absurd ruled in the theater, in the plays of Ionesco and Adamov. In the films of Antonioni and Resnais, the cinema witnessed the triumph of incommunicability. The same despair, the same rejection of civilization, the same controlled anger inspired the canvasses of Dubuffet, the novels of Beckett, the aphorisms of Cioran.[1] In its extreme forms, this despair was liable to lead to suicide. From Paul Celan to Primo Levi, from Nicolas de Staël to Mark Rothko, from Lucien Sebag to Niko Poulantzas, a disturbing number of artists and thinkers chose in the decades following 1945 to take their own lives.

More numerous still were those who, out of disenchantment with the world, moved away from politics. Convinced of their powerlessness to influence events, these disillusioned intellectuals preferred to content themselves with observing the world with a distant eye, feeling that their mission was not to change it but, at most, to understand it. Among this group, two movements arose in the aftermath of the war. The first proposed to recover the lost meaning of modern culture through interpretation; the second, to illuminate the functioning of symbolic processes through analysis of their constituent structures. Philosophical hermeneutics and scientific structuralism thus emerged, on the threshold of the second half-century, as competing ways of responding to the crisis of Europe, to its spiritual distress as well as to the inexorable loss of political independence.

IN ITS ORIGINAL SENSE, hermeneutics (from the Greek hermēneia, meaning "interpretation") designated a method of critical exegesis applied to biblical texts, going back to the eighteenth century and illustrated particularly by the work of the German Protestant philosopher and theologian Friedrich Schleiermacher (1768–1834). But at least since the time of Dilthey it has been realized that interpretation, identified with internal understanding (Verstehen) as opposed to external explanation (Erklären), is a common activity in many other fields, particularly in the humanities and social sciences.

With Hans-Georg Gadamer (b. 1900)—who, having briefly served as rector of the University of Leipzig just after the war, passed the rest of his career at Heidelberg, where he retired in 1968—hermeneutics assumed a larger meaning associated with an attempt at "deciphering" that was applicable to all the sciences and, beyond these, to all cultural productions, considered as sets of signs. This attempt was necessary for two reasons. First, if the crisis of reason had first arisen in the 1920s, the catastrophe of the Second World War—the ultimate disaster of modernity—had created a situation in which the meaning of humanity's highest cultural productions now seemed totally lost for Europeans. Second, now not only the conditions under which objective knowledge is possible needed to be identified, as in Kant's time, but indeed the conditions under which understanding itself was possible.

The recovery—or, more exactly, the "recollection"—of meaning therefore became for Gadamer the proper business of philosophy. Implicit in his doctoral thesis, composed under Heidegger's supervision and devoted to the ethical meaning of Plato's dialogue Philebus, this project furnished the main lines of his work after 1945, culminating with the publication in 1960 of Truth and Method. In this monumental work, which exercised a decisive influence on the subsequent development of the hermeneutic movement, Gadamer tried both to formulate its methodological ambitions and to put these to the test in three fundamental fields: art, history, and language.

For Kant, a work of art is a pure "form" presented to the judgment of taste. Gadamer held, to the contrary, that a work of art invites us, provided we know how to elucidate its ontological significance, to experience a "truth content" that cannot be reduced to the understanding of the author's intentions and whose objective richness is not inferior to that of scientific knowledge. History, like art, transmits the traditions that constitute a culture. Because each culture has its own share of truth, history must be rescued from historicist relativism. This dual analysis led Gadamer to assert the fundamental role played by language in all human activities: to understand is to be in agreement with others about the meaning attributed to certain signs. The task of philosophical hermeneutics, on this view, is to facilitate both intersubjective comprehension and communication while saving language from the "technicist" reduction imposed upon natural languages by the formalism of modern science.

If it remains unclear upon what ground—metaphysical or theological—such a project is to be based, and if in this respect *Truth and Method* constitutes a typical production of German idealism—the latest in a long line, and surely the only great Heideggerian-style work published in Germany since the end of the war—the conclusions at which Gadamer arrived were rather far removed from those of his teacher. The importance he attached to language places him nearer to Wittgenstein than to Heidegger. In fact, Gadamer is the first major German philosopher to have attempted to provide a link between Continental phenomenology and analytic philosophy. This emphasis on language—together with the quality of his aesthetic intuitions, his characteristic faith in the virtues of dialogue, and the optimism that supports his Platonic quest for meaning—explains the widespread appeal of Gadamer's approach, not only in Germany but also in Italy and France, particularly upon Gianni Vattimo (b. 1936) in *Poetry and Ontology* (1967) and *The Adventure of Difference* (1980), and upon Paul Ricoeur.

Born in 1913, Ricoeur obtained his *agrégation* in philosophy and then, following a period of imprisonment in Germany during the war, passed the main part of his career in higher education, first at Strasbourg and the Sorbonne and later, after 1965, at the University of Nanterre. A humanist of vast learning, keenly interested in literature as well as in the social sciences, and an avid traveler open to Anglo-American culture as well as to the German tradition, he initially associated himself with the Christian existentialist movement, represented in France in the 1930s by Gabriel Marcel (1889–1973), and with the personalist doctrines of Emmanuel Mounier. In Marcel he discovered the model for a style of philosophical reflection that accorded a central place to religious questions without renouncing conceptual rigor. It was also because of Marcel that Ricoeur took up the study of phenomenology before the war, particularly Husserl—whose *Ideas* he translated into French in 1950—and Jaspers, to whom he devoted his first book, *Karl Jaspers and the Philosophy of Existence* (1947), written in collaboration with Mikel Dufrenne.

Preoccupied by the theme of sin, Ricoeur sought to respond to his own concerns as a believer in a way that would be worthy of the requirements of phenomenological method, which, by virtue of its desire to be faithful to things themselves, seemed to him the sole rigorous reflective method. Ricoeur then undertook a massive project entitled *Philosophy of the Will*, the first volume of which (*The Voluntary and the Involuntary*) appeared in 1950; two subsequent volumes (*Fallible Man* and *The Symbolism of Evil*), both of which came out originally in 1960, were later collected under the title *Finitude and Guilt*. In the course of these three volumes, the classical questions that inspired his work—How can one wish evil? What is bad faith? What is the meaning of an involuntary act?—led him to explore the depths of the unconscious beneath the surface layer of consciousness as well as the symbolic universe in which the major religions attempt to deal with the problem of evil. He thus came into contact with psychoanalysis and hermeneutics simultaneously, taking from each the idea that human reality is constituted above all by signs, the actual deciphering of which is endless. This intuition was developed in his next two books, *Freud and Philosophy: An Essay on Interpretation* (1965) and *The Conflict of Interpretations: Essays in Hermeneutics* (1969).

All these books approached the question of language in terms of symbolism. But it was mainly as a result of political disillusionment that Ricoeur decided to go into partial exile in the United States, where he taught regularly after 1970 at the University of Chicago (convinced of the need to modernize the French university system, he was disappointed by the turn of events in 1968–69 and elected to take early retirement from Nanterre), and to take a closer interest in the linguistic sciences. Along with Gadamer, then, he became one of the first Continental thinkers to strike up a dialogue with analytic philosophy, which produced two more important works on language, *The Rule of Metaphor* (1975) and the three-volume *Time and Narrative* (1983–85).

The first of these two works contemplated metaphor in terms of the creation of meaning and the enrichment of literary texts that arises from it. *Time and Narrative* went beyond linguistic analysis, moving from a consideration of the literature of the past to pose the very question of the possibility of historical knowledge, of its nature and use. It is true, of course, that a work of history always comes under the head of narrative, even when its author intends—in the spirit of the *Annales* school, for example—to attack factual history by substituting for it a long-term perspective; but this sort of account is not a narrative form like others. Historians may introduce various plots in order to bring back the past, but the reality that they are speaking to us about is indeed *our* reality. The past belongs to us to the extent that we belong to it and that our present actions fit into a continuous memory—to this extent, for individuals as for peoples, identity is not something given but an unfinished construction whose only possible medium is time.

Finally, in *Oneself as Another* (1990), the semantic and pragmatic analysis of the subject was linked together with a provisional ontology of the person in order to sketch the outlines of an ethics. Ricoeur sees this as the business of practical reason, whose requirements the philosopher must try to satisfy without, however, renouncing his independence vis-à-vis his own religious faith and political commitments.

For Ricoeur, then, as for all partisans of hermeneutics, the meaning of the world and of life indubitably exists beyond the signs that express it—a view vigorously contested by structuralists, for whom the "signified" is always a simple effect of the "signifier," and the subject an effect of the invisible linguistic, unconscious, and social structures that generate it, unbeknownst to the subject itself.

THE ORIGINS OF STRUCTURALISM lie in an epistemological revolution carried out at the beginning of the century by the Swiss linguist Ferdinand de Saussure. Saussure sought to lay the basis for a genuine science of language, distinct from classical philology, which was more concerned with the historical evolution of languages than with their internal organization. At the heart of this science was a most promising idea, namely, that a language is not a haphazard collection of words but a system of signs that are connected with each other according to specific rules. It constitutes an autonomous totality, referring only to itself and possessing its own structure. Accordingly, it was the analysis of this structure that henceforth had to guide the linguist's approach.

Saussure's *Course in General Linguistics* (1916), published by two of his former students three years after his death, thus appears in retrospect as one of the founding works of modern social science. At the time, however, it was hardly noticed, except by a small group of Russian writers and linguists who dreamed, amid the swirling winds of revolution, of elaborating a new theory of literature. Among these young theorists an exceptional figure emerged: Roman Jakobson (1896–1982).

Born in Moscow, Jakobson displayed at a very young age a remarkable facility for learning languages. As an adolescent he was an enthusiastic admirer of the artistic avant-garde of the day; his friends included the painter Malevich and the poets Khlebnikov and Mayakovsky. In March 1915 he took part in the founding of the Moscow Circle, a result of the encounter between futurist theorists and the Russian linguistic school, represented by Prince Nikolai Sergeevich Troubetskoy (1890–1938). During this time he also read Husserl's *Logical Investigations*, which he later claimed had a great influence upon him. In 1917, a few months before the October Revolution, he established a society for the study of poetic language in Petrograd. Its members proposed to study literature as a purely linguistic construction and saw in poetry—a sort of language about language—its very essence. Conscious of their Slavic roots, the formalists (as they called themselves) were also concerned with ethnography and folklore, in particular popular poetry, whose typically anonymous productions seemed to be the product of verbal invention that was at once spontaneous and subtle.

It soon became clear that official approval of such innovative but "elitist" researches was weakening, and in 1920 Jakobson departed for Czechoslovakia. In Prague he got to know Carnap and discovered Saussure's *Course in General Linguistics*, whose ideas redirected the course of his own work. Also during this period, in Vienna, he met up again with Troubetskoy, who had likewise chosen exile. Their exchanges soon gave birth to phonology, the fundamental branch of structural linguistics. In the years that led up to the founding of the Cercle linguistique de Prague (later better known as the Prague School) in 1926, then, Jakobson decisively turned away from formalism toward structuralism.

Forced once again by events to emigrate, he settled in 1941 in the United States, where he finished out his career. But before joining the faculty at Harvard—where in 1951 he first met the young Noam Chomsky, then a junior member of the Society of Fellows—and later the Massachusetts Institute of Technology—where he and Chomsky were colleagues—Jakobson taught for several years in New York at the École Libre des Hautes Études, a French university-in-exile founded during the winter of 1941–42. The dean of the École was not unknown to him—a fellow countryman, the Russian (later French) philosopher Alexandre Koyré. Their reunion in New York was to be decisive for the future of structuralism.

ALEXANDRE KOYRÉ (1892–1964) was born at Taganrog, on the Sea of Azov in southwestern Russia, into a Jewish family of the commercial bourgeoisie. While still very young he participated in the political movement stemming from the 1905 Revolution, was arrested by the police, and completed his secondary studies in prison. There, it is said, he first read Husserl's *Logical Investigations*. From 1908 to 1911 he attended lectures by Husserl and Hilbert at Göttingen. From Husserl's phenomenology, which remained for him more a method than a metaphysics (although fascinated by the eidetic reduction, he rejected Husserl's turn in the direction of transcendental idealism), Koyré retained the critique of positivism and the Platonic insistence on the intellectual objectivity of scientific and philosophical concepts.

After a brief stay in Paris, during which he wrote a paper on the idea of God in the philosophy of Saint Anselm (published in 1923), he moved to Switzerland. When the First World War broke out he returned to Moscow and fought on the Russian front. A socialist but not a Leninist (he took part in the February Revolution of 1917 but not the October Revolution), he emigrated once more in 1919, returning to Paris. There he continued his studies in medieval religious philosophy, composing an essay entitled *Philosophy and the National Problem in Russia at the Beginning of the Nineteenth Century* (1928) in which he uncovered the ideas that in his view linked German idealism to the speculative mysticism of the Renaissance. Then, while doing research for his next book, *The Philosophy of Jacob Boehme* (1929), he realized that Boehme could not be understood without reference to the new astronomy elaborated a half-century earlier by Copernicus.

Consequently Koyré threw himself into the study of the history of science from antiquity through the eighteenth century. He was guided along the way by the advice of his teacher and friend Émile Meyerson (1859–1933), the French (originally Polish) epistemologist whose *Identity and Reality* (1908) sought to develop a theory of knowledge that was distinct from both positivism and conventionalism. Koyré was influenced too by the works of Duhem as well as those of Cassirer, who was one of the first to have emphasized the philosophical interest of the history of ideas. At the same time he joined the faculty of the fifth section (religious sciences) of the École Pratique des Hautes Études and, in 1932, founded the journal *Recherches Philosophiques*, which helped make Heidegger known in France and published the whole of the Parisian avant-garde of the period, including Sartre, Klossowski, Bataille, and Lacan.

Two works by Bachelard, *The New Scientific Spirit* (1934) and *The Formation of the Scientific Spirit* (1938), persuaded Koyré that scientific progress came about not in a linear, but in a discontinuous, fashion by means of "breaks" and "ruptures" that were provoked more often by the emergence of new theoretical conceptions than by empirical observation of facts. He later applied Bachelard's thesis to the history of modern physics and astronomy in two great books, *Galilean Studies* (1939) and *From the Closed World to the Infinite Universe* (1957). Koyré convincingly showed that the mathematization of physics inaugurated by Galileo was neither a detailed reformulation nor a purely technical innovation. Quite to the contrary, it signaled an intellectual revolution—a transformation of man's picture of the world. The medieval belief in a closed and hierarchical *cosmos* was now done away with, replaced by the idea of a universe that was infinite and homogenous in three directions. This transformation amounted, in short, to a global change in habits of thought, as much in the domain of science as of philosophy and religion. Such a discontinuist and deliberately antipositivist interpretation of the advance of knowledge exercised in its turn, as we will see later, a decisive influence on the early investigations of Michel Foucault and Thomas Kuhn.

These books alone would have sufficed to establish the importance of Koyré's work. But there were other grounds for his reputation as well. For Koyré was not only a philosopher and historian but also a formidable *passeur*, a man who understood—as Père Mersenne had in the seventeenth century—how to put himself at the center of the most innovative thinking of the day and, by virtue of this, to give it added force. In addition to introducing Heidegger's philosophy in France, he also helped make the early works of Hegel known—the point of departure for a revival of Hegelian studies presided over by his disciple Kojève. It was also Koyré who, during his New York exile, had the happy idea of putting Jakobson in touch with the French anthropologist and ethnographer Claude Lévi-Strauss.

BORN IN 1908, Lévi-Strauss was an *agrégé* in philosophy who published his first paper in 1927 on the philosophical assumptions of dialectical materialism. After teaching for a few years at the secondary level he came to feel the need to flee both Europe and a style of philosophy that offered no contact with the outside world. With the help of the sociologist Célestin Bouglé (1870–1940), at the time the director of the École Normale Supérieure, he was given the opportunity to go to South America, doing research in ethnology. Appointed to the University of São Paulo, he led a first expedition among the Caduveo and Bororo Indians, and then in 1938 a second expedition, again in Brazil, among the Nambikwara and the Tupi-Kawahib. The story of these expeditions he later related with humor and nostalgia in a memoir noted for its literary style, Tristes Tropiques (1955).

The coming of the war brought Lévi-Strauss to New York. There he made the acquaintance of Koyré, who, as we have mentioned, introduced him to Roman Jakobson in 1942. From Jakobson he first learned about structural linguistics and quickly grasped its possibilities. Sensing that all symbolic social phenomena could be treated as a system of signs possessing its own specific structure, it occurred to him to apply the Saussurian method to a nonlinguistic field, using it to explain kinship relations in illiterate societies. This remarkable intuition, which Jakobson played a major role in shaping, gave rise after the war to a book called Elementary Structures of Kinship (1949). By subjecting a vast and diffuse collection of empirical observations to clear and rigorous logical analysis, it revolutionized social anthropology. Nonetheless it had trouble winning acceptance in the Anglo-American world, where less theoretical styles of research prevailed.

Several other important works followed: Structural Anthropology (the first volume of which appeared in 1958 and the second in 1973), Totemism (1962), The Savage Mind (1962)—the last chapter of which challenged both Lévy-Bruhl's notion of a "prelogical mentality" as well as the Sartrian conception of dialectic—and, most notably, the four-volume Introduction to a Science of Mythology, consisting of The Raw and the Cooked (1964), From Honey to Ashes (1967), The Origin of Table Manners (1968), and Naked Man (1971). This last work, aimed at showing that the religious myths of the American Indians constitute a unified corpus whose various internal elements are organized by means of rules, demonstrated the fruitfulness of the structural method. But it also demonstrated its limits. In the same way that Descartes, in order to provide a ground for physics, had to reduce matter to extension, so Lévi-Strauss found himself obliged, in order to construct a science of mythology, to extract myths from the sociocultural context in which they were produced and transmitted, and to reduce them to pure series of semantic units, combinable with each other according to rules that evidently owed less to history than to algebra.

Having in the meantime, thanks to the support of Merleau-Ponty, been elected to the Collège de France in 1959, Lévi-Strauss reigned over French anthropology for two decades while continuing to develop his materialistic, atheistic, and pessimistic view of the world in three final books: *The Way of the Masks* (1975), *The View from Afar* (1983), and *The Jealous Potter* (1985). In these works one also finds an increasingly marked interest in music and art (especially the primitive art that Max Ernst and André Breton had taught him to appreciate during their years of joint exile in New York), understood as the sole means available to humanity to raise itself above the mediocrity of life. In his later years the very model of the great man of letters shut up in an ivory tower, Lévi-Strauss remained a devout conservative when it came to Western music and art (where his interest in modernity hardly went beyond Wagner and the impressionists) as well as politics (owing to his conviction that human societies cannot be improved).

But the real interest of his thought obviously lies elsewhere. Lévi-Strauss was a man of immense learning who—like two of his teachers, the sociologist Marcel Mauss (1872–1950) and the sinologist Marcel Granet (1884–1940)—was able to bring to the strangest features of exotic cultures a critical eye no less objective than the one brought to bear by the biologist upon a section observed through a microscope. His originality consisted in the ambition to establish a science of society that could equally claim to be a science of mind while at the same time making it possible to avoid reliance on psychology, a discipline of questionable standing in his view. The coherence of his approach is seen in its three fundamental aims: to define societies as symbolic systems; to show that these systems cannot be hierarchically ranked, each one being entitled to the same dignity as the others; and to establish their profound unity at the structural level—the ultimate measure of the unity of the human mind.

Lévi-Strauss's other great achievement, namely, that for a half-century he led the structuralist movement in the social sciences, was not less important. He was responsible, in particular, for bringing the psychoanalyst Jacques Lacan (1901–81) into contact with structuralism.

LACAN'S THOUGHT, although it displays incontestable similarities with that of Lévi-Strauss, nonetheless went beyond structuralism in so many different ways that it can be grasped in its full complexity only by retracing its development step by step.

Born into a provincial bourgeois family, Lacan was briefly tempted in his youth by the doctrines of the extreme Right. His move to Paris, his medical studies, and his attraction to the avant-garde produced a rapid evolution in his thinking. Fascinated by an article published in July 1930 by Salvador Dali in the first issue of *Surréalisme au service de la Révolution*, "The Rotten Ass," he made the painter's acquaintance. Dali explained to him the meaning of the "paranoiac-critical" method, based on systematic investigation of visual hallucinations. Lacan's doctoral thesis, *On Paranoiac Psychosis in Relation to Personality* (1932), showed the influence of this discovery and revealed his early interest—stimulated by one of his professors, the psychiatrist Gaetan Gatien de Clérambault—in the relationship between madness and artistic creation. It also represented an awkward first attempt to provide psychiatric theory with a psychoanalytic dimension.

This work passed unnoticed outside surrealist circles, however, except by Nizan, who devoted an admiring article to it in the Communist daily *L'Humanité*. The surrealists invited him to contribute to their new journal, *Minotaur*. Two provocative essays by Lacan, who had just entered into analysis, appeared in it in 1933, "The Problem of Style and the Psychiatric Conception of Paranoiac Forms of Experience" and "Motives for Paranoiac Crime." From this period of feverish activity dates his worship of style (both literary and sartorial), his taste for secret societies, and a penchant for hermeticism that he was never to lose.

Lacan was increasingly intrigued in the following years by the vast perspectives opened up to reflection by psychoanalysis. He therefore embarked upon the task of rereading the basic writings of Freud while at the same time exploring the work of Nietzsche—a new interpretation of which had recently been proposed by his friend Georges Bataille (1897–1962), at once aestheticizing and individualistic—and attending lectures by the Russian-born philosopher Alexandre Kojève (1902–68) aimed at arousing a new interest in Hegelian thought in France.

A nephew of the painter Kandinsky, Kojève had left the Soviet Union in 1920 to go to Germany. At Heidelberg, where he studied under Jaspers, he became friends with Alexandre Koyré and married Koyré's sister-in-law in 1927. The year before he defended a thesis, directed by Jaspers, on the Russian theologian Vladimir Soloviev (1853–1900) and then decided to settle in Paris, where Koyré had been an associate lecturer at the École Pratique des

Hautes Études since 1922. Under his guidance Kojève immersed himself in the history of mathematics and physics in order to compose *The Idea of Determinism in Classical and Modern Physics* (1932). That same year, he began to attend Koyré's lectures on the religious philosophy of the young Hegel. During the summer of 1933, Koyré, shortly due to leave to teach in Cairo, proposed that Kojève give the course in his absence. Kojève accepted and in the fall became in his turn an associate lecturer at the École Pratique. His seminar, devoted primarily to a reading of the *Philosophy of Spirit* (then not yet translated into French), continued regularly until the fall of 1939. Organized around the theme of the "end of history"—a theme that, with the rise of fascist regimes, had an odd resonance at the time—it was attended by a small but dedicated group of avant-garde intellectuals and writers: Henry Corbin, Raymond Queneau, Georges Bataille, Raymond Aron, Maurice Merleau-Ponty, Jean Hyppolite, and, from 1934, by Lacan himself.

Thanks to Kojève, therefore, Lacan discovered in Hegel's writings a theoretical elaboration of the concepts that preoccupied him—a philosophy of desire, language, and intersubjectivity. The phenomenological dialectic of "master" and "slave," in particular, helped him develop the theme of the struggle between two consciousnesses, brought face-to-face with each other in search of mutual recognition. Similarly, the Hegelian problem of alienation overlapped with his own thinking about mental illness. Lacan considered collaborating with Kojève on an article that would give systematic expression to this intertwined reading of Hegel and Freud, an idea he then abandoned in favor of writing what was to be his first personal contribution to psychoanalytic theory—a paper on the "mirror stage,"[2] read in August 1936 in Marienbad at a conference chaired by Freud's English disciple Ernest Jones, who abruptly cut him off after ten minutes. Seventeen years later, Hegel resurfaced in the central thesis—"the unconscious of the subject is the discourse of the other"—of a paper Lacan delivered at a conference held in Rome in September 1953, "The Function and Field of Speech and Language in Psychoanalysis."[3]

But in the meantime other influences came to be grafted upon this Hegelian base. First, in 1949, at the time of its publication, Lacan read Lévi-Strauss's *The Elementary Structures of Kinship*. He arranged to meet the author and the two became friends. Then some months later, in 1950, Lévi-Strauss introduced him to Roman Jakobson. Shortly afterwards, with the help of Jean Beaufret (from 1951 one of his patients), Lacan deepened his knowledge of the philosophy of Heidegger, whom he later visited in Germany and subsequently, in 1955, received in turn at his own home. He also translated an essay by Heidegger, "Logos," which appeared in the first issue of the journal *La Psychanalyse* in 1956.

Still, there was not any real convergence, not in any deep way at least, between Heidegger's thought and Lacan's work, even if the two men shared, among other things, an identical taste for the oracular style of pronouncement. It does appear, however, that Heidegger may have ended up convincing Lacan that philosophy was finished. Nonetheless Lacan had no intention of embracing a "thought of Being," no matter what ideas—evident in the paper presented at the Rome Congress in 1953—he may have borrowed from *Being and Time*. Only Freudian theory, in the reformulation he would attempt to give it, seemed to him adequate to take over (in the Hegelian sense of the term *Aufheben*) from philosophy. This, in any case, is the conclusion that seems to emerge from the exchange that took place between Lacan and Jean Hyppolite during Lacan's 10 February 1954 seminar.

It remained to work out on what basis and in what terms psychoanalytic theory was to be reformulated. For Lacan this meant going back to the letter of Freudian texts—the central tenet of his approach since July 1953—and, more importantly still, rereading these texts in the light of structural linguistics. Here Jakobson's role was once again decisive, this time doubly so. On the one hand it was Jakobson who, in 1950, had introduced Lacan to Saussure's work. Lacan immediately grasped, as Lévi-Strauss had done previously with regard to anthropology, the potential significance of importing the method of structural analysis into psychoanalysis and sought to apply it to the "signifying" productions of the unconscious, dreams, and symptoms. In June 1954 at his weekly seminar, officially begun the year before at the Hôpital Sainte-Anne in Paris, he first discussed Saussure's theory of the sign. By 1958 he was prepared to assert that the unconscious is in fact "structured in the most radical way like a language."[4] This amounted to proclaiming, in the tradition of the discontinuist philosophy associated with Koyré, the fundamental identity of the two great ruptures represented by the discoveries of Saussure and Freud.

On the other hand, it was Jakobson's 1956 article "Two Aspects of Language and Two Types of Aphasia" that suggested to Lacan a new approach to what Freud regarded as the two fundamental mechanisms of the dream, "condensation" and "displacement."[5] Taking substantial liberties with Jakobson's analysis, Lacan henceforth saw condensation as equivalent to metaphor and displacement to metonymy. From this he drew an original interpretation of Freud's great work, *The Interpretation of Dreams*, enriched by references to classical rhetoric and expounded in a paper given at the Sorbonne on 9 May 1957, "The Agency of the Letter in the Unconscious, or Reason since Freud."[6]

In the hall of mirrors thus created at the intersection of psychoanalysis and linguistics, it very quickly became apparent that one no longer knew whether language was to be considered as the condition of the unconscious, or the reverse: both formulas are found in Lacan. But at least two things were clear, namely, that the unconscious is structured like a language and that the function of the "I" in this "signifying chain" is analogous to that of a "shifter" (a term borrowed from Jakobson); that is, to a grammatical unit responsible for designating the subject of an utterance without, however, signifying it. This conception of a subject divided by the unconscious—echoing the Freudian notion of the splitting of the ego (*Ichspaltung*) and radically opposed to the Cartesian, Husserlian, and Sartrian philosophies of the *cogito*—came to be completed in September 1960 by the thesis, introduced at a Royaumont colloquium organized by Jean Wahl, that the subject is a simple element in the symbolic structure ("a signifier is that which represents the subject for another signifier"[7]). In the years that followed, the systematic use of "graphs" permitted Lacan to embroider many variations on this theme.

With the collection of selected articles and lectures in a volume entitled *Écrits* (1966), Lacan finally achieved fame. Of course, the details of the various conflicts that opposed him to the psychoanalytic establishment and complicated relations among rival interpreters of his teaching hardly interested the general public, but they were of intense interest to the attentive crowd of students that flocked to hear him lecture, now at the École Normale Supérieure (1964–69) and later at the law faculty of the Panthéon (1969–80). This belated renown both pleased and tired him, however. As Lacan grew older, he stepped back from his own discourse. He made unforeseen detours through the work of Wittgenstein (during the 1969–70 academic year) and of Joyce. Convinced that at bottom he had been misunderstood, even by those who tried to listen to him carefully, he took refuge during the 1970s in increasingly enigmatic reflections upon the structure of the psyche. Gradually abandoning the linguistic model, he now tried to understand the mind in mathematical terms, through braids and other complex topological figures, such as Borromean rings (wrongly called "knots" by Lacan).

In the last sessions of his class at the Panthéon in the spring of 1980,

Lacan scarcely talked, contenting himself with drawing mysterious diagrams on the blackboard that left his audience perplexed. He died the following year, leaving the presumptive heirs to his intellectual legacy deeply divided over how it was to be communicated. This, combined with numerous technical difficulties of transcription, caused a considerable delay in the publication of the complete twenty-six-volume edition of his oral lectures, covering the period 1953–80. Begun in 1973, it is still far from being finished.

Lacan's thought was rejected by a part of the psychoanalytic community, which disapproved his very personal conception of "cure," and poorly received by professional philosophers, with a few exceptions (Hyppolite, Merleau-Ponty, Althusser, Derrida, and Badiou in France; Cavell in the United States). Nonetheless, of all the approaches to philosophy in the twentieth century that have tried to fully acknowledge the consequences of the end of metaphysics, it remains one of the most important and one of the most coherent.

WITH THE CONCURRENT PUBLICATION of Lacan's Écrits and Lévi-Strauss's *Introduction to a Science of Mythology*, structuralism became the dominant ideology of the European social sciences of the 1960s. In France this fashion was also promoted by the spectacular development of linguistics proper (associated with the work of Émile Benveniste), semiology (with Roland Barthes, whose *Mythologies* had appeared in 1957), new forms of literary criticism (with Tzvetan Todorov and Gérard Genette), and historical analysis (with Jean-Pierre Vernant, whose *Myth and Thought among the Greeks* appeared in 1965), as well as by the belated discovery of the writings of Georges Dumézil (1898–1986), a linguist and historian who from the end of the 1930s, following in the footsteps of his teacher Marcel Granet, used a kind of structural method to compare the religious myths of Indo-European peoples, culminating in his three-volume *Myth and Epic* (1968–73).

It was also in France, as we have seen, that this fashion produced its first specifically philosophical consequences, at least in a polemical way. For despite their many differences, Lévi-Strauss, Lacan, Dumézil, Barthes, and their followers share certain fundamental orientations. Materialist, antidialectical, anti-Marxist (with some qualification in the latter regard, since neither Vernant, nor even Barthes when he started out, completely rejected Marxism), they were above all anti-Sartrian, which is to say antihumanist. As advocates of a "philosophy of the concept," they wished to put an end to the primacy of consciousness insisted upon by the author of Existentialism and Humanism.

The scientific study of structures—whether of language, the unconscious, myths, and social relations—demonstrated, in their view, that the autonomy of the subject was illusory. Now that it stood exposed as a purely imaginary effect of narcissism, the subject had to be ousted from the throne it had occupied since Descartes. As a result, Sartre's voluntarism, his optimistic belief in the possibility of influencing the course of history, and his taste for engagement lost all justification. The structuralists, by contrast, were skeptical of political action (even if Lévi-Strauss had been a socialist in his youth and Dumézil a monarchist); in the 1960s they were positivists or aesthetes, or both at once. Although they admitted the necessity of an objective knowledge of symbolic phenomena, they did not expect it to help change the world. Moreover, they did not consider themselves—if one takes them at their word—to be philosophers, but at most practitioners of this or that form of knowledge.

Must we take them at their word? One would have to conclude, then, that there is no such thing as structuralist philosophy. However, while the structuralists (Lacan included) denied that they were philosophers, Althusser, Foucault, Derrida, and other professional philosophers found themselves characterized as structuralists by the media and public opinion. With the exception of Michel Serres (b. 1930)—whose encyclopedic thought, nourished by study of Leibniz and Bachelard, particularly in the five-volume Hermès (1969–80), nonetheless bears less upon the concept of structure than on that of communication—these philosophers explicitly rejected the label in question: Althusser because he considered himself a Marxist; Foucault and Derrida because, in spite of their occasional interest in certain insights of Lacan or Dumézil, the original inspiration for their work either diverged from structuralism on important points (in the case of Foucault) or claimed even to call it into question (in the case of Derrida).

No doubt Foucault's case is the more complex of the two from this point of view. For if he occasionally resorted to structural tools, above all in his early works, the use that he made of them and, still more significantly, the personal (and politically committed) interest that he brought to the study of history had the practical effect of shattering the positivist conception of knowledge on which structuralist methodology was founded and, beyond that, of casting doubt upon the very notion of truth.

A History of Truth

Born in Poitiers, Michel Foucault (1926–84) entered the École Normale in 1946. There, under the supervision of Jean Hyppolite, he wrote an essay for his master's degree on Hegel while at the same time dedicating himself to the study of psychology. Beginning in 1948 he also attended Althusser's lectures and formed a lasting friendship with him. For two years, between 1950 and 1952, he belonged to the French Communist Party. He abandoned it as quickly as he did in large part because Marxism, as a theory, held few charms for him. Although he was skeptical of all established ideologies and distrusted the heroic conception of engagement personified by Sartre, he nonetheless felt an intense desire at the time to understand history, particularly the way in which the various faces of what, for the sake of convenience, we call "truth" successively appear and disappear in it.

His formative years were marked by varied reading—of Lacan and Lévi-Strauss, naturally, but also of Nietzsche. Nietzsche he discovered through the interpretation that had been given in the 1920s and 1930s in France by Georges Bataille, for whom Nietzsche's subversive writing constituted the perfect antidote to the tyranny of Hegelian rationalism. This aestheticizing interpretation of the author of Zarathustra was later developed by Maurice Blanchot (b. 1907) and Pierre Klossowski (b. 1905)—the first translator of Wittgenstein into French—and received further impetus with the publication in 1962 of a book by the philosopher Gilles Deleuze (1925–95), Nietzsche and Philosophy. For Deleuze, an opponent of all philosophies of Being and of representation, Nietzsche's thought was first and foremost a philosophy of the will. Noting that, in the absence of any objective criterion of truth, only the philosopher's "will to truth" exists, Deleuze argued that this will provided the philosopher with the means of affirming his own personal language, and therefore of creating his own concepts, without having to make reference to transcendent norms, which by definition were unknowable.

Foucault—fascinated by the linguistic, indeed ludic, nature of literary creation, to which he devoted a number of papers influenced by his discovery of Raymond Roussel and the "psychotic" writings of Jean-Pierre Brisset—was profoundly captivated by the readings of Nietzsche proposed by Bataille, Klossowski, and Deleuze, and in his later years he looked increasingly to Nietzsche for inspiration. The masters he acknowledged when he first began to write, however, were mainly historians: professional historians like the ones who gravitated to the journal Annales, founded in 1929 by Marc Bloch and Lucien Febvre, as well as Philippe Ariès, who pioneered the history of *mentalités* in the 1950s; but also philosophers and historians of science such as Bachelard and Koyré and their common disciple Georges Canguilhem (1904–95), who was both a philosopher and a physicist, Bachelard's successor at the Sorbonne, and the author among other works of *The Normal and the Pathological* as well as an influential article, first published in 1956, aimed against the scientific pretensions of academic psychology.[8] This is not to forget, of course, Foucault's friendship with Georges Dumézil, to whom he looked for advice his whole life. It is hardly surprising, then, that the three works that established his early reputation, situated at the yet relatively unexplored intersection of the study of mentalities, myths, and knowledge—*Mental Illness and Personality* (1954; revised and reissued in 1962 under the title *Mental Illness and Psychology*), *Madness and Civilization* (1961), and *The Birth of the Clinic* (1963)—should have been both works of history and of philosophy.

A new tone could be detected in them at once. Foucault's style was not that of a scholar who lived in the past. His learning, although considerable, was not without its flaws. Better informed, although not unbiased, specialists were relentless in picking out the errors and inaccuracies that sprinkled his first works. From their point of view, they were right to do so. But they missed the essential point: hostile to traditional academic institutions in France—which he regularly left, accepting posts abroad in Sweden, Poland, and Germany, only returning to take part in the creation of an alternative university at Vincennes in 1968 before finally being elected to the Collège de France two years later, where he succeeded Hyppolite—Foucault did not claim to be engaged in antiquarian study. His ambition lay elsewhere. It consisted in writing a history of truth, in illuminating the bonds that link it with the social and political arena, as much through its conditions of possibility as through its effects; in short, in destroying the positivist pretention (and that of classical rationalism) to establish knowledge on a stable and assured ground.

Madness and Civilization—his doctoral thesis in philosophy, directed by Canguilhem—provides the best illustration of this undertaking. Working from a corpus of old medical records discovered at Uppsala in Sweden (where, thanks to Dumézil, he had been hired as director of the Maison Française), Foucault reconstructed the history of the successive ways in which madness had been perceived within Western culture. During the Middle Ages, the madman was free and tolerated, seen as the bearer of a sacred sign, the beneficiary of divine election. With the consolidation of the absolute monarchy, and the creation of a centralizing state freed from the domination of the church, he became an element of social disorder. The great lockup of the seventeenth century did not suffice, however, to isolate madness from other forms of deviance. It was necessary to wait until the end of the eighteenth century when, from 1780 to 1820, madness came to be redefined as a mental illness by the medical establishment. Now an object of positive knowledge, it came within the purview of psychiatry, a new branch of medicine that grew up in the course of the nineteenth century, thus providing the procedure of internment with a measure of scientific justification. As the guarantor of familial order, psychiatry was to be the source of a great many abuses of power.

The implication of such a rereading of history is twofold. On the one hand, madness, far from being the name of a familiar concept with recognized contours, is—like the majority of the concepts of psychology and the social sciences in general—only a notion whose content has widely varied over the course of history as a function of political concerns, or "practices" in the broad sense of the term, which in any case are foreign to the pure search for truth. In short, truth is not the sole motive of knowledge. In every age, the social function of knowledge has depended on the place it occupied within a given network of power.

On the other hand, there is nothing immutable about this network of power itself. Very often it is enough to expose the false pretense of the knowledge on which it claims to be based in order to render it curiously vulnerable. This conviction led Foucault and his first disciples in the late 1960s and the 1970s to engage in selective struggles against the psychiatric establishment, which found itself under the attack at the same time, only from a Sartrian perspective, by the British "antipsychiatrists" Laing and Cooper. Meanwhile Gilles Deleuze launched a bombshell in collaboration with the psychoanalyst Félix Guattari, *Anti-Oedipus* (1972), that, in celebrating human "desiring-machines," opposed the repressive dogmas of Freudianism and "familialism." The effect of this opposition, which rapidly spread throughout Europe, was to force a partial retreat from abusive internment practices everywhere, while leading psychiatrists themselves at least momentarily to revise certain of their assumptions.[9]

It is plain, then, that Foucault's thought—despite its individualism, its "minimalism," and its refusal of pathos—was closely connected with issues of social conflict. His two principal works of epistemological reflection—*The Order of Things* (1966) and *The Archaeology of Knowledge* (1969), to which may be added (as in fact Foucault's American publishers later did) his inaugural lecture at the Collège de France, the *Discourse on Language* (1971)—gave further proof of this. The first of these books, subtitled "An Archaeology of the Human Sciences," returned to the period studied in *Madness and Civilization* (the end of the sixteenth century to the beginning of the nineteenth century) with the aim of showing that, far from illustrating the continuous progress of reason, it was framed instead by two "subterranean ruptures"—hidden breaks with the past that were to give historically quite distinct forms to subsequent ways of thinking.

A first rupture was marked by the emergence at the end of the Renaissance of what in France is referred to as the classical age. For the theoreticians of the seventeenth century, intellectual and artistic activity could be conceived only in terms of representation, a worldview illustrated by the linguistics of Port-Royal, for example, and the *Las Meninas* of Velásquez. A second rupture, in the late eighteenth and early nineteenth centuries, caused the supremacy enjoyed by representation to pass to a mode of thought centered on the notion of the subject. Then a new idea appeared, according to which man was both the author and the actor of his own history, and with it the promotion of historical science to the rank of "mother of all the sciences of man."[10] This second rupture opened a new age, modernity, from which we have not yet emerged but whose end, no less than that of the preceding age, is assured.

Leaving to one side the question whether Foucault's definition of modernity is not overly expansive, to the extent that it underestimates the quite considerable scientific and artistic transformations of the years between 1880 and 1914, let us concentrate instead on the theoretical and practical conclusions that he drew from this inquiry. First, the theoretical conclusion: human thought does indeed evolve, as Bachelard and Koyré had claimed earlier, in a discontinuous fashion. In each era, thought is constrained by the empirically determined structure that underlies the culture of the age. Foucault called this structure *epistēmē* since it constitutes, in a general way, the common base of all forms of knowledge. Therefore a rupture in our way of regarding the world—at once secret, violent, and anonymous—is required for the *epistēmē* to change, for the limits of the thinkable to shift, for it to become possible, in a word, to think in a different way. It should be noted in passing that this implication was directly responsible for the mistaken view of Foucault's thought among journalists (expressed as early as 1966 with the appearance of *The Order of Things*) as a form of structuralism. Foucault himself challenged this view three years later in the *Archaeology of Knowledge*, saying that the study of structures in themselves interested him less than understanding how our "discourses" are both produced and limited by prior historical circumstances that, at the same time, rob the notion of authorship of all its romantic prestige.

On the other hand, there are practical consequences: if "man is neither the oldest nor the most constant problem that has been posed for human knowledge,"[11] if the concept of man is "only a recent invention"[12] that appeared at the end of the eighteenth century and that there is every reason to suppose is now "nearing its end,"[13] then theoretical humanism also finds itself utterly condemned. As a result, all the dialectical philosophies of history—founded, like Hegelianism and Marxism, on the belief in a progress generated by the negativity of human action—fall apart, one after another, giving way to new figures of sociological knowledge as well as to novel forms of political intervention.

Which figures and forms might these be? This is what Foucault tried to imagine—not without difficulty, as it turned out—in the years that followed. He managed neither to explain his reasons for rejecting Marxism clearly, despite the many interviews in which he was invited to do so (for example, the one he gave to Duccio Trombadori in 1978[14]), nor to avoid certain lapses in judgment (here one thinks of his praise for the Islamic revolution in Iran in its early stages). By the beginning of the 1970s, in any case, his desire to practice an individual style of activism, independent of parties and centered on the politicization of the problems of daily life, had drawn him nearer to the extreme libertarian Left. He thus arrived, almost in spite of himself, at positions close to those of Sartre, with whom he was never able to establish a real dialogue, however.

Foucault's initiatives in both scholarship and politics henceforth proceeded from a fundamentally anti-authoritarian motivation. Whether concerned with the history of the notion of exclusion or—as in his first lectures at the Collège de France (soon to be published)—the genealogy of the penal system, these researches announced a new project: working out a "microphysics" of power. Far from being a monolithic entity, power, Foucault held, must be spoken of in the plural. Its forms are diffuse. Because the networks that they constitute are not all mutually connected, gaps exist through which resistance may infiltrate. Their interaction with networks of knowledge, themselves perpetually shifting as well, is particularly complex. Sometimes it happens that knowledge and power coincide with each other. Such a situation then leads to violent episodes of censorship that arouse dramatic displays of opposition on the part of those who are excluded and seek to reclaim the voice of which the system deprives them.

For the excluded have a point of view as well, as Foucault proved in 1973 by publishing the confession of a young Norman peasant who had committed parricide ("I, Pierre Rivière, Having Cut the Throats of My Mother, My Sister, and My Brother"). Buried since 1835 in the judicial archives, this moving document not only cast an interesting light upon the legal and psychiatric manipulation of the evidence linking Rivière to this triple murder at the time of his trial, in order to make him appear as a madman; but it also attested to the existence among even the most helpless of the oppressed of a singular ability to speak, and therefore to know—a power that continues to this day to be stifled by authorities of all kinds, beginning with the academic authorities, the licensed possessors of legitimate knowledge.

Two years later, in *Discipline and Punish* (1975), Foucault recounted the birth of the modern prison. Coming after the *History of Madness*, this new book attempted to retrace developments in the medical, criminal, and psychological sciences—or pseudo-sciences—that led to the emergence at the end of the eighteenth century of a system for disciplining bodies and minds by means of which the centralizing state was able to extend its hold over the rest of society. Breaking with the practice of *supplices*, or torture, favored by the ancien régime, this system was intended (among other things) to reeducate prisoners by forcefully subjecting them to a disciplinary and punitive pedagogy. The modern prison, descended from Bentham's "panopticon," now became the chief instrument of social control.

But here Foucault's purpose was more openly subversive than in the 1961 book, for the prison, still more than the hospital, was the very symbol of a bourgeois order anxious to repress all forms of deviance. Foucault himself took part during this period in militant actions aimed at closing the maximum security wings of French prisons. In France, and to a certain extent in the United States (at least in intellectual circles), *Discipline and Punish* inspired a new leftism critical of all forms of authority (especially the authority associated with the police power of the state or symbolic of it) but relatively indifferent to the socioeconomic conditions that permitted authority to be exercised.

At the same time the book's success created problems for its author. Although he was skeptical of the ideology of liberation with which some wished to associate his name, and annoyed by the growing attention shown by the media to his work, it was nonetheless difficult for Foucault to give up publicizing his ideas. Evidence of this ambivalence is the anonymous interview he gave to the newspaper *Le Monde* in 1980 under the mysterious name "the masked philosopher"[15]—a title echoed by this sentence from *The Archaeology of Knowledge*: "I am no doubt not the only one who writes in order to have no face."[16] At a deeper level, Foucault felt a need for self-renewal. Wishing to enlarge the limits of his own thought by creating new objects and new objectives, he attempted secretly to reinvent himself. He did this during the years that separated *The Will to Knowledge* (1976), the first volume of what was to be his last work, the *History of Sexuality*, from the next two volumes, *The Use of Pleasure* and *The Care of the Self*, which appeared only after a long silence, in June 1984—the same month that Foucault, a victim of AIDS, disappeared prematurely from the philosophical stage at the age of fifty-eight.

The Will to Knowledge, intended as the preface to a projected but ultimately unwritten work, seemed to herald a new enterprise of "demystification" aimed for the most part against psychoanalysis. Psychoanalysis maintained that sex in the Western world had been inhibited by Christian morality for so long and so completely that the mere fact of speaking about sex, in the face of such a taboo, would by itself constitute a liberating act. This, Foucault retorted, was an illusion. He proposed to establish instead that Western culture, through the habit of confession required by the Catholic church, had made sex not only the object of a flood of words but, from the moment the psychologist, psychoanalyst, and sexologist took over from the priest, the object of a pseudo-science with pretensions to medical authority whose real function was to normalize the diversity of possible sexual practices by reducing it to the monotony of a single schema.

The promised demonstration, however, was never provided. Confident, perhaps too confident, that he could see it through, Foucault grew tired of what was at bottom an academic task before he had even begun. Moreover, around 1980 his interest shifted from the sexual morality of the Church Fathers to that of the Greek and Latin authors they combatted. His purpose in writing a history of sexuality had changed as well. He no longer wished to free sexuality from the hold of Christianity—so often denounced since Nietzsche—but simply to rediscover, in their positive aspect, the doctrines of the ancients on this subject.

Foucault therefore took up again the study of classical languages. With the guidance of one of his colleagues at the Collège de France, the Roman historian Paul Veyne, he discovered that these doctrines were much more complex than Platonic and Aristotelian theories of love had led scholars to believe. For Hellenistic moralists, the Stoics and Epicureans in particular, sex was, like sport, personal adornment, and diet, an element of "regimen"; that is, a way of life followed by the sage to construct his own personality—a way of attaining pleasure, health, and serenity, all at once, in a world ravaged by violence and forgetfulness of God.

Such a dispassionate, depsychologized inquiry into the art of living could not fail but appeal to a confirmed individualist like Foucault. The notion that regimen makes the construction of oneself possible also enabled him to effect a synthesis between his hedonistic conception of ethics and his libertarian vision of politics. The wise man, by intensifying his pleasures, free from repressive preoccupations and emancipatory obsessions alike, succeeds in escaping the fixed role that Western culture has imposed on the humanist subject and, in doing this, helps subvert social conventions more effectively than any ideology could do—a position that, once again, was not dissimilar to the one sketched by Deleuze and Guattari in *Anti-Oedipus* and developed in *A Thousand Plateaus* (1980).

Unfortunately, a disease itself tragically linked to sexuality killed Foucault before he had time to draw all the conclusions of his inquiry. As a result his work is marked, like that of Althusser, by a sort of essential incompleteness, having been cut off at just the moment when it was poised to evolve in new directions. Like Althusser's work, too, it is obscured today in part by an unhealthy interest in the fate of its author. The latest example of this is the success of a recent biography of Foucault centered on his homosexuality that by its systematic search for the scandalous ends up missing everything, the work and the man both.[17]

CERTAIN SHIFTS in contemporary philosophical thought brought about by the work of these two figures, the effects of which seem to be irreversible, remain to be discussed. It is no longer possible, after Althusser, to go on talking of Marx without having first tried to read him in the way that Althusser showed he could be read. In the same way, after Foucault, it is no longer possible to speak of truth and knowledge without acknowledging that in and of themselves, as Foucault showed, these categories are too general to be useful. Nor can we any longer fail to see that these categories, far from designating transcendental realities as Husserl and Russell believed, themselves have an empirical history that is tied to that of Western culture, having emerged with Plato, and that in a strict sense comes under the head of archaeology.

Foucault surely was not the first to have made this point. His archaeology obviously proceeded from the Nietzschean notion of genealogy, a concept whose fertility escaped neither Bataille, on the one hand, nor Benjamin, Horkheimer, and Adorno on the other. But, although he recognized at the end of his life that his views had been anticipated in part by the Frankfurt School, Foucault was the first to give this kind of analysis its full critical force, freeing it from the metaphysically worn-out language of dialectic in order to reformulate it within the language—inherited from Koyré—of a discontinuist theory of history.

That such a rediscovery of Nietzschean relativism should have been made in France in the 1960s was probably not an accident. Having come of age under the sign of Auschwitz and Hiroshima, in a country weakened by colonial wars as well as by the Cold War, Foucault was in fact altogether representative of a generation that, having lost confidence in the great social utopias and no longer believing that history had a meaning, could only regard the ideals in the name of which historical progress had been legitimized until then with a thoroughgoing skepticism. To the same generation belonged his countrymen Gilles Deleuze, who with the publication of *Difference and Repetition* (1968) and *The Logic of Sense* (1969) had become the most influential of contemporary Nietzscheans, and Jean-François Lyotard (1924–98), originally a member of the "Socialism or Barbarism" movement who went on to systematize his critique of the great Marxist and Freudian narratives in *Discourse/Figure* (1971) and *Libidinal Economy* (1974).

If we are right in grouping together Foucault, Deleuze, and Lyotard—three nomadic, deliberately marginal thinkers who nonetheless shared an affirmative, energetic, and pluralist conception of philosophical practice—their work can be seen as illustrating a moment of strategic consequence in the recent history of philosophy. The crisis of philosophy of history, aggravated by the many consequences of the Second World War and the worldwide triumph of a "society of spectacle" (as the situationists called it[18]), in which ideas themselves are no longer anything more than merchandise, led as a result to a veritable crisis of reason that called into question the very possibility of scientific knowledge itself. One effect of the crisis was to prompt these philosophers to make a clean break with structuralism, severing whatever occasional or merely apparent connection they had with it. For structuralism—no more than neopositivism, of which, finally, it was the last avatar—never challenged the transcendental nature of truth.

Thanks largely to Foucault and to the "poststructuralist" current that originated with him, the debate over the foundations of reason, its powers and its future, has for some twenty years now been the central debate of contemporary philosophy. But before examining the various positions to which it has given rise, we ought to remind ourselves that the discontinuist conception of history was not inevitably connected with relativism of one kind or another. In the work of the American philosopher and historian of science Thomas S. Kuhn (1922–96), likewise descended from Koyré but developed entirely independently from that of Foucault, it led to quite different conclusions.

BORN IN CINCINNATI, OHIO, Kuhn entered Harvard in 1939 with the intention of studying theoretical physics. In his freshman year, however, he became interested in philosophy upon reading Kant's *Critique of Pure Reason*—whose notion of category, understood as the condition of the possibility of knowledge, made a great impression on him—and shortly afterwards Arthur O. Lovejoy's *The Great Chain of Being* (1933), which convinced him of the existence of a dynamic specific to the development of ideas.

After the war (Kuhn was one of the first Americans to enter Paris, on 25 August 1944, the day of France's liberation), he returned to Harvard to continue his studies. As a graduate student he was asked by the university's president, James B. Conant, to teach a course during the 1947–48 academic year for undergraduate nonscience majors intended to give them an understanding, on the basis of specific cases, of how science is practiced. This chance assignment—which obliged him to read Aristotle, in order to be able to describe how the transition from Greek physics to that of Galileo and Newton came about—unexpectedly made him realize that the picture of scientific progress given by logical empiricism did not correspond to the reality actually experienced by scientists in their research. As a result, once his dissertation was finished Kuhn decided to give up physics in order to devote himself to the history of science.

This new orientation led him in turn to immerse himself in Koyré's *Galilean Studies*, the methodological principles of which he embraced at once. In 1950, in Paris, he met Koyré, who arranged for him to have a brief interview with Bachelard. Kuhn scarcely knew Bachelard's work and did not read it later, perhaps because his philosophical interests were so different. By contrast, the work of other French scholars did help shape his thinking: Meyerson's *Identity and Reality* (a celebrated work in American universities at the time) as well as the writings of Pierre Duhem on medieval physics (which treated it as an essential step on the road leading from Aristotle to Galileo) and those of Hélène Metzger (1889–1944) on the birth of modern chemistry, *Chemical Doctrines in France from the Beginning of the Seventeenth Century to the End of the Eighteenth Century* (1923) and *Newton, Stahl, Boerhaave and Chemical Doctrine* (1930).

In addition to the French school of history of science, Kuhn was influenced by *Gestaltpsychologie*, on the one hand, and on the other by the discoveries of the Swiss psychologist Jean Piaget (1896–1980) confirming the discontinuous character of the child's intellectual development. On the American side, Kuhn was particularly influenced by two philosophers, W. V. Quine and Wilfred Sellars. He endorsed both the thesis defended by Quine in "The Two Dogmas of Empiricism" that truth depends on both language and facts and the critique proposed by Sellars of the "myth of the given." These arguments, it seemed to him, made it clear that one could not go on defining the truth of a theory—as Popper did, following Tarski—by its simple correspondence with external reality; it was also necessary to take into account another dimension, every bit as important as the facts against which the theory is tested, namely, the language in which it is formulated. Indeed, the transformations of this language constituted the real object of history of science.

In 1957—the same year that Koyré's *From the Closed World to the Infinite Universe* appeared—Kuhn published *The Copernican Revolution*, which had the similar aim of placing the strictly astronomical aspects of this revolution in their cultural, philosophical, and religious context. Consideration of additional case studies led him five years later to propose a more general set of conclusions in *The Structure of Scientific Revolutions* (1962). Drawing upon history, philosophy, and the sociology of knowledge, this work broadened the basis for the claim that scientific progress occurs not in a linear and cumulative fashion but by abrupt shifts. Such discontinuities or leaps, Kuhn held, occur when a set of theories enters into "crisis" and eventually finds itself eliminated in favor of another set of differently organized theories.

The views of the world that underlie the work of scientists from one era to the next Kuhn called "paradigms." A paradigm is a "disciplinary matrix" composed of general theoretical hypotheses as well as of a set of laws and techniques necessary for testing them. It defines the norm of what counts as legitimate activity in a given scientific domain and, to a large degree, determines what kind of facts the researcher is effectively permitted to observe. Over time, of course, any paradigm finds itself faced with certain experiments that seem to contradict it. Its ability to resist such "anomalies" for a longer or shorter period of time, Kuhn argued, depends on how well its constituent theories agree with the majority of known facts.[19] This is why Kuhn rejected both falsificationism[20]—in both its sophisticated form, associated with Imre Lakatos (1922–74), and its classical form, associated with Popper—and the inductivist conception of knowledge developed by Carnap.

By contrast, when the observed anomalies become too numerous and too intractable there come about in the minds of scientists those mysterious transformations—hidden from conscious view and always difficult to date with precision—that end up producing a "paradigm shift," which is to say a change in the way of looking at the world that signals a scientific revolution. For Kuhn, such shifts in our manner of apprehending reality are analogous to religious conversions. New concepts do not come to be promptly substituted for old ones; rather, in designating new objects and in posing new questions, they suggest a different way of "seeing" the world that ultimately prevails. But if scientific revolutions are, at bottom, linguistic in character, new theories generally cannot be translated back into the language of the old theories—old and new theories, Kuhn asserted, are "incommensurable."

Is it nonetheless the case that they are in some sense consistent? A relativist might be tempted to point out that Kuhn gives no transcendental criterion that would make it possible to establish the superiority of one paradigm over another. Nothing proves, for example, that an outdated paradigm is obsolete in its entirety: the Galilean revolution itself went back beyond Aristotle to a mathematical conception of nature issuing from Plato; and even when it is, this means that our beliefs have changed, not that older beliefs were erroneous at the time they were held. Neither the phlogiston theory nor the geocentric thesis was globally contradicted by the majority of observations available during the era in which these beliefs were considered to be true.

A variation on this line was, in fact, urged by logical empiricists rather than relativists. The Columbia philosopher of science Ernst Nagel (1901–85), whose major work The Structure of Science (1961) had the misfortune, as has often been pointed out, of appearing a year before The Structure of Scientific Revolutions, stressed that the advent of Einsteinian relativity did not suddenly make Newtonian mechanics wrong: Newtonian mechanics still applied perfectly well to our immediate terrestrial environment, only its scope of application was now severely curtailed. Einstein's theory, by providing a more satisfactory explanation of a larger field of physical phenomena, subsumed the older theory without invalidating it. The critique of Kuhn's doctrine of incommensurabilty was subsequently deepened by Nagel's student Joseph Epstein (1917–93), who had earlier established his reputation as a penetrating critic of Ayer's philosophy and of Quine's attempt to reconstruct empiricism.[21]

With the benefit of hindsight, however, in view of the rise of more extreme forms of relativism in the interval, the differences between these two schools seem today rather less pronounced than they did in the 1960s and 1970s. Indeed, Kuhn, in an epilogue added to the second edition of The Structure of Scientific Revolutions (published in 1970), as well as in later writings collected in The Essential Tension (1977), vigorously denied being a relativist. It is always possible, he argued, to reach a conclusion that is preferable to others on objective grounds. Scientific progress, in particular, is not a delusion. If our current theories are superior to the ones that they replaced, this is not only for sociological reasons; that is, because the community of scientists today would agree in asserting their superiority. It is also because they actually do succeed in solving more problems, or in explaining a greater number of phenomena on the basis of more economical hypotheses, or in permitting quantitatively more precise predictions to be made.

In short, Kuhn doubted neither the objectivity of reason nor that science constitutes the highest form of rationality. The most he would concede was that scientific progress could not be conceived as a process by which the human mind ineluctably draws nearer to some preexisting truth, since the definition of truth always depends in part on language, and therefore on history. This modest concession to relativism explains the liveliness of the attacks mounted upon Kuhn's theses by Popper and his disciples, partisans of an ahistorical conception of scientific objectivity.[22] It also justifies, on the other hand, the comparison that has often been made between Kuhn and Foucault.

This comparison has its limits, however. For one thing, in spite of the unarguable similarity between the concepts of paradigm and epistēmē, all the evidence seems to suggest that Foucault never really read Kuhn and that Kuhn, for his part, only belatedly discovered Foucault's work. Moreover, the approaches of the two thinkers are quite different. Foucault correctly described the fundamental features of the epistēmē that became established in European culture at the end of the eighteenth century, opposed to that of the previous two centuries; but he did little to explore the ensemble of economic and ideological causes that provoked this transformation. In this sense, he was more of an anthropologist than a true historian.

Finally, Foucault expected his inquiry into the archaeology of knowledge to produce directly political consequences, subversive in character, whereas Kuhn did not believe that it was in the nature of philosophical activity to contribute by itself to the liberation of humanity. The French philosopher's conviction that "everything is political" stands in sharp contrast to the American's far more compartmentalized view of social practices—a cleavage that could only serve to perpetuate the one that divided the Frankfurt School from Popper and the neopositivists.

Foucault, an avowedly radical thinker, had no difficulty accepting the idea that reason should find itself deprived of all objective foundation, whereas Kuhn, whose purposes were fundamentally conservative, maintained that reason did in fact have a foundation, unchanging beneath the diversity of its historical forms. In the final analysis, however, both of them—the one deliberately, the other in spite of himself—helped cast doubt upon the existence of such a foundation. It remained to draw from this doubt its ultimate consequences, which is precisely what two other philosophers, Jacques Derrida in France and Richard Rorty in the United States, undertook to do in the 1960s.

From Deconstruction to Neopragmatism

Born at El Biar in Algeria, in 1930, Jacques Derrida entered the École Normale Supérieure in 1952, six years after Foucault. He returned to teach philosophy in 1964 during Althusser's tenure as deputy director, before becoming director of studies at the École des Hautes Études en Sciences Sociales, itself the result of a schism within the École Pratique des Hautes Études after the war.

One of Derrida's first articles, in which he admitted to being a "disciple" of Foucault,[23] was devoted to a discussion of Madness and Civilization. Despite their early divergences, which were only to increase, the two philosophers nonetheless were united by their determination to work outside the structuralist tradition. Indeed, Derrida went much further in his critique of structuralism; for if, like Foucault, he was influenced by the interpretation of Nietzsche proposed by Bataille and Blanchot, he relied additionally on Husserlian phenomenology, whose antipositivist orientation he lost no time in radicalizing.[24]

Derrida's fundamental criticism of structuralism was that it remained the prisoner of the problem of signification, which itself was closely tied to the most classical assumptions of Western metaphysics. Contrary to what Saussure's followers seemed to suppose, the thesis that "everything is language" was not really new. It only revived one of the central conceptions of Greek philosophy, namely, the supremacy of discourse (*logos*), identified with actual speech or "voice" (*phônē*) and considered as the original source of meaning. This "phonologism," or "logocentrism," has rested in its turn since Plato and Aristotle on a metaphysics of Being confused with the Supreme Being— that is, on an "onto-theo-logy"—since, if everything is significant, the signifier itself cannot help but rest upon a transcendental signified, the ultimate guarantor of every provision of meaning. Unfortunately, such a system of hierarchical references could only lead to the same impasses that had long been familiar. If philosophy aspires to free itself from them, it must therefore begin by freeing itself from the domination of *logos* and, by the same token, by recognizing the insurmountable "difference" that separates Being from being.

From the beginning, then, Derrida acknowledged his debt to Heidegger's initial project in *Being and Time*. As he readily admitted in an interview with Henri Ronse, published in *Positions* (1972), "What I have attempted to do would not have been possible without the opening [provided by] Heidegger's questions."[25] Beyond this, again following Heidegger's example, he did not believe that one could get rid of metaphysics by turning it on its head, or by attacking it head-on in the name of a diametrically opposed position, which would in all likelihood only be another—albeit camouflaged—metaphysical position.

His strategy was more subtle. Nothing illustrates it better than the two-part work Derrida devoted to Husserl: a long introduction to his translation of *The Origin of Geometry* in 1962 and then in 1967 a commentary entitled *Voice and Phenomenon* on the first chapter of the first of the *Logical Investigations*. Whether it was a question, in the one case, of the fundamental notions of geometry or, in the other, of the concept of *Bedeutung* (which may be translated as "reference" or "meaning"), Husserl was trying to arrive at a pure form of thought that would be at once the origin and the essence of all scientifically rigorous discourse. He managed, however, to grasp such a form of thought only through the mediation of the signs that expressed it, and particularly of the *written* signs that served to note it. Contaminated by the secret presence of that writing without which no scientific statement would be possible, the point of origin that Husserl believed himself to have reached was only an "impure" origin or, more exactly, not an origin at all—indeed, on Derrida's view, there is no origin. Husserl himself refused to draw this conclusion, though it was implied by his own analysis, in the futile hope of saving his ideal reconstruction of science.

It is tempting to regard this paradoxical reading as the source of all the others that followed. Its main outlines are to be found, in any case, in Derrida's great theoretical work, *Of Grammatology* (1967). An elaborate hall of mirrors, the book is organized around the *mise-en-abyme* of two texts that, at different moments in the history of Western metaphysics, expressed the same disparaging opinion of the written sign: Rousseau's *Essay on the Origin of Languages* and the account given by Lévi-Strauss in *Tristes Tropiques* of the discovery of writing by the Nambikwara. From their comparison Derrida draws a conclusion similar to the one he drew in his works on Husserl: while they claim to demonstrate the supremacy of *logos*, understood as living speech, these texts nonetheless end up—by the very way they pose the problem—undermining this supremacy since there is no alternative but to presuppose the existence of an original *archi-écriture* ("arche-writing"), prior to *logos*, in order to account for the "articulation" that defines it. As a result, the "appearance" of the origin is seen, through the introduction of this "supplement" (or prior form of expression), to be "deferred" indefinitely, and meaning condemned to an irrevocable "dissemination" or dispersal.

The theory of arche-writing Derrida called grammatology—literally, the theory of the "stroke" or "line" (*grammé* in Greek) involved in writing, the theory of the inscription and erasure of letters. Grammatology was thus proposed as the name of a new science or, at least, of a particularly devastating form of textual subversion. In subsequent works Derrida nonetheless decided against trying to develop the methodology of such a project systematically, no doubt because the very notion of theory seemed to him still dependent upon the metaphysics that he wished to challenge. He set out instead to make good on this challenge, which at first went by the name of "différance"—a noun constructed out of the present participle of the French verb *différer*, meaning both "to differ" and to "defer"—and which later was popularized by his followers under the simpler term "deconstruction," probably suggested to Derrida by the Heideggerian term *Abbau* and commonly used by him from 1966 on.[26]

In the case of Rousseau and Levinas, as of Hegel and Freud, the "absent presence" of writing—present through the symptoms of its denial—always, and from the very beginning, corrupts the origin itself. It explains both the failure of the metaphysical enterprise and the need we feel to overcome metaphysics. There is no proof, however, that such an overcoming is possible; in a sense, even Heidegger's attempt failed. Taking the image of a circle to suggest the closure of metaphysical discourse upon itself, Derrida preferred to say that attempting to escape the circle means having to go around it indefinitely. In practice that meant rereading Western philosophy with a view to destabilizing the center of the circle from a point on its periphery; in other words, in bringing to bear against it all those semantic elements that could serve to dislocate the great binary and hierarchical oppositions around which philosophy has been organized since Plato: soul/body, mind/matter, masculine/feminine, signified/signifier, speech/writing, theory/practice, and so on.

Derrida's rereading, like the one Heidegger proposed in the case of the Greeks, was attentive to the etymology of words as well as to their multiple meanings; but it was attentive also (like the psychoanalyst's floating attention as listener) to the gaps, the contradictions, the "unthought" of metaphysical discourse—in a word, to all that which is symptomatic of some unconscious or hidden meaning. Finally, it required that texts be interpreted without making a priori assumptions about their relative importance. If one wishes to renounce the very idea of a hierarchy of concepts, all texts have to be accorded the same value. Thus Derrida examined the minor writings of well-known philosophers, such as Rousseau's *Essay on the Origin of Languages*; the writings of minor philosophers, such as Condillac, treated in *The Archaeology of the Frivolous* (1973); the writings of authors who are not considered philosophers, such as Jabès and Artaud, in *Writing and Difference* (1967), or Genet, in *Glas* (1974); and even works from the worlds of painting and design that, although not texts, can be seen as having been constructed on the same model, as Derrida argues in *The Truth in Painting* (1978) and *Memoirs of the Blind* (1990).

How are the results of this exercise, practiced in unceasingly novel ways for almost thirty years, to be judged? Inevitably, there have been some disappointments and not a few instances of misinterpretation. In the literature departments of American universities—where, in large part owing to the influence of Paul de Man (1919–83) at Yale, Derrida's thought penetrated in the 1970s—deconstruction today amounts to a style of textual criticism that, when it is not felicitously practiced, very often reduces to a mere denunciation of the reactionary character of metaphysical concepts; which is to say, finally, to a denunciation of Western culture as a whole. Moreover, Derrida's attack on the patriarchal character of this culture, associated with the portmanteau term *phallogocentrism*, has made his thought influential among American feminist theorists. Under these circumstances, it is not at all surprising that the transatlantic deconstructionist offensive has sometimes been regarded by its adversaries as a leftist menace having no other aim than to undermine the foundations of knowledge and of democracy.

This situation formed the background to a campaign launched against deconstruction (as part of a dispute over the interpretation of J. L. Austin's work) by John Searle, a former student of Austin well known for his conservative views, as we have noted earlier. Searle's counterattack was prompted by the English translation in 1977 of Derrida's essay "Signature Event Context," which originally appeared in *Margins of Philosophy* (1972). His sharp reply, "Reiterating the Differences," provoked in turn a riposte from Derrida, "Limited Inc a b c," which did nothing to end the controversy.[27] In the United States, deconstruction remains an academic fashion vigorously contested by most professional philosophers. Although a few thinkers outside the analytic mainstream such as Stanley Cavell and Richard Rorty have lent a sympathetic ear to Derrida's work, they have not been able by themselves to dispel the various misunderstandings that have attended its reception in America.[28]

Nonetheless, it is not unfair to see in Derrida's work a revolutionary ambition of a sort. Metaphysics cannot be deconstructed without deconstructing reason itself, without going forward with a radical dissolution of both its basic principles and the cultural and social space they organize. As one might expect, a project of this kind does not aim just at doing away with structuralist logocentrism. It necessarily has larger consequences, though Derrida himself has been reluctant to characterize them as revolutionary, wishing to avoid all "ideologization" of his thought. While admitting that deconstruction inevitably produces effects of a political nature, he has been careful to ensure that these are not reducible to oversimplified formulas. This did not, however, prevent him from publicly opposing racism and apartheid, or from supporting Czechoslovak dissidents—which in 1981 earned him a brief stay in prison in Prague—or from tackling, more recently and more directly, the question of the future of Marxism in what remains to this day one of his best books, *Specters of Marx* (1993).

Anxious to denounce the myth of the "end of history" propagated by Francis Fukuyama, Derrida points out in this book that liberal democracy has not actually been established in most of the world and that it is not by itself capable of solving the problems caused by the relentless advance in the West and elsewhere of injustice and poverty. By showing the usefulness of certain aspects of Marx's thought in trying to make sense of the historical juncture at which we presently find ourselves, and by following Benjamin in a return to the "messianic" inspiration of Marxism,[29] Derrida has been able to anchor his own thought in a critical tradition that unequivocally led back—beyond *Capital*—to the positive side of the Enlightenment.

He has not yet managed, however, to free himself completely from doubts about the theoretical origins of deconstruction, arising from its dual connection with Heidegger and Blanchot, both of whom were attracted in the 1930s to revolutionary ideologies of the extreme Right, National Socialism in the one case, Maurassian fascism in the other. Strangely silent for many years on this sensitive subject, Derrida finally addressed it in two books, *Of Spirit: Heidegger and the Question* and *Psyche: Inventions of the Other*, that appeared in 1987. Nonetheless, his purpose was not to condemn Heidegger but rather to try to patiently untie the strands in the fabric of Heidegger's own writings that still link the attempt to overcome metaphysics with the odysseys of a "metaphysics of presence" and to rescue it from such wanderings.

These two books, in which Derrida observed that Heidegger's National Socialist discourse is also mixed up with the humanist discourse of Husserl and Valéry in strange and obscure ways, marked the beginning of a long-term project. No sooner had he made a start on the tedious job of disentangling them completely than the media mini-circus triggered by the appearance in France of two previously mentioned biographies of Heidegger (the one by Farias in 1987, the other by Ott in translation in 1990) forced him temporarily to retreat into a defensive position. At the same time as the "Heidegger affair" was unfolding in France, another scandal cast a shadow over Paul de Man in the United States with the discovery, four years after his death in 1983, that during the war he had been a contributor to anti-Semitic newspapers in his native Belgium. Derrida, though distressed by this revelation, responded with a long essay, *Mémoires: For Paul de Man* (1988), in which he tried both to clarify the situation in which his old friend had found himself and to clear up the doubts that these two affairs had succeeded in arousing about deconstruction.

More generally, we need to inquire into the close connection between Heidegger's thought and that of Derrida and Levinas, both of whom came from Jewish families, as well as the complex relationship that existed between the two of them. Levinas, one of the first to study Husserl and Heidegger in France, as we have seen, was a friend of Blanchot (whom he met at Strasbourg in the 1920s) and a student of Bergson, Jean Wahl, and Gabriel Marcel. From 1945 he attempted to elucidate the metaphysical foundations of ethics in an existentialist style while refusing to separate ethics from the requirements of religious tradition. For Levinas, the truth yielded by Heidegger's analysis of *Dasein* amounted to a "revelation" of absolute transcendence by which man could not help but be flooded. In his two major books, *Totality and Infinity* (1961) and *Otherwise Than Being* (1974), he embraced a form of thought in which—unlike what one finds in the work of Marcel or Ricoeur—the strictly philosophical element is displaced by faith. This turn toward theology decisively distinguished his thought from that of both Husserl and Heidegger and won him a belated measure of media attention as well.

Derrida never lost his youthful interest in phenomenology and remained an attentive reader of Levinas's work, devoting several essays to it.[30] Both philosophers recognize in their different ways the primacy of the Law and therefore that of Writing (with a capital W); but Derrida clearly rejects Levinas's idea of God as "absolutely other," "otherwise than being," pure and uncontaminated origin. Must we then conclude that, if the attachment of Levinas and, to a lesser degree, of Derrida to Heidegger is explained by a will to assimilation that goes back to their youth, the distance Derrida placed between himself and Levinas signals an interest in going further in the direction of emancipation from the Mosaic conception of the Law?

The secularization of Writing may indeed be one of the purposes, albeit an implicit one, of Derrida's approach. If so, it would represent an additional point of convergence between his work (which has to be understood in the light of Derrida's moving account of his own childhood in an autobiographical essay, "Circumfession"[31]) and that of Benjamin, who also was torn by his allegiance to two traditions—Judaism and the Enlightenment—separated by an imperceptible but essential difference. It is interesting in any case to note that two of Derrida's most recent books, *Politics of Friendship* and *Force of Law* (1994), deal in part with the critique of the *Aufklärung* sketched by Benjamin and with the ambiguous affinities that this critique sustained, at least until 1933, with the antirationalism of Schmidt and Heidegger.

Derrida, while he is alert to the similarities between these two styles of thought, realizes too that each risks drifting in the direction of violence and fascism. At the end of *Force of Law* he does not hesitate to give a clear statement of the differences that separate the Benjaminian and Heideggerian theme of destruction from his own position, which he characterizes as a "deconstructive affirmation." It is rather as though, after so many years in this strange hall of mirrors, he had finally managed to identify the one trap that deconstruction, like every critique of reason, must make every effort to avoid.

IF KUHN AND FOUCAULT showed that truth has a history, and Derrida that Western metaphysics has deconstructed itself, Richard Rorty (b. 1931) has gone a step further, denouncing as illusory every attempt to found reason on a stable and assured ground.

Formerly professor of humanities at the University of Virginia, having previously taught philosophy at Princeton for twenty years, Rorty first attracted attention as the editor of an anthology of papers on analytic philosophy, The Linguistic Turn (1967). Doubts about the legitimacy of this approach were already apparent, however, in the introduction he wrote for this volume. A growing conviction that neither ordinary language philosophy nor logical empiricism were in a position to give definitive answers to philosophical questions, and that neither one met the rigorous standards of rationality to which each aspired, led Rorty over the course of the next decade to develop with characteristic clarity a conception of rationality that amounted to denying it any permanent basis. In reducing science and philosophy to the rank of simple cultural practices, he dismissed out of hand their claim to tell the truth—a claim that seemed to him not only unrealizable but, even on its own terms, unjustifiable and useless. Since then Rorty has adhered to this position, on account of which he stands as the leading representative of philosophical relativism in the United States.

To piece together the logic of this rapid evolution in Rorty's thinking, it needs to be kept in mind that at least three distinct influences made themselves felt. The first was Dewey's pragmatism. The second was Continental philosophy, in the line running from Heidegger to Derrida. The third derived from certain aspects of analytic philosophy, from which he drew very personal conclusions.

Dewey was known to Rorty from childhood.[32] His father, a former Communist sympathizer who accompanied Dewey to Mexico in 1937, was also a friend of Dewey's student Sidney Hook, a pragmatist of Marxist sympathies and, as we have noted, a staunch opponent of Stalinism. Rorty thus inherited both a progressive political sensibility and an early interest in Dewey's thought, which by the 1960s had gone out of fashion in the United States. To Dewey he owes his concern for human solidarity as well as the conviction that the value of an idea is measured by the effects that it produces and therefore has no need, in order to be considered "right," of having an a priori foundation.

Rorty also took an early interest in European philosophy, on which he is (along with Stanley Cavell) one of the foremost American experts. At the beginning of the 1960s he discovered Derrida's work. This in turn led him back to Heidegger, at the time persona non grata in the American academy. The main idea Rorty took from Heidegger, whose thought he interpreted in a free and individual way, was that metaphysics—the quintessential expression of Western philosophy—was finished and that it was time at last to go on to something new. If the questions of classical philosophy were no longer our questions, this was because they belong to an era in Western culture that began with Plato and have meaning only in terms of the language peculiar to this era. With its end, which we are witnessing in the twentieth century, the old language has broken down, carrying away with it the old questions. Far from being eternal, these questions no longer have anything more than historical interest and therefore can be abandoned.

Paradoxically, in the course of making his exit from classical philosophy Rorty found encouragement in the work of Thomas Kuhn and, through this, the critique of logical empiricism proposed by Quine and Sellars. Pushing the arguments developed by Quine in "The Two Dogmas of Empiricism" to an extreme, he came to conclude that there are neither givens (here echoing Sellars's argument) nor facts, but only language. Facts, Rorty held, do not exist independently of the manner in which we reconstruct them using words. Put differently, the question of knowing whether our propositions are true (that is, whether they agree with some reality) matters less than our capacity for inventing new vocabularies to express what we think and feel.

Such an attitude may seem forced or, at least, at variance with actual scientific practice. It is not far removed, however, from the "anarchist" theory of knowledge defended by another philosopher and historian of science, Paul Feyerabend (1924–94), whose work—contemporaneous with that of Kuhn—led to even more subversive consequences, spelled out in his principal book, *Against Method* (1975). Feyerabend, a determined adversary of the falsificationism represented by Popper and Lakatos, argued that the history of the great transformations of scientific thought shows these frequently occurred by chance, that progress does not obey fixed rules, and that, as far as discovery is concerned, any method will do provided that it works. It follows that the boundary between science and nonscience is perpetually shifting, and that the very norms of scientific discourse are neither immutable nor universal. For Feyerabend, scientific rationalism is only one cultural paradigm among other possible ones. These paradigms being incommensurable with each other, none can be said to be superior to any other, neither in an absolute way nor even—as Kuhn maintained—in a relative way. Furthermore, to assure that individual liberty of choice will be protected against all restriction, the state should refrain from championing one paradigm over another—science over religion, for example—and limit itself to offering each citizen the opportunity to study whichever one he or she prefers.

Rorty found the new perspectives of such a relativism liberating and openly broke with analytic philosophy in the late 1970s. Because it claims to be scientifically rigorous, and so goes on subscribing to the classic metaphysical myth, he argued, analytic philosophy still belongs to the pure Kantian tradition. To combat this myth, Rorty did not hesitate to rely on Heidegger, as well as Derrida and Foucault, aspiring in effect to the same role of "murderer" in relation to analytic philosophy that Popper had claimed for himself in relation to logical positivism. In any case he was—again, along with Stanley Cavell—one of the first American philosophers since Quine's trip to Vienna in 1933 to provide a bridge to European philosophy, but this time in the direction of its most antiscientific tendencies.

The manifesto of Rorty's new thinking, *Philosophy and the Mirror of Nature*, published in 1979,[33] is laid out in three parts dealing with the nature of the mind, the status of the theory of knowledge, and the end of philosophy, respectively. In the first part, Rorty argues that Western culture since Plato has embraced the religious dualism of mind and body, the source of innumerable false problems. From this dualist perspective, the mind is conceived as a mirror in which nature—that is, the universe of physical bodies—finds itself reflected. So far from being universally obvious, this view is a historical construction that today has become obsolete.

In the second part, Rorty holds that since Descartes and Locke our knowledge has been defined on the mirror model as an adequate representation of reality, which likewise has given rise to many false problems. Not only is there nothing necessary about such a definition, but it may profitably be replaced by a pragmatic conception of truth. Like James and Dewey, Rorty thinks that truth is simply "the fittest thing to believe in"; in other words, the set of statements that have been shown most useful for making sense of reality and for living better lives. Empirical psychology and philosophy of language, the two pillars of analytic philosophy, succeed only in confining it to the outdated problem of representation.

Finally, in the third part, Rorty asserts that every philosophy pretending to explain rationality and objectivity in terms of adequate representations is likewise obsolete. Moreover, classical metaphysics never actually managed to ground beliefs by virtue of their supposed correspondence with reality; it served only, in the best case, to furnish people with the means for freeing themselves from outmoded forms of discourse and for inventing visions of the world better suited to their own individual development. The thought of Dewey, Heidegger, and Wittgenstein in his later period is mentioned in this connection as being useful in a pragmatic sense. The effect of these philosophers has been chiefly therapeutic, liberating the minds of their day from the hold of metaphysics just as the philosophers of the Enlightenment had freed the minds of theirs from the hold of theology. These philosophers thus helped secularize culture, since metaphysics is at bottom only an elaborate form of religious illusion—in effect, a lay religion.

In 1982 Rorty brought together under the title *Consequences of Pragmatism* a number of articles he had published between 1972 and 1980. Here he explained in what sense he felt justified in considering himself a pragmatist, claiming to take inspiration from the solidarist concerns of Dewey while at the same time praising the works of Heidegger and Derrida for the particularly original and creative language games they contain. He also defended the view that there exists a "later" Wittgenstein, distinct from the Wittgenstein of the *Tractatus*. On this view, the *Philosophical Investigations* constitute the most polished attempt to show that philosophy as a foundational enterprise—as a transcendental project in the Kantian sense, of which the *Tractatus* provided one of the last examples—was dead.[34] If one were to take this interpretation seriously, philosophy was now only a form of conversation cut off from any privileged access to truth and, by virtue of this alone, free to go where it pleased. Philosophy could only survive as a literary genre permitting its practitioners to express themselves as the spirit moves them and its readers to take aesthetic pleasure from their performance.

In *Contingency, Irony, and Solidarity* (1982) Rorty returned to the attack, again opposing the notion that the duty of philosophy is to supply a foundation for our beliefs. Because our beliefs are by definition contingent, the hope of providing them with a foundation is futile. But this does not mean that all beliefs are of equal value. Some are more useful than others. It is well and good, for example, to believe in the need for individual development as well as in the necessity of improving the society in which we live. But these two aspirations, pushed to their logical extreme, may prove hard to square with each other. As a practical matter, however, in order to prevent this situation from giving rise to a metaphysical problem, one must simply cease seeing a contradiction in it.

In the utopia that (by his own admission) Rorty is attempting to construct, the ideal philosopher would be a "liberal ironist." As a liberal, judging cruelty to be the worst of evils, he would work to develop solidarity among peoples; as an ironist, he would know that this conviction has no transcendental foundation and that it does not prevent him from seeking, within the framework defined by his rejection of cruelty, his own personal happiness. In short, his "public" language and his "private" language could be deployed simultaneously and, because they are situated on different levels, without incoherence. A similar irony inspires the last book by Paul Feyerabend published during his lifetime, *Farewell to Reason* (1987),[35] which provided grist for Rorty's mill. Feyerabend developed the thesis that the meaning of the terms *rationality* and *objectivity* may vary in different times and places, as in fact historically it has in Western culture. Moreover, he proposed to put art, science, and philosophy on the same level, arguing that they should no longer be considered as imitative, but rather as creative, activities. The "farewell" of the title does not mean that we must give up behaving as rational beings. It is simply a matter of recognizing that, depending on the context, the notion of rational behavior can cover a range of quite different types of conduct.

Thus, to take Feyerabend's example, the attitude of Pygmy peoples who shun all contact with Western civilization does not supply proof of their irrationality. It shows only that these peoples have made a strategically sensible decision to avoid a civilization that, from their point of view, threatens to destroy a way of life to which they remain attached. One might object, however, that the choice of the Pygmies is objectively grounded in the usual sense in which we ourselves understand the term; in other words, that their capacity for analyzing situations, for arguing and drawing conclusions, does not at all differ from what we in the West regard as rational behavior. In that case, rationality is not a mere ethnological peculiarity—a simple "tribal creed" that happens to be ours[36]—but instead has a universal vocation. Moreover, it is plain that in order to make such arguments Rorty and Feyerabend themselves must submit to the norms of the very rationality whose pretensions they challenge.

Conscious of the precariousness of his position, Rorty sought to consolidate it by collecting various papers together in two further volumes, both published in 1991, *Objectivity, Relativism, and Truth* and *Essays on Heidegger and*

Others. Two aspects of his defense, in particular, are worth noting. On the one hand, because alliance with some kind of universalism was closed to him, Rorty tended more and more to take shelter behind the notion of language games. Just as Heidegger's main achievement was to have devised an antimetaphysical "vocabulary,"[37] so Rorty's originality can be seen as consisting in an attempt to cure the conceptual illnesses caused by the agonizing obsession with foundations. According to Rorty, this therapy does not aim at discrediting a concern with argument as such but simply at getting rid of the illusion that, in order to defend a given conviction, one argument is absolutely better than any other.

On the other hand, while conceding—like Feyerabend—that there may exist, if not one, then at least some acceptable scientific methods, and that one cannot do without reason—that is, the faculty of judgment—in everyday life, Rorty maintained that certain intellectual choices, insofar as they can be judged by their effects, remain objectively superior to others. Thus he affirmed, for example, that democracy is preferable to its opposite and even advanced this proposition as a fact that is more certain than any philosophical argument that claims to justify it by reference to some ahistorical criterion.[38]

These two theses served in effect to establish the bounds that Rorty's brand of relativism finally decided not to overstep. Do they suffice, however, to protect him against all danger of drifting into irrationalism? The French philosopher Jacques Bouveresse (b. 1941), although sympathetic to Rorty's undertaking, strongly doubts it.[39] Relativism, Bouveresse argues, is open to a dual objection. On the one hand, it is incompatible with the realism that, despite its own inadequacies, continues to inform the daily activity of the majority of scientists. On the other hand, in accepting a priori all possible language games, it works to devalue the practice of reasoned debate—until now essential to philosophy—in relation to the invention of new vocabularies. From this point of view, Bouveresse remarks, nothing separates Rorty's relativism from the Nietzscheanism of Deleuze and Guattari, who in *What Is Philosophy?* (1991) see philosophers only as creators of concepts, exempted from any obligation to defend them before their peers.

If one is to avoid slipping into philosophical autism it therefore matters that a solid foundation can be constructed for an ethics of communication. This aim has been pursued for more than twenty years, along two distinct but parallel routes, by the German philosophers Jürgen Habermas and Karl-Otto Apel.

Communication or Investigation?

Jürgen Habermas was born in 1929 in Düsseldorf. As a student of philosophy in the years following the war, he found to his dismay that National Socialist ideas had by no means disappeared from German university life. What is more, they were not the object of systematic critical analysis. Habermas's first reaction, attesting to his early interest in sociology and politics, was to break this oppressive silence. When in 1953, and without a word of explanation, Heidegger published the lectures of the course he gave in 1935 under the title Introduction to Metaphysics, the twenty-five-year-old Habermas ventured to reply in an article in the Frankfurter Allgemeine Zeitung that caused a great stir. Entitled "On the Publication of Lectures of 1935," it summed up the whole matter in a few sentences.

Habermas pointed out the profound connection between the denunciation of metaphysics and the political convictions of the former rector of Freiburg[40] and he condemned Heidegger for his silence about Nazi crimes. Above all, Habermas warned his fellow citizens against the danger they would face if they identified themselves—even in a passive way—with the most regressive tendencies of German culture. "Does fascism," he asked, "perhaps have more to do with the German tradition than one would ordinarily like to admit?" If this were in fact the case, the problem must be brought out into the open. It now became necessary, as he said in conclusion, "to think with Heidegger against Heidegger."[41] In short, every effort needed to be made, as Jaspers had said in 1946, to prevent Germany from remaining, or from becoming once again, the enemy of the West—in other words, the enemy of the Enlightenment.

In 1961 Habermas returned to the charge, recalling the eminent role played by Jewish thinkers in German philosophy since the eighteenth century.[42] In 1968 he took an active part in the student movement while criticizing certain of its excesses. Since then he has frequently intervened in political and academic debates and remained a vigilant presence on the German intellectual scene. He has combatted the hermeneutic movement represented by Gadamer, whom he criticized for adopting a neutral and aestheticizing attitude with regard to modern history. He vigorously took sides in the Historikerstreit (or historians' debate) in 1986 against the revisionism of Ernst Nolte, the conservative historian (and disciple of Heidegger) who justified Nazism by the need to fight Communism, asserting that the extermination of the Jews amounted only to a copy of Stalin's purges and reducing

Auschwitz to the level of a mere technological innovation—the gas chamber—prompted by the fear the Nazis felt at the time that they themselves might fall victim to aggression from the East.[43] The publication of Farias's biography led Habermas in 1988 to return to the question of the politico-ideological presuppositions underlying Heidegger's thought.[44] Since then, the reunification of Germany, the ensuing debate about Germany's role in Europe's future, and the simultaneous resurgence of xenophobia and racism have kept his attention focused on current events.

Habermas's rationalism naturally finds expression as well in his strictly theoretical work, which rests on the idea that it is important to go beyond, not philosophy itself, but the traditional opposition between philosophy and science. Even if it could not carry on as though nothing had happened between 1933 and 1945, philosophy must pursue its critical mission. In Habermas's view, it can do this only by allying itself more closely with the social sciences, by working with them in an interdisciplinary spirit and drawing upon their combined resources (including those of linguistics, psychoanalysis, and sociology) to give new content to the project of the Enlightenment—in short, by candidly analyzing what goes unspoken in social relations, that dark side of the human soul exploited by conservatism and conformism to block social progress.

Habermas's intellectual development places him squarely in the tradition of the Frankfurt School. Indeed, after defending his doctoral thesis on Schelling's philosophy of history, in 1954, he became Adorno's assistant at Frankfurt two years later. While Adorno appreciated his talent as a writer, Horkheimer found Habermas's first book, an inquiry into the political consciousness of West German students, too far to the Left for his taste and imposed conditions for obtaining the habilitation degree that were so strict Habermas gave up and got it instead at the University of Marburg, on the strength of a thesis published in 1962 as *The Structural Transformation of the Public Sphere.* After a brief stay at Heidelberg, where Gadamer and Löwith were among his colleagues, he returned to Frankfurt in 1964. There he succeeded to Horkheimer's chair and taught until 1971, when he accepted the directorship of the Max Planck Institute in Starnberg. He held this post for ten years, resigning it to return once again to Frankfurt.

Habermas, the last representative of the Frankfurt School, carried on the tradition of its founders to the extent that he was inspired by Marxism and adopted the materialist critique of positivism. He interpreted these positions in a very personal way, however, and before long he had moved away from what might be called the classical version of critical theory. Like Marcuse, he was more interested in the young Marx of the 1844 manuscripts than by the Marx of Capital and believed that Marxism was seriously in need of renewal if it were to be able to adapt itself to the conditions faced by industrial societies in the technocratic age, a stage of historical development he called late capitalism (Spätkapitalismus). Marcuse had begun the project of renovating Marxism. Habermas followed him in stressing the inadequacy of the notion of the proletariat. Workers had in fact seen their quality of life improve, so much so that they now benefited from all the advantages of the welfare state. As a result, the class struggle had passed into a dormant phase and the socialist model no longer applied. By contrast, the administrative system established by the technocracy had saddled the working class with constraints that, little by little, emptied democracy of its meaning while at the same time a growing number of the young and unemployed found themselves abandoned on the edges of the system. To reintegrate them, to make the system more open, democratic debate had to be given fresh meaning through the creation of new forms of communication within the public sphere. How this was to be done subsequently became one of Habermas's chief concerns.

As for the Frankfurt critique of positivism, Habermas criticized Popper in the 1961 Tübingen debates, as we have seen, for his failure to reflect upon the assumptions of scientific activity. To Popper's way of thinking, mounting a critique of society was not a proper project for the social sciences to undertake—a view that seemed wholly arbitrary to Habermas and altogether lacking in justification. He stood opposed to any a priori limitations being placed upon scientific research, arguing that the strictly philosophical requirements of such a critique could not be kept separate from actual empirical inquiry. Habermas did not, however, condemn positivist science out of hand. In this respect his own approach was more truly sociological than that of Horkheimer and Adorno. Not only did he draw upon the results of anthropology in his work; he also took a close interest in the philosophy of language and, in particular, Anglo-American treatments of it. In this he was encouraged by one of his colleagues at the University of Frankfurt, the philosopher Karl-Otto Apel.

Born in 1924, Apel was one of the first Continental thinkers, after Gadamer and Ricoeur, to take into account the pragmatic turn by which Anglo-American philosophy had moved, thanks to Austin and his successors, from a strictly formalistic approach to syntax and semantics to an approach centered upon the social uses of speech, which is to say upon the notion of communication. Nonetheless it became clear in his major work, *Towards a Transformation of Philosophy* (1973), that Apel intended to remain within the Kantian transcendental tradition, seeing the very structure of language (itself constitutive of an ideal "community of communication") as one of the conditions of intersubjective comprehension. What Apel then tried to do was to use this pragmatic and transcendental a priori to ground a discourse ethics (*Diskursethik*)—a set of norms governing public debate—that would shelter reason from any relativist type of criticism.

Habermas, although he was greatly influenced by this point of view, relocated the problem within a perspective that was at once less ambitious and more materialist. For him, the community of communication is an objective datum rather than a dimension of transcendental subjectivity and so cannot be separated from empirical social reality. This position furnished the point of departure for the researches that he pursued during the 1970s, the results of which were laid out in the two-volume *The Theory of Communicative Action* (1981) and then in *Moral Consciousness and Communicative Action* (1983). Habermas's motivation in both these works was to detach critical theory from its idealist origins in order to give it a more solid foundation. Horkheimer and Adorno, on his view, remained prisoners of a philosophy of history (more precisely, a dialectic of culture) inherited from Hegel. For Habermas, by contrast, as for Marx and the majority of sociologists, history must be understood above all as a set of *social* interactions. It was therefore the logic of these interactions—and above all their discursive logic, since every interaction occurs by means of verbal communication—that needed to be reconstituted.

Habermas began by recalling that because philosophers since Marx had already traveled a long road in order to escape metaphysics it was no longer necessary to dramatize this way out in the Heideggerian manner. The overcoming of metaphysics had been largely accomplished by Peirce (to whom Apel devoted an important work in 1975) and, still more fully, by the linguistic philosophy issuing from Frege and Russell. The road that remained to be traveled, while taking care not to fall into the trap of positivism, was clearly indicated in the preface to the French edition (1987) of *The Theory of Communicative Action*. It still remained to ground the concept of communicative activity, itself tied to that of the "lived-in world," upon a new definition of scientific and critical reason—in other words, of putting reason in its proper place, as Sartre and Heidegger wished to do, only without making it dependent upon a philosophy of consciousness or one of *Dasein*, since the proper place of communication itself is located in the reality of social life, which by definition is intersubjective.

Habermas's solution therefore encompassed a pragmatic description of language as an instrument of communication, which rested in turn upon an empirical analysis of social integration. Indeed, the better part of the *Theory* is devoted to a reconsideration of the related sociological conceptions of Max Weber (in the first volume) and of Durkheim, George Herbert Mead, and Talcott Parsons (in the second volume), not omitting those of Marx himself. Habermas's specific contribution consisted in showing, on the basis of this empirical analysis, how the communicative situation by its very existence creates the conditions of authentic debate. Participants in any discussion must jointly agree upon certain logical norms if the course of argument is to lead to conclusions that they can all accept. Thus reason can be unambiguously defined as that set of norms guaranteeing the democratic and rigorous character of all debate.

Of the various objections brought against the *Theory*, at least one was admitted by Habermas. The foundation that he proposed for reason, being empirical in character rather than transcendental (as Apel's was), takes for granted the existence of a certain number of results deriving from linguistics and sociology. It appeared, therefore, to involve a vicious circle. But this awkwardness seemed minor to Habermas, who as a convinced materialist considers the objectivity of the sciences to be beyond question. The advantages of such a conception, on the other hand, are many. The chief advantage, as the essays collected in *The Philosophical Discourse of Modernity* (1985) argued, is that now it becomes possible to save reason from the philosophers—Nietzscheans, Heideggerians, subjectivists, and poststructuralists—who have been bent on attacking it, from Foucault and Lyotard to Derrida and Rorty.

The last three openly challenged Habermas's approach. Lyotard was skeptical of the humanism that inspires it. Is it true, he asked, that men really wish to understand each other and that they seek consensus above everything else? Derrida sees such an approach only as a way of returning to a metaphysics of science, doomed to fall captive to the very positivism it seeks to avoid. Rorty, for his part, regards the communicative reconstruction of reason as a legitimate game but one that lacks any absolute value. For ten years Habermas has labored to answer these objections. With regard to the first, he argues for the necessity of privileging consensus over disagreement (what Lyotard called "dissensus"). Derrida he criticizes for confining himself—like Gadamer and Adorno—to an aestheticizing view of reality, which amounts to economizing on history. As against Rorty, he emphasizes the contradictory nature of a position that in rejecting out of hand the concept of foundation deprives itself of a solid base without, however, offering any worthwhile resistance to the threat represented by the revival in the late twentieth century of a diffuse and polymorphous irrationalism.

These polemics are still far from being over. In the meantime, the debate over the foundation of reason has been enriched by the contributions of three Americans, all of whom teach philosophy at Harvard: John Rawls, Stanley Cavell, and Hilary Putnam.

BORN IN 1921, John Rawls is known above all for one book, *Theory of Justice* (1971). Its remarkable worldwide success is due to three innovations. First, although Rawls's views owe almost nothing to logical empiricism, with this book he was nonetheless the first to apply to political debate an analytic style of thinking. Next, because he rejected the utilitarianism of Bentham and Mill, and because he revived—and raised to a level of maximum abstraction—the theory of the social contract associated with the jurisprudence of the seventeenth and eighteenth centuries, he succeeded in renewing the debate over the principles on which modern society is to be organized. Finally, to the extent that his work represented a continuation of the struggles waged in the United States during the 1950s and 1960s on behalf of civil rights for black citizens, he gave new life to a leftist tradition ("liberal" in the American sense of the term) that had been in decline since the death of Dewey.[45]

Moving from an "original position" equivalent to a "state of nature" in which people, deprived of information, are placed under a "veil of ignorance" with regard to the position they might occupy in the society to be constructed, Rawls tries to show that every reasonable person would, under such circumstances, wish to belong to the fairest possible system. What fundamental principles, then, underlie the notion of justice as fairness? Rawls distinguishes two, the first logically prior to the second. The first asserts the equal right of each person to basic individual liberties and thus implies the choice of democracy. The second insists upon the equality of individual opportunity, that is, the reduction of natural and social inequalities. It thus follows that the state must play a regulatory role vis-à-vis the free market in order to ensure a redistribution of wealth and income sufficient to provide those least favored by birth with the necessary means (access to education, health care, and so on) to improve their initial condition.

This brand of liberalism, tempered by a moral concern for fairness in a way that recalls the aims of nineteenth-century European social democracy, obviously exposes Rawls's system to two quite different kinds of objections. On the one hand, because Rawls, like all liberals, treats society as a simple aggregate of identical—and therefore abstract—individuals, he has been criticized by communitarians who maintain that the social good is superior to that of the individual, indeed that the individual does not exist outside the many groups—from the family to the nation—that help shape his personality. These critics include Michael Sandel (b. 1953), Charles Taylor (b. 1931), and Alasdair MacIntyre (b. 1929), whose *After Virtue* (1981) argues against purely rational justifications of morality issuing from the philosophy of the Enlightenment, proposing a return instead to Aristotelian ethics. On the other hand, the regulatory and interventionist function that Rawls confers upon the state has been contested by libertarians who, like Robert Nozick (b. 1938) in *Anarchy, State, Utopia* (1974), remain attached to the classical version of liberalism defended by Adam Smith in the eighteenth century and consider that any state equipped with more than a minimal set of powers violates the sacred rights of the individual. In the United States this thesis was advanced by the Republican Party against the Clinton administration in its first term with considerable effect: although the administration won a second term, its success was largely a result of moving to the Right in response to the perceived popularity of this view among voters. Rawls, it must be said, has had some trouble responding to both groups of adversaries at once.[46]

From his replies, spread out over more than ten years and consolidated in his most recent work, *Political Liberalism* (1993),[47] it has become clear that, despite its Kantian heritage, Rawls's conception of justice as fairness— summed up in the biblical formula "Do unto others as you would have them do unto you"—is to be understood as expressing a political rather than a metaphysical position. In foreswearing the transcendental, Rawls meant simply to claim that such a conception is the best one available to ground a reasonable politics; in other words, to place on a solid basis the set of rules that, in our social lives, each of us must accept if we wish others to do the same. Moreover, in response to the objection that his theory is at bottom only a hasty generalization of the principles of the American Constitution, Rawls affirmed the suitability of its application to every society, including the society of nations.

In asserting this much he supplied a justification for the "duty to interfere," or the obligation that falls upon democratic nations not only to help those that have not yet made the transition to democracy to do so, but also to oppose unjust wars and to prevent—by military means if necessary— tyrannies from crushing peoples who are helpless to resist. Because Rawls's ideas have encouraged those disappointed by the experience of the past century with socialism in practice to try once again to gradually transform the capitalist system from within, they are perhaps more fashionable today in Europe than in the United States. It is nonetheless true that they have lent support to the leading contemporary theory of law in America—somewhat paradoxically since the fundamental thesis of this theory, advanced by Ronald Dworkin (b. 1931) in *Taking Rights Seriously* (1977), consists in the individualist claim that citizens enjoy moral rights (among them, a right to privacy) that may be asserted against the state, which in Rawls's scheme enjoys less circumscribed powers.

The thought of Stanley Cavell (b. 1926), although it derives from a wholly different set of concerns connected with his study of aesthetics, likewise speaks to anxieties peculiar to Continental philosophy. Convinced, like Rorty, that the analytic approach is only the final avatar of an exhausted Kantianism, Cavell wishes by contrast to clear a new path that will help philosophical thought assert itself against an increasingly one-dimensional world. He locates the starting point for this project in the work of Austin— whom he met in 1955 at Harvard, where Austin delivered the William James lectures that year, and whom he regards as his real teacher—and in the later work of Wittgenstein, whose interest in the most ordinary aspects of language and life he shares.

Why, Cavell came to wonder, do most philosophers tend to ignore these aspects, when to do so amounts to rejecting one's own identity? Having written an extraordinarily deep and intelligent book on Wittgenstein, *The Claim of Reason* (1979), he began to inquire into his own identity in *Pursuits of Happiness* (1981) by studying the ways in which Hollywood cinema, the popular American art form par excellence, embodies the aspirations of the modern individual. Then, moving from the screen to the stage in *Disowning Knowledge* (1987), he examined six plays by Shakespeare. In these plays, written between the time of Montaigne and Descartes, he detected the emergence of a skepticism (the "disowning of knowledge" of the book's title) that obscured all subsequent Western metaphysics. To escape this skepticism he turned toward the transcendentalism of Ralph Waldo Emerson (1803–82), showing how the ethics developed by Emerson (whose influence on pragmatism, Nietzsche, and Wittgenstein has until recently been underestimated) could help restore confidence and even help bring about the new world that remains for us to create if we wish to survive—thus the message conveyed by the enigmatic title of one of his first books on Emerson, *This New Yet Unapproachable America* (1989). Cavell is also indebted to European philosophers, as noted earlier, Heidegger and Derrida in particular, but also Freud and Lacan; indeed, his most recent work, *A Pitch of Philosophy* (1994), is presented as a sort of free autobiographical confession interweaving psychoanalysis and cultural theory, in which the interplay of "voice" and "listening" (echoing that of operatic performance) occupies a central place.

Surely the most atypical representative, or ex-representative, of analytic philosophy is Hilary Putnam (b. 1926). Trained both as a philosopher and as a mathematician specializing in recursion theory, he first came to be known for his work on logic and epistemology in the tradition of Quine and subsequently made important contributions to cognitive science. But he has also had, from an early age, an abiding interest in politics. His father was a Communist,[48] and he himself was drawn to Maoism briefly in 1968. Although he returned in later years to a more classical conception of democracy, he nonetheless continues to think of himself as a man of the Left, which leads him to remind Rawls, for example, that justice is not merely a concept and that the oppressed cannot be left to go on waiting indefinitely for a better world to come.

In 1974, in an article devoted to Popper,[49] Putnam denounced as mistaken the strict demarcation insisted upon by Popper between, on the one hand, the concepts of science, whose task is taken to be purely explanatory, and political and philosophical ideas, on the other, which are taken to have no scientific value. By so radically separating theory from practice, and moreover by devaluing practice within the framework of a conception of knowledge defined by the principle of falsification—that is, by the necessity of referring to experience—Popper was shown to be caught up in a peculiar inconsistency. Moreover, without claiming either that historical laws exist or that, if they do exist, they can be known, Putnam rightly pointed out that to affirm the contrary, a priori, is an arbitrary, scientifically unjustified, and politically dangerous decision.

One might suppose that Putnam's critique of Popper makes him a natural ally of Habermas, who is similarly concerned to provide reason with a foundation in order to strengthen both science and democracy. But Putnam, wary of the German idealist tradition, rejects the possibility of a social and linguistic foundation along the lines proposed by the *Theory of Communicative Action*, finding Habermas still too much of a Kantian, too much influenced by Apel's transcendental philosophy. Like Rorty, Putnam claims to be inspired by the pragmatism of Peirce and Dewey; unlike Rorty, however, he feels that it is necessary to try to give an answer to philosophical problems.

On Putnam's view, a foundation for reason is to be found neither in some a priori assumption nor in a particular concept such as communication but only in the concrete practice of what he calls *investigation*. By this he means experimental research in all its forms, which is to say the method of trial and error. Moreover, far from restricting the field of application of this method to the natural sciences, he considers it perfectly applicable to the social sciences, ethics, and politics. The necessity of respecting the data of experience, of advancing only theses justifiable by universally comprehensible arguments, of never trying to extort the agreement of one's adversary—these things have no need of being grounded a priori. They can quite readily be drawn from human experience by a simple process of abstraction. It suffices for the purposes of philosophical reflection to take seriously the notions that we hold to be indispensable in daily life.

One thus arrives at a pragmatic definition of reason as the capacity to distinguish good from bad and right from wrong. As a consequence of his opposition both to skepticism and to the metaphysical realism of the neopositivists, Putnam defends an "internal," or minimal, realism that he traces to the great tradition of Peirce and Dewey. As a direct descendent of these two philosophers (but also of Austin as well), he challenges Carnap's dichotomy between facts and values. Like Dewey, he holds that the implied distinction between science and ethics must be relativized and that moral concepts can themselves be justified in a way that is both rational and experimental[50]—in short, that philosophy is not an empty discourse but a method that has, to the contrary, the dual function of helping us to live better lives while making society more just.[51]

Habermas, although he cannot be expected to accept Putnam's assault on the basic assumptions of his own theory, nonetheless does join Putnam in subscribing—as do Apel, Rawls, and Cavell—to the idea that philosophy has a social mission to carry out. These thinkers also share the belief that some intellectual choices are better than others. No doubt on this last point, at least, they are in agreement with Rorty, but in seeking to support their convictions they place these on a much firmer footing than Rorty does, namely, reason—the only ground, it would appear, on which a philosophical discourse concerned with its own coherence can now stand.

The Unfinished Cathedral

To draw up the balance sheet for a century of philosophy is a perilous undertaking, all the more since during the course of the present century there has not always been agreement among philosophers themselves about the meaning of the term *philosophy* or about the boundaries of the domain it encompasses. How is one to know whether a discipline has made progress when one does not know exactly what end it was trying to reach? Any reckoning seems bound to be inadequate.

In concluding this survey I shall therefore limit myself to a few brief observations. If they are hardly likely to arouse immoderate optimism—something that perhaps does not need to be apologized for, however—it is because they are intended simply to furnish the reader with a few suggestions that may stimulate his or her own thinking, and not to foster a triumphalist vision, as shallow as it would be illusory, of the powers of the mind.

FIRST OBSERVATION: the crucial debate of philosophy today, between rationalists and relativists, is far from being a purely theoretical affair. Let us recall the terms of the debate. The question at issue is whether a firm foundation can be found for reason or whether reason constitutes only one cultural model among others, possessing only a relative superiority—or, indeed, no superiority at all—over other historically possible models. It needs to be added that this debate has developed simultaneously in two related fields: science and politics. At stake in the first of these fields is the question of *knowledge*; that is, whether science tells us something about reality or whether it is merely a linguistic construction having no direct connection with it. At stake in the second field is the question of *democracy*; that is, whether rational government is—by definition—a regime that proposes to establish social justice with strict respect for individual liberties or whether other forms of government having different objectives might not be every bit as good.

Second observation: the debate over rationalism and relativism originated in a particular historical moment that must not be forgotten. Since the Enlightenment, rationality has continually enlarged its hold over Western culture, bringing in its train prodigious advances in science, technical knowledge, and material wealth. The ruthless exploitation of man by his fellow man during the industrialization of the nineteenth century planted doubts about the myth of progress that were aggravated in the early twentieth century by the absurdity of the First World War, which sowed the seeds of confusion on all sides. The atrocity of the Holocaust, finally, in revealing how far the complicity of this same rationality with the worst crimes ever committed by mankind could extend, represented a point of no return. It comes as no surprise, then, that the critique of rationalism—whose premises had been laid down between the two wars by Wittgenstein, Rosenzweig, Benjamin, and Heidegger—should have taken a form that was both radical and systematic after the Second World War, of which it was for the most part the consequence.

Third, and final, observation: although the debates over knowledge and democracy involve apparently distinct problems, they cannot be completely dissociated from each other. No doubt a preference for democracy does not imply, a priori, that one must renounce epistemological relativism.[1] But this relativism, to the extent that it amounts to depriving our intellectual choices of objective foundation and declaring them all to be of equal worth, risks fatally undermining even the most earnest attempts to justify such a preference.

If the ambition of providing a sound foundation for reason is abandoned, the possibility of showing that some arguments are better than others vanishes as well. Indeed, certain relativists consider that the principal achievement of philosophy in the twentieth century has been to rid us of philosophy itself—to produce its own overcoming. Whether one understands this term in Heidegger's sense or in Rorty's, the result is the same: philosophy sees itself reduced in either case to the rank of a mere cultural practice, to which one might conceivably devote oneself with an aesthetic purpose in mind but whose social utility is limited, to say the least. Such a position affords really only one advantage, namely, that it makes room, atop the rubble of philosophy, for new forms of intellectual creativity. But even relativists must nonetheless admit that they have not yet witnessed the birth of any such forms.

Its disadvantages, on the other hand, are considerable. Apart from the fact that it seems as arbitrary to announce the end of philosophy as to proclaim the end of history, or the end of painting or the end of marriage, the renunciation of any objective conception of reason carries with it immense dangers for the future of humanity—dangers that have become all the more visible now that even the least doubtful moral values find themselves more threatened by the day as the twentieth century draws to a close. The resurgence all over the world of racism and ethnic nationalism, which were the chief ingredients of Hitlerite National Socialism; the rise of religious fundamentalisms of all sorts, inevitably hostile to freedom of thought; the proliferation of quasi-religious sects and the explosive increase in credulity and irrationalism, to say nothing of the diffusion via the audiovisual media of standardized ideas that anesthetize the critical spirit—all these phenomena raise fears that a decline into obscurantism may occur on a global scale.[2]

The only possible barrier against such a decline remains, despite its fragility, a return to the ideals of the Enlightenment, suitably revised and corrected, and fortified by rational argument and debate. This practice, and the purposes it supports, have historically formed the core of what is called philosophy. They alone can give the struggle for human respect, no less urgent now than it was two centuries ago, the universal foundation it yet lacks.

NOT ONLY EPISTEMOLOGICAL CONSIDERATIONS but also ethical ones, in light of which the future of democratic values seems decisive by comparison with the status of knowledge, ought therefore to lead us to choose rationalism in spite of its shortcomings, which it falls to us to make up for. This choice makes it possible in turn to reread the history of philosophy in the twentieth century in a less skeptical fashion than before and to see that, far from being incoherent or purely negative, it has in fact registered certain limited but nonetheless real advances while, at the same time, producing irreversible shifts in the ways the oldest philosophical questions are treated.

On the positive side of the ledger, under the head of progress, we should note first the disappearance of certain problems or, more exactly, their transfer to other disciplines better equipped to solve them. Thus the question of the foundation of mathematics has become a mathematical question, while questions concerning the nature of matter and of life have come once again, and rightfully so, within the purview of the physical and biological sciences. Similarly, it is now the business of the cognitive sciences to throw light upon the functioning of the mind, so far as such a thing is possible, and of linguistics to assume responsibility for explaining the workings of language.

If, on the other hand, the ambition of philosophy to become a rigorous science in the Husserlian and Russellian sense is today no longer anything more than a distant dream, the linguistic turn initiated by Frege, Moore, Russell, and Wittgenstein has given philosophers new instruments of analysis that have helped improve techniques of argumentation by refining our notions of knowledge, meaning, and truth. Although they have yet to radically redirect research in ethics and politics, these fields have nonetheless undergone profound transformations over the course of the century.

With regard to political inquiry, perhaps the most important change is connected with the attempt to develop a critical theory of society. First formulated by Marx and then elaborated by various thinkers from Lukács and Horkheimer to Foucault and Habermas, this theory has gradually managed to free itself from the ideological inertia that, in conjunction with other factors, brought about the failure of European communism. Freed at last from the tyranny of materialist and dialectical dogmatisms, it ought now to be possible to envisage in a pragmatic way the radical reforms that our societies desperately need. The urgency of this task, of which the condition of the oppressed throughout the world ought to remind us daily, is insisted upon by philosophers such as Adorno, Sartre, and Putnam who have also proposed original solutions to the problem of reconstructing ethics on an autonomous basis, independent of all religious presuppositions. This reconstruction is difficult, but by no means impossible. It is in any case indispensable if our societies, democratic and nondemocratic alike, are to survive the mounting onslaught of violence and hatred.

Even if such advances are only in their early stages, they are important. They constitute so many steps forward along the long road that reason has yet to travel, redefining its ends and the means appropriate to them, and taking into account the harsh failures it has experienced during the last century as well as the criticisms, often justified, that have been brought against the "imperialism" to which the Enlightenment gave rise on account of an excessive faith in the power of technology—the destructive and perverse effects of which our recent past has amply demonstrated.

NOTHING IS ACTED OUT once and for all on the stage of history, no more on that of the history of philosophy than on any other. Nonetheless, disturbing signs of the reemergence of obscurantism; the loss of historical memory to which the West seems strangely prone, at regular intervals, with regard to its errors and crimes; and the disastrous tendency to consider that the end of the Cold War, in delivering the world from communism, has rescued it from its worst scourge, when quite obviously its true enemies lay in wait elsewhere—all these things lead one to fear that, once again, philosophy may not be equal to the tasks that face it.

Philosophy, this vast and unfinished cathedral whose completion no one shall ever see, nonetheless remains today the only space dedicated to rational debate within which our societies can construct the future—provided, of course, that they are able to come to terms with the past, and that they can contemplate the present with fewer illusions.

Notes

Introduction

1. Immanuel Kant, *Critique of Pure Reason*, trans. Norman Kemp Smith (New York: St. Martin's Press, 1965), 93.
2. Preface to the second edition (1787), ibid., 21.
3. See ibid., 17.

Chapter One | The Sure Path of Science

1. Charles S. Peirce, "How to Make Our Ideas Clear," in *The Essential Peirce*, ed. Nathan Hauser and Christian Kloesel (Bloomington: Indiana University Press, 1992), 124–41.
2. Gottlob Frege, to Bertrand Russell, 22 June 1902, in *Philosophical and Mathematical Correspondence*, ed. Brian McGuinness and trans. Hans Kaal (Chicago: University of Chicago Press, 1980), 132. An alternate and more restrained translation, by Beverly Woodward, may be found in *From Frege to Gödel: A Source Book in Mathematical Logic, 1879–1931*, ed. Jean van Heijenoort (Cambridge, Mass.: Harvard University Press, 1967), 127–28; this volume also contains Russell's remarkable 1962 letter to van Heijenoort recalling the circumstances of his correspondence with Frege and paying tribute to Frege's intellectual courage: "As I think about acts of integrity and grace, I realize that there is nothing in my knowledge to compare with Frege's dedication to truth."
3. Gottlob Frege, "Review of *Philosophy of Arithmetic*—I of Edmund Husserl," in *Collected Papers on Mathematics, Logic, and Philosophy*, ed. Brian McGuinness, trans. Max Black et al. (Oxford: Blackwell, 1984), 195–209.
4. See Husserl to Scholz, 19 February 1936, in Karl Schuhmann, ed., *Edmund*

Husserl: Briefwechsel, vol. 3, part 6 of *Husserliana: Dokumente* (Dordrecht: Kluwer, 1994), 379.

5. Edmund Husserl, *Logical Investigations*, trans. J. N. Findlay (London: Routledge & Kegan Paul, 1970), 1:249. Husserl makes it clear here that he is referring not merely to the "experiences of thinking and knowing" but to a broader, more inclusive category—what in its French translation is called the "pure ontology of lived experience."

6. Ibid., 1:43.

7. Ibid., 1:222–24.

8. See Martin Heidegger, "My Way to Phenomenology" (1963), in *On Time and Being*, trans. Joan Stambaugh (New York: Harper & Row, 1972), 74–82.

9. Edmund Husserl, "Philosophie als strenge Wissenschaft" (1911), in *Phenomenology and the Crisis of Philosophy: Philosophy as Rigorous Science, and Philosophy and the Crisis of European Man*, trans. Quentin Lauer (New York: Harper & Row, 1965), 71.

10. See ibid., 145.

11. Ibid., 122.

12. Edmund Husserl, "Philosophy and the Crisis of European Man" (1935), in *Phenomenology and the Crisis of Philosophy*, 157.

13. Ibid., 185.

14. Ibid., 172. Lauer translates the Greek term as "overseer."

15. Edmund Husserl, *The Crisis of European Sciences and Transcendental Phenomenology: An Introduction to Phenomenological Philosophy*, trans. David Carr (Evanston, Ill.: Northwestern University Press, 1970), 389; note that this text, found in appendix 28 in the German edition, appears as part of appendix 9 in the English edition.

16. Bertrand Russell, *My Philosophical Development* (London: Allen & Unwin, 1959), 38.

17. Bertrand Russell, *Principles of Mathematics*, 2d ed. (London: Allen & Unwin, 1938), §427, 451.

18. Bertrand Russell, "Mathematics and Metaphysicians," in *Mysticism and Logic* (London: Longmans Green, 1918), 92; this article first appeared as "Recent Work on the Principles of Mathematics," *International Monthly* 4 (1901): 83–107.

19. See Russell to Lady Ottoline Morrell, 18 January 1914, cited in Ray Monk, *Bertrand Russell: The Spirit of Solitude, 1872–1921* (New York: Free Press, 1996), 339.

20. Bertrand Russell, *My Philosophical Development*, 208.

21. Bertrand Russell, *The Practice and Theory of Bolshevism*, 2d ed. (London: Allen & Unwin, 1949), 73.

22. Ibid., 76.

23. Ibid., 131.

24. See Bertrand Russell, "La démocratie politique peut-elle s'adapter aux problèmes de 1950?" *Politique étrangère* 15 (1950): 5–13. This article, prepared for French publication, has no exact English counterpart.

25. Ludwig Wittgenstein, *Notebooks, 1914–1916*, ed. G. H. von Wright and G. E. M. Anscombe (Oxford: Blackwell, 1961), 77ᵉ.

26. Ludwig Wittgenstein, *Tractatus Logico-Philosophicus*, trans. D. F. Pears and B. F. McGuinness (London: Routledge & Kegan Paul, 1961), 3.

27. Ibid., 5. Reference is likewise made, in the quotations from the *Tractatus* that follow in the text, to the Pears-McGuinness translation.

28. Friedrich Engels, *Socialism: Utopian and Scientific*, trans. Edward Aveling (New York: International Publishers, 1935), 14.

29. Some readers may prefer the literal Ogden-Ramsey rendering of the famous seventh and final proposition, as well or better known than the modern version: "Whereof one cannot speak, thereof one must be silent" (Wovon man nicht sprechen kann, darüber muß man schweigen).

30. Quoted in Ray Monk, *Ludwig Wittgenstein: The Duty of Genius* (New York: Free Press, 1990), 272.

31. See Wittgenstein's conversations with Schlick and Waismann, recorded in the latter's *Wittgenstein and the Vienna Circle*, ed. Brian McGuinness (Oxford: Blackwell, 1979), 69.

32. Ibid.

33. See Cora Diamond, ed., *Wittgenstein's Lectures on the Foundations of Mathematics: Cambridge, 1939* (Hassocks: Harvest Press, 1976), 237.

34. See Ludwig Wittgenstein, *Remarks on the Foundations of Mathematics*, trans. G. E. M. Anscombe, rev. ed. (Cambridge, Mass.: MIT Press, 1978), part 5, §10–12, 268–71.

35. Ibid., part 6, §21, 322.

36. This version of the incident, given by Popper in *Unended Quest: An Intellectual Autobiography* (La Salle, Ill.: Open Court, 1976), 122–24, has been challenged by certain persons who were present at the lecture, most recently by Wittgenstein's student Peter Geach in response to the account contained in a memoir of Popper by John Watkins, a former colleague at the London School of Economics, published in the *Proceedings of the British Academy* (1996). A heated debate ensued in the pages of the *Times Literary Supplement* (see Letters to the Editor, 13 February, 20 February, 6 March, and 27 March 1998), to which other eyewitnesses joined in. For a balanced account of this latest controversy, which the

Cambridge philosopher Hugh Mellor has characterized as "an example of Popper's own thesis of the fallibility of observation reports," see "The Red-Hot Poker and the Frosty Quip: 52 Years Later, They're Still Dueling" (*New York Times*, 21 March 1998, A15, 17). The chief interest of the original incident, as the historian Peter Munz has pointed out, lies in the fact that it symbolizes the clash of two opposed tendencies in twentieth-century philosophy and, beyond this, demonstrates the impossibility of dialogue where there is no common ground. The event is also described in the context of Wittgenstein's life at the time in Monk, *Wittgenstein*, 489–95.

37. See Bertrand Russell, *My Philosophical Development*, 216–17.

38. The quotations that follow are taken from G. E. M. Anscombe's translation of the *Investigations*, edited with R. Rhees (Oxford: Blackwell, 1953). The reader may wish, however, to consult the third edition (New York: Macmillan, 1968), which preserves the various revisions made in the second edition and includes an index.

39. See Saul A. Kripke, *Wittgenstein on Rules and Private Language* (Cambridge, Mass.: Harvard University Press, 1982), 7.

40. Ludwig Wittgenstein, *Culture and Value*, ed. G. H. von Wright in collaboration with Heikki Nyman, trans. Peter Winch (Oxford: Blackwell, 1980), 49e.

Chapter Two | Philosophies of the End

1. Paul Valéry, "The Intellectual Crisis," in *Variety*, trans. Malcolm Cowley (New York: Harcourt, Brace, 1927), 7–8.

2. Franz Rosenzweig, *Der Stern der Erlösung* (Frankfurt, 1921). A translation of the 2d edition (1930) by William W. Hallo is available as *The Star of Redemption* (Notre Dame, Ind.: Notre Dame University Press, 1985).

3. Karl Löwith, "Martin Heidegger and Franz Rosenzweig, or Temporality and Eternity," *Philosophy and Phenomenological Research* 3 (1942).

4. Martin Heidegger, *Being and Time*, trans. John Macquarrie and Edward Robinson (New York: Harper & Row, 1962), 2.

5. Ibid., 32.

6. Ibid., 34.

7. Ibid., 38.

8. Ibid., 39; passage italicized in the original.

9. Ibid., 378; passage italicized in the original.

10. Ibid.

11. Martin Heidegger, "What Is Metaphysics?" in *Existence and Being*, ed. Werner Brock (Chicago: Henry Regnery, 1949), 342.

12. Ibid., 348.

13. Ernst Cassirer and Martin Heidegger, *Débat sur le kantisme et la philosophie* (*Davos, mars 1929*), ed. Pierre Aubenque (Paris: Beauchesne, 1972), 24.

14. Karl Marx and Friedrich Engels, *Theses on Feuerbach*, in *The German Ideology, Parts I and II*, ed. R. Pascal (London: Lawrence and Wishart, 1938), 199; translation slightly modified.

15. Except for a single occurrence, in the title of the fourth chapter of Engels's *Ludwig Feuerbach*, but this is an interpolation of Soviet origin, dating from 1949.

16. See Edmund Husserl, *Logical Investigations*, 1:197 ff.

17. See V. I. Lenin, *What the "Friends of the People" Are*, in *Works* (Moscow: Foreign Languages Publishing House, 1960), 1:163 ff.

18. See the section entitled "Parties in Philosophy and Philosophical Blockheads" in V. I. Lenin, *Materialism and Empirio-Criticism: Critical Comments on a Reactionary Philosophy* (New York: International Publishers, 1927), 348–69.

19. V. I. Lenin, *Philosophical Notebooks*, in *Works*, 38:180.

20. Stalin, *Oeuvres Choisies* (Tirana: Éditions 8 Nèntori, 1980), 18.

21. Ibid., 19.

22. See Dominique Auffret, *Alexandre Kojève* (Paris: Grasset, 1990), 305.

23. See Richard Rorty, ed., *The Linguistic Turn* (Chicago: University of Chicago Press, 1967).

24. Rudolf Carnap, "Intellectual Autobiography," in *The Philosophy of Rudolf Carnap*, ed. Paul A. Schilpp (La Salle, Ill.: Open Court, 1963), 9.

25. W. V. Quine, "Le combat positiviste de Carnap," in *Le Cercle de Vienne: doctrines et controverses*, ed. Jan Sebestik and Antonia Soulez (Paris: Méridiens-Klincksieck, 1986), 170.

26. Rudolf Carnap, *The Logical Structure of the World*, trans. Rolf A. George (Berkeley: University of California Press, 1967), xviii.

27. "The Scientific View of the World: The Vienna Circle," in Otto Neurath, *Empiricism and Sociology*, ed. Marie Neurath and Robert S. Cohen, Vienna Circle Collection, vol. 1 (Dordrecht: Reidel, 1973), 304–5.

28. Ibid., 306.

29. Ibid., 307.

30. Ibid., 316; passage italicized in the original.

31. Ibid., 317.

32. Ibid., 318; passage italicized in the original.

33. Moritz Schlick, "Experience, Cognition and Metaphysics," in *Philosophical Papers, Volume II (1925–1936)*, ed. Henk. L. Mulder and Barbara F. B. van de Velde-Schlick (Dordrecht: Reidel, 1979), 110–11.

34. Immanuel Kant, "Introduction to Transcendental Dialectic," *Critique of Pure Reason*, 297 ff.

35. Rudolf Carnap, "The Elimination of Metaphysics through Logical Analysis of Language," in *Logical Positivism*, ed. A. J. Ayer (Glencoe, Ill.: Free Press, 1959), 63.

36. Ibid.

37. It should be noted, by contrast, that for a Platonist such as Frege the negation of this statement would be a well-formed proposition.

38. Carnap, "Elimination of Metaphysics," 76.

39. Ibid., 80.

40. In Martin Heidegger, *Vorträge und Aufsatze* (Pfullingen: Neske, 1954); see *Essais et conférences*, trans. André Préau (Paris: Gallimard, 1958), 80–115. An English translation by Joan Stambaugh appeared in Heidegger, *The End of Philosophy* (New York: Harper & Row, 1973).

41. Rudolf Carnap, *The Logical Syntax of Language*, trans. Amethe Smeaton, Countess von Zeppelin (London: Routledge & Kegan Paul, 1937), xiii.

42. Ibid., 222.

43. In Karl Popper, *Conjectures and Refutations*, 3d ed. (London: Routledge & Kegan Paul, 1969), 253–92.

44. See chapter 17 ("Who Killed Logical Positivism?") in Popper, *Unended Quest*, 87–90.

45. In G. E. Moore, *Philosophical Papers* (London: Allen & Unwin, 1959), 32–59.

46. Karl R. Popper, *Unended Quest*, 90.

47. In P. F. Strawson, *Logico-Linguistic Papers* (London: Methuen, 1971), 1–27.

48. See Michael Dummett, *The Origins of Analytical Philosophy* (London: Duckworth, 1993).

49. John Dewey, *Democracy and Education: An Introduction to the Philosophy of Education* (New York: Free Press, 1966), 331.

50. Hook attracted notice early in his career for his original synthesis of Marxism and pragmatism. A major figure in the dissident politics of the 1930s, he later broke with the entire revolutionary tradition and became a prominent critic of Soviet Communism. Although his politics and philosophy were directly influenced by Dewey, the work for which in the end he may be best remembered, *From Hegel to Marx: Studies in the Intellectual Development of Karl Marx* (1936), does not depend on his pragmatism. After the war Hook enjoyed a considerable reputation as a public intellectual and wrote extensively on issues of the day in popular magazines and newspapers, but his influence as a political theorist was greater among philosophers than among politicians. See Theodore

Draper, "Sidney Hook's Revolution," *New York Review of Books* (9 April 1998): 52–54.

51. The favorable attention given to Alan Ryan's recent intellectual biography, *John Dewey and the High Tide of American Liberalism* (New York: W. W. Norton, 1995), may be a welcome sign that this situation is changing, however.

52. See W. V. Quine, "Two Dogmas of Empiricism," in *From a Logical Point of View*, 2d ed. (Cambridge, Mass.: Harvard University Press, 1960), 20–46.

53. It is, however, possible to give a purely linguistic, and therefore materialistic, definition of intentionality, as Roderick Chisholm (b. 1916)—the American translator of Brentano—did in *Perceiving* (1957), anticipating Quine's notion of "referential opacity." On the latter point see Jean-Pierre Dupuy, *Aux origines des sciences cognitives* (Paris: Éditions La Découverte, 1994), 99.

54. See W. V. Quine, *The Times of My Life: An Autobiography* (Cambridge, Mass.: Harvard University Press, 1985), 194.

55. One of these, Gérard Genette, has himself emphasized this convergence in a recent book, *L'Œuvre de l'art* (Paris: Seuil, 1994).

56. Turing, a Cambridge mathematician and logician who attended Wittgenstein's lectures during the Easter term of 1939, succeeded in a famous article that laid the theoretical basis for modern computers ("On Computable Numbers, with an Application to the *Entscheidungsproblem*," completed in 1936 and published the following year) in ruining the Leibnizian and Hilbertian ambition of reducing all reasoning to a simple calculus. During the same term Turing was himself giving a course entitled "Foundations of Mathematics." For an account of his differences of opinion with Wittgenstein over the nature and importance of mathematical logic, see Monk, *Wittgenstein*, 417–20.

57. See John R. Searle, *The Rediscovery of the Mind* (Cambridge, Mass.: MIT Press, 1992). For an overview of the current state of debate over artificial intelligence and related issues, see also the interviews with Searle and other figures in *Speaking Minds: Interviews with Twenty Eminent Cognitive Scientists*, ed. Peter Baumgartner and Sabine Payr (Princeton: Princeton University Press, 1995).

58. On the importance of subjective experience, see in particular Nagel's famous 1974 paper, "What Is It Like to Be a Bat?" in *Mortal Questions* (New York: Cambridge University Press, 1979).

59. See Paul M. Churchland, *The Engine of Reason, The Seat of the Soul: A Philosophical Journey into the Brain* (Cambridge, Mass.: MIT Press, 1995).

60. The source of this interest may be traced back to the publication by one of Quine's former students, the philosopher Dagfin Føllesdal, of an article in 1969 comparing the Husserlian concept of *noēma* and the Fregean concept of sense (*Sinn*). But it must not be forgotten that Wittgenstein, in his later writings

exploring the foundations of psychology, particularly *Remarks on Colour* (1950), had already recognized the existence of phenomenological problems even if he questioned phenomenology as a theory and as a method.

Chapter Three | Conceiving Auschwitz

1. See Stéphane Mosès, *L'Ange de l'histoire* (Paris: Seuil, 1992), 22.

2. See Gershom Scholem, *Walter Benjamin: The Story of a Friendship*, trans. Harry Zohn (Philadelphia: Jewish Publication Society of America, 1981).

3. Although "Holocaust" (deriving from the Greek *holócauston* of the Septuagint) is the term usually used in English to refer to the extermination of European Jewry during World War II, I should like to express my reservations about its use in this context for it seems to give the Nazi destruction of the Jews a religious significance that it does not possess. In French, it is more common to use the Hebrew term *Shoah*, which has the merit of being more specific, since it limits itself to designating a particular historical event—"the Catastrophe."

4. Some of these texts were later reprinted (at Heidegger's expense) by Guido Schneeberger under the title *Nachlese zu Heidegger: Dokumente zu seinem Leben und Denken* (Bern, 1962); a partial French translation appeared in the journal *Le Débat* 48 (January–February 1988): 176–92.

5. See Hugo Ott, *Martin Heidegger: A Political Life*, trans. Allan Blunden (New York: HarperCollins, 1993), 190. Since the original publication of this work an excellent and still more comprehensive biography by Rüdiger Safranski has appeared in Germany, now available in English as *Martin Heidegger: Between Good and Evil*, trans. Ewald Osers (Cambridge, Mass.: Harvard University Press, 1998), that confirms Ott's analysis.

6. See ibid., 270–74.

7. Martin Heidegger, *An Introduction to Metaphysics*, trans. Ralph Mannheim (New Haven: Yale University Press, 1959), 199.

8. See Karl Löwith, *My Life in Germany before and after 1933*, trans. Elizabeth King (Urbana: University of Illinois Press, 1994), 59–60.

9. A French translation of this text ("Das Rektorat 1933–1934: Tatsachen und Gedanken") was first published in the journal *Le Débat* in November 1983 and subsequently reprinted in Martin Heidegger, *Écrits politiques, 1933–1966*, ed. and trans. François Fédier (Paris: Gallimard, 1995), 215–38. See also Martin Heidegger, "Letter to the Rector of Freiburg University" (4 November 1945), in *The Heidegger Controversy: A Critical Reader*, ed. Richard Wolin (Cambridge, Mass.: MIT Press, 1993), 61–66.

10. This interview was first published in the 31 May 1976 issue of *Der Spiegel*,

a few days after Heidegger's death, in strict accordance with the terms of his will. A French translation later appeared under the title *Réponses et questions sur l'histoire et la politique* (Paris: Mercure de France, 1988).

11. This letter was published for the first time in 1988 in Ott's previously cited biography; see *Martin Heidegger: A Political Life*, 192–93.

12. Cited by Wolfgang Schirmacher in *Technik und Gelassenheit* (Freiburg: Karl Alber, 1984); see also Philippe Lacoue-Labarthe, *Heidegger, Art and Politics: The Fiction of the Political*, trans. Chris Turner (Oxford: Basil Blackwell, 1990), 34.

13. Gadamer's position is summarized in an article published in French by the weekly magazine *Le Nouvel Observateur* (22–28 January 1988): 45.

14. Jean Beaufret, *De l'existentialisme à Heidegger* (Paris: Vrin, 1986), 18.

15. See Martin Heidegger, "Lettre à Richardson," *Questions III et IV* (Paris: Gallimard, 1990), 344.

16. See, for example, Heidegger's paper "Overcoming Metaphysics" (1936–1946), in *The Heidegger Controversy*, 72–73; see also "Moira (Parmenides VIII, 34–41)" (1952), in Martin Heidegger, *Early Greek Thinking*, trans. David Farrell Krell and Frank A. Capuzzi (New York: Harper & Row, 1975), 79–101. The latter translation renders this term as "the twofold."

17. Martin Heidegger, *Letter on Humanism*, in *Martin Heidegger: Basic Writings*, ed. David Farrell Krell, 2d ed. (San Francisco: HarperCollins, 1993), 234.

18. See Martin Heidegger, "Overcoming Metaphysics," in *The Heidegger Controversy*, 73–74; see also "The End of Philosophy and the Task of Thinking" (1964), in *Basic Writings*, 433.

19. See, for example, Heidegger's 1952 lectures, published in 1954 as *Was Heisst Denken?* and available in English as *What Is Called Thinking?* trans. Fred D. Wieck and J. Glenn Gray (New York: Harper & Row, 1968), 8.

20. Martin Heidegger, "Overcoming Metaphysics," in *The Heidegger Controversy*, 68.

21. Martin Heidegger, *Introduction to Metaphysics*, 45. The French translation of this work reproduces the German text more faithfully: Russia and America are metaphysically the same, Heidegger says, displaying "the same sinister frenzy of unbridled technology"; see *Introduction à la métaphysique* (Paris: Gallimard, 1967), 49.

22. The results of Faye's work on Heidegger, sketched in various articles that have appeared since the 1960s, are laid out in *La Raison narrative* (Paris: Balland, 1990) and summarized in *Le Piège: la philosophie heideggérienne et le nazisme* (Paris: Balland, 1994).

23. See Martin Heidegger, *The Question of Being*, trans. William Kublack and Jean T. Wilde (New Haven: College & University Press, 1958), 87. The rendering

found here has been altered, following the standard French translation of *Verwindung* in preference to Kublack's and Wilde's "restoration."

24. Ibid., 93. The French philosopher Gérard Granel proposed in 1968 that *Abbau* be translated as "deconstruction," which is very close to its literal sense of "dismantling."

25. These lectures were reprinted after the war in two volumes as *Nietzsche* (Pfulligen: Neske, 1961).

26. Martin Heidegger, "What Are Poets for?" in *Poetry, Language, Thought*, trans. Albert Hofstadter (New York: Harper & Row, 1971), 91.

27. See Emmanuel Levinas, "Comme un consentement à l'horrible," *Le Nouvel Observateur* (22–28 January 1988): 48.

28. See Victor Farias, *Heidegger and Nazism*, trans. Paul Burrell and Gabriel R. Ricci (Philadelphia: Temple University Press, 1989) and Hugo Ott, *Martin Heidegger: A Political Life*. Farias's book (written in Spanish but never published in its original form) first appeared in French in 1987; Ott's, first published in German the following year, appeared in a French translation in 1990. The errors for which Farias's book has been widely criticized may be due at least in part to its complicated publication history, having subsequently been translated from French into German with substantial modifications and additions by the author; for further information see the foreword by the American editors, Joseph Margolis and Tom Rockmore. See also the recent book by Hans Sluga, *Heidegger's Crisis: Philosophy and Politics in Nazi Germany* (Cambridge, Mass.: Harvard University Press, 1993).

29. See Henri Meschonnic, *Le Langage Heidegger* (Paris: Presses Universitaires de France, 1990).

30. Martin Heidegger, "The Word of Nietzsche: 'God Is Dead,'" in *The Question Concerning Technology and Other Essays*, trans. William Lovitt (New York: Harper & Row, 1977), 112.

31. On this revisionist movement, see *Histoire de l'antisémitisme (1945–1993)*, ed. Léon Poliakov (Paris: Seuil, 1994), especially 145–49.

32. The first of these expressions is due to Adorno (see *Negative Dialectics*, part 3, chap. 3, §1). The second constitutes the subtitle of a book by Jean Améry, *Janseits von Schuld und Sühne: Bewaltigungsversuche eines Überwaltigen* (Stuttgart: Klett-Cotta, J. C. Cotta'sche Buchhandlung Nachfolger, 1977).

33. Daniel Jonah Goldhagen, *Hitler's Willing Executioners: Ordinary Germans and the Holocaust* (New York: Knopf, 1996). On everyday life inside the camps, see Wolfgang Sofsky, *The Order of Terror: The Concentration Camp*, trans. William Templer (Princeton: Princeton University Press, 1997).

34. See Léon Poliakov, "Histoire et polémiques: à propos du génocide," *Com-

mentaire 53 (spring 1991): 202–5. The recent publication by Stéphane Courtois and others of *Le Livre noir du Communisme: Crimes, terreur, répression* (Paris: Laffont, 1997), arguing that the record of Communism was indeed superior to that of Nazism in respect of evil, has aroused a storm of controversy in France. Although for the moment at least most scholars reject both its documentation and its conclusions, the book's thesis has been favorably received in some quarters; see, for example, the review by the Berkeley historian Martin Malia, "The Lesser Evil?" *Times Literary Supplement* (27 March 1998): 3–4.

35. See Hans-Georg Gadamer, *Philosophical Apprenticeships*, trans. Robert R. Sullivan (Cambridge, Mass.: MIT Press, 1985).

36. See David S. Wyman, *The Abandonment of the Jews: America and the Holocaust, 1941–1945* (New York: Pantheon, 1984), 20.

37. On Arendt's romantic involvement with Heidegger, see Elzbieta Ettinger, *Hannah Arendt/Martin Heidegger* (New Haven: Yale University Press, 1995).

38. See Hannah Arendt, *The Origins of Totalitarianism* (New York: Harcourt, Brace, 1973), 222.

39. Ibid., xxiii.

40. Nathan Tarcov and Thomas L. Pangle, "Epilogue: Leo Strauss and the History of Political Philosophy," in *History of Political Philosophy*, ed. Leo Strauss and Joseph Cropsey, 3d ed. (Chicago: University of Chicago Press, 1987), 930.

41. Letter from Horkheimer to Adorno, cited by Rolf Wiggershaus, *The Frankfurt School: Its History, Theories, and Political Significance*, trans. Michael Robertson (Cambridge: Polity Press, 1994), 162.

42. This formula is found in the preface composed in 1969 by Horkheimer and Adorno for a new edition of *Dialektik der Aufklärung*; see *Dialectic of Enlightenment*, trans. John Cumming (London: Verso, 1979), x.

43. Ibid., 200.

44. Max Horkheimer, *Dawn and Decline: Notes 1926–1931 and 1950–1969*, trans. Michael Shaw (New York: Seabury Press, 1978), 138. Note that the first German edition of the *Notizen* (1974) covers the period 1950–69, whereas the slightly expanded second edition, corresponding to the sixth of the nineteen volumes of Horkheimer's collected papers (Frankfurt: Fischer, 1985–96), covers the period 1949–69.

45. Ibid., 153.

46. See Theodor W. Adorno, *Negative Dialectics*, trans. E. B. Ashton (New York: Seabury Press, 1973), 97–131.

47. Ibid., 144.

48. Ibid., 203.

49. Ibid., 153.

50. Ibid., 361.
51. Ibid., 366–67.
52. Ibid., 365.
53. Ibid.
54. Ibid., 404.
55. Ibid., 405.
56. Theodor W. Adorno, *Aesthetic Theory*, trans. C. Lenhardt (London: Routledge & Kegan Paul, 1984), 1.
57. Ibid., 369.

Chapter Four | In the Cold War

1. See Henri Bergson, *Les Deux sources de la morale et de la religion* (Paris: F. Alcan, 1932).
2. See Karl R. Popper, *La Société ouverte et ses Ennemis* (Paris: Seuil, 1979), 1:168.
3. Karl R. Popper, *The Open Society and Its Enemies*, 4th ed. (London: Routledge & Kegan Paul, 1962), 2:28.
4. Ibid., 2:122.
5. Ibid., 2:329 (n. 13).
6. Ibid., 2:211.
7. Ibid., 1:1.
8. Ibid., 2:246.
9. Ibid., 2:237.
10. See ibid., 2:60.
11. Ibid., 1:124.
12. See Karl R. Popper, "Reason or Revolution?" *Archives européennes de sociologie* 11 (1970): 252–62.
13. See *Revolution oder Reform? Herbert Marcuse und Karl Popper: eine Konfrontation*, ed. Franz Stark (Munich: Kösel-Verlag, 1971).
14. See Francis Fukuyama, *The End of History and the Last Man* (New York: Free Press, 1992).
15. Simone de Beauvoir, *Memoirs of a Dutiful Daughter*, trans. James Kirkup (New York: Harper & Row, 1974), 339–41.
16. Simone de Beauvoir, *The Prime of Life*, trans. Peter Green (New York: Paragon House, 1992), 112.
17. Jean-Paul Sartre, *The Transcendence of the Ego: An Existentialist Theory of Consciousness*, trans. Forrest Williams and Robert Kirkpatrick (New York: Hill & Wang, 1960), 104–6.

18. Jean-Paul Sartre, *Being and Nothingness: A Phenomenological Essay on Ontology*, trans. Hazel E. Barnes (New York: Washington Square Press, 1956), 157.

19. Ibid., 703.

20. Ibid., 707.

21. Ibid., 798.

22. See ibid., 558.

23. Ibid., 546.

24. Ibid., 671.

25. Ibid., 675.

26. Ibid., 330.

27. See ibid., 498.

28. See ibid., 556.

29. See ibid., 698.

30. See Martin Heidegger, *Letter on Humanism*, in *Basic Writings*, 232–33.

31. Jean-Paul Sartre, "Merleau-Ponty" (1961), in *Situations*, trans. Benita Eisler (New York: George Braziller, 1965), 245.

32. Reprinted in Jean-Paul Sartre, *Situations Philosophiques* (Paris: Gallimard, 1990); see "Materialism and Revolution," in *Literary and Philosophical Essays*, trans. Annette Michelson (London: Rider, 1955), 185–239.

33. Maurice Merleau-Ponty, *Humanism and Terror: An Essay on the Communist Problem*, trans. John O'Neill (Boston: Beacon Press, 1969), 148.

34. Jean-Paul Sartre, "Merleau-Ponty," in *Situations*, 287.

35. Reprinted in Jean-Paul Sartre, *Situations VI* (Paris: Gallimard, 1964).

36. Reprinted in Jean-Paul Sartre, *Situations VII* (Paris: Gallimard, 1965); see also Sartre, *The Ghost of Stalin*, trans. Martha H. Fletcher with the assistance of John R. Kleinschmidt (New York: Braziller, 1968).

37. Jean-Paul Sartre, *Search for a Method*, trans. Hazel E. Barnes (New York: Vintage Books, 1968), 83.

38. Ibid., xxxiv.

39. Ibid., xxxv.

40. Ibid., xxxiv.

41. Reprinted in Jean-Paul Sartre, *Situations VIII* (Paris: Gallimard, 1972).

42. Benny Lévy, *Le Nom de l'homme* (Lagrasse: Verdier, 1984), 191.

43. See Marcuse's 1948 essay "Sartre's Existentialism," reprinted in *From Luther to Popper*, trans. Joris De Bres (London: Verso, 1972), 157–90.

44. Herbert Marcuse, *One-Dimensional Man* (Boston: Beacon Press, 1964), 187.

45. Alfred North Whitehead, *The Function of Reason* (Boston: Beacon Press, 1959), 5; quoted in Marcuse, *One-Dimensional Man*, 228.

46. See Max Horkheimer, "Materialism and Metaphysics" (1933), in *Critical Theory: Selected Essays*, trans. Matthew J. O'Connoll et al. (New York: Herder and Herder, 1972), 22.

47. Herbert Marcuse, *One-Dimensional Man*, 257.

48. Ibid.

49. Reprinted in Louis Althusser, *Écrits sur la psychanalyse* (Paris: Stock/IMEC, 1993).

50. See Maurice Merleau-Ponty, *The Adventures of the Dialectic*, trans. Joseph Bien (Evanston, Ill.: Northwestern University Press, 1973), 74–94.

51. The coherence of this triple reading will become clearer with the forthcoming publication of the lectures given by Althusser at the École Normale between 1950 and 1980.

52. Jean Cavaillès, *Sur la logique et la théorie de la science*, 4th ed. (Paris: Presses Universitaires de France, 1987), 78.

53. Louis Althusser, *Lenin and Philosophy and Other Essays*, trans. Ben Brewster (New York: Monthly Review Press, 1971), 43.

54. Twenty pages, entitled "On Spinoza," are reproduced in Louis Althusser, *Éléments d'autocritique* (Paris: Hachette, 1974), 65–83.

55. Louis Althusser, "Soutenance d'Amiens," reprinted in *Positions* (Paris: Éditions Sociales, 1976).

56. Louis Althusser, *Reply to John Lewis* (1973), in *Essays in Self-criticism*, trans. Grahame Lock (London: NLB, 1976), 39.

57. Reprinted in Louis Althusser, *Écrits philosophiques et politiques*, vol. 1 (Paris: Stock/IMEC, 1994), 527.

58. These articles were republished in a volume of the same title, *Ce qui ne peut plus durer dans le Parti communiste* (Paris: François Maspero, 1978).

59. This essay is reprinted in the first volume of the previously cited *Écrits philosophiques et politiques*, 539–76.

60. See Louis Althusser, *L'Avenir dure longtemps* (Paris: Stock/IMEC, 1992).

61. See Cornelius Castoriadis, *L'Institution imaginaire de la société* (Paris: Seuil, 1975) and *Domaines de l'homme* (Paris: Seuil, 1986).

62. New impetus has also been given to Marxist thought by the work of the so-called Analytical Marxists, who have tried to reformulate Marxist sociology in terms of rational-choice theory, borrowed from neoclassical economics. Three works in particular are worthy of note: G. A. Cohen, *Karl Marx's Theory of History: A Defence* (Princeton: Princeton University Press, 1978); John E. Roemer, *Analytical Foundations of Marxian Economic Theory* (Cambridge: Cambridge University Press, 1981); and Jon Elster, *Making Sense of Marx* (Cambridge: Cambridge University Press, 1985). For a post-1989 assessment of the prospects of Marxist

theory and practice see Roemer, *A Future for Socialism* (Cambridge, Mass.: Harvard University Press, 1994). Dick Howard, who is not a Marxist, has also written extensively on Marx and Marxism; see, for example, his *From Marx to Kant*, 2d ed. (Basingstoke: Macmillan, 1993).

63. See Manuel de Diéguez, *Le Combat de la raison* (Paris: Albin Michel, 1989), 273–79.

Chapter Five | Reason in Question

1. Romanian by birth, Emil Cioran (1911–95) wrote the greater part of his work in French; among his books translated into English are *A Short History of Decay* (1949), *Syllogisms of Bitterness* (1952), and *Temptation to Exist* (1956). Although he always refused to be considered as a professional philosopher, his meditations on the absurdity of existence are of direct interest to philosophy.

2. See Jacques Lacan, "The Looking-Glass Phase," *International Journal of Psychoanalysis* 18, no. 1 (January 1937). A substantially revised version of this paper was later delivered at the sixteenth International Psychoanalytical Congress in Zurich on 17 July 1949; an English translation of this version has been published under the title "The Mirror Stage as Formative of the Function of the I" in *Écrits*, trans. Alan Sheridan (New York: Norton, 1977), 1–7.

3. Jacques Lacan, "The Function and Field of Speech and Language in Psychoanalysis," in *Écrits*, 55.

4. Jacques Lacan, "The Direction of the Treatment and the Principles of Its Power," in *Écrits*, 234.

5. See Roman Jakobson, "Two Aspects of Language and Two Types of Aphasic Disturbances," in Jakobson and Halle, *Fundamentals of Language*, 2d ed. (The Hague and Paris: Mouton, 1971), 69–96.

6. See Jacques Lacan, "The Agency of the Letter in the Unconscious or Reason since Freud," in *Écrits*, 146–78.

7. Jacques Lacan, "The Subversion of the Subject and the Dialectic of Desire in the Freudian Unconscious," in *Écrits*, 316.

8. Georges Canguilhem, "Qu'est-ce que la psychologie?" in *Études d'histoire et de philosophie des sciences* (Paris: Vrin, 1968).

9. On this movement as a whole, see Christian Delacampagne, *Antipsychiatrie* (Paris: Grasset, 1974).

10. Michel Foucault, *The Order of Things*, trans. Alan Sheridan-Smith (New York: Pantheon, 1971), 367.

11. Ibid., 386.

12. Ibid., xxiii.

13. Ibid., 387.

14. Reprinted in Michel Foucault, Dits et écrits (1954–1988), vol. 4 (Paris: Gallimard, 1994), 41–95.

15. Interview with Christian Delacampagne, reprinted in ibid., 104–10.

16. Michel Foucault, The Archaeology of Knowledge, trans. Rupert Sawyer (New York: Pantheon, 1972), 17.

17. See James Miller, The Passion of Michel Foucault (New York: Doubleday, 1993).

18. Founded in 1957 by the French writer and filmmaker Guy Debord (1931–94), the Situationist International was a thoroughly informal movement aiming to produce the most radical and subversive critique possible of politics, society, and culture in capitalist systems during the technocratic age. Debord's fundamental thesis in The Society of the Spectacle (1967) was that everything in these systems—as well as the Marxist challenge to them—had become a matter of "image" and "merchandise." After riding the wave of 1968, the movement dissolved in 1972. Debord committed suicide in 1994.

19. See Thomas S. Kuhn, The Structure of Scientific Revolutions, 2d ed. (Chicago: University of Chicago Press, 1970), 147–48.

20. See Thomas S. Kuhn, "Logic of Discovery or Psychology of Research?" in The Essential Tension (Chicago: University of Chicago Press, 1977), 266–92.

21. See Joseph Epstein, "Professor Ayer on Sense-Data," Journal of Philosophy 53, no. 13 (1956): 401–15, and "Quine's Gambit Accepted," Journal of Philosophy 55, no. 16 (1958): 673–83. Epstein's review of Kuhn's Essential Tension, for which the author expressed his gratitude in private correspondence, appeared in the American Journal of Physics 47, no. 6 (1979): 568–70. An authority on pragmatism, and a keen student of Peirce, Epstein came to Columbia as a graduate student while Dewey was still active. He taught for more than forty years at Amherst, where in February 1994 Hilary Putnam delivered the memorial lecture in his honor, suggestively entitled "Was Wittgenstein a Pragmatist?" Putnam's approach to the problem of how we describe the world, described in greater detail below, may provide a natural way of bridging the gap between the followers of Nagel and of Kuhn.

22. This conception was expounded by Popper from the time of his earliest writings and further developed in Objective Knowledge (Oxford: Clarendon Press, 1972).

23. Jacques Derrida, "Cogito and the History of Madness" (1963), reprinted in Writing and Difference, trans. Alan Bass (Chicago: University of Chicago Press, 1978), 31.

24. Derrida began studying phenomenology as early as 1953 (witness his first published article, which appeared that year, "The Problem of Genesis in the

Philosophy of Husserl"), convinced from the outset that neither Sartre nor Merleau-Ponty were reliable interpreters of Husserl.

25. Jacques Derrida, "Implications," in *Positions*, trans. Alan Bass (Chicago: University of Chicago Press, 1981), 9, translation slightly modified.

26. See, for example, Jacques Derrida, "Freud and the Scene of Writing" (1966), in *Writing and Difference*, 196. On the sense of *différer*, see Derrida's interview with Henri Ronse, "Implications," in *Positions*, 8.

27. The three texts (Searle's in summary form) can be found in Jacques Derrida, *Limited Inc*, trans. Samuel Weber and Jeffrey Mehlman (Evanston, Ill.: Northwestern University Press, 1988).

28. In 1996 the journal *Social Text* accepted for publication a paper by Alan Sokal, a professor of physics at New York University, devoted to a deconstructionist interpretation of quantum theory that afterwards was recognized as a deliberate piece of nonsense. "Sokal's Hoax" naturally delighted Derrida's opponents—although it proves nothing, except that the editorial boards of certain journals are not as careful in scrutinizing submissions as they should be. The subsequent publication in France of a book by Sokal and Jean Bricmont, *Impostures Intellectuelles* (1997), created a small storm on both sides of the English Channel, thus giving new life to the debate across the Atlantic.

29. See Jacques Derrida, *Specters of Marx*, trans. Peggy Kamuf (New York: Routledge, 1994), 55.

30. Several pieces by Derrida on Levinas have been published, one in *Writing and Difference*, another in *Textes pour Emmanuel Levinas*, ed. François Laruelle (Paris: Jean-Michel Place, 1980); the latter piece may also be found in Derrida's *Psyche: Inventions de l'autre* (Paris: Galilée, 1987). See also his opening paper at the commemorative conference "Hommage à Emmanuel Levinas" held at the Sorbonne in December 1996 entitled "Le mot d'accueil," which has recently been published together with Derrida's funeral oration for Levinas as *Adieu à Emmanuel Levinas* (Paris: Galilée, 1997).

31. See "Circonfession," in Geoffrey Bennington and Jacques Derrida, *Jacques Derrida*, trans. Geoffrey Bennington (Chicago: University of Chicago Press, 1993).

32. On this point see Rorty's autobiographical essay, "Trotsky and the Wild Orchids," *Common Knowledge* 1, no. 3 (winter 1992): 142 ff.

33. See Richard Rorty, *Philosophy and the Mirror of Nature* (Princeton: Princeton University Press, 1979).

34. On this point see Rorty's essay "Keeping Philosophy Pure," in *Consequences of Pragmatism: Essays 1972–1980* (Minneapolis: University of Minnesota Press, 1982), 19–37.

35. Feyerabend's interesting autobiography, finished a few weeks before his

death and published posthumously as *Killing Time* (Chicago: University of Chicago Press, 1995), is marred by an awkward omission—his reluctance to express any regret about his active participation in World War II wearing the Nazi uniform. His relativism was not, in those years, so very different than that of Heidegger (whom, tellingly perhaps, he declined the opportunity to meet in 1966).

36. Paul Feyerabend, *Farewell to Reason* (London: Verso, 1987), 301.

37. On this point in particular see Rorty, *Essays on Heidegger and Others* (New York: Cambridge University Press, 1991).

38. See, in particular, Rorty's essay "The Priority of Democracy to Philosophy," in *Objectivity, Relativism, and Truth* (1991), 175–96.

39. See Jacques Bouveresse, "Sur quelques conséquences indésirables du pragmatisme," in Jean-Pierre Cometti, ed., *Lire Rorty* (Combas: Éditions de l'Éclat, 1992), 19–56.

40. This connection has, of course, been explicitly rejected by some—most notably, perhaps, by George Steiner in his *Heidegger* (1978). See too Steiner's recent endorsement of what might be called the "Gadamer defense" of Heidegger—"'Martin was the greatest of thinkers and the most petty [kleinlich] of men'"—in "An Almost Inebriate Bewitchment," *Times Literary Supplement* (15 August 1997): 11.

41. Jürgen Habermas, "Zur Veröffentlichung von Vorlesungen vom Jahre 1935," *Frankfurter Allgemeine Zeitung* (25 July 1953); see the translation by William S. Lewis in *The Heidegger Controversy: A Critical Reader*, 196–97. Another version of this article was previously published in chapter 6 of *The New Conservatism: Cultural Criticism and the Historians' Debate*, ed. and trans. Shierry Weber Nicholsen (Cambridge, Mass.: MIT Press, 1989).

42. See Jürgen Habermas, "The German Idealism of the Jewish Philosophers" (1961), in *Philosophical-Political Profiles*, trans. Frederick G. Lawrence (Cambridge, Mass.: MIT Press, 1983), 21–43.

43. See the articles by Habermas constituting his contribution to the "historians' debate" in chapter 9 ("A Kind of Settling of Damages") of *The New Conservatism*: "Remarks from the Roemerberg Colloquium" (209–11), "Apologetic Tendencies" (212–28), "On the Public Use of History" (229–40), and "Closing Remarks" (241–48).

44. See Jürgen Habermas, "Martin Heidegger: Werk und Weltanschauung," in *The New Conservatism*, 140–72.

45. Similarly, Ronald Dworkin's work in the philosophy of law has been deeply marked by the historical legacy of the Vietnam War.

46. Rawls's ideas have also been criticized from a leftist perspective not

very far removed from the humanism of the young Marx by Michael Walzer in *Spheres of Justice: A Defense of Pluralism and Equality* (New York: Basic Books, 1983).

47. John Rawls, *Political Liberalism* (New York: Columbia University Press, 1993); see also the collection of his articles published in French under the title *Justice et Démocratie* (Paris: Seuil, 1993).

48. In this connection see Putnam's review in the 22 May 1998 issue of the *Times Literary Supplement* of Rorty's most recent book, *Achieving Our Country: Leftist Thought in Twentieth-Century America* (Cambridge, Mass.: Harvard University Press, 1998), based on lectures given at Harvard in 1997 in which Rorty recalls his experience growing up as the child of fellow travelers who broke with the Communist Party the year after he was born.

49. See Hilary Putnam, "The Corroboration of Theories," in *The Philosophy of Karl Popper*, ed. Paul A. Schilpp (La Salle, Ill.: Open Court, 1974).

50. See chapter 11 of Hilary Putnam, *Realism with a Human Face* (Cambridge, Mass.: Harvard University Press, 1991).

51. This issue lies also at the heart of Charles Larmore's moral philosophy; see his *Patterns of Moral Complexity* (Cambridge: Cambridge University Press, 1987).

Epilogue

1. This in any case is the position adopted by Rorty, who does not always recognize himself in the descriptions that are given of his relativism and who prefers to consider himself as an "ultra-pragmatist" disciple of Davidson.

2. This decline has rightly been denounced in France by Bernard-Henri Lévy, one of the few philosophers to have courageously spoken up on behalf of the Bosnian Muslims, in *La Pureté dangereuse* (Paris: Grasset, 1994).

Select Bibliography

An exhaustive bibliography of Western philosophy since 1880 would by itself fill several volumes. In view of the fact that a great many titles have already been cited in the text, this list will limit itself to mentioning certain general works and, in the case of major philosophers, their most significant books and essays. For ease of reference, works are cited in their English editions except where no translation exists.

Adorno, Theodor W. *Aesthetic Theory*. Edited by Gretel Adorno and Rolf Tiedemann; translated by C. Lenhardt. London: Routledge & Kegan Paul, 1984.

———. *Minima Moralia*. Translated by E. F. N. Jephcott. London: New Left Books, 1974.

———. *Negative Dialectics*. Translated by E. B. Ashton. New York: Seabury Press, 1973.

Adorno, Theodor W., Hans Albert, Jürgen Habermas, and Karl R. Popper. *Der Positivismusstreit in der deutschen Soziologie*. Darmstadt and Neuwied: Hermann Luchterhand Verlag, 1969. [The main texts of the 1961 Tübingen debate]

Althusser, Louis. *Écrits philosophiques et politiques*. Volume 1. Paris: Stock/IMEC, 1994.

———. *For Marx*. Translated by Ben Brewster. New York: Pantheon, 1969.

———. *The Future Lasts a Long Time and The Facts*. Edited by Olivier Corpet and Yann Moulier Boutang; translated by Richard Veasey. London: Chatto and Windus, 1993.

———. *Writings on Psychoanalysis: Freud and Lacan*. Edited by Olivier Corpet and François Matheron; translated with a preface by Jeffrey Mehlman. New York: Columbia University Press, 1996.

Améry, Jean. *Janseits von Schuld und Sühne: Bewaltigungsversuche eines Überwaltigen*. Stuttgart: Klett-Cotta, J. C. Cotta'sche Buchhandlung Nachfolge, 1977.

Apel, Karl-Otto. *Towards a Transformation of Philosophy*. Translated by Glyn Adey and David Frisby. London: Routledge & Kegan Paul, 1980.

Arendt, Hannah. *Eichmann in Jerusalem: A Report on the Banality of Evil*. New York: Viking Press, 1963.

——. *The Human Condition*. Chicago: University of Chicago Press, 1958.

——. *The Origins of Totalitarianism*. New York: Harcourt, Brace, 1973.

Aron, Raymond. *The Opium of the Intellectuals*. Translated by Terence Kilmartin. Garden City, N.Y.: Doubleday, 1957.

Auffret, Dominique. *Alexandre Kojève*. Paris: Grasset, 1990. [A very good biography]

Austin, John L. *How to Do Things with Words*. Cambridge, Mass.: Harvard University Press, 1962.

——. *Philosophical Papers*. Edited by J. O. Urmson and J. L. Warnock. 2d edition. Oxford: Clarendon Press, 1970.

——. *Sense and Sensibilia*. Oxford: Clarendon Press, 1962.

Bachelard, Gaston. *The New Scientific Spirit*. Translated by Arthur Goldhammer, with a foreword by Patrick A. Heelan. Boston: Beacon Press, 1984.

——. *The Philosophy of No: A Philosophy of the New Scientific Mind*. Translated by G. C. Waterston. New York: Orion Press, 1968.

Benjamin, Walter. *Reflections: Essays, Aphorisms, Autobiographical Writings*. Edited by Peter Demetz; translated by Edmund Jephcott. New York: Schocken, 1986.

——. *Selected Writings*. Edited by Marcus Bullock and Michael W. Jennings. Cambridge, Mass.: Belknap Press, 1996.

Bergson, Henri. *Matter and Memory*. Translated by Nancy Margaret Paul and W. Scott Palmer. New York: Zone Books, 1988.

——. *The Two Sources of Morality and Religion*. Translated by R. Ashley Audra and Cloudesley Brereton, with the assistance of W. Horsfall Carter. London: Macmillan, 1935.

Bloch, Ernst. *The Utopian Function of Art and Literature: Selected Essays*. Translated by Jack Zipes and Frank Mecklenberg. Cambridge, Mass.: MIT Press, 1988.

Bouveresse, Jacques. *La Parole malheureuse*. Paris: Éditions de Minuit, 1971. [On Wittgenstein's later philosophy]

Buber, Martin. *I and Thou*. Translated by Walter Kaufmann. New York: Scribner's Sons, 1970.

Canguilhem, Georges. *La Connaissance de la vie*. 2d revised and enlarged edition. Paris: Vrin, 1969.

Carnap, Rudolf. "The Elimination of Metaphysics through Logical Analysis of Language." Translated by Arthur Pap. In A. J. Ayer, ed., *Logical Positivism*, 60–81. Glencoe, Ill.: Free Press, 1959.

——. *The Logical Structure of the World*. Translated by Rolf A. George. Berkeley: University of California Press, 1967.

Cassirer, Ernst. *The Philosophy of Symbolic Forms.* Translated by Ralph Mannheim. 4 volumes. New Haven: Yale University Press, 1953–96.

Castoriadis, Cornelius. *The Imaginary Institution of Society.* Translated by Kathleen Blamey. Cambridge: Polity Press, 1987.

Cavaillès, Jean. *La Connaissance de la vie.* 2d revised edition. Paris: Vrin, 1992.

Cavell, Stanley. *The Claim of Reason: Wittgenstein, Morality, and Tragedy.* New York: Oxford University Press, 1979.

———. *Conditions Handsome and Unhandsome: The Constitution of Emersonian Perfectionism.* Chicago: University of Chicago Press, 1990.

———. *A Pitch of Philosophy.* Cambridge, Mass.: Harvard University Press, 1994.

Cohen, Hermann. *Religion of Reason: Out of the Sources of Judaism.* Translated by Simon Kaplan. New York: F. Ungar, 1972.

Courtine-Denamy, Sylvie. *Hannah Arendt.* Paris: Belfond, 1994. [An intellectual biography that is also a portrait of the age]

Davidson, Donald. *Essays on Actions and Events.* New York: Oxford University Press, 1980.

———. *Inquiries into Truth and Interpretation.* New York: Oxford University Press, 1984.

Delacampagne, Christian. *Antipsychiatrie.* Paris: Grasset, 1974.

Delacampagne, Christian, and Robert Maggiori, editors. *Philosopher: les interrogations contemporaines.* 2 volumes. Paris: Presses Pocket, 1991. [The major questions of classical philosophy treated by some forty contemporary French philosophers]

Deledalle, Gérard. *La Philosophie américaine.* Brussels: De Boeck-Wesmael, 1987. [One of the best accounts presently available of two centuries of American philosophy]

Deleuze, Gilles, and Félix Guattari. *Anti-Oedipus: Capitalism and Schizophrenia.* Translated by Robert Hurley, Mark Seem, and Helen R. Lane. New York: Viking Press, 1977.

———. *What Is Philosophy?* Translated by Hugh Tomlinson and Graham Burchell. New York: Columbia University Press, 1994.

Dennett, Daniel. *Consciousness Explained.* Boston: Little Brown, 1991.

Derrida, Jacques. *Of Grammatology.* Translated by Gayatri Chakravorty Spivak. Baltimore: Johns Hopkins University Press, 1976.

———. *Specters of Marx.* Translated by Peggy Kamuf. New York: Routledge, 1994.

———. *Writing and Difference.* Translated by Alan Bass. Chicago: University of Chicago Press, 1978.

Dewey, John. *Democracy and Education: An Introduction to the Philosophy of Education.* New York: Free Press, 1966.

————. *Logic: The Theory of Inquiry.* New York: H. Holt, 1938.

Dummett, Michael. *The Origins of Analytical Philosophy.* London: Duckworth, 1993.

Faye, Jean-Pierre. *Le Piège: la philosophie heideggérienne et le nazisme.* Paris: Balland, 1994.

Ferry, Jean-Marc. *Habermas: l'éthique de la communication.* Paris: Presses Universitaires de France, 1987. [A solid and well-documented study of Habermas's thought]

Feyerabend, Paul. *Against Method: Outline of an Anarchist Theory of Knowledge.* 3d edition. New York: Verso, 1993.

Fisette, Denis. *Lecture frégéenne de la phénoménologie.* Combas: L'Éclat, 1994. [A careful and illuminating analysis of some Anglo-American interpretations of Husserl's thought]

Fodor, Jerry A. *The Language of Thought.* Cambridge, Mass.: Harvard University Press, 1975.

Foucault, Michel. *Discipline and Punish: The Birth of the Prison.* Translated by Alan Sheridan. New York: Vintage Books, 1977.

————. *Madness and Civilization: A History of Civilization in the Age of Reason.* Translated by Richard Howard. New York: Pantheon, 1965.

————. *The Order of Things: An Archaeology of the Human Sciences.* Translated by Alan Sheridan-Smith. New York: Pantheon, 1971.

Frege, Gottlob. *Collected Papers on Mathematics, Logic, and Philosophy.* Edited by Brian McGuinness; translated by Max Black et al. Oxford: Blackwell, 1984.

Freud, Sigmund. *Civilization and Its Discontents.* Translated and edited by James Strachey. New York: Norton, 1989.

————. *The Future of an Illusion.* Translated and edited by James Strachey. New York: Norton, 1989.

Gadamer, Hans-Georg. *Truth and Method.* Translation revised by Joel Weinsheimer and Donald G. Marshall. 2d revised edition. New York: Continuum, 1993.

Goodman, Nelson. *Languages of Art: An Approach to the Theory of Symbols.* 2d edition. Indianapolis: Hackett, 1976.

————. *The Structure of Appearance.* 3d edition. Dordrecht: Reidel, 1977.

————. *Ways of Worldmaking.* Indianapolis: Hackett, 1978.

Gramsci, Antonio. *Prison Notebooks.* Edited by Joseph A. Buttigieg; translated by Joseph A. Buttigieg and Antonio Callari. 2 vols. New York: Columbia University Press, 1992–96. [An ongoing project based on the authoritative four-volume edition, *Quaderni del carcere,* prepared by Valentino Gerrentana (Turin: Einaudi, 1975)]

Habermas, Jürgen. *The New Conservatism: Cultural Criticism and the Historians' Debate.* Edited and translated by Shierry Weber Nicholsen. Cambridge, Mass.: MIT Press, 1989.

————. *The Philosophical Discourse of Modernity*. Translated by Frederick G. Lawrence. Cambridge, Mass.: MIT Press, 1987.

————. *Philosophical-Political Profiles*. Translated by Frederick G. Lawrence. Cambridge, Mass.: MIT Press, 1983.

————. *The Theory of Communicative Action*. Translated by Thomas McCarthy. 2 volumes. Boston: Beacon Press, 1984–87.

Heidegger, Martin. *Being and Time*. Translated by John Macquarrie and Edward Robinson. New York: Harper & Row, 1962. [A new translation by Joan Stambaugh has recently been published by the State University of New York Press]

————. *The Heidegger Controversy: A Critical Reader*. Edited by Richard Wolin. Cambridge, Mass.: MIT Press, 1993.

————. *An Introduction to Metaphysics*. Translated by Ralph Mannheim. New Haven: Yale University Press, 1959.

————. *Martin Heidegger: Basic Writings*. Edited by David Farrell Krell. 2d revised edition. San Francisco: HarperCollins, 1993.

————. *The Question Concerning Technology and Other Essays*. Translated by William Lovitt. New York: Harper & Row, 1977.

————. *The Question of Being*. Translated by William Kublack and Jean T. Wilde. New Haven: College & University Press, 1958.

————. *What Is Called Thinking?* Translated by Fred D. Wieck and J. Glenn Gray. New York: Harper & Row, 1968.

Heijenoort, Jean van, ed. *From Frege to Gödel: A Source Book in Mathematical Logic, 1879–1931*. Cambridge, Mass.: Harvard University Press, 1967.

Horkheimer, Max. *Dawn and Decline: Notes 1926–1931 and 1950–1969*. Translated by Michael Shaw. New York: Seabury Press, 1978.

Horkheimer, Max, and Theodor W. Adorno. *Dialectic of Enlightenment*. Translated by John Cumming. London: Verso, 1979.

Husserl, Edmund. *The Idea of Phenomenology*. Translated by William P. Alston and George Nakhnikian. The Hague: Nijhoff, 1964.

————. *Ideas: General Introduction to Pure Phenomenology*. Translated by W. R. Boyce Gibson. New York: Macmillan, 1952.

————. *Logical Investigations*. Translated by J. N. Findlay. 2 volumes. London: Routledge & Kegan Paul, 1970.

————. *Phenomenology and the Crisis of Philosophy: Philosophy as Rigorous Science, and Philosophy and the Crisis of European Man*. Translated by Quentin Lauer. New York: Harper & Row, 1965.

Hyppolite, Jean. *Figures de la pensée philosophique: Écrits de Jean Hyppolite (1931–1968)*. 2 volumes. Paris: Presses Universitaires de France, 1971.

Jakobson, Roman, and Morris Halle. *The Fundamentals of Language*. 2d revised edition. The Hague: Mouton, 1971.

James, William. *Essays in Radical Empiricism*. Cambridge, Mass.: Harvard University Press, 1976.

———. *Pragmatism: A New Name for Some Old Ways of Thinking*. Cambridge, Mass.: Harvard University Press, 1978.

Janicaud, Dominique. *Le Tournant théologique de la phénoménologie française*. Combas: L'Éclat, 1991. [A useful reminder that philosophy and religion are not to be confused]

Jankélévitch, Vladimir. *L'Imprescriptible: Pardonner? Dans l'honneur et la dignité*. Paris: Seuil, 1986. [A reprinting of the two works given in the subtitle]

Jaspers, Karl. *The Question of German Guilt*. Translated by E. B. Ashton. New York: Dial Press, 1947.

Jorland, Gérard. *La Science dans la philosophie*. Paris: Gallimard, 1981. [An excellent introduction to the thought of Alexandre Koyré]

Klossowski, Pierre. *Nietzsche and the Vicious Circle*. Translated by Daniel W. Smith. Chicago: University of Chicago Press, 1997. [Translation of a landmark 1969 essay in contemporary Nietzsche studies]

Kojève, Alexandre. *Introduction to the Reading of Hegel*. Edited by Allan Bloom; translated by James H. Nichols Jr. New York: Basic Books, 1969.

Kolakowski, Leszek. *Main Currents of Marxism: Its Origins, Growth, and Dissolution*. 3 volumes. Translated by P. S. Falla. New York: Oxford University Press, 1981. [A work remarkable for its objectivity and thoroughness]

Koyré, Alexandre. *From the Closed World to the Infinite Universe*. Baltimore: Johns Hopkins University Press, 1957.

———. *Galileo Studies*. Translated by John Mepham. Atlantic Highlands, N.J.: Humanities Press, 1978.

Kripke, Saul A. *Naming and Necessity*. Cambridge, Mass.: Harvard University Press, 1980.

———. *Wittgenstein on Rules and Private Language: An Elementary Exposition*. Cambridge, Mass.: Harvard University Press, 1982.

Kuhn, Thomas S. *The Essential Tension*. Chicago: University of Chicago Press, 1977.

———. *The Structure of Scientific Revolutions*. Chicago: University of Chicago Press, 1962.

Lacan, Jacques. *Écrits*. Translated by Alan Sheridan. New York: Norton, 1977.

Levinas, Emmanuel. *Totality and Infinity: An Essay on Exteriority*. Translated by Alphonso Lingis. Pittsburgh: Duquesne University Press, 1979.

Lévi-Strauss, Claude. *The Savage Mind*. Translated by John Weightman and Doreen Weightman. Chicago: University of Chicago Press, 1966. [The last chapter is devoted to a critique of Sartre's conception of dialectic and history]

Löwith, Karl. *My Life in Germany before and after 1933*. Translated by Elizabeth King. Urbana: University of Illinois Press, 1994.

Lukács, Georg. *History and Class Consciousness: Studies in Marxist Dialectics*. Translated by Rodney Livingstone. Cambridge, Mass.: MIT Press, 1971.

Lyotard, Jean-François. *Libidinal Economy*. Translated by Iain Hamilton Grant. Bloomington: Indiana University Press, 1993.

Marcuse, Herbert. *Eros and Civilization: A Philosophical Inquiry into Freud*. 2d edition. Boston: Beacon Press, 1966.

———. *One-Dimensional Man: Studies in the Ideology of Advanced Industrial Society*. Boston: Beacon Press, 1964.

Merleau-Ponty, Maurice. *Phenomenology of Perception*. Translated by Colin Smith. New York: Humanities Press, 1972.

Monk, Ray. *Bertrand Russell: The Spirit of Solitude, 1872–1921*. New York: Free Press, 1996.

———. *Ludwig Wittgenstein: The Duty of Genius*. New York: Free Press, 1990.

Mosès, Stéphane. *L'Ange de l'histoire: Rosenzweig, Benjamin, Scholem*. Paris: Seuil, 1992. [A fundamental work for the understanding of Judeo-German philosophy]

Nozick, Robert. *Anarchy, State, and Utopia*. New York: Basic Books, 1974.

Ott, Hugo. *Martin Heidegger: A Political Life*. Translated by Allan Blunden. New York: HarperCollins, 1993. [The work of a historian, lacking in philosophical perspective but flawless in its precision and objectivity]

Peirce, Charles S. *The Essential Peirce*. Edited by Nathan Hauser and Christian Kloesel. Bloomington: Indiana University Press, 1992.

Petrosino, Silvano. *Jacques Derrida e la legge del possibile*. Naples: Guida, 1983.

Popper, Karl R. *The Logic of Scientific Discovery*. 3d revised edition. London: Hutchinson, 1968.

———. *The Open Society and Its Enemies*. 4th revised edition. London: Routledge & Kegan Paul, 1962.

Putnam, Hilary. *Realism with a Human Face*. Cambridge, Mass.: Harvard University Press, 1991.

———. *Words and Life*. Edited by James Conant. Cambridge, Mass.: Harvard University Press, 1994.

Quine, W. V. *Quiddities: An Intermittently Philosophical Dictionary*. Cambridge, Mass.: Belknap Press, 1987.

———. *Word and Object*. Cambridge, Mass.: MIT Press, 1960.

Rawls, John. *Political Liberalism*. New York: Columbia University Press, 1993.

———. *Theory of Justice*. Cambridge, Mass.: Belknap Press, 1971.

Ricoeur, Paul. *Time and Narrative*. 3 volumes. Translated by Kathleen McLaughlin and David Pellauer. Chicago: University of Chicago Press, 1984–88.

Rorty, Richard. *Consequences of Pragmatism: Essays 1972–1980*. Minneapolis: University of Minnesota Press, 1982.

―――. *Contingency, Irony, and Solidarity.* New York: Cambridge University Press, 1989.

―――. *Philosophy and the Mirror of Nature.* Princeton: Princeton University Press, 1979.

―――. *Reading Rorty: Critical Responses to Philosophy and the Mirror of Nature (and Beyond).* Edited by Alan R. Malachowski with Jo Burrows. Cambridge, Mass.: Blackwell, 1990.

Rosenzweig, Franz. *The Star of Redemption.* Translated by William W. Hallo. Notre Dame, Ind.: Notre Dame University Press, 1985.

Russell, Bertrand. *Introduction to Mathematical Philosophy.* London: Routledge, 1993.

―――. *Logic and Knowledge.* Edited by Robert C. Marsh. London: George Allen & Unwin, 1956.

―――. *My Philosophical Development.* London: George Allen & Unwin, 1959.

―――. *The Problems of Philosophy.* Oxford: Oxford University Press, 1967.

Ryle, Gilbert. *The Concept of Mind.* London: Hutchinson, 1949.

Sartre, Jean-Paul. *Being and Nothingness: A Phenomenological Essay on Ontology.* Translated by Hazel E. Barnes. New York: Washington Square Press, 1956.

―――. *Critique of Dialectical Reason.* Volume 1: *Theory of Practical Ensembles.* Edited by Jonathan Rée; translated by Alan Sheridan-Smith. Atlantic Highlands, N.J.: Humanities Press, 1976. [The unfinished second volume is translated by John Mathews in *Between Existentialism and Marxism* (London: Verso, 1983)]

―――. *The Transcendence of the Ego: An Existentialist Theory of Consciousness.* Translated by Forrest Williams and Robert Kirkpatrick. New York: Hill and Wang, 1960.

Sartre, Jean-Paul, and Benny Lévy. *L'Espoir maintenant: les entretiens de 1980.* Paris: Verdier, 1991.

Saussure, Ferdinand de. *Course in General Linguistics.* Edited by Charles Bally and Albert Sechehaye with the collaboration of Albert Riedlinger; translated and annotated by Roy Harris. La Salle, Ill.: Open Court, 1986.

Scholem, Gershom. *Walter Benjamin: The Story of a Friendship.* Translated by Harry Zohn. Philadelphia: Jewish Publication Society of America, 1981.

Searle, John R. *The Rediscovery of the Mind.* Cambridge, Mass.: MIT Press, 1992.

―――. *Speech Acts: An Essay in the Philosophy of Language.* London: Cambridge University Press, 1969.

Sebestik, Jan, and Antonia Soulez. *Le Cercle de Vienne: doctrines et controverses.* Paris: Méridiens-Kliencksieck, 1986. [The proceedings of a colloquium held in Paris in 1983]

Sellars, Wilfrid. "Empiricism and the Philosophy of Mind." In Herbert Feigl and

Michael Scriven, eds., *The Foundations of Science and the Concepts of Psychology and Psychoanalysis*. Minnesota Studies in the Philosophy of Science, volume 1. Minneapolis: University of Minnesota Press, 1956.

Shusterman, Richard. *Practicing Philosophy: Pragmatism and the Philosophical Life*. New York: Routledge, 1997. [An original and illuminating study of American pragmatism]

Strauss, Leo. *Persecution and the Art of Writing*. Chicago: University of Chicago Press, 1988.

Strauss, Leo, and Joseph Cropsey, eds. *History of Political Philosophy*. 3d edition. Chicago: University of Chicago Press, 1987.

Strawson, Peter F. *Analysis and Metaphysics: An Introduction to Philosophy*. New York: Oxford University Press, 1992.

———. *Individuals: An Essay in Descriptive Metaphysics*. London: Methuen, 1959.

Taylor, Charles. *Sources of the Self: The Making of the Modern Identity*. Cambridge, Mass.: Harvard University Press, 1989.

Vernant, Denis. *La Philosophie mathématique de Russell*. Paris: Vrin, 1993. [A precise and detailed account of Russell's ideas on logic and mathematics]

Whitehead, Alfred N. *Process and Reality: An Essay in Cosmology*. Corrected edition, edited by David Ray Griffin and Donald W. Sherburne. New York: Free Press, 1978.

Wiggershaus, Rolf. *The Frankfurt School: Its History, Theories, and Political Significance*. Translated by Michael Robertson. Cambridge: Polity Press, 1994.

Wittgenstein, Ludwig. *The Blue and Brown Books*. Oxford: Blackwell, 1975.

———. *Culture and Value*. Edited by G. H. von Wright in collaboration with Heikki Nyman; translated by Peter Winch. Oxford: Blackwell, 1980.

———. *Lectures and Conversations on Aesthetics, Pyschology and Religious Belief*. Edited by Cyril Barrett. Oxford: Blackwell, 1978.

———. *Philosophical Investigations*. Edited by G. E. M. Anscombe and R. Rhees; translated by G. E. M. Anscombe. Oxford: Blackwell, 1953.

———. *Remarks on the Foundations of Mathematics*. Edited by G. H. von Wright, R. Rhees, and G. E. M. Anscombe; translated by G. E. M. Anscombe. Revised edition. Cambridge, Mass.: MIT Press, 1978.

———. *Tractatus Logico-Philosophicus*. Translated by D. F. Pears and B. F. McGuinness. London: Routledge & Kegan Paul, 1961.

Index

Library of Congress Cataloging-in-Publication Data

Delacampagne, Christian, 1948–
     [Histoire de la philosophie au XXe siècle. English]
     A history of philosophy in the twentieth century / Christian Delacampagne ;
translated by M.B. DeBevoise.
          p.   cm.
     Includes bibliographical references and index.
     ISBN 0-8018-6016-4 (alk. paper)
     1. Philosophy—History—20th century.   I. Title.
B804.D3713   1999   99-11237
190'.9'04—dc21   CIP